WEST AFRICAN MASKING TRADITIONS AND DIASPORA
MASQUERADE CARNIVALS

ROCHESTER STUDIES IN
AFRICAN HISTORY AND THE DIASPORA
Toyin Falola, Series Editor

The Jacob and Frances Sanger Mossiker Chair in the Humanities
and University Distinguished Teaching Professor

University of Texas at Austin

*Muslim Fula Business Elites
and Politics in Sierra Leone*
Alusine Jalloh

*Race, Decolonization, and Global
Citizenship in South Africa*
Chielozona Eze

*Plantation Slavery in the Sokoto
Caliphate: A Historical and
Comparative Study*
Mohammed Bashir Salau

*African Migration Narratives:
Politics, Race, and Space*
Edited by Cajetan Iheka and
Jack Taylor

*Ethics and Society in Nigeria:
Identity, History, Political Theory*
Nimi Wariboko

*African Islands: Leading Edges of
Empire and Globalization*
Edited by Toyin Falola, R. Joseph
Parrott, and Danielle Porter-Sanchez

*Catholicism and the Making of Politics
in Central Mozambique, 1940–1986*
Eric Morier-Genoud

*Liberated Africans and the Abolition
of the Slave Trade, 1807–1896*
Edited by Richard Anderson and
Henry B. Lovejoy

*The Other Abyssinians:
The Northern Oromo and the
Creation of Modern Ethiopia*
Brian J. Yates

*Nigeria's Digital Diaspora:
Citizen Media, Democracy,
and Participation*
Farooq A. Kperogi

A complete list of titles in the Rochester Studies in African History and the
Diaspora series may be found on our website, www.urpress.com.

West African Masking Traditions and Diaspora Masquerade Carnivals

History, Memory, and Transnationalism

Raphael Chijioke Njoku

UNIVERSITY OF ROCHESTER PRESS

First published 2020
University of Rochester Press
668 Mt. Hope Avenue, Rochester, NY 14620, USA
www.urpress.com
and Boydell & Brewer Limited
PO Box 9, Woodbridge, Suffolk IP12 3DF, UK
www.boydellandbrewer.com

ISBN-13: 978-1-58046-984-5
ISSN: 1092-5228
Cataloging-in-Publication data available from the Library of Congress.

This publication is printed on acid-free paper.

In
memory of
Nne Nkáru Anosike,
Njoku Timothy Anosike,
Peter Njoku,
Francis Joseph Ayozieuwa Njoku,
Ukaerueze Ejimofor,
Ejimofor Nwaiwu,
and
Francisca Ulumma Uzodinma

CONTENTS

FIGURES AND TABLES

Figures

Tables

PREFACE

My conceptual journey to this study began before I learned how to read and write. Growing up in the 1970s while the Igbo recuperated from the traumas of the 1966–1970 Nigerian Civil War, my grandmother, a keen host for our regular moonlight tales, would jokingly chide the kids arriving late from the composite households with the *au fait:* "He who arrives at the middle of a story leaves with a disjointed narrative." Her words echo an Igbo saying: "When a man who was absent at a burial exhumes the corpse, the village should be prepared to deal with a disembodied cadaver." While both proverbs underscore the imperative of complete and accurate mastery of a subject in general, they particularly challenge students of Africana Studies to ensure grounded knowledge of the complex and intricate nuances of the African roots of African American history and culture they market. Otherwise, the ominous risk is to produce incoherent and disjointed accounts.

In this book, I bring an African voice to the copious volumes of studies on African and African Diaspora linkages by focusing on African-styled masquerade carnivals. Taking into account the unique roles masquerades played in the indigenous society, the voice with African linguistic, ethnic, and cultural roots is crucial so not to have the details muddled in translation in an age of modernist thinking. The book informs the reader where, when, and how the African masquerade genre was invented and explains the life force behind the festival play.

Masquerading in the Africana world was a dynamic device of narratology. For the enslaved people, the art of masquerade *engagee* was one of the most potent survival devices in the Americas. By exploring the origins, religious idioms, symbols, internal and diasporic diffusions, and the music, dance, and drama that accompany the masquerade tradition, the result is to see beyond the jamboree displays, which most people have identified with carnivals everywhere today.

With a Pan-African approach contextualized in change-over-time-and-space argument, this book also speaks to the connection between Bantu migration and the ethnic complexity and spread of masquerade culture across the continent and beyond. In addressing this theme, I provide a richer and fuller account of both the internal dynamics and the multiple and multifaceted cultural connections between Africa and the African Diasporas without reifying culture as something cast in stone. The Bantu-African masquerade genre that evolved from the Bight of Biafra hinterland is adaptive and was in constant flux prior to the beginning of the transatlantic slave trade. Its presence in the Americas was an extension of the fluid Bantuization process outside Africa by way of creolization.

Bearing in mind the agitated debates it conjures, the Bantu paradigm deserves further clarification. As employed here, Bantu as a concept is more than the language question; it is symbolic for precolonial cultural inventions and the hybridities that connect African societies across regional lines. Colonial scholars who pioneered Bantu studies and classified African languages into different families admitted that they did not understand fully the etymologies and complex nuances of African languages and the culture they carry. As a result, the early Bantu scholars placed the Igbo language among the Kwa subfamily of the parent Niger-Congo family. The colonial scholars discounted the fact that the Cross River Igbo (including Ábám, Ábiribá, Áfikpo, Arọchukwu, Èddá, Ezzikwo, Ihe, Igbèrè, Ikwo, Isu, Nkporo, Ọháfiá, Ọkpọsi, Uburu, Unwáná, and Ututu) share similar history, culture, and language with their Èfik, Ibibio, Ijọ, and Èkọi neighbors who were classified into the Bantu subfamily group of the Niger-Congo group. In a field of history where the word of the colonial scholar often carries the same weight as a papal bull, it is critical to start rethinking some of the serious flaws inherent in these received sweeping ideas in order to turn a new corner in African history. After eminent scholars such as Adiele Eberechukwu Afigbo, Ogbu Kalu, and Ebiegberi Joe Alagoa, I reiterate here that the Igbo language, particularly the various dialects spoken among the Cross River Igbo, align more to the Bantu subfamily than the Kwa subgroup.

I owe numerous individuals immense gratitude for their assistance in completing this project. From the very beginning, Baldwin Anyasodo, Chidi G. Osuagwu, Joseph Bangura, Emmanuel Amadife, Apollos Nwauwa, Dimeji Togunde, John McLeod, Thomas Mackey, Tracy K'Meyer, Christine Ehrick, and Francis O. C. Njoku offered their support that saw to the successful completion of this book. Additionally, Alaba Kajobola, Francis and Ngozi Njoku, Bryce Turner, and Rachael Johnston provided the critical logistics that advanced the pace of my research. My sincere gratitude to all those who funded this research, including Idaho State University's College of Arts and Letters, the Department of History, and the Department of Global Studies and Languages at ISU. A National Endowment for the Humanities (NEH) grant made possible my extended work at the Schomburg Center for Research in Black Culture in Harlem and the New York Public Library in New York. At Schomburg, I met mentors and colleagues who were very generous with their ideas and time. My weekly discussions with Colin A. Palmer, Howard Dodson, Carolyn Brown, Venus Green, Barbara Krauthammer, Malinda Alaine Lindquist, Kezia Ann Page, Chad L. Williams, Lisa Gail Collins, Valerie Babb, Carla Kaplan, and Diana Lachatanere will ever remain priceless.

I am greatly indebted to Toyin Falola, Chima J. Korieh, Kristine Hunt, Malliga Och, and Douglas Chambers for their insightful and critical comments on the earlier versions of this manuscript. I am very thankful to the Editorial Board and acquisition editors at the University of Rochester Press for their keen interest in this project.

Raphael Chijioke Njoku
Idaho State University, Pocatello
April 2019

ABBREVIATIONS

Arọ   Arọchukwu
CAR   Central African Republic
DRC   The Democratic Republic of the Congo
MDU   Mbieri Development Union
NAK   National Archives Kew
NNAE   Nigerian National Archives Enugu
NNAI   Nigerian National Archives Ibadan

Introduction

THIS BOOK EXPLORES THE origins, religious idioms, symbols, internal and diasporic diffusions, and the music, dance, and drama that accompany African and African Diaspora masks and masquerade performances. The relevance of an inquiry of this nature cannot be overemphasized. Masquerades embody the essence of African civilization and the spirit of culture and customs that translate meanings to certain dimensions of the continent's complex history. The songs, dance, drama, poetry, proverbs, and other accouterments of practices that go with the masquerade performances also represent a repertoire of intellectual traditions crucial to the recovery of aspects of lost African pasts. The rituals associated with masking define the fluid structures of power and authority, patterns of civil society networks, and the people's social consciousness. The changing faces of African-styled masquerade carnivals hold a mirror on the variegated impact contacts with alien cultures have brought upon Africans and their diasporic descendants.

In examining the changes that have permeated the masquerade spectacle in the last four centuries, this study probes the interconnections among masquerade narratives, memory, reinventions, and transnationalism. Centering on the role of the Igbo, one of the most visible Bight of Biafra hinterland ethnic groups involved in transatlantic commercial exchanges, the inclination toward ethnicization of African cultural artifacts in the Americas is problematized. The argument is put forth that enslaved Africans should be understood as Bantu-African culture modeling agents or culture carriers who tried to reenact vestiges of their inherited traditions in alien societies. While the Bantu culture is contagious, often the traditions the modelers enacted were not exact replicas of the African prototypes—and they need not be. Cultural diffusions or modeling are dynamic and do not usually re-create the original. Modeling agents use simulations or scaled-down versions of the original to show how an event might occur under specific circumstances, and they may not work in an exact way or as the object or system they represent. Beginning from the sixteenth century, African-themed cultural activities in the New World were dilutions of a conglomerate of practices from several ethnic African and European nations nurtured on American soil. As models help scientists develop explanations about a natural phenomenon that may be difficult to observe, so should we appreciate African American cultural artifacts and study them within the dialectics of traditions and adaptations.

The terms *adaptation, time,* and *space* are central to this study because Africana masquerades are not just entertainment tools in static mode. In the Bight of Biafra hinterland Bantu Culture Area, masquerades, in their adaptive nature, served as a genre of literary engagee in the oral and performative style. Masquerade narrative is interpreted here as a method of committed and organic literary discourse in performative form. Customarily, African masquerades symbolize the conscience of a society. They provide a platform to promote identity; propagate, defend, or pursue a cause or ideology; and recover or reshape collective consciousness in a constantly changing world. While enslaved Africans extended this dynamic role of masquerades to the slaveholding American society, the challenges that they were confronted with in the new society were quite different from those they were acquainted with in the Bight of Biafra Culture Area, which, as the original homeland of the Bantu, gave birth to the larger Bantu Culture Area.

The notion of culture areas is not new in academic discourses, but the idea of a Bantu Culture Area has not been applied to any study on African culture transfers to the New World. Proponents of the diffusion theory in America, otherwise known as the "American School of Diffusion," hold the view that people learn and appropriate rudiments of culture they encounter and as the rate of interaction between cultures increases, so do the probability of borrowing and learning. Melville Herskovits argues that cultures in an area tended to form clusters that are "sufficiently homogenous in regions on which they occur [that] can be delimited on a map."[1] Nita Mathar defines culture area as "the geographical space in which similar cultures are found."[2] The American diffusionists believe that by mapping spatial distribution of traits in specific geographical spaces, one can then easily illuminate the parallels and variances among cultures.[3] The initial articulation of culture areas as a paradigm in the American ethnographic academy go back to 1895 when Otis T. Mason used the term *culture area* in his work.[4] Other scholars building on this have since expanded the theory by correlating dominant cultural traits with geographical spaces.[5] Clark Wissler provided a conceptual and methodological approach to the study when he stated that if "we take all traits into simultaneous consideration and shift our point of view to the social or tribal units, we are able to form fairly definite groups. This will give us culture areas, or a classification, of social groups according to their cultural traits."[6] In other words, social groups may be geographically dispersed but still form a common cultural identity.

The African presence in the New World was a Pan-African project. Thus, rather than pursuing a narrow ethnic model, which arbitrarily assigns agency to certain African groups while ignoring others, I have adopted the Bantu Culture Area model as a more embracing paradigm for the hundreds of ethnic nations represented by the enslaved Africans in the Americas. This inclusive approach precludes disjointed and disembodied stories. It offers a nuanced explanation of the inherent distance crossings, fluidity, similarities, and variables associated with African and African American cultural complexes. The distinction brought into purview is the degree of changes that were already affecting the masquerade tradition in Africa prior to its departure to the Americas. The counterpoints include the interface among the centuries of internal and cross-regional exchanges, changes brought upon the culture by Islamization, Christianization, and colonization within the continent and in the African Diasporas; the (re-) secularization of the institutions that were in the past exclusively for male initiates; and the masquerades' intersections with the European culture as globalization deepens and expands.

In the past four decades, masquerade studies have attracted a significant amount of scholarly curiosity as new study methods continue to boost our understanding of the manifold and multifaceted processes that created the African Diasporas. Early on in the 1940s, the broad subject of cultural transfers and retentions (of which masquerading is a big part) among enslaved Africans emerged as one of the dominant topics of debate among scholars of the Black Atlantic. The attraction to this idea soon created two opposing schools of thought. The first school, identified heretofore as the "African Culture Retention School," was championed by Melville Herskovits, while the second, the "Tabula Rasa School," was advocated by Stanley Elkins. With *The Myth of the Negro Past* (published in 1941), which aimed to dignify the frontiers of new traditions the enslaved Africans fostered in the Americas, Herskovits launched the canon of studies that has today grown exponentially.[7] But in 1959, Elkins challenged the Retention School with his declaration that the cultural difference between Africans and African Americans was wider than one could imagine. Elkins provocatively affirmed that the African slaves who survived the perilous Middle Passage suffered memory blackout or cultural annihilation: "Nearly every prior connection had been severed." In a rhetorical question as to where the slaves would look for new knowledge, traditions, values, etiquette, standards, and cues, Elkins concluded that it was the White planters of America who owned the slaves.[8] In 1978, Albert Raboteau, who studied African traditional religious survivals in the American South, backed the tabula rasa hypothesis with a bold declaration that the slaves' "African religious heritage was lost."[9]

It is not that the Elkinses and Raboteaus are completely off the mark with their views. The violence and cruelty that characterized the Middle Passage incontestably depleted the victims' physical, psychological, and mental well-being. However, the idea of a permanent memory blackout is an overreach at the fringes of pseudoscience. First, a misrepresentation of this magnitude betrays a lack of elementary knowledge of human psychology, which recognizes the role of nature and nurture in the molding of life-long characters and skills.[10] Second, the advocates of the tabula rasa argument tend to forget that ellipsis of memory is not unique to enslaved Africans. Amnesia often goes with remembering, and the critical issue is not essential that amnesia or forgetfulness might occur. What matters most is which realities gave the individual or group a full sense of identity or relevance and making the memory or what we remember to respond to the challenges of life experiences. Third, how anyone can completely strip a grown-up person of agency and then reduce him or her to the level of Pavlov's dog, in this case, subject to an operant culture reconditioning, is altogether difficult to contemplate.

Like the Tabula Rasa School, the culture retention argument also betrays serious conceptual and heuristic flaws. Partly fueling the culture transfer/retention debate is the attempt by the previous studies to ethnicize African Diaspora slave cultural artifacts. This is a tricky monologue because the paradigm tends to ignore the dynamism and centrality of spatial reasoning—that is, the tendency to imagine things with limited information. Cultural diffusion and modeling, as the accounts of the Bantu migrations and the transatlantic slave trade conjure, could hinder narrow ethnic thinking. Like transatlantic slavery, Bantu population movements show that cultures in motion are like a rolling stream; they acquire new tastes and colors in relation to the ecosystem. Although not often emphasized, results from recent studies on African masquerade arts carnivals expose the intricate intersections among diffusion, spatial reasoning, complex interactions, and the role of memory in masquerade narratologies responsive to the pressing needs of the present.

A closer look at Abner Cohen's seminal studies on masquerade carnivals, for instance, reveals a continuous reinvention of village-based customs in both the urban centers of Africa and the African Diasporas by migrants arriving from the countryside.[11] As Cohen discloses, these city-based masquerades are never the same as their village-based prototypes because, as the social setting has changed, so did the narrative and presentation. Philip Scher's *Carnival and the Formation of the Caribbean Transnation* takes a global perception of carnivals as contested arenas of politics and identity formation in both the island state of Trinidad and Trinidadian communities in England, the United States, and Canada.[12] Again, the cosmopolitan carnivals are adapted to the dictates of modern politics in new environments rather than the same versions associated with the slave planta-tion era. Norman Stolzoff and Gerard Aching have further explored a similar theme in their separate studies on the Caribbean, including Cuba. The authors investigated the use of masks as an instrument of power and political mobiliza-tion in these racially bifurcated societies as the contours of power and author-ity continue to shift.[13] Put together, these studies communicate a clear message that to grasp and predict masquerades and their behaviors, scholars must look at the interactions between location and realities of a sociopolitical milieu rather than the shape of a past tradition found in one area. This calls to mind Stan-ley Littlefield, Dele Jegede, and Esther Dagan's description of African masks and masquerades as a continuing art form paralleling shifting religious belief systems, theater performances, artistic productions, nationalistic identities, and much more.[14]

The constant shifts demand revisions and new approaches that sometimes present conceptual challenges. In 1990, John Gray came to an epiphany when he advocated for a Pan-African approach as a future direction of research on the resilient Afro-Creole masquerade culture.[15] Perhaps this may have motivated Ivor Miller's works on the Abákuá masquerade of Cuba, which he sees as an ex-tension of Èfik-style Èkpè masquerade in modern Nigeria; and Robert W. Nich-olls's *Old-Time Masquerading in the Virgin Islands*, which links the masquerade carnival in that island enclave with the Igbo prototypes. Similarly, Toyin Falola and coauthors' volume, *Orisa*, explored various aspects of Yoruba gods and spir-itual identities in Africa and the African Diasporas.[16] Other related studies such as *Igbo in the Atlantic World: African Origins and Diasporic Destinations*, edited by Toyin Falola and Raphael Chijioke Njoku; Linda Heywood's edited volume *Central Africans and Cultural Transformations in the American Diaspora*; and *The Yoruba Diaspora in the Atlantic World*, edited by Toyin Falola and Matt D. Childs, have respectively explicated the dynamism of slavery and Igbo, Kongo/ Angolan, and Yoruba contributions to African diasporic cultures.[17] Revisiting these studies offers a perspective on how to better comprehend African and African American masquerade carnivals as an active and fluid device for sociopolitical dialogue in a world in constant flux.

In essence, this study acknowledges that several millennia prior to the transatlantic slave trade, African culture was already experiencing changes through Bantuization, and studying African American culture in the Americas is a continuation of that change outside the African continent. As the Bantu population movements subjected African culture to a process of intense and dramatic refinements and harmonization, so did the transatlantic slave trade extend this process of harmonization to the Americas by way of creolization. In this process, both African and African American cultures became a collective programming, a mobile community of practices constructed on shared and pragmatic habits, values, maxims, and need-based observances within a group thought. Thus, situating the African Diaspora culture transfer discourse within the Bantu migration history makes sense: It helps further our appreciation of the far-reaching impacts of the Bantu beyond sub-Saharan Africa. While the story of the Bantu in relation to Black Africa is well known, frequently ignored is the influence of the migrations and the masquerade culture it brought to Islamized North Africa.

Second, positioning the discourse within the Bantu studies literature shows that long before the waterscapes began to serve as conduits of economic and cultural sharing between peoples and lands in the First Global Age (c. 1400–1800), landscapes (such as the Bantu migratory routes, the trans-Saharan trade routes, and the Silk Roads) have been serving as conduits of cross-regional exchanges on the global scale. This demonstrates how conventional arguments in history writing about the dynamics of the maritime world, distance crossings, the rise of the West, and the charm of colonial empires can be overturned by emphasizing dynamic, collaborative, and nonlinear networks as opposed to formal networks based on power, the Maxim gun, and social classes. The land-based networks in the Ancient Global Age (c. 2500–1400) and First Global Age reflect a different picture of global interactions. Landscapes emphasize the centrality of peoples, distance crossings, the materialities of cultures in motion, and other exchanges at different times in different parts of the world. Additionally, this book challenges certain chronological readings such as attempts to periodize the origin and spread of cultural traditions like masking and masquerading. It imposes a multivalent approach and urges scholars to think spatially and thematically instead—that is in a way that relates to the position, size, and relevance of ideas and concepts within specific geographical locations.

Spatial reasoning, as the accounts of the Bantu population movements and the transatlantic slave trade reveal, allows us to see what happens when culture modelers migrate with inherited tropes of values and symbols and the history they convey flows in multiple directions and across regions and culturescapes. Theophilus Okere explains that some values or symbols were destined for a transnational mission. Some "values are not only more permanent in time but seem destined for a universal vocation, eventually being accepted beyond their time and place of birth."[18] The imperative is a more nuanced construal, a cognition that recognizes the complexities inherent in the cross-regional diffusion of ideas and symbols.

Thus, rather than forcing the ethnic cloak on African American culture complexes, *West African Masking Traditions and Diaspora Masquerade Carnivals* prioritizes the subtleties of persistence, nostalgia, practices, memories, institutions, coping strategies, and structures that provided succor and character for those in bondage. The consideration is more on ways through which African epistemologies of religion, music, dance, and other repertories of ideas embedded in the masquerade phenomenon aided enslaved people to survive oppression. The conscious or unconscious desire to reinvent African-themed cultural prototypes in the New World—whether successful or not—contributed to the subsequent growth of what we know today as African American art, music, and literature in particular and the Grand American culture in general.

Accordingly, contra the Tabula Rasa School, this study is also mindful of what Judith Bettelheim has noted about the "Herskovitsian retention model," which she wearily describes as "a *retardataire* analysis, which stresses a continuous historical connection with Africa."[19] The Retentionists have contested that with the African presence, new cultural practices sprouted in the Americas and the realm of ritual and belief systems constituted the force around which African Americans organized themselves into a people with an identity.[20] The point, however, remains that the overall intent of enslaved Africans' cultural expressions was primarily geared toward survival rather than reinventing proto-African ethnic practices as many have passionately argued. Such ideas fail to capture the harsh circumstances confronting the slaves that we study of their history. Narrating her family experience, ex-slave Louisa Adam, born in Rockingham County, North Carolina, reminds us that "I tell you de truth, slave time wuz slave time wid us. My brother wore his shoes out, and had none all thu winter. His feet cracked open and bled so bad you could track him by the blood" [*sic*].[21]

Louisa Adam's picturesque is the actualities of slavery that should never be lost. The onus of inquiry then is on memory or the art of remembering surrounding the global journey of the brand of masquerade culture that the Biafra hinterland people invented and through the Bantu movements shared with their fellow Africans. The birth of this tradition goes back several millennia prior to the transatlantic slave trade and the European colonial expansions that followed. I have identified a culture zone in southeastern Nigeria where the Cross River Igbo, in partnership with their neighbors—the Èfik, Ibibio, Èkoi, and Ijọ—nurtured a very contagious brand of masquerading. The tradition was propagated as a device of representation that makes use of memory and narratology to safeguard social norms, restore harmony in the midst of chaos, and resolve societal issues. Exploring the materiality of cultural inventions of the various societies native to the original Bantu homeland, which encompasses the historic Bight of Biafra slave embarkation port, offers a path to a better appreciation of the diachronic interchanges between the Old World/Old Time masquerade traditions and the New World/New Time masquerade carnival culture.

In other words, this is a transregional, transatlantic world inquiry with emphasis on one of the most popular and continuing cultural dialogues between Africa and the Atlantic world. Colin A. Palmer has underscored that the name "Atlantic world" is not merely "a geographic expression but also a metaphor for the organic and human linkages that characterize it."[22] Along with this line of thought, Thomas Benjamin accentuates how the new transatlantic linkages the Europeans established in the fifteenth century "shall unloose the bonds of things."[23] This means that the merging of the Old and the New Worlds created opportunities for closer relationships between Africa, Europe, and the Americas. But the timeline and scope of the present study predate the beginning of the transatlantic exchanges. It incorporates the timeless precolonial African era, which I have named the Ancient Global Age, the supposed First Global Age, and the New Global Age (1800–present). Building on the theory of cooperation, human social networks, nonlinear dynamics, and the coupling of human and natural complex systems, as propounded by Steven H. Strogatz, among others, some perspective lights are shed on periods of African history, chiefly as it relates to cultural productions and regional exchanges in the ancient, medieval, and modern times.[24] One of the major innovations provided is the use of "agent-based modeling" (also known as artificial intelligence) to simulate information about people or historical actors such as the Bantu in areas of the world and/or periods of time for which written sources are poor or nonexistent.

The Bantu as Culture Modeling Agents

The history of Bantu migration and cultural cross-fertilizations or diffusion highlights the theory of human social networks and the agent-based modeling system. The Bantu phenomenon remains one of the greatest migrations in human history considering the huge number of people involved, the time span, and more important, its extensive cultural impacts. Oral, linguistic, and archaeological sources show that the proto-Bantu group lived precisely in the areas bordering parts of the Benue-Cross River Basin of southeastern Nigeria, and western Cameroon. It is believed that the first Bantu migrants left this area earlier than 2500 BCE on what would become intermittent movements involving hundreds of generations now dispersed across the entire continent. The Bantu resettled everywhere with the appurtenances of material and nonmaterial cultures: religious ideas, new languages, and sociopolitical institutions. Some scholars have characterized the Bantu as violent and disruptors of established cultures in their environmental predation, while others see them more positively as culture carriers who helped in spreading sociocultural institutions that encouraged development across the continent.[25]

It is not the intention of this study to adjudicate the characterization of the Bantu. Rather, the Bantu are highlighted as culture modeling agents. Andre Grow and Jan Van Gavel have noted that the agent-based modeling paradigm is an emerging field in demographic studies with the potential to help scholars close "the gap between the conventional and an alternative approach to population studies by combining the advantages and limitations of both."[26] It is consequent to state that a study of the Bantu population movement embodies both the challenges and advantages of the conventional and the unconventional in historical narrative and social science research. In lieu of conformism, the Bantu migrations occurring several millennia ago are not entirely different from the influx of Europeans into the Americas between the fifteenth and nineteenth centuries or the more recent refugee movements involving millions still unfolding in Western Europe and North America. Migration, which sometimes results in total displacement, is a constant part of human history. The unconventional implication, however, is apparent in assessing the impact of the Bantu in the framework of cultural inventions, syncretism, and hybridities in the ancient times. Daniel Courgeau and Jakub Bijak have outlined four successive but complementary sequences in agent-based modeling that, as the demographers noted, have been evolving since the seventeenth century. These are the period (*time of the study*), cohorts (*number of people treated as a group*), event-history (*a longitudinal record of when events happened for a number of people*), and multilevel perspectives (*multiple approaches and viewpoints involved in a change process*).[27]

Both Bantu population movements and transatlantic slavery linked with the restless Bight of Biafra hinterland people have all the features outlined by Courgeau and Bijack: period, cohorts, event-history, and multilevel perspectives. The *periods* are twofold: 2500 BCE to 1400 CE and 1400 to 1800 CE. The *cohorts* are also twofold: the Bantu migrants crossing regional boundaries, and lending to and borrowing ideas and material cultures from alien societies; and the African slaves involved in the transatlantic exchanges sharing their memories of African culture in the Atlantic world while internalizing Western/American ideas and ways of life. Both historical episodes define the *event-history* and the inherent analytical *multilevel perspectives*, viewpoints, and challenges the events pose. With the spread of African cultural traditions, including religion and masquerading, agent-based modeling helps us to respond to three main challenges: how to overcome complexity in social history research of this nature, how to reduce its uncertainty in terms of clear-cut evidence and specific timelines, and how to reinforce its theoretical foundations. For demography, interactions between various populations systems are specifically examined. We then show how this approach enhances a study of this nature and the benefits it brings. Though the impact of the Bantu migration on Africa south of the Sahara is well known, there is nothing on the impact of the Bantu and the masquerade culture they brought to North Africa and of course the Americas. Original studies by anthropologist Edvard Westermarck have shed some light on how the Bantu culture extended its influence beyond the sub-Saharan region to North Africa with mask and masquerade observances in the pre-Islamic indigenous Berber North African society.[28]

In respect to the transatlantic slave trade and the evolution of African American culture, the modeling approach, applied with the aid of information from available primary and secondary literature preserved in multiple languages—English, French, Igbo, Èfìk, Ibibio, Ijọ, and so on—furthers the nexus between migration and cultural invention and adaptations. The emergent cue is that cultural production and adaptation is a function of "cleave and compare": when two or more alien cultures come in contact, they first form a cleavage (or a sharp division), which results in a dialogue or struggle—momentarily causing a confusion or chaos.[29] Over time, however, the opposing cultures tend to find accommodation or outlet within a syncretic/hybridized context through comparison. Thus, hybridization is the soul of culture transfers: a product of nonlinear dynamics and chaos, made possible by the ability of the carriers of the cultures in opposition to compare the practices they were more familiar with and adapt to some degree that which they have encountered. It is within this framework and the ensuing dialogue that the idea of cooperation is negotiated. Not only is this the setting in which African cultures developed; it is also the underlying premise that led to the birth of African American culture in the Americas.

Conceptual Approach and Sources

It is crucial to be aware of this inquiry's multiple layers of multidisciplinary and comparative analytical praxis before peeling them off. For clarity, this is an African perspective on diaspora history. Throughout, the connecting thread across the various chapters is masquerading and the music, dance, and drama that accompany the festivities as sites of memory. The performances are conceived as a moving watercourse on a global journey. As it navigates through regions, landscapes, and waterscapes, masquerading acquire diverse idioms, tastes, and attributes with the masquerade culture modelers drawing their ideas from the archives of human memory. It is also obvious that African masquerades cannot be studied in isolation of the indigenous religion in which it is embedded. As the people's religion shifted, so would the masquerade tradition as its offspring. In essence, this is a multidisciplinary inquiry crisscrossing diverse disciplines in the humanities and social sciences. While accentuating the intellectual episteme of masquerade dances, capturing the symbols and meanings inherent in African masking tradition furthers our state of knowledge in the ethnology and historical anthropology of African and African Diaspora cultures.

The main laboratory for this investigation is the Bantu original homeland where the Igbo, Èfik, Ibibio, Èkoi, and Ijọ of southeastern Nigeria live. As the evidence shows, the traditions native to this region are contagious, but not all Bantu culture traits are Igbo, Èfik, Ibibio, Kálábári or Ijọ in origin. The historical footprints left behind by the autochthonous inhabitants who have traversed the rainforest region for centuries not only edified the Bantu migratory routes but also shaped the prominence of the West African economic emporium known today as the Bight of Biafra, with Calabar as its main port. The assertion that the Bight of Biafra hinterland is the birthplace of the masquerade culture is predicated on three crucial historical facts. First, as expounded in the coming chapters, the most intricate masquerade rituals with out-of-this-world costuming were developed among the Igbo/Èfik/Ibibio/Ijọ. Moving out from this culture area, the masquerade traditions found in other parts of West and Central Africa exhibit a clear regressive involvement with religious ideologies, the exercise of political authority, and the weight of privileges assigned to masquerade cults. Second, as culture carriers, the Bantu began to emigrate from this area before 2500 BCE, and as they traversed the sub-Saharan African region, they lent their traditions, including governmental systems, religion, and masquerading, and borrowed ideas and practices from their host societies. Third, the Igbo/Èfik/Ibibio/Ijǫ geographical axis produced one of the highest numbers of victims of the transatlantic slave trade. Millions of captives from the Bight's hinterlands forcefully relocated to the Americas starting from about the late sixteenth century joined forces with other enslaved Africans in the struggle for freedom using their inherited Bantu culture, including ritual observances, music, dance, and street theatre.

Accounts left behind by people of African descent in the New World and eyewitness accounts by European travelers, planters, and administrators in colonial America repeatedly mention the Igbo and the Bight of Biafra in African-themed masquerade carnivals, music, and dance activities involving the enslaved. However, these sources cannot be used without caution. The Igbo did not live in isolation of their Èfik, Ibibio, Ijǫ, and other neighbors. They shared close cultural traditions with these neighbors centuries prior to the beginning of the transatlantic slave trade. Additionally, the Igbo did not form a single ethnic bloc. Some Igbo communities found today in southeastern Nigeria have lived here since the prehistoric era. Others moved in at different times. Therefore, cultural immersions into the ancient Bantu traditions differed from place to place within and outside Igboland. These differences challenge strict ethnicization of African American cultural artifacts as Igbo, Èfik, Akán, or Mande for that matter.

On the other side of the Atlantic, the comparative focus is placed more on Jamaica, the Virgin Islands, Trinidad and Tobago, and other places in the Caribbean where many Igbo slaves disembarked. These islands took in more Bight of Biafra slaves than other places, and, more important, African-style masquerades were not widely dispersed in North America other than in Louisiana. In the New World, Igbo migrants shared everyday life with other enslaved Africans, European planters, and Native Americans. The Igbo culture and their journey started from the Igbo country in Nigeria.

Over the course of this research, I made ten different trips to southeastern/southwestern Nigeria, Senegal, Mali, and Ghana between 2006 and 2017 to conduct ethnographical research. The present study is the first to combine both the big and small pictures to deeply probe the question of origins in order to identify multiple specific cultural practices associated with an ethnic group, a culture area, and/or a demographic group in Africa and closely examine all these along with African diasporic genres using the multilevel agent-based modeling paradigmatic approach.

Partly, some of the theoretical underpinnings of this book are sourced from pertinent agent-based modeling ideas related to cooperation studies. Much current agent-based modeling produces results that are either ahistorical or anachronistic if applied either to the Ancient Global Age or to the First Global Age. Cooperation, as Robert Keohane has noted, "Requires that the actions of separate individuals or organizations—which are not in pre-existent harmony—be brought into conformity with one another through a process of policy coordination."[30] A modified form of this theory is employed to further support the assertion that when alien cultures cross parts, they first engage in a process of dialogue and negotiation. Over time, the superior civilization tends to gain authority over the weaker culture. In West African history, for example, the Fulani militarily conquered the Hausa city-states in the early nineteenth century, but the Hausa language ended up emasculating the Fulani (Fula) language. Globally, the superior strength of Western education has triumphed over other traditional forms of socialization found in Asia, Africa, and pre-Columbian America. Likewise, the masquerade culture of the original Bantu homeland has claimed a prominent place within the mantra of popular cultures. This came about through its proven relevance as a tool of political administration, social mobilization capacity, and entertainment value. One unique part of this study on masquerades, which the African village elders cleverly promoted as political actors in spirit forms, is that it gives a sense of how the tradition has changed over time as the contexts and concepts continue to respond to changes both on the local and global arenas—from the ancient, medieval, colonial, and postcolonial eras.

Given the paucity of written works on precolonial Africa, snippets of data on masking from oral accounts are augmented with information from rare books and memoirs left behind by Arab and European visitors to Africa. These materials cover the period from the thirteenth to the late nineteenth-century colonization of Africa. Few examples include the writings of Ibn Battuta (1324); Leo Africanus (1526); Manuel Álvares (1526–1583); Anna Maria Falconbridge's memoir published in series of letters (1794); John Barbot, who made a voyage to Old Calabar (1699); Thomas Astley and John Churchill (1732); C. G. A. Oldendorp, a missionary in Sierra Leone who wrote on Calabar (1777); Olaudah Equiano (1789); and many others.[31]

Sources of information on the activities of African slaves in the colonial Americas—beginning from the fifteenth century European colonization of the

New World—came from newspaper reports and records left behind by colonial administrators, planters, and visitors. Examples include Hans Sloane (1752), Edward Long (1774), James Barclay (1777), Matthew Gregory Lewis (1816), Michael Scott (1836), Joseph Tuckerman (1837), Isaac Mendes Belisario (1838), Joseph John Gurney Charles (1840), and William Day (1852).[32] These works, despite their flaws, provide a solid source of information when used along with the copious secondary literature on Caribbean masquerade carnivals.

Of course, a comparative study of this nature poses some anecdotal and logistic problems. First, Igbo (or any other ethnic) masks and masquerades cannot be studied in isolation from similar traditions found among the Èfik, Ibibio, and Ijọ neighbors. Before the late nineteenth-century beginnings of European colonialism in Africa, the Igbo and their various neighbors had been exchanging cultural institutions and ideas through ritual, economic, trading, political, war, and marriage interactions. In essence, Igbo traditions and institutions are products of both internal and external forces. This is where the idea of a Cross River Basin Bantu Culture Area model is found relevant. However, critics such as Julian Steward and Marvin Harris have accentuated three main shortfalls of the culture area approach: "(1) center and boundary change with passage of time, (2) culture within the area may change so that it resembles cultures in different areas at different times, and (3) portions of the area may be regarded as containing radically different cultures despite sharing of many features."[33] While these problems rather enhance the Bantu Culture Area approach, being conscious of them is important in order to avoid generalization and romanticism.

Second, though the Igbo comprised one of the largest populations of Africans shipped off from the Bight of Biafra entrepôt between the mid-sixteenth century and the 1850s, there is no cohesive African Diaspora community solely constituted by the Igbo. Not even the so-called Maroon communities found in large numbers in the swamps and forests of Surinam, the mountains of Jamaica, and the Brazilian Amazon jungle could claim ethnic homogeneity. Where a precise ethnic identification is possible, as some related studies of the early Igbo communities in the U.S. Virgin Islands, Jamaica, Maryland, and Virginia imply, it is still important to acknowledge that the succeeding descendants of the Igbo ex-slaves have, over the centuries, lost this sense of Igboness.[34]

Third, for individuals who had lived in small village communities, the enslaved Igbos in Americas, with a knack for adaptation, had successfully transformed their village consciousness into a larger Pan-African and transnational/transatlantic identity. Example of the Igbo mentality in the African Diasporas is found with the demeanor exhibited by James Africanus Horton (1835–1883), the legendary surgeon, intellectual, and African nationalist born of recaptive Igbo parents in Sierra Leone. Christopher Fyfe informs us that while Horton actively identified with his Igbo cultural association in Freetown, he was first and foremost a Pan-Africanist who never desired to go back to the Igbo country.[35] This corroborates Michael Gomez's assertion of a Pan-Africanist ideology as held by the African Diasporas.[36] Thus, a comparative examination of the underlying premises of African masks and African Diaspora carnivals promises a rich harvest of culture and ethnohistorical ideas.[37] In a broader sense, this inquiry is in agreement with the UNESCO initiative aimed at bridging the gap that "separates the academic study of slavery and the slave trade from a full and general appreciation of the heritage of Africa in the diaspora and the modern world."[38]

Chapter Outline

This book consists of eight chapters beyond this introduction. Chapter 1, "On Origins of Masking: History, Memory, and Rituals Observances," explores the discernment of the early development of masks and masquerades between the prism of religion and ritual abstractions and the ingenuity of physically costuming "spirit beings" for the public theater. In line with the nonlinear principle in which this inquiry is situated, characteristics, forms, and rhythms in both artistic and performance art forms are seen as growing from multiple sources cutting across world regions and timelines. In preindustrial European agrarian communities, for instance, masquerades served as vehicles for social regulation much as they did in precolonial Africa. Also, mindful of the fact that the earliest recorded evidence of masked art forms existed in ancient Egypt, the elevation of abstract notions of spirits to a physical entity in "bodily forms" was first conceived and appropriated in the Igbo/Èfik/Ibibio/Kálábári or Ijọ homelands. Michael Echeruo corroborated this idea in 1981 with the conclusion that "the Igbo will do what the Greek did, expand ritual into life and give that life a secular base."[39] However, Echeruo's theater-based analysis did not fully capture the strength of Igbo costumed spirit-regarding masquerade invention. In fact, Victor Ukaegbu has aptly argued that because of the uniqueness of the symbolism it connotes, Igbo masking tradition "cannot be squeezed into any other model because of its cultural praxis."[40] In the ensuing discussions, the religious observances, political frameworks, practices of gender, and other values defining the sociopolitical milieu in which the mask and masquerade tradition emanated in the Biafra hinterland area are explained.

Chapter 2, "Aspects of Society and Culture in the Biafra Hinterland," offers a unique laboratory for testing the process of cultural globalization developing from a small corner of the world in West Africa in the Ancient Global
Age. A synthesis of ethnographic and anthropological accounts of culture,
religion, government, and masquerade plays of the main groups like the Igbo,
Èfik, Ibibio, and Ijọ are covered.[41] Also included are the different classifications
of African masks and masquerades and their sociopolitical functions. While
Abner Cohen defined masquerade "carnival" in its Western understanding as
"a season of festive popular events that are characterized by revelry, playfulness,
and overindulgence,"[42] Ben Enweonwu reminds us "African art is not really the
Western context but an invocation of ancestral spirits through giving concrete
form or body to them before they can enter into the human world."[43] Thus, the
functions of African masks and masquerades are analyzed under two classes: (1)
"spirit-regarding art" and (2) "man-regarding art." In the former category, masquerade plays are infused with religious rituals and ideas for social control. The
latter art form is the more secular carnival culture that was easily reinvented in
the African Diaspora. The result is an illustration of how the practice of masking developed and became entrenched in society as a force of imperial culture
par excellence.

Chapter 3, "Bantu Migrations and Cultural Transnationalism in the Ancient
Global Age, c. 2500 BCE–1400 CE," focuses on the Cross River-Igbo masquerade's travels within the continent. The copious literature on the Bantu details
the culture and customs of groups in the Bantu Culture Area. However, it is no
longer a secret that these studies are fraught with serious errors and conjectures
that often miss the facts. An important corrective in this chapter is that the
Cross River Igbo, Èfik, Ibibio, and Ijọ belong to the same linguistic culture and
the present areas they occupy are part of the Bantu cradle. The history of the
Bantu migration is an inquiry in agent-based modeling—that is a study in the
dispersal and spreading of culture across the continent. This excursion on Bantu
cultural artifacts reveals that across the continent, diverse aspects of Bantu traditions have been adapted to local needs. Within Africa, masquerade forms such as
the Ágábá and Okoroshá masquerade festivals of the Ábágáná, Ífákálá, Umunneọhá, Mbieri, Ọgwá, and Ubomiri Igbo communities have been adapted even
in non-Bantu areas as seen with the masquerade dances of the Bamana, Bozo,
and Sòmonò groups in Mali and Guinea.[44] By the beginning of the transatlantic
slave trade in the late fifteenth century, the culture of masking (like the spread
of agricultural practices, pottery, family traditions, age-grade associations, marriage institution, and metallurgy) had completed its sub-Saharan Africa-wide

journey, thus making it one of the most important forms of sociopolitical mechanisms of religion, identity formation, social control, as well as a mode of artistic/intellectual expression.

Chapter 4, "Bight of Biafra, Slavery, and Diasporic Africa in the Modern Global Age, 1400–1800," provides an account of the masquerade expansion to the Americas. The centuries of transatlantic slavery (c. 1480–1840s) gave impetus for the slaves to serve as modeling agents in the New World, and the specific nature that masquerade carnivals assumed there is explained as a function of the agents' culture competencies, structures of power in the Americas, the slaves' social location, racial and ethnic conglomerations, and competing ideologies. The transformations undergone by African-born masquerade societies like the Ékpè, Kéléké, Ágábá, Okoroshá, and Ojiǫnu are illustrated with the Abakuá, Mocko Jumbies, Bamboula, and Jonkonnu. The changes are situated not as a retainer of the African versions but as a coupling of ideas drawn from multiple African nations to fit the needs of the new society.

Chapter 5, "Igbo Masquerade Dances in the African Diasporas: Symbols and Meanings," uses the Igbo traditions as demarcated in this study to make a potpourri prolegomena exploration of agent-based modeling and cultural diffusion in the development of New World carnival performances. The Caribbean examples are analyzed in light of possible precedents in Africa, without negating the obvious Western European contributions. Previous studies by Miller, Chambers, and Nicholls have established some linkages between the Èfik and Igbo traditional practices with the evolution of Creole culture in the African Diasporas—Cuba, Virginia, Jamaica, the United States, and the Virgin Islands.[45] This chapter attempts to put this historiography in a more nuanced context, with the caveat that elements of Igbo culture found in the African Diasporas also contain dilutions of Èfik, Igbo, Ibibio, Ijǫ, and other African ethnic traditions. For example, a closer study of the Bamboula dances of Saint Thomas, which an editorial in the Saint Thomas *Tidende* newspaper of December 28, 1872, repudiated as "a remnant of barbaric Ebo [Igbo] drum," reveals that it was a diffusion of practices from West and Central Africa, with perhaps more doses of the Kongo and Igbo prototypes.[46] One cannot also discount European and Taino cultural influences. The same pattern of cultural diffusion explains the evolution of the Jonkonnu in Jamaica and Bahamas; the Cuban Abakuá, as a re-creation of the original Ékpè masquerade of the Èfik, Ibibio, Efut, and Quá Ejághám groups of Calabar and the Árǫ, Ngwá, and Ábịrịbá communities of the Igbo.[47] The chapter reiterates that our study of African cultural practices in the New World must be pursued in the realm of "culture areas"—that is, in the metanarrative of transnationalism, because the frontiers of ideas and practices that emerged in the African Diasporas are dilutions of practices from several parts of Africa and the boundary of cultural inventions spurred the social flux that characterized the slave plantations, the abolition movements it prompted, and the postabolition social reengineering that followed.

Chapter 6, "Unmasking the Masquerade: Counterideologies and Contemporary Practices," focuses on the various meanings of masks and masquerades and the processes of transformation that include the continuing influences of the Islamic religion starting from medieval times, the transmutations resulting from the transatlantic slave trade, and the enslaved Africans' deployment of masquerade processions as an instrument of resistance against oppression. The counterpoints reveal the interface among Islamization, Christianization, and colonization of the masquerades in both Africa and in the African Diasporas; the (re)-secularization of the institutions that were in the past exclusively for the initiates; and their intersections with the European culture and its globalization. The nature of the relationship between the two unequal forces (Western and African roots) explains the characteristics masquerade carnivals assumed in the African Diasporas.

Chapter 7, "Idioms of Religion, Music, Dance, and Africana Art Forms," highlights the integral meanings of the various cultural forms in the lives of people of African descent. It shows that music and dance constitute legitimate spheres of intellectual production. The elder who legitimized the tradition, the artist who carved the mask, the chief priest who infused the art object with sacred powers, the singer who composed the songs and poems for the festivities, and the dancer who moves to the rhythms—all must be understood as producers of texts. Their studied philosophical ideas deserve more than a casual attention; a more insightful interpretation is offered in order to appreciate the unique wisdom and value constructs packaged in the practice of masking. Diverse musical genres and dance forms in both Africa and the African Diasporas are interpreted along with some masquerade songs, incantations, words of wisdom, puzzles, poetries, and proverbs as intellectual expressions.

Chapter 8, "Memory and Masquerade Narratives: The Story of Remembering," furthers our appreciation of the effectiveness of masquerade carnivals in structuring narrative forms that have, across the centuries, responded and continue to respond to the needs of those societies that created them. Masquerade narratology changes as the society transforms. This dynamism ties into the central argument of this study—that African masks and masquerades may be prototypes of the African Diaspora genres but the latter need not be judged as a replica or one-on-one retentions of the African mother culture.

In whole, this book offers pristine ideas of how to imagine the rise and spread of African masquerades as a product of clusters of ideas echoing the needs of the societies that produced them. In the modernist praxis, the global detours of African masking style have followed the progression of culture "psychologization"— that is, a process of adaptation of culture to needs and habits of the present. One cannot agree more with Leonard Binder and Joseph La Palombra that "modern culture is self-conscious about functional sequences of its patterns." Definitely, "the rejection of nonrational symbols has gone hand in hand with the rejection of various forms of group mystique."[48] Within this dynamism, the African-styled masquerade carnivals have, over time, mutated and adapted to the needs of those that play them.

CHAPTER I

On Origins of Masking

History, Memory, and Ritual Observances

The masquerade edifies my existence
I, arriving from the nether world
The drummers and flutists announce my arrival
I, the earth goddess who rides the heavenly galaxies
The music in the air honors my ancestry
I, whose offspring have crossed mighty seas to distant places
The dancers and onlookers acknowledge my motherhood
I, whose being twirls to the rhythms of memory.

— Ezeowu, Okoroshá masquerade dancer (2008)

OZZY EZEOWU'S POETICS (*UBE*) associated with the Christmas and
New Year Okoroshá masks and masquerade festivities in the Achi-
Mbieri in Owerri-Igbo area of southeastern Nigeria mirrors the power
of this African culture as a site of history, memory, ritual observances, self-rein-
vention, intellectual episteme, and cultural identity. The *mask*, for the purpose
of clarity, is literally a camouflage, covering or disguise used to hide one's physical appearance either wholly or partially during a public performance. Richard
Woodward elucidates that the "full drama of a mask includes an entire custom
and even more important, a human setting with music, dance, and song."[1] Thus,
the *masquerade* is the theatrical or performing art form of the mask—that is,
wearing the mask and its accessories and costumes—which electrifies the participants into a festive spirit. The art of costuming—which usually makes use of
fabrics and other items of clothing, ornaments, accessories, and colors adorned
by actors and actresses for the purpose of defining and establishing the circumstances of the character's existence in time and space—is the critical tool with

which the Igbo and their neighbors literally turned lifeless objects created by humans into mobile spirits and divinities.

In African precolonial society without a well-developed and widely shared writing culture, masquerade celebrations were constituted and observed in due times and seasons as living histories. For example, among the Yoruba of south-western Nigeria (who are also found in the present-day Francophone Republic of Niger), the Gélédé masquerade purportedly honors the earth spirits and the ancestors, and celebrates "Mothers" (*áwon iyá wá*)—chief among them, the earth goddess, female spirits, and elderly women.[2] The annual Gélédé (or Èfé) fiesta highlights the status of women and pacifies their hypothetically dangerous mystical powers. As performers ascribe honor to women in a male-controlled society, the Gélédé, "the festival of supplication," effectively serves a purifying role in society.[3] Of course, the purpose, utilities, or needs of masks and masquerades change as new ideas and other forces change society. In the context of transatlantic slavery (c. 1440s–1880s) for instance, the Gélédé was invoked by the Yoruba elders to soothe the colossal pains afflicted on mothers whose offspring were kidnapped by slavers and sold off to overseas destinations. During the course of the Gélédé fêtes, gender conflicts and other sociopolitical issues are considered in public. The preparation of Gélédé masks and masquerade runs for months, and celebrations usually commence at midnight when the big mask heralds start of the festivities. On the next day, the lesser masks take turns to entertain the audience, satirizing even the most vexing and daunting sociopolitical issues.[4] Corroborating this idea, Sachin Dete adds that like the other Yoruba masquerades including the Egungun (a manifestation of Yoruba ancestors), the Gélédé uses "satirical devices as a means of enforcing conformity in society."[5]

Neither the functions ascribed to the Gélédé nor the specific value of finding balance in the midst of chaos that the masquerade festival represents is solely unique to the Yoruba. Across the continent in the precolonial era, diverse African communities deployed masks and masquerades for similar functions: they aided governments as an arm of law enforcement, supported justice administration, compelled social conformity, and fought crimes in order to maintain balance and a more peaceful order in a world fraught with disorder and chaos. While scholarly interest in masquerades and carnival jamborees has grown exponentially in the past four decades, the primary and perhaps most pertinent questions that have not been fully addressed in the copious literature remain when, why, and how the masquerade tradition came about.

In surveying these intriguing questions, the theory of nonlinear dynamics and chaos is adopted, albeit in a modified form, to explore an opportunity for scholars to test the processes of cultural emergence and expansion in a transregional/transnational context. Additionally, we interrogate the tie between memory and discourse embodied in this genre of African literal art form, using clearly identified specific regional case studies. Moreover, since masquerade displays are mass oriented, an attempt here is made to reorient social, economic, and intellectual endeavors toward the masses rather than the elite in contradistinction to what the theory of elitism often purports. In Gramscian theory, elite domination of the lower classes is called "the 'normal' exercise of hegemony," and Gramsci sees hegemony to be the spontaneous acceptance of the moral and cultural values, as well as the general world outlook and its influence on various practical activities of the ruling class by the majority of the people of the subordinate classes.[6] But diverging from the idea that elite culture dominates popular ideologies, here the agency is accorded to the masses with the contention that cultural production and observances are a two-way dialogue, a collaborative project between the masses and the elite. Together, the low and the high in society contribute to the production of dominant cultures.

Ideology, Nonlinear Dynamics, Order, and Chaos

There have been mostly inconclusive and contrary views as to when and where the masquerade culture began, but hardly any discussion of how. One suggestion on origins emanating from Europe and by extension the colonial Caribbean and colonial South America purports that masking originated in Italy where the term *maschera* gained currency in the thirteenth century with the Carnival of Venice (Italian: *Carnevale di Venezia*). According to this view, masking evolved and expanded from Venice to France (French: *mascarade*) around 1393, and subsequently to other European countries, including Great Britain.[7] Venetian masks are today recognized by their ornate design, with bright colors such as gold or silver and the adaption of intricate designs in the baroque style. The bulk of Venetian mask designs come from commedia dell'arte, either full-face masks (e.g., the *bauta*) or eye masks (e.g., the Columbina). The Italians wore their masks with decorative beads matching in color.

The Italian masking and masquerade carnival has been cast as a purely secular rather than religious observance. But Samuel Glotz and Marguerite Qerlemans's study of European masks reveals that "originally, the European masks assumed the same religious function as those of other continents and other civilizations."[8]

FIGURE 1.1. European mask, 1555. Used with permission
from the Rijksmuseum, Amsterdam.

Linda Carroll adds that "the fundamental themes" of European masks "were
rooted in the Indo-European belief that cosmological and vegetation cycles fostered the life of spring by eliminating the deadening influence of the old and by
emphasizing the bodily functions that would generate and sustain the new."[9]
The ancient religious roots began to change with the emergence of urbanization,
the Enlightenment movement, and spread of industrialization in the continent.
Over the centuries, the masking celebrations that often came during the winter
season assumed a more secular nature during which the participants tended to
abandon decency for reverie and overindulgence in the fun, food, unconventional manners of dressing, noisemaking, erotic dances/parades, slothfulness,
wastefulness, and antigovernment rhetoric. In her study of the Venetian masks,
Carroll argues that angry young men like Angelo Beolco "used the tradition of
anti-establishment criticism and obscenity associated with Carnival as a vehicle

for protest against his exclusion and the greed and hypocrisy of the ruling class which he felt lay at its root. His espousal of the peasants, whom he portrayed as impoverished by the city people's rapacious desire for money and food, was inspired not only by a concern for their plight but by their symbolization of his own."[10] As a result, by the eighteenth century, wearing masks in everyday life in Italy was considered by many religious and political groups as a public nuisance. The elite, therefore, limited the masked carnivals only to three months, from December 26 to the end of March—that is, the end of the Lenten period or Easter eve.[11]

Implicit in the Venetian-origins hypothesis, encountered in the early literature on masquerade carnivals, is the suggestion that African slaves in the colonial Caribbean and Latin America were inspired by watching White planters indulge in masquerade plays. With regards to origins of the Trinidadian masquerade carnival, Michael Anthony reports that it all began when "the French settlers and their slaves from the Windward Islands began to crowd into Trinidad"[12] following the "Cedula of Population for Trinidad," a decree proclaimed by King Carlos IV of Spain in 1783 to allow immigrants into the island in the face of the imminent threat of British colonization.[13] According to Anthony, the immigrants "were the people who brought the carnival to Trinidad. They came from Grenada, Guadeloupe, and Martinique."[14] As the "French Whites, who in the main owned the estates, celebrated the Roman Catholic feast of Carnival in their great houses," the Africans, as some of the historical literature emphasizes, reportedly started mimicking and ridiculing the White elite as a mode of protest against the oppressive plantation culture in the Americas.[15]

Errol Hill, in *The Trinidad Carnival*, acknowledges that during the period of British rule of this Caribbean island nation—that is prior to emancipation, from 1797 to 1834, "carnival was an important institution for Whites, and free coloreds, particularly in the towns."[16] Hill echoes previous studies such as those by Andrew Pearse, Andrew Carr, and Raphael DeLeon, who all claimed that masked carnivals originated from Europe.[17] At best, these studies suggest that the elite White culture was in existence earlier than the emergence of the Negro-Creole-themed masquerade carnival dances in this American island nation. A similar potpourri assessment has been concluded by John Chasteen in regard to the pre-Lenten Samba carnival dancing in Rio de Janeiro. Chasteen underscores that the *lundu* carnival dance in Rio (Brazil) predated the subsequent Creole-led samba dances that began from late nineteenth century and grew in popularity in the twentieth century to become the part of national culture it

FIGURE 1.2. Masquerade dress, Europe, 1596–1635. Used with permission from the Rijksmuseum, Amsterdam.

FIGURE 1.3. The Carnival of Venice, 1726. Used with permission from the
Rijksmuseum, Amsterdam.

has assumed today.[18] It is useful to recall to memory an Igbo proverb: "He who
joins a story midway runs the risk of a gross misunderstanding."[19] What these
different but similar accounts that point to Europe as the birthplace of carnival
tell us is *when* the masquerade carnivals arrived in the Caribbean but not *how*
and *where* they originated.

In line with the nonlinear approach in which this entire inquiry is situated,
characteristics, forms, and rhythms in both artistic and performance art forms
are perceived as growing from multilinear sources rather than from a single
source or timeline. Within European agrarian communities in preindustrial
times, masquerades operated as vehicles for social regulation much as they did
in West Africa. Violet Alford maintains that the horned masquerade known
as the Ooser of Melbury Osmond in Dorset, England, could be "brought out
for the punishment of village wrongdoers in a Skimmington [a rowdy parade]
or Rough Music."[20] Alford notes that in parts of Germany during yuletide, a
mask portraying the kindhearted Saint Nicholas appeared accompanied by a
grotesque figure (a Bad Santa) called Knecht Ruprecht, clad in skins, or straw,
with a fierce deportment.[21] The "good children get cakes for saying their prayers;
the bad ones are beaten with ash-bags."[22] Robert Nicholls explains that those
identified as "bad children" were hit with a bag full of ash until they are covered
in dust. Nicholls further notes that ash is part of "funeral wake adornment in
much of West Africa," and that during Christmas and New Year festivities in
Saint Thomas, participants going out without costumes were pestered with flour
or confetti—obvious substitutes for ash.[23] It is a fact that Christmas was adapted

from the ancient Germanic Yule celebration of the winter solstice observed in many parts of Europe featuring antlers, horns, and animal skin costumes to mark the onset of the sun's rebirth; renewal rituals in most societies are deeply spiritual.[24]

There is no overriding need to dismiss the European influences on masquerade carnivals in the New World. It is worth mentioning though that John Picton has noted that the term *masquerade* entered into the European lexicon from the Arabic verb *sakhira* meaning "to laugh, scoff, jeer, ridicule, mock, deride, and make fun."[25] This means that the Arab masking practices may have predated the European genre; while Caribbean or Latin American antecedents may have provided factual social milieus in which the African players would rediscover their rich repertoire of inherited masquerade dances, the fact of the matter is that masking is as old as human civilization, which started in Africa. Murals and other paintings by artists of ancient Egypt reveal that masks and their imageries were present in the social and political traditions of ancient people. As early as the 3000 BCE, Egyptians produced masks and invoked them in their religious observances as "death masks" and "ritual masks." The Egyptians believed that it was important to preserve the dead body as a dwelling place for the soul or spirit that lives on; hence the science of mummification was widely practiced as part of the unending interchange between the dead and the living.[26] For the departed soul to be able to identify the lifeless physical body to which it would return, the Egyptians considered it a necessity to design their death masks (often made from wood and papyrus) in the likeness of the deceased. Some of the most famous funerary masks left behind by these ancient people are the masks of the eighteenth-dynasty pharaoh Tutankhamen, who reigned 1332–1324 BCE and Ramses II (r. 1279–1213 BCE), the third king of the nineteenth dynasty.[27] Usually, royal death masks were made from precious metals, such as gold (or gold leaf) and bronze.

Like the Egyptians, the Aztecs of pre-Columbian Mexico followed the tradition of many ancient peoples: they used death masks in celebration of the "Day of the Dead," Dia de los Muertos.[28] In other words, the early Aztec arts also reveal religious themes such as ancestor worship, a practice that goes with music and dancing dating back to about 3000 BCE. One of the notable aspects of Aztec culture and mask designs is that they were primarily for display, not to be worn as apparel or gear as in performance art. This explains why there are masks with no eye-holes, or masks placed on stone or on skulls. With certain exceptions, the eyes are closed as one in a state of death.[29] In contrast, all death masks of ancient Egypt were made after the likeness of the deceased but with slightly enlarged

FIGURE 1.4. Death mask of Ramses II of
ancient Egypt. Used with permission from the
Rijksmuseum, Amsterdam.

eyes and a faint smile. The depictions of earliest masks of Egypt also revealed the
fashion of their times with painted jewelry and makeup. Painted ritual masks,
made from cartonnage (layers of papyrus covered with plaster) in the likeness of
animal heads and heads of gods of Egypt (such as Anubis, god of death), were
worn by priests during funeral ceremonies such as the "Opening of the Mouth,"
which was a symbolic animation of a mummy. At these occasions, the priest, the
privileged interpreter between the worlds of the dead and the living, would wear
a head mask that concealed his head and shoulders so that he was constrained to
peep through a couple of tiny holes cut on the neck of the mask.[30]

In Asia, masks featured in highly archetypal religious and profane dramas
of China, Sanskrit Ramlila in India, and in Korean, Tibetan, and Mongolian
shamanism.[31] For several millennia, masks featured in the Indian tradition as

a vehicle to express belief systems, dance, and festival moods. Writing in *The Tribune* in 2006, K. D. L. Khan recalls that the ancient people of India treated religious-themed masks as sacred cult objects: "Each mask seems to be unique. But after viewing many, we begin to see that they fall into iconographic groups. Most strong masks, such as tribal masks, Sikkim lama masks, masks of demonic characters (devils and evil spirits), and masks used in sacrificial rites and cult initiation, reflect integral relationships of icon, mask, and movement."[32] The stylized Noh drama masking tradition of Japan that features in the popular theater goes back to the thirteenth century as the oldest surviving performing art form.[33]

The ancient Egyptian, Asian, American, and European genres show that it is difficult to conclude categorically when and where the masking tradition was first observed. In other words, it is also anecdotal to suggest that the Egyptian tradition predated the Igbo observances or even insinuate that Asians borrowed their masking tradition from the ancient Egyptians or vice versa. The overriding point is that religion is used by these ancient societies as a baseline in a nonlinear impulse-response and multistep phenomenon with a leverage effect. One vital fact offered by Herodotus on the origin of carnival as a public parade is found when he described the ancient Egyptians as "the first who introduced public festivals, processions, and solemn supplications." Herodotus further concluded that "the Greek learned from them [Egyptians] for these rites appear to have been lately introduced" in Greece.[34] If we accept Herodotus literally, the Greeks borrowed religious-themed public processions from Egypt, but the exact time this took place is not clear.

In a complex historical work of this nature with confusing timelines, the relevance of thinking spatially and reasoning in line with the science of nonlinear dynamics, order, and chaos becomes crucial. Nonlinear dynamics, according to its proponents, arise whenever multifarious entities of a system cooperate, compete, or interfere.[35] One is not by any means implying that ancient peoples were in competition among themselves or that specifically Egyptians were competing with Europeans, Asians, or Aztecs. Rather, the symbolism and fascination each of these cultures found with dead masks were part of the quest to resolve the conflict and chaos associated with the mysteries of life and death. The ancient peoples, through their paintings, took the first courageous steps to ascribe to the gods and spirits some form of physical features that aligned with the fashion and artistic traditions of their times, as revealed in the ancient Egyptian dead masks. But the ancients came short of providing the spirits and divinities with unique costumes—that is, the out-of-this-world attire, mobility, and mannerisms that

have come to be uniquely associated with Igbo/Èfik/Ibibio/Kálábári or Ijọ masquerades in particular and African masquerades in general.

Also, there is no intent here to use the ancient Egyptian practices to either
degenerate or privilege the North American (Aztec) or Asian (Indian, Chinese)
cultures. In his *Muqaddimah: An Introduction to History* (1377), Ibn Khaldun
(1332–1406), the eminent medieval Arabic philosopher-historian, declared:
"History is an art of valuable doctrine, numerous in advantages and honorable
in purpose; it informs us about bygone nations in the context of their habits,
the prophets in the context of their lives and kings in the context of their states
and politics, so those who seek the guidance of the past in either worldly or
religious matter may have that advantage."[36] With those words, Ibn Khaldun
stated the obvious: nonlinear dynamical systems defy understanding based on
the traditional reductionist approach, in which one attempts to understand a
system's behavior by combining all constituent parts that have been analyzed
separately. Available techniques on nonlinear dynamics are either not concerned
with historical analytical objectives or fail to closely look at the big picture (baseline) along with the case study (or small picture) with the potential to extract
useful information for improving understanding of multiplier ideas. While taking advantage of both the big picture and small picture approaches, the obvious
challenges of cultural complexity in historical analysis involving multilinear/
multivariate dimensions are tackled using two new approaches. As encountered
in the natural and applied sciences where multilead electrocardiogram (ECG)
signals are generated through orchestrated depolarization and repolarization of
cells and manifest significant nonlinear dynamics, here, we harness an understanding of the origins of the masquerade culture within depolarized and repo-
larized interfaces of religion.

To proceed, depolarization and repolarization, as relating to the origin of
masking, reminds us that religion, in its diverse and time-honored forms, has
always provided the incubator in which humanity's proclivity for answers to life
challenges have been sought. The fact allows one to assert the obvious—that
cultural inventiveness associated with masks and masquerades were hatched in
the ancient times within the incubator of religion. In the past three decades following Steven Strogatz's work, the ideas and techniques of nonlinear dynamics
and chaos have found resonance in new fields such as systems biology, evolutionary game theory, and sociophysics.[37] Extending this to the field of religion as a
universal practice makes sense in the context of cultural contact or cultures in
opposition, chaos, adaptation, and order.

Religion in human society came about to bring order to a world in which humans encounter chaos in every event, especially in those natural phenomena and mysteries associated with death, darkness, processes of birth, natural disasters, and so on. In light of this, we impose a theory of first-order differential equation and bifurcation in nonlinear dynamics with the assertion that religion-borne masking was not solely African/Egyptian, Asian/Indian, or Aztec/American. It was a natural response to life mysteries as detected by mortal humanity's powerlessness within the natural environment. To further explore this idea, using African cosmology, what follows is a culture's reinterpretation of Strogatz's configuration of phase plane analysis, limit cycles, and their bifurcations, based largely on the "Lorenz equations" characterized by "chaos, iterated maps, period doubling, renormalization, fractals, and strange attractors."[38]

African Cosmology and Religion

Like in all cosmologies, the indigenous African belief system is shrouded in mystery, and the existentialism of masquerades emerged as part of the indigenous belief in the pantheon of gods and spirits that have been roaming the African universe. This is a world in which the belief is strongly held that the living and the dead share a continuing relationship. Africans transplanted to the New World during the era of transatlantic slavery did not copy the masquerade tradition both as a religious entity and an art form from their host societies. Rather, the captives learned about masks and masquerades back in Africa where it served, not only as an embodiment of the indigenous religion, but also an important arm of the political administration, civil society mobilization, and identity expression. Masquerading was more pronounced in those communities such as the Igbo and Ibibio with decentralized political systems. Chike Aniakor's study of Igbo social space through analysis of household objects and architecture identifies the principles of dualism and complementarity as profound in the sociocultural and political domains. The pairing of concepts such as human and spirit, men and women, old and young, Black and White, and a cyclical relationship between paired beings or objects, underlies the shaping of Igbo material culture and space.[39] The Igbo ascription to the bifurcation ideology is encountered in the everyday saying: *Ife kwulu, ifé ákwudobé yá, ife di, ife ádidobe yá* (Where one thing stands, something else stands beside it. Or where one thing exists, something else exists besides).[40] Chidi G. Osuagwu has distilled this concept in *Truth and Chaos: Dynamics of Truth within Igbo Cosmology* with the explanation that the pairing of visible and invisible objects and things in the Igbo world could variously manifest as an alter ego, a protagonist, or a complementarity.[41]

At this juncture, the question as to how and why the masquerade performances came to be in Africa is addressed, using relevant legends and traditions found in the continent as specific examples. Guest-historian Richard Igwebe is perhaps the first to attempt an explanation of the origin of masquerades in his native town of Arọndizuọgu. The legend tells us that one Okoye Nwaobi, aka Okoye Mmọnwu ("Okoye the Masquerade") "introduced masquerade in Arondizuogu."[42] According to the story, Nwaobi was involved in a land dispute with a formidable opponent with whom he could not match. After the usurper had forcefully taken over Nwaobi's family inheritance, he proceeded to hire laborers to start cultivating on the farm. But Nwaobi had a plan that involved frightening his opponent with masquerades he had hidden in the farm. Pretending that these masked beings were the ghostly manifestation of his late father, Nwaobi screamed "My father! My father! Wherever you are; come and save your only son." While repeating these words in a more desperate tone, "one of the masquerades jumped [out of his hiding place] to the farm; both the workers and their leaders started to run home. This served as the introduction of masquerade."[43] Like most legends, the story is contextualized in the contemporary era and it is bereft of exact timelines. Also, the narrative neither provides the name of Nwaobi's opponent nor from where the protagonist brought the masked beings. Thus, this is only an explanatory myth rather than a valid historical fact. William Bascom has noted, "Legends are prose narratives which, like myths, are regarded as true by the narrator and his audience, but they are set in a period considered less remote when the world was much as it is today." Bascom further explains that "legends are more often secular than sacred and their principal characters are human."[44] Among other things, legends offer accounts of deeds of past heroes, migrations, wars and victories, and succession in ruling dynasties. While they are usually the verbal equivalent of written history, they also involve local tales of ghosts, saints, buried treasure, and fairies.

In a more nuanced and paradigmatic context, Alex Asigbo has offered some theories on the origin of the masquerade art in Africa. One of these has been branded the *power-balancing theory*, which vindicates Michel Foucault's notion of dispersed centers of power.[45] In many African communities, the practice of witchcraft (i.e., sorcery or invocation of malicious spirits for selfish and often harmful purposes) is used to punish and/or intimidate rivals and critics. This ancient form of science is dominated by women, who supposedly execute it under the cover of darkness. To counter this problem, considered potent enough to cause disorder and chaos in society, the power-balancing theory says that the male elders came together to institute the exclusive male masquerade cult. Whenever witches attacked at night and something strange occurred, masquerades were beckoned to unravel the mystery and expose the perpetrators behind the mischief. In the awareness that there is an extraordinary power coming to expose them, naturally, witches and similar mischief-makers tended to observe more caution.[46] The similar ideology of social control has been linked to the Gélédé and Egungun masquerades among the Yoruba. Olakumbi Olasope argues that the tremendous power women appropriate and their dreadful capacity as witches have therefore been been offered as the primary cause patriarchal elders instituted the masquerade art and excluded female involvement in the night activities of *Eku 'rahu* (masquerade).[47]

Standing alone, the power-balancing theory does not provide a convincing explanation for the masquerade origin; at best, it is a part of the story within a broader narrative centered on religion, politics, and social control. For instance, while the theory recognized women as having the upper hand in the practice of sorcery, it says nothing about the equally destructive role of wizards in the exercise of intimidation and injustice in the indigenous society. In African culture, notions of witchcraft include a view of extremely rich people whose size of wealth was considered abnormal—and these individuals were often men. Perhaps more noticeably absent in power-balancing theory is its silence on how women acquire the powers that enable them to fly about at night punishing their enemies. Is this power specifically reserved for women, and by whom? Additionally, the theory tends to suggest that witchcraft was the sole source of social problems and that religious decadence stemmed solely from sorcery. Implicit in this line of reasoning is the idea that the only duty assigned to the masquerades was combating the menace of witches in society or social control in general. The truth of the matter is that there are other potent threats to society, and masquerades served a broader purpose, including addressing spiritual and secular afflictions encountered in everyday life such as theft, murder, incest, adultery, arson, spiritual madness, and other related problems threatening individuals, households, and society with chaos and social disorder, inhibiting natural laws, and rule of justice.

Echoing the influence of geography in shaping human cultures, Ogbu Kalu argues in specific reference to the use of masquerades in Igbo, "it would be useful to examine the impact of ecology and cultural differentiation in Igboland on modes of social control."[48] The pertinent question arises as to whether societies design control techniques suitable to the imperatives of their culture theatres.

The present study agrees with Kalu to affirm that social control or coercion alone as the primary role of the precolonial masquerade societies in Africa is not enough to fully appreciate the multifaceted roles the masquerades played. In other words, the study of an element of custom like the masquerade institution cannot be reduced to a single story. A society controls the behavior of its members in four different but related ways that are relevant to this study. First, every society enunciates and inculcates acceptable values in its members through the approved processes of socialization/enculturation: family, school, marriage, peer influence, sports, and so on.[49] Second, the society takes appropriate steps to restrain members from breaking those values. In this regard, prescription of punishment and threats alone are not enough to deter offenders. Rather, modeling and encouraging individuals to identify with civil society engagements are crucial. Third, on the side of negative reinforcement, the society punishes those who break its norms and values, and the punishment is tailored to effectively convey the message that consequences abound for those who violate the law. Fourth, there is the advantage of rewards or what psychologists call "positive reinforcement" in human behavior conditioning.[50] Society rewards those who respect and uphold social norms and values in order to emphasize that the community appreciated those virtues. It is the totality of these four processes that constitute "social control," which denotes the means by which a society preserves itself from social and moral chaos and extinction.[51]

To further illustrate the point, a quick look at a recent event in Yemen allows us to better understand the tenor of justice administration served by masquerades societies in indigenous African society. In the incident that occurred in July 2017, Mohammed Saad Mujahid al-Maghrabi, a forty-one-year-old man, was found guilty in Sanaa (the Yemeni capital) by a Houthi-run court of the attack on Rana al-Matan, a three-year-old girl whom he raped and killed. His public execution with bullet shots at point blank was in response to the societal outrage that condemned this act of spiritual madness.[52] In the precolonial Igbo, Éfik, Ijọ, or Ibibio society, the appropriate punishment for acts similar to Mujahid al-Maghrabi's misdeeds would have been carried at the late hours of the night by an equally vicious Ékpè, Èkpo Ọnyohọ, Egungun, Egwurugwu, or Ágbálá masquerades. Eyewitness accounts from the medieval period have revealed that among other things, masquerades were employed by the Africans to perform crucial social control functions by enforcing discipline and upholding natural laws. Speaking of the rule of justice in the ancient Mali Empire, Ibn Battuta, the medieval Arab traveler and jurist who visited West Africa in 1352, observed that of "the small number of sets of injustice that there [in Mali] for of all peoples, the Negroes abhor it [injustice] the most" [*sic*]. Battuta further noted that the ruler of Mali, whom he referred to as "the sultan," "never pardons anyone guilty of injustice."[53] This shows that the utilitarian role of religion in the adjudication of justice in society and the powers appropriated by the masquerade cults in precolonial Africa were such that even kings were under their authority, as they were believed to be agents of supernatural wisdom.[54]

The second paradigm on masquerade origin, offering a stronger *conceptual*[55] and rounded explanation is the *omnipresent theory*. It posits that masquerades are ancestors in a momentary visit to the world of the living. This idea emanates from the conception of the African world as cyclical and interdependent. In this order as typified by the various seasons of the year, the sun, the moon, the stars, and natural events, in general, repeat themselves in an interminable way.[56] Mircea Eliade described this repetitive order in nature as the "myth of eternal return."[57] In the indigenous philosophy, the orderly succession of times and seasons symbolized harmony, persistence, and dynamism and must not be disrupted in the universe in which the different levels of space as perceived are inhabited. This corroborates the psychological and sociological approaches to the study of religion, which argue that religion is a response to strain or deprivation caused by events in society. Accordingly, when stability and peace are in society, its members deploy their efforts and energy to those pursuits that promote human well-being and happiness. These together sustain social equilibrium. However, when the peace of the society is threatened by internal conflict, selfish and mischievous people, or by outside forces, society may seek to renew itself by various means, not least through a new cult, sect, or denomination, or a brand new religion. David Aberle has maintained that relative deprivation, whether economic or social, is the cause of the stress that generates new religious movements.[58] A. E. C. Wallace suggested that the threat of societal breakdown forces people to examine new ways to survive.[59] This led Émile Durkheim to assert one of his most audacious analytical leaps—that religion is transcendental, in fact, not only a social creation but "society divinized." In a method evocative of Ludwig Feuerbach's *Essence of Christianity*,[60] Durkheim asserts that the deities that people worship are only projections of the power of society. Religion is eminently communal: it occurs in a social context and, more important, when men celebrate sacred things, they unwittingly celebrate the power of their society. This power so transcends their own existence that they have to give it sacred meaning in order to visualize it.[61] In other words, the preservation of a religious moral order is the central intent of social control techniques, while the religious ritual is used to reinforce the basic tenets of the religion and the values it promotes in society.[62]

The omnipresent theory resonates in the dead masks of ancient Egypt linked with the belief that the departed soul must return to a recognizable body, hence mummification became a preparation for life after death. In the Igbo system, Asigbo asserts, "the ancestors overcome by a perplexing nostalgia and yearning for the company of man, manifest as masquerades to commune with the living."[63] As the dead masks in ancient Egypt were modeled after the image of the dead, so did the Igbo design their masquerades to precisely mimic the character of known individuals who were deceased and now considered ancestors. The ancestral spirits and divinities "can, as the occasion demands, foretell the future and perform other ritual functions."[64]

At the level of abstraction, it is immediately obvious that while the omnipresent theory is holistic in its treatment of masquerade origins; however, its proponents did not offer an explanation as to when and how the physical creation of a mobile masquerade was accomplished. To drive the point home, an analogy from the Bible is in order. After his resurrection, Jesus Christ appeared to the ten Apostles while apostle Thomas was away.[65] At his return, Thomas found it hard to believe that his master Jesus had returned to them in his physical body after death. Thomas's demonstration of unbelief prompted Jesus Christ to reappear to his disciples a second time, during which he asked Thomas to put his hand on his side so Thomas could feel where Jesus had been stabbed on the cross with the spear by the Roman centurion guard (John 20:19–29). In light of this allegory, the Africans in essence realized that without concretizing the belief in the existence of spirits with its physical manifestations in bodily forms, the burden of proving the abstract belief in continuous presence and interest of the gods and departed ancestors in the everyday affairs of the living would have remained elusive if not utopian.

It is in the task of equipping "spirits" with masks and cladding them in unique attire that the African genius is revealed in the act of masquerading. The Africans perfected the phenotypical efficacy of masquerades as sacred entities across time and space through stretches of the imagination, philosophical thoughts, artistic designs, intricate costuming laced with awe and absurdity, secrecy, humor, and ritual observances. As Mircea Eliade summed up in his authoritative studies of the sacred and the profane, "When the sacred manifests itself, man becomes aware of the sacred because it manifests itself, shows itself, as something wholly different from the profane—[that is] a hierophant."[66] In fashioning bodily forms to invisible spirits and gods, Africans demonstrated a level of ingenuity that did not hitherto exist elsewhere.[67] They successfully created an archetypical being, a product Ola Rotimi described as "through whom the spirits breathe."[68]

At what specific point or the date the Africans of Bantu extraction mastered this aspect of masquerade is not clear, but it is safe to say that it is likely before 3000–2500 BCE—that is, prior to the first waves of Bantu population movements. This assertion is supported by the fact that the migrants could not have been able to propagate the idea outside their original homeland if they were not already well acquainted with the diverse ramifications of its practice. Between the ancient Egyptian dead masks and similar elements of belief systems found in other parts of the world, the African spirit-regarding masquerade is unique because of its ability to walk, talk, and dance; express emotions and drama or create humor; fight, carry out justice, and even predict the future in language forms the audience and onlookers could understand. Driving this point home, René A. Bravmann aptly noted that throughout the Islamic world, among the clerical elite, theologians, jurists, and the mass of believers, the concept of *djinn* (spirits) is an ever-present feature. In everyday language, folklore, and literature such as the *Thousand and One Nights*, descriptions of djinns abound in their perhaps vividly engaging and widely shared forms. But, it was in the Islamized Zara Bobo-Dyula of southwest Upper Volta that the ambiguous world of the djinn was better defined: "In a totally unique way through the agency of mask and its surrounding artistry and ritual, the Zara gave form and body to the ephemeral spirit, thereby enabling members of their society to comprehend and relate more fully to this important element within Islam."[69]

In the great majority of African folklores, masquerades are said to emerge from the earth below, from ant holes or groves hidden from inquisitive eyes of humans. The timelessness of these mythologies signifies that the origin of masquerades is buried in antiquity. The connection to Mother Earth is not by accident. The earth divinities are those no one wants to offend in the Igbo cosmos. This notion is embodied in the ritual with such songs as:

> Oh! Please, Mother Earth!!
> The land of my sojourn!
> Come and lead us.
> Famous Arusi of all lands.
> Haste and lead us.[70]

As all lives, at death, return to Mother Earth, the powers associated with this divinity are second to none other but the Creator God. Confirming the usual visits of the ancestors to the world of the living, John Illah notes, "the ancestors are believed to travel back to the living, through the mediant persona [represented by the masquerades] to partake and celebrate with their living offspring, in a re-invigoration of their relationship."[71] Masquerades are thus believed to be divinities, sons of the heavenly realm who get involved in the affairs of men through engagements that balance religious, social, and individual emotions.[72] Through this device, communities are able to moderate human vices and uphold social control since the masquerades speak with the authority of the ancestors.[73] To make the essence and functions of African masquerades more intelligible in the mutually reinforcing worlds of religion and politics—that is, the nether world and the physical world—it is crucial to examine, in detail, how the political administrations of the precolonial African societies functioned in the absence of a standing police, army, or other modern apparatuses of government and law enforcement.

Religion, Masquerades, and Politics of Control

African societies are marked by different patterns of cultural dynamics evolving over several centuries. The heart of these cultural patterns has endured with some modifications despite the exertions brought about by both internal and external forces of change. Africanus Beale Horton (1835–1883), the African émigré and a pioneer West African nationalist of Igbo parentage, was one of the first modern scholars to study West African indigenous political systems. Writing in 1868, Horton broadly identified two principal forms of the government in the region, which also applies to most parts of sub-Saharan Africa in the precolonial era. In the first category are political systems in which power is vested in a single individual called *basileus*—a Greek word for "king" or "sovereign." Horton explains that such a kingly figure, as found among the precolonial Ashanti (Asante) and Dahomey kingdoms, for example, enjoyed implicit power over life and property and were as such held in awe by their subjects. The kings were surrounded by a number of headmen, who had pledged their loyalty to his power. Horton identified the second category of governmental system as a limited monarchical system, while the third category was the village democracies. According to Horton, in the limited monarchical systems, just like in the village democracies, democracy was the modus operandi.[74]

As if furthering Horton's pioneering work, in a 1951 study Paula Brown identified four systems of political organizations indigenous to Africans: (1)

kinship-based authority; (2) kinship and associations-based authority; (3) kingship, associations, and centralized authority state; and (4) consolidated centralized state authority.[75] Brown's study was motivated by a similar study in 1940 by M. Fortes and E. E. Evans-Pritchard, who distinguished two major categories of African political organizations. In the "A" group are the centralized systems, and in the "B" group are the decentralized groups or what the authors labeled "stateless societies."[76] Among those included in the latter are the Igbo, Angas, Birom, Idoma, and Ibibio of modern Nigeria, Tallensi of Ghana, Tonga of Zambia, Langi of Uganda, the Western Dinka and the Nuer of Sudan, and the pre-nineteenth-century Nguni of South Africa.[77] A more nuanced division would be one that transcends the temptation of categorizing cultures into the "stateless" and "centralized." None of these ideas accurately represents the indigenous political structures or the premises of cultural values on which they were operated. As a matter of rule, government in both governmental systems not only made use of the sublineage, lineage, and village-level government structures involving direct or representative decision-making processes, but also all the various forms of government were anchored on religious ideologies and symbols.

As the most crucial foundation of the sociopolitical organization, religion was intricately interwoven with the government, authority figures, and exercise of power. Religious symbols reflected the civic and political culture, and masks and masquerades featured in both the centralized and decentralized societies enforcing discipline, upholding natural laws, and reinforcing political legitimacy as mediated through the ideology of ancestral spirits. Among the centralized political systems, the notion held about divine kingship implies that the human and natural worlds are interdependent for their continued existence on the person and ritual activities of the king. From ancient Egypt to the forest kingdoms of Dahomey and Oyo in the nineteenth century, religion remained a powerful tool for political legitimacy. According to Michael Kenny, who has studied the kinship system of precolonial Buganda, the position of the king in this type of political system is cast in doubt when through personal illness or natural or political disaster the continuance of his tenure in office is threatened by rising pressure in favor of his replacement.[78] Among the Yoruba of southwestern Nigeria, for example, while the Alaafin (king) of the Old Oyo Empire enjoyed absolute powers, he was at the same time vulnerable to the Oyomesi (a council of senior hereditary chiefs), who adjudicated suicide for the king should he breach the laws of the gods of the land.

Randall Packard's study of chiefly power among the Bashu people of Eastern Zaire further reveals that precolonial African politics is only comprehensible when basic constitutional and cosmological ideas that motivate and legitimate power and exercise of authority are also understood. Packard asserts that "African kinships have shown that kings were frequently defined by members of society as ritual mediators between society and the forces of nature ... they were closely associated with well-being of the land and society"[79] This tells us that royal power, though substantial, was still subject to limitation. The indigenous belief system played a crucial role in the unity of a polity, whether decentralized or centralized. It also provided legitimacy to the position of the ruler and the citizens while serving as a mechanism for checks and balances. This structure of authority and power was not cast on a rigid and unchanging context. In peculiar circumstances, there might be disagreement among the priests, the people, the elders (in case of the decentralized systems), kings (in the centralized systems), and so on. Such disagreements usually led to changes in the existing structures of authority, as well as to reinvention and reinterpretation of relationships between the deities and humanity, the ruled and the ruler.

Additionally, religion figured prominently in gender ideologies, notions of power, and exercise of authority. As in all patriarchal societies, including Igboland, women depended on their men for guidance in certain decisions, roles, and tasks, but they did not depend on men to the degree of dependence the early missionaries and colonial anthropologists had believed. Originally, African women, particularly those who served as priestesses, agents of deities, or oracular authorities, enjoyed unhindered powers and authority, and their roles were central to the smooth functioning of the social order. Women appropriated separately controlled social and political spheres of power, and through their organizations handled legal and other matters specifically reserved for them. Women also participated in issues that affected both genders, and in some communities, elderly women and priestesses welded more influence and respect than most men in indigenous politics.

To recap, questions about when, why, and how masks and masquerade carnivals came into existence have been surveyed. These critical questions were tackled in light of the principles of the nonlinear approach using the occurrences of order, chaos, and bifurcation as constant realities of society and existentialism. As the evidence reveals across all regions of the world, masking has been with humanity for thousands of years, and its journey began as an offshoot of religion. Judging solely by evidence of recorded history, ancient Egyptians, Asians, Europeans, and Native Americans of the Aztec Empire should all be credited with the initial attempts to objectify the link between the souls of the dead and the gods with a myriad of celebrations, rituals, and artistic representations of dead masks. In other words, there is no suggestion here that perhaps similar forms of religious objects were not created elsewhere prior to 2500 BCE. However, the breakthrough with costumed masquerades as an advanced form of spirit objectification resulted when the elders in sub-Saharan Africa found a way to combine human performances with a ritual art form into a single entity in the form of masquerades. Packaged with the ability to walk, jump, run, dance, talk, express anger, engage in dramatics or humorous displays, execute justice, and even predict the future in language forms the audience and onlookers could understand, masks and masquerades acquired a wholly different utilitarian ex-istentialism or manifestation that the people in the communities in which they were fashioned could relate with in more meaningful ways. Shrouded in secrecy, mythologies, legends, and ritual observances and initiation rites, African mas-querades retained and bolstered their "godly" images in attire made of different physical media found within their local environments.

Through the appearance of the masquerades, disputes are reconciled through the use of judicial sanctions, punishment in forms of fines, physical threats, clan-destine and nocturnal killings, and mediated settlements. When the occasion demands, the masquerades also settled sensitive conflicts without any individual involved in the conflict having to admit guilt or blame. In his informative work on Ibibioland where the dreaded Èkpo Ọnyohọ reigned as the most powerful spirit-regarding masquerade, Edet A. Udo provides an insight into what happens when the masquerade delivers a wrong punishment or miscarried justice. The first step was to keep the problem secret from noninitiates. This means that the matter will be deliberated upon at the Èkpo Ọnyohọ village square. This is an arena exclusively reserved for the cult members. At the trial, the offending Èkpo Ọnyohọ member was branded Okpokko Ibit Èkpo (Èkpo drummer). He was then indicted for stirring the Èkpo Ọnyohọ to act wrongly through his untimely drumming and singing. Meanwhile, the guilty Èkpo Ọnyohọ members that performed at the occasion were believed to have disappeared to the land of the ancestors soon after the incident, and "the Èkpo drummer was held responsible for the crime and was charged accordingly, and if found guilty, was punished by the Èkpo Ọnyohọ. The public was informed that the Èkpo drummer had been found guilty and punished."[80]

The Europeans arriving in Africa in the late nineteenth century tended to misunderstand many elements of the indigenous practices, including the use of masquerades as a mechanism of political control and conflict resolution. Next, we explore the society and culture in the Bantu/Biafra hinterland in order to fully treat the mechanisms and sociopolitical milieu in which the mask and masquerade culture developed and gained popular appeal among Africans. Using the Igbo as a precise example, it is shown that the environment of the people structured the indigenous religion. The cosmology, in turn, determined the cultural ideas that gave birth to the masquerade tradition in this region.

CHAPTER 2

Aspects of Society and Culture in the Biafra Hinterland

As men imagine gods in human form, so also they suppose their
manner of life to be like their own.
— Aristotle, *Politics* (Part II), 350 BCE

ARISTOTLE APPOSITELY OBSERVED THAT humanity's imaginings
of the gods, their physical attributes, and their mannerisms tend to
align with human ideas and physical shapes of earthly things. This
explains why cosmologies are produced after the peculiar experiences of those
societies that behold them. In fact, Toyin Falola's study of *Culture and Customs
of Nigeria* informs us that the masquerades of the various Nigerian ethnic groups
including the Yoruba, Èfik, Kálábári, and Igbo "communicate with the gods
and the ancestors, relaying people's wishes to the gods and dramatizing for the
worshippers the gods' assumed habits and behavior."[1] One way through which
the Igbo and their neighbors honored and depicted the gods and ancestors was
by commemorating masquerade festivals in their names. Some masquerade festivals celebrated gods of human and agricultural fertility and harvest during
which time the Igbo renewed their belief in such deities as Ogbom, Njǫku, or
Ahịajǫku.[2] While the Ahịajǫku deity is connected with agriculture, the festival
masks and masquerades found among the Ibéku, Olokoro, and Obono communities associated with the fertility goddess Ogbom were performed in honor of
the earth deity (Álá). In a predominantly farming society where big family sizes
were highly desirable, Ogbom was believed to help in making children more
plentiful.[3] Other masquerades honored outstanding individuals who had made
remarkable contributions to their society during their lifetimes. Because of the
belief in the sustenance of life through interaction with the ancestors, it was
fundamental for these Africans to maintain social harmony and this required
constant consultation, dialogue, and honoring the ancestors.[4] If a taboo is vio-
lated, there must be a penalty and an appeasement (*ịkwá álá*) to the gods of the
land and ancestors or kinship forebears.

43

In context, the Aristotelian thought on the human conception of the gods and their mannerisms that is profoundly shared by other scholars has a couple of mutually reinforcing implications for a deeper appreciation of the sociocultural ambiance in which the masquerade arts play and the rituals it carries are articulated, nurtured, and appropriated. First, it helps us to reiterate the close association among worldview, political culture, and modernization.[5] Second, it validates the shared understanding that family and kinship creeds constituted the bedrock on which contemporary political systems were crafted. Hence, French historian Numa D. Fustel de Coulanges (1830–1889), who studied the ritual underpinnings of ancient Greece and Rome, concluded that ancestor worship and family ideology were not only the nursery beds for modern religions but also the roots of sociopolitical and economic organizations and cooperation.[6]

The immediate task here is to use the essentials of religio-cultural and sociopolitical traditions found in the original Bantu/Bight of Biafra's hinterlands, mainly in the Igbo area, to illustrate how the practice of masks and masquerades became entrenched in society. For the purpose of this study, it is important to restate that the "Bantu/Biafra hinterland" refers to the areas inhabited by the Igbo and the neighboring borderland communities of southeastern Nigeria and western Cameroon identified by scholars as the Bantu cradle.[7] There are two entangled and overlapping layers involved in masquerade cult politics and its operationalization in southeastern Nigeria. To unpack the webs of multifaceted roles masquerades played in the indigenous societies of this region and the ideologies that supported them, one must first capture the underlying cosmological and philosophical foundations. These foundations also explain the political and social structures of power and authority that the masquerade tradition was a huge part.

Cosmology: Ideological and Metaphysical Foundations

To proceed, it is important to see cosmology as how societies conceive the world and the order of things around them. In today's world in which access to the Internet and information is at our fingertips, it is almost inconceivable how the ordinary people were made to believe and invest in what one may regard today as the spiritual scam that promoted masquerades as gods and ancestral spirits and political actors. The key to the rationale is found in the unique ways the Igbo and their Ibibio, Èfik, and Ijọ neighbors understood and structured the world around them. It was a universe with an intricate affinity between the sacred and the profane, and politics and morality. Everything in this universe is articulated through the prism of religion—both in the context of dogmas as a set of belief systems and in the context of religion as something that binds a community together.

In the framework of this study, Igbo or Ibibio, Èfik, and Ijǫ philosophy— connote the application of reason, thought, and vision to human challenges— and the interrelationship of human existentialism, religion, politics, and moral order are one. Accordingly, C. B. Nze argues, "African philosophy is not a mere objective, abstract science, but a practical science, a lived philosophy such that whatever is conceptualized metaphysically is translated into action."[8] Through an action-oriented approach to metaphysical ideas, the indigenous religion helps the believer comprehend and embrace a style of life and the forces that regulate everyday practical living. In other words, unlike the major world religions, African traditional religions are neither articulated in a holy book like the Bible or Quran nor codified and formulated into systematic dogmas. However, the indigenous religions of the various communities found in the Bantu homeland are all defined by a certain set of beliefs, which come with paralysis: beliefs have the power to imprison the mind of the believer and direct actions toward a preordered or telescopic view of things. As a result, the believer becomes a victim of delusions, fears, and zealousness.

But what we want to avoid is the suggestion that religion in general lacks rationality, as atheists often argue. In consideration of this, scholars have theorized that African traditional religions developed as a response to the psychosomatic needs of the people, converging on safety and continued survival.[9] This corroborates Émile Durkheim and the functionalist school of thought's explanation of social phenomena in regard to how the needs of a people are served—that is, to help them adjust and adapt to shifting social settings.[10] In perspective, the indigenous cosmology and the nature of religion it gave birth to emerged as a direct message from the Supreme God (Chukwu) or Creator God (Chinéké) to the first Igbo forebears. In the course of time, the succeeding Igbo patriarchs, pressured by the challenges of life, seemingly deviated from God's original plans to venerate some entities and objects made by the Creator God. Thus, environment and ecology are crucial factors in the development of religious systems.

Among other things the Igbo recognized as gods are the galaxies and celestial bodies, lightning and thunder (from where the deities Igwe and Ányánwu were founded),[11] rivers and creeks (which led to the worship of Orimiri and Nne Nmiri or Mammy Water spirits), trees and forests (out of which the Ámádiǫhá or Ámádiǫrá deity was created), and the earth goddess (Álá or Áni). But the fundamental idea of a Creator God was retained alongside the belief in the existence of chimera divinities and lesser deities to which the departed ancestors belong. The Igbo regard the smaller divinities as intermediaries in the hierarchy of gods with the earth goddess acknowledged as the prefect and custodian of the morally sanctioned customs, taboos, and traditions (*ọmenálá*). The ọmenálá corpus of statuettes regulates interhuman, intergroup relationships as well as humanity's association with the gods.[12] A violation of the moral laws is equal to an open challenge to the powerful earth goddess, and the penance for acts of transgression is usually devastating. In the indigenous religion, the chief priests (*Eze Mmụọ*), priestesses, and masquerades communicate to the culprit and the people the anger and demands of the deities.

Therefore, unlike Christianity and Islam that are about going to either heaven or hell, paradise or damnation, the African indigenous religion was about humanity and its lived tradition; it was focused on improving interpersonal and intergroup relationships and promoting harmony—hence, the religion was an intrinsic part of the people's culture, the totality of knowledge and human behaviors, ideas, and objects that constitute the common heritage of a given society. The culture, therefore, embraces every aspect of the society's life in relation to the environment, interpersonal, and intracommunal relationships as well as the ideational elements within the society.[13] The immediate understanding from this is that cultures like jewelry cameos are wired; they transmit the electricity that lights up the senses with certain patterns of knowledge, emotions, and actions. The erected idea of knowing and feeling connect the material with the immaterial worlds. This implies that there are several layers of culture, with the philosophical level at its core. In the indigenous society, the notion of the philosophical is met in reality rather than in the Western tradition of abstractions. In other words, in the Igbo, Ibibio, and Ijọ indigenous knowledge episteme, philosophy explicates precise answers to life's problem.[14]

Coming next to the philosophical level of culture is the mythical level. This level of reasoning is concerned with myth making, that is, the corpus of stories, legends, taboos, emblems, and ideologies that make up the elementary beliefs of the people—the beliefs that inspire action and thought that provide meanings to life, the customs the people observe, and those manners and observances that define the sacred and the profane in the moral order.

The foregoing explains why the precolonial Igbo, Ibibio, Èfìk, and Ijọ were deeply involved in the masquerade institution. It was part of everyday life for both diviners and ordinary mortals to dream about or actually run into ancestral spirits appearing as guests to the human world on lonely afternoons or in the darkness of the night. Here, epiphanies, as portrayed in the *Iliad* and the *Odyssey* in the ancient Greek tradition, were a part of religious experience, though more often than not masquerades represented visitations of the ancestral spirits.[15] The Èkáng of Bende and Aba Divisions; the Odo and Ọmábe masquerades of Nsukka Division and Imufu community in Enugu-Ezike, Igboeze; *mmánwu* among the southwestern Igbo, and host of other societies (Ékpè, Ebiabu, Ákáng, and Ọbọn) among the Cross River Igbo—all signify the infiltration of the spirit world into the realm of the living with profound ethical implications. The seasonal factor—that is, the timing in the appearances of these masquerades—reflects the genuine concerns of the community at various points in the agricultural cycle.[16]

Having explained the cosmological and philosophical foundations on which the masks and masquerade tradition were embedded in the Igbo, Ibibio, Èfik, and Ijọ worlds, the next task is to further clarify the political and social structures on which they were justified. First, to quickly recap, it has been argued that while elements of culture can be recognized from the people's religion, the system of belief itself is an intrinsic part of the people's culture, in a broader sense, and as applied to the African world embraces politics and other institutions. Culture and religion are inseparable. But philosophy, the application of reason to life experiences—that is, the theoretical basis of a particular branch of experience, and the fundamental nature of knowledge, reality, and existence—constitutes the heart of culture and politics.[17] The point of emphasis here is to capture the sociocultural milieu in which masquerades operate as both religious entities and political actors, and the reasoning behind it.

Masquerade Politics and Associational Life

The role assigned to the masquerades in the Igbo, Ibibio, Èfik, and Ijọ societies is better comprehended when explained in the context of the indigenous political constructs rigged with imageries of associational life, ancestors, and spiritual ideations. First, it must be recognized that we are concerned with local societies functioning on indigenous democratic ideals and with no formalized or institutionalized security agencies like the police or the army. The precolonial Igbo, like their Ibibio neighbors, operated one of the most outstanding systems of indigenous structures of republicanism, while the Èfik and Ijọ transitioned from this form of village-based democracy to a quasi-traditional monarchical system around the sixteenth century. In both the republican and monarchical systems, the ancestors personified in artistic representations of masks and masquerades played prominent roles. In broad terms, the Igbo (the largest ethnic group among the four in focus here) operated two varieties of political systems: the monarchical and village republic. The monarchical systems as found in Onitsha, Ogutá, and Arochukwu, for instance, developed as result of these communities' history of close contacts with those non-Igbo neighbors who were under centralized state systems, like the Benin to the west, Èfik to the east, Ijọ to the south, and Igálá and Idomá to the north.[18] In both the Igbo presidential monarchy and the village republic, however, the distribution of power, authority, and the processes of local administration are the same. The council of elders ruled their communities by representation, participation, and negotiation. And the various social clubs, age-grade associations, secret societies, and masquerade cults shared political roles with elders and kings. The notion of a difference between the monarchical and village republics was found primarily in the king's ceremonial protocols, kingly regalia, other material objects, and titles.[19]

For the Igbo, like in the Ibibio practice of direct democracy, heads of the various households discussed the affairs of the units at the sublineage and lineage levels. The village assembly, which was the largest unit of political organization, comprised those villages that have reconciled their land use rights, co-opted individual families in the defense of the area they occupied, venerated the same major deity, and acknowledged the right of the same village group head to supervise land use and oversee the rituals connected with the observance of common laws.[20]

In the village assembly, all the adult members of the group participated in decision making. The village assembly had an inner council made up of the lineage heads (the Ámálá or Senate in modern parlance) that deliberated on village affairs.[21] The sublineage, the lineage, and the village assembly were levels of direct democracy where every adult male, or female in some cases, was directly involved in the affairs of the group. In all deliberations, the majority opinion carried the day, though the councils of the elders (including men and women of superior chronological age, chief priests and priestesses, titled men and women, and other categories of respectable figures who have served their society with distinction) counseled the people from their experiences. The procedure for such counseling or shaping of public opinion varied. Sometimes it followed the usual and secretive acts of political lobbying; in other times the elders employed more secretive but necessary forms of intimation or spiritual sanctions, including threats, poisoning, or psychological warfare.

Thus, for the village communities without a professionalized standing police or army, social control through psychological or metaphysical means was crucial. This is where the masquerade cults became even more relevant, along with the age-grades, social clubs, and secret societies that managed their affairs.

The implied vision makes room for role differentiation and social solidarity while these agencies implant the fear of God in the minds and heads of individuals, thus moderating disruptive behaviors and curtailing the propensity of individuals and groups to cause harm to society through disrespect to the laws of the land. This brings us to one of the critical strategies through which Igbo/ Èfik/Ibibio/ Ijọ elites continuously renewed the relevance of the masquerade culture. They ensured that the masses imbibed in, protected, and invested in the traditional religious belief systems. As already explicated, Igbo religion, and indeed the indigenous religions of the Èfik, Ibibio, and Ijọ, is culturally bound and learned through processes of socialization; in this domain, powerful and gripping ideologies of myth making, secrecy, and ritual observances were cultivated, including those connected with socialization and rites of passage (birth, coming of manhood, marriages, death, and so on) that introduced new members of the society into a plethora of village-based age-grade associations, secret societies, and masquerade cults. Within these agencies, members were schooled to uphold the myths and legends constructed and offered as authentic history of the people.

Ogbu Kalu has noted correctly that the bequest of these agents of socialization with the sacred order in the Bantu world also led to the sacralization of the rites of passage, to the point that social events like the naming ceremony were elevated to a serious religious event. "So pervasive was the sacralization of life's journey that religion and identity of persons and communities were ineluctably bound."[22] Chidi G. Osuagwu, who has studied the indigenous culture from the standpoint of his expertise in the natural sciences argues "the Igbo society was the most scientific of all [African] societies."[23] Culturally cultivated, the mind of inquiry inspired the Igbo, Ibibio, Èfik, or Ijọ parent, at the arrival of the newborn, to summon diviners (human agents with powers to peep into the mysteries of the unseen world) to identify which progenitor has reincarnated and or even whether a deity was visiting in human form. The result of this investigation determines the choice of a name for the newborn. Francis O. C. Njoku explains that the Igbo is ruled by those things he could not understand, hence the quest for meanings in a world fraught with chaos that dominates his senses, leading to an endless quest for solutions to mysteries.[24] With this mindset, regular naming ceremonies are clad in religious garb and ritualized in a convivial festivity for a returning progenitor. In some villages, a first son is given the name of his paternal grandfather (Nnánná in Igbo; Ètébọm in Ibibio), whereas a first daughter bears the name of her paternal grandmother (Nnenná in Igbo and Èkaette in Ibibio/Èfik).

In the same vein, puberty rites are turned into intricate religious affairs. Other rites of passage such as Íwá Ákwá among the Mbieri, Íwá Ǹjá among the Owerri, and the Isiji in Áfikpo are examples of these practices. Colonial anthropological reports on the Èddá documented between 1928 and 1934 detailed the sacrifices, traditions, and idioms associated with the Erusi-Èddá cult.[25] The reports reveal that such naming ceremonies and rights of passages are consolidated into several functions: a symbolic rebirth, an educative experience, a rite of passage into adolescence or early manhood, sex differentiation, inculcation of survival values, and a means of communal cohesion and identity formation. Among the Èddá, as colonial anthropologists further reported, the cult of Erunsi would literally subject the initiate to an ordeal, a life-altering direct encounter with Èddá's most powerful deity.[26] This religious observance was also found among the Ábiribá as colonial anthropologist G. I. Jones recorded between 1932 and 1939, carried huge moral and psychological symbols, mystery, secrecy, awe, and at times provided entertainment and recreation for both the young and the old in an agrarian setting.[27]

Thus, one must first appreciate masquerade societies as part of the larger body of religious and civil society networks that shared political functions with tutelary monarchs, village chiefs, elders, age-grade associations, social clubs, and secret societies. In this system, the elders ensured that all masquerades are not equal; they came in different hierarchies, grades, functions, and operationalization. Two classes of masquerades have been demarcated in the system. First are the high-grade masquerade cults that were either run by the village elders or the powerful secret societies. This class of masquerades was invoked once in a while as ancestral spirits and sociopolitical actors to physically execute a myriad of tasks, chiefly social control functions. Second are the lesser-grade masquerade cults that were owned and operated by lesser-grade secret societies, age-grade associations, or social clubs in those villages without age-grade institutions. Both the higher-and lesser-grade masquerades were established on religious idioms in alignment with the essential needs of the community that instituted them.

The crucial place of masquerades and secret societies in the traditional order needs more clarification. Some masquerades, such as Ọmábe of the Nsukka people that appears every five years, were directly connected with moral control, as well as "to celebrate peace and unity in the community and also rejoice with our ancestors for taking care of us."[28] Some other masquerades performed double functions of social control and entertainment, depending on the specific occasion and season. Yet, some others such as the Ojiọnu and Ágábá of the Mbáitoli people were solely for entertainment or what the colonial officials categorized

FIGURE 2.1. Dancing initiation masks, boys' initiation, Cross River. This image
is copyright. Reproduced by permission of University of Cambridge Museum of
Archaeology & Anthropology (N.13095.GIJ).

as "harmless dances."[29] This brings us to the second crucial scheme through
which the indigenous religion, politics, and masquerades were intricately bound:
entertainment. In this domain, the masses and the Igbo, Èfìk, Ibibio, and Ijọ
elites used artistic designs, theatricals of songs, proverbs, folklore, drama, dance,
satires, musical instrumentation, and cultural observances to foster communal
ownership of the masks and masquerade institutions.

To fully appreciate their functions, a further classification of these masquerades is required in light of Ben Enweonwu's assertion that "African art is not

really art in the Western context but an invocation of ancestral spirits through giving concrete form or body to them before they can enter into the human world."[30] The distinction in costuming corroborates Margaret Trowell's tripartite classification of African art into the "spirit-regarding art," "art of ritual art display," and "man-regarding art" forms. Frank Willett emphasizes that Trowell's groupings are better seen as a "classificatory device" for understanding the extensive and diverse art forms of Africa.[31] Trowell's analytical framework is adapted here somewhat in deeply analyzing the functions of African masks and masquerades under two broad categories: "spirit-regarding art" (or "ritual art display") and "human-regarding art" (or secular art/carnival display).

Although the two genres of art are in many ways related, and their functions sometimes overlap, the spirit-regarding art displays conform to what Henri Kamer considers as the "authentic" art form because they are intricately embedded in religious rituals and political idioms. In contrast, the human-regarding art form serves mostly for civic engagement, social mobilization, and aesthetic and entertainment purposes. According to Kamer, an authentic piece of African art is "a sculpture executed by an artist . . . and destined for the use of the tribe in a ritual or functional way."[32] Barbara Thompson authoritatively asserts, "through ritual, an object can be physically and symbolically transformed into the tangible embodiment of intangible powers and can be perceived as having a life of its own."[33] This implies that unlike most of what obtains in the African Diaspora today, not all African masks and masquerades were intended for entertainment, public fun, or jamboree. The spirit-regarding or ritual art forms of masquerades portray more than the ingenious secular creativity of the African. This is in line with John MacAloon's theoretical postulation: "Cultural performances are more than entertainment, more than didactic or persuasive formulations and more than cathartic indulgences. They are occasions in which as a culture or society we reflect upon and define ourselves, dramatize our collective myths and history, present ourselves with alternatives, and eventually change in some ways while remaining the same in others."[34] For instance, when the Njimá masquerade Arọndizuọgu, festooned in a shaggy costume and bullhorns, appeared at the village square on January 5, 1988, on the occasion of the interment of the traditional ruler (Èzé Árọ) of Arọchukwu, the crowd roared in ecstasy.[35] However, the primary message it brought to the onlookers was that the ancestors have come to bless the transition of one of theirs from the human world to that of the ancestors.[36] This leads to the question as to why certain art forms of Igbo masquerades are viewed as spirit-regarding while others are human-regarding art forms.

Spirit-Regarding (Ritual) Art Forms

This group of arts of Africa includes the performances and artworks produced with some reference to spiritual observation, reservation, and appeasement. The mask, as a form of spirit-regarding art, is supposed to represent either the spirit of the ancestors or the gods of the land. This is why the Igbo literally referred to the mask as the "head of the spirit" (*isi-mmụọ* or *isi-mmánwu* in Igbo, *ekpo etubọm* in Ibibio). When the Igbo or Ibibio mask appeared with all the customs and paraphernalia of a masquerade, it was called "spirit" (*mmụọ* in Igbo, *ekpo* in Ibibio). The spirit-regarding masks, which may also be referred to as the "upper-class masks," were spiritually imbued with religious beliefs—hence they are also called "big spirits" (*nnukwu mmụọ* in Igbo, *ekpo ákámbá* in Ibibio). This genre of masquerades was performed mostly at night and was created to terrify and invoke the fear that compelled conformity to social expectations and etiquette. Onuora Nzekwu's eyewitness description of the appearance of one of these genres of Igbo masquerades after a burial ceremony in the late 1950s perhaps best captures the fear and respect they conjured:

> Entering a small Eastern Nigerian village one morning, I was surprised by the pandemonium which had replaced the usual calm that precedes dawn. Men, women, and children rushed towards their houses and disappeared through doors which they slammed behind them. One of the men who passed by me stopped long enough to ask what I was doing just standing and staring. Did 'a deaf and dumb' need to be told when a battle was on?[37]

That this form of public reaction was possible in the 1950s provides an insight into the degree of effect of these masquerades on the people's psyche. As in the past, most of these masquerades are still depicted in public theaters today, but with caution, as violent, aggressive, and destructive spirits.

Membership and participation in the upper-class/spirit-regarding art displays were highly restricted. Alex Grecian has noted that once individuals secure membership in exclusive, often secret societies, including the Freemasons, the Yakuza, Illuminati, Skull and Bones, Rosicrucians, Bilderberg, Knights Templar, and so on, they are granted privileged access and considerations: political favors, financial opportunities and credits, appointments to influential positions, business and. Some societies with a more religious (or perhaps sacrilegious) bent believed they could gain mystical abilities or accrue [occultist] powers and artifacts.[38] Likewise, Igbo, Ibibio, Ijọ, and Èfik precolonial secret societies leveraged their positions of authority to not only secure access to power and influence but

FIGURE 2.2. Spirit (*mmụọ*) masquerade

also garner occultist powers and mystical abilities.[39] As Falola observes, such art forms "reveal the power structure of each community."[40] For example, only the initiates in the Okumkpá play of Ámurọ village in Áfikpo, as well as the more secretive Ègbélé or Ogo village cult of Áfikpo and Unwáná communities of Igboland, were welcome to participate in their masquerade and other spirit-regarding activities.[41] The male noninitiates (or *ennás*) were often pilloried by members and were barred from any kind of involvement in its activities. A similar sanction also applied to women and strangers.[42] This aligns with the common notion that African art is characterized by secrecy as encountered in certain categories of physical art, oral literature, and the indigenous belief system. As Dennis Duerden elucidates, "knowing too much about a man's ancestors gives another man power over him."[43] This kind of power, Nancy Millington concurs, "originates from an invisible and incomprehensible source, yet, becomes visible and tangible in effect. It is expressed as a concealed or revealed force, channeled through religious or chiefly authority."[44]

Yet, members of the same spirit-regarding masquerade society were often graded according to age and individual abilities. In this hierarchy, the most senior members of the masquerade societies usually served as the custodians of the values and aspirations the culture embodied. They ensured that the rules, regulations, and secrecy surrounding their group's activities were maintained and respected. Mostly, the more vigorous people below the age of forty-five operated the warlike powerful masks. This was because the operation of the masks required much vigor and dexterity.[45]

The spirit-regarding Igbo, Èfik, Ibibio, and Ijọ art forms were always appeased, feared, and believed to give protection to the community by seeking out and destroying any evil forces trying to intrude into the society. They also dealt with individuals considered as morally bankrupt either by relieving them of their maladies or completely destroying them. Among the Igbo, for instance, the appearance of the Ụlágá masquerade is usually accompanied by songs speaking out against secrets like taboos, murders, poisonings, and incestuous acts committed by members of the community. Among the Achi-Mbieri people, an elder remembered that the Ụlágá masquerade is fearless and "tells the truth as it is. There was an incident in the past," he recalled, "involving a couple of mysterious deaths of young people that threatened the peace of our community." As the community struggled to understand why these young people died within a period of two weeks, "the Ụlágá masquerade appeared one night and disclosed the name of the culprit who allegedly poisoned the victims. The culprit was banished from the community and that was how peace returned."[46]

FIGURE 2.3. Ghost police, Amobia Village. This image is copyright.
Reproduced by permission of University of Cambridge Museum of
Archaeology & Anthropology (N.13163.GIJ).

Also, like the Amobia village "Ghost Police," the Èkpè (or Leopold) masquerade society among the Èfik, Ibibio, and Arọ communities of the Cross River Valley of southeastern Nigeria served as an important arm of village administration.
Besides their usual policing functions, members of the secret society could visit
civil transgressors like thieves, adulterers, and so on at night to warn them to
desist from their dastardly acts or be killed. A resident of Aba in the early 1960s
recalled a case of adultery involving one Kanu and his mistress, Ikwuo, a married
woman from Etinam, in Cross River State. According to the source, Ikwuo's

husband was a civil servant resident in the industrial city Aba while his wife and kids lived in Oron, about thirty miles away. Unknown to the husband, Ikwuo was having an affair with Kanu, who was a friend to the family. The event came to a climax when Ikwuo got pregnant by Kanu and the incident was revealed to Ikwuo's husband, who was a member of the Ékpè society. "Kanu died a shameful death, while Ikwuo had a stillbirth."[47] According to Falola, these masquerade festivals that made use of secrecy, sanctions, and intimidation, "strike fear in the guilty, as they may not even know that the public will come to their houses to ridicule them." Actions or "statements made in such carnivals are not considered libelous or defamatory." Ogbu Kalu recalls that in his native community, a burlesque figure called Udu performs "at the same time and runs an unedited social commentary as it leads children, like a pied-piper, around the village." Falola adds that under such a climate of culture that shames antisocial behaviors in public, "the only protection one has is to behave according to community norms and values."[48] Thus, Kanu's fate reminds us that these masquerades, when sojourning among the living, "probed human conduct and morals, and their return to the spirit world would leave the community tense and expectant thus providing a compelling reason to observe moral codes."[49]

The spirit-regarding Ékpè masquerades that perform during the Ikeji festival among the eastern Igbo and Cross River Igbo were not only spirit bound but also spirit infested. Both the Ékpè of Èfik, and Ekpo of Ibibio that comes out at the climax of the New Year festival, play the same role as the Njǫku or Ifejiǫku, god of yam of the Igbo. The Ékpè masquerade festival renews the symbols of cultural relationships between the people, the ancestors, and the gods of agriculture such as Njǫku. When it cuts off a goat's head in a lone strike, the community is assured of a rewarding farming year. The Ikeji festival is held during the time of harvest and may be understood as a period of identity renewal and thanksgiving.[50]

The Ijélé (the beautiful elephant) masquerade of Enugukwu of Igboland, another spirit-bound mask, is one of the biggest masquerades found in Africa. With an average height of about twenty feet (six meters), the masquerade purports to symbolize the incarnated ancestral spirits.[51] Whenever the bellicose Ijélé appeared in public, usually other rivals went underground to avoid a deadly confrontation with the monster. This masquerade, like other categories of militant societies, most likely grew out of the indigenous warrior groups. Their membership was solely open to individuals who had distinguished themselves in war or other brave acts.[52] This implies that in the precolonial order, different masquerade societies often competed for power and influence in society.

In such competitions, victorious masquerade clubs usually claimed to have the support of the gods and ancestors of the land. Prior to 1970, the Ijélé was seen only once in a decade or two, except when occasions of serious concern called for its appearance. Since the end of the Nigerian Civil War (1967–1970), the Ijélé masquerade has lost most of its secrecy and aura; it has now become an annual cultural exhibition among the Enugukwu people. Also, membership in the Ijélé cult has embraced Christians and non-Christians, the educated and illiterate, the poor and the rich, and urban and rural dwellers alike. This heterogeneous membership has brought some new ideas. The Ijélé still ranks among the most intricate and beautifully decorated masquerades in the world.[53]

Another set of masquerades, the Mmánwu, are personifications of danger-ous spirits who punish both overt and covert offenses. Generally, this genre of masquerades features in communities where secret societies are a part of the political system. Otherwise, their wild behaviors during the seasonal appear-ances could become dysfunctional. In the Igbo south and Cross River areas, where Ọkọnkọ exists, including among the Ngwá people, these masquerades served as enforcement agencies in some places, while they were merely entertain-ment masquerades in others. In other words, the Ọkọnkọ performs double roles as both an arm of administration and public entertainment. While primarily serving spiritual and ritual functions, some spirit-regarding masks also provide good sources of recreational activities for both the performers and the onlookers. They serve to bring the people together, particularly at the festivals and also promote economic growth through tourism.[54] The Ékpè-Ọkọnkọ, according to Victor Ukaegbu, an authority on Igbo masking traditions, was bequeathed to the Ngwá by the Arọchukwu Ékpè lodge.[55] Traditionally, the Ọkọnkọ, a very tall, surreal figure, was adorned with an overall dress made from raffia palms, and complete with headgear bearing antelope horns and a partially concealed mask made of fabric with the eyes and nose delineated with cowry shells. Today, the Ọkọnkọ may dress in an unconventional manner, especially when it is out to entertain in the public sphere.

In fact, without costumes, there would have been no masquerades in the mold of thought, designs, and performance held by the Igbo, Ibibio, and their neigh-bors. Costumes breathed life into a time-honored tradition of ritual and artistic representations of spirits and gods—thereby transforming them into the mobile and do-it-all ancestral spirits whose appearances invoked fears of unimaginable proportions intended to astound and enchant the audience. Usually, in the concept of masking, the maskers, and the cult members select the appropriate costumes and makeups to be invested in a mask. While partial coverage of the masker's body may be allowed in some communities, it is unacceptable in others because it nullifies the entire idea of spirit manifestation.

All the spirit-regarding masquerades—Ékpè and Ikeji masquerades of Arọ, the Ijélé of Enugwukwu, the Ékpè-Ọkọnkọ, of Ngwá, and the Mmánwu that feature during important religious and political seasons and festivals were believed to possess the powers (*Átịkpá*) or "the science of alchemy" to drive away evil spirits from the community. According to Chukwukadibia Nwafor, Átịkpá Ágwu science was well known and practiced in Igboland even today by those, including priests and priestesses, whose trade "actually predates humanity."[56] In precolonial times, some performers, as well as onlookers, were allegedly either struck dead or disabled by the magical powers of the performers of Ékpè at the Ikeji festival and their unseen evil rivals. Today, with the expansion of Western education, Christianity, and secular modern government, the performers still flex their juju powers, but there are no longer reports of careless murders and injuries because of the obvious legal consequences. In recognition that the spirit-regarding art concept is truly spirit bound, artists whose works are associated with the ritual performances are referred to in Igboland as "inspirational artists" (*Ndi-ọka*).[57] The spirit-regarding masks were usually produced after the likeness of particular late ancestors, and they were displayed in imitation of those individuals' human characteristics and mannerisms. The artist who carved the mask was expected to use his imagination to reproduce something representative of the invisible power and virtue of an ancestor. In this way, the mask is used to project and protect the ancestral belief without completely misplacing the human characteristics and mannerisms of the past ancestors.

The works of other craftsmen who also mass-produce art objects and relics for commercial purposes are generally referred to as "gifted craftsmen" (*Ndi-nká ọká*). From this Igbo interpretive standpoint, African arts in the African Diaspora that have enriched tourist interests, where they exist, are more or less works of "gifted craftsmen" rather than "inspirational artists." The rationale for this differentiation is that the works of the "gifted craftsmen" mainly serve secular and commercial purposes.

Human-Regarding (or Carnivaleering) Art Forms

Human-regarding Igbo masquerades are primarily designed for entertainment. For analytical convenience, this category of masks and masquerades are simply referred to here as the human-regarding art forms. They are less secretive and thus create the right atmosphere for performer-audience interaction. This genre of masquerade arts provides Africans with what the erudite scholar and art historian Dele Jegede has aptly described as "total theater."[58] They are aesthetically designed for public entertainment and revelry. The human-regarding art forms are not intimately associated with any particular ancestors, although some pretend to be within that realm in order to invoke awe among the ignorant, women, children, and strangers.[59] As Geoffrey Nwaka's excellent study reveals, early colonial authorities in eastern Nigeria believed that the masks and masquerades of the colonial era were a "menace to the peace and good government of the country."[60] This was because they constituted a challenge to colonial authorities.

In appearance, the human-regarding masks are usually very beautiful art pieces with neat finishing. Closely connected with this group of arts are the utility crafts, and the decorative art forms such as fabric designs, wall decorations, ceramics, pottery, basketry, tapestry, calabash carving, and other artistic paraphernalia that accompany masquerades and carnival displays around the globe. Artworks produced or acquired under this genre are easily commercialized, circulated, and published. However, any of these secular items automatically becomes a ritual (or holy) object when consecrated and employed in the services of a deity, oracle, god, shrine, or associated with an ancestor-honoring masquerade. In this context, Christopher Steiner underlines the raison d'être behind Western collectors and appraisers' categorization of certain art forms as either authentic or inauthentic artworks. It is held in Western understanding that authentic objects of African arts no longer exist because contemporary objects produced in the continent are no longer employed in the service of deities and other similar ritual undertakings.[61] Such ideas are not completely correct because certain aspects of precolonial practices have survived in the countryside although with increasing corruption.

Therefore, there are different grades and levels of spirit infestation in the human-regarding art forms depending on what services they may be employed for. For example, such grades of human-regarding masks as the junior forms of Èkpo, Ágábá, Ojiọnu, and the Okoroshá of Ibibio, Oru, Mbieri, Ubommiri, Umuáká, Orodo, Ifákálá, Ọgwá, and other surrounding communities of old Mbáitoli-Ikeduru local government areas of Imo state are performed by young people between the ages of five and fourteen. The youngsters design a very simple mask to cover the performer's face. The boy behind the mask will take his cane-stick to chase other kids and their colleagues around, pretending to be one of the authentic and awe-inspiring masquerades, while also dancing to the music produced by their playmates. In his ethnography of children and the masquerade tradition in West Africa, Simon Ottenberg argues that this indigenous form of

FIGURE 2.4. Boys' masquerade (Ibibio style mask) Abiriba. This image
is copyright. Reproduced by permission of University of Cambridge Museum
of Archaeology & Anthropology (N.71839.GIJ)

socialization "in association with a reordered communication employs paralan-
guage as against everyday speech and normal kinesic activity, [and] permit[s] the
masqueraders to deal with psychologically repressed materials that often have
references to early life experience."[62]

Young men between the ages of fifteen and forty perform a higher grade of
the human-regarding art form. They use masks produced after the images of
certain persons, birds, or any other animals.[63] Generally, all the lower classes of
Igbo masquerades—the Èkpo, Èkpè, Ụlágá, Átunmá, Ojiọnu, Ọgbá ngbádá,

Igá, and Kéléké, are physically characterized by a smooth wooden face or head mask (except the Igá). The dancers have a few layers of raffia around their waists and necks. They dance publicly and receive gifts of money from their onlookers and admirers. It is the human-regarding class of masquerades that bear much influence on the ordinary members of the society because they allow for a wider participation of people including visitors, women, and children in the festivities. This openness, which promotes performer-audience intercourse, makes the human-regarding form of masquerades a carnival complete with sharing of greetings, food, drinks, gifts, souvenirs, and other items of interest. Oftentimes, the onlookers are so mesmerized by the dances to the point that they get transformed from admirers to participants. Under such conditions of high cultural tempo, onlookers dole out gifts of money to the masquerades.

The human-regarding masquerades provide much-desired entertainment and revelry particularly during festivals and some ceremonies such as traditional weddings, chieftaincy installations, burial ceremonies of important figures, outing ceremonies of nursing mothers, and new yam festivals. Since the beginning of colonialism, African masks and masquerade performances, like other institutions in Africa, have experienced some radical transformations. Because the details of the colonial impact are not the primary concern of this analysis, it must simply be noted that indigenous culture has become an important part of Christmas and Easter celebrations. For the old traditional society, these radical changes have necessitated an unavoidable accommodation of new forces and meanings.

It will be judicious to end this chapter by addressing one of the evidently wrong notions held by Igbo scholars on the origin of secret societies and masquerades in Igboland. In his eminent Ahịajọku Lecture in 2002, Emmanuel Onwu hypothesized that the Igbo borrowed secret societies, most of which were also synonymous with masquerade plays, from their Èfik and Ibibio neighbors. This is similar to the view held by Adiele Afigbo that the Igbo may have borrowed secret societies and age-grade associations from their Ibibio, Ijọ, and Èfik neighbors. Afigbo promoted this assertion with the argument that the absence of highly developed age-grade associations in the core-Igbo heartland areas of Owerri, Mbáno, Ikeduru, Mbáitoli, Mbieri, and Orlu indicates that the institution was new to the areas.[64] Similarly, Onwu, whose work tapped heavily on Afigbo's, asserted, "the Arọ brought secret societies from Èfik-Ibibio areas into Igboland, such as Ékpè, Ọkọnkọ, Ọbong, Ákáng. The Arọ made great use of them and because of their influence cult houses were erected for them at the village centers of several Igbo communities, for effective control of communities.

They also made use of *nsibidi* sign for communication which made the need for initiation quite attractive."[65] It is only fair to include that Onwu attempted to inoculate himself from criticism with the caveat that his thought about Ibibio/Èfik influence on the development of secret societies does not presuppose that these agencies were absent in Igboland until the Arọ arrived with their slave trade oligarchic practices. Several studies on intergroup relations in precolonial southeastern Nigeria recognize the imperialistic influences of the Arọ-owned oracle named Ibinukpabi, which the Europeans called "The Long Juju."[66] The oracle, which served as an instrument of slavery, created a climate of awe throughout Igboland (from about 1600–1900) to the point that individuals who could afford it desired to secure memberships in Arọ-owned cults like the Èkpè as a form of protection against kidnapping and enslavement.[67]

While the mid-seventeenth-century rise of the Arọ as uncrowned kings of Eastern Nigeria marked a new dawn in Igbo history, it is important to say that it was not by any means the genesis of masquerade cults, secret societies, age-grades, and social clubs among the Igbo. If we reexamine Onwu's hypothesis in the context of Igbo identity discourse, it is immediately seen that the Arọ did not originally ascribe to Igbo ancestry as highlighted by the text of the Ajali-Arọchukwu Agreement of August 17, 1911, which reads as follows:

> Now we, the Arọs recognize that the land we live on and our forefathers lived on is not our property but the property of the Ibos, the original inhabitants of the country. We therefore agree on behalf of ourselves and our people to pay the Ibos . . . an annual nominal rental of five pound sterling . . . and we the Arọs and the Ibos fully understand the agreement we are signing.[68]

Originally, the Arọ self-identified as Èkọi, Èfik, and Ibibio—all their closest Cross River Valley neighbors. This reflects Amaury Talbot, Daryll Forde, and G. I. Jones, and Adiele Afigbo's classification of the Igbo into different cultural areas: Western Igboland (Ásábá axis); North-Western Igboland (Onitsha axis); Northern Igboland (Udi-Nsukka axis); North-Eastern Igboland (Nkanu-Awgu-Abakaliki axis); Central Igboland (Okigwe-Nkwerre-Orlu-Owerri, Mbáise axis); Southern Igboland (Ngwá, Umuahia, Bende, Ndọki axis); and the Cross River/Eastern Igboland cultural axis to which Arọchukwu, Ábám, and Ọháfiá people belong.[69] Thus, what comes to light is that Onwu was only referring to the Cross River/Eastern Igboland culture area, and the period in his purview is the mid-seventeenth century when the Arọ and their military allies (Ọháfiá, Ábám, and Èddá) literally seized control of the Igbo world.

In essence, Onwu's and Afigbo's views on the origin of secret societies in Igbo-land is an example of the problem of forcing certain chronological readings when the prerogative should be to think spatially and thematically—that is, in a way that relates to space and the position, area, and size of things within it, and the relevance of ideas and concepts within specific geographical locations. Neither Afigbo nor Onwu considered the timelessness of Igbo life and culture preceding the seventeenth-century developments or the thousands of diverse masquerade cults and secret societies found across the various Igbo areas.[70] The majority of them have nothing to do with either the Arọchukwu or Ibibio/Èfik/Èkọi elements in origin. The Igbo traditions pre-dated the later cross-cultural borrowing between the Igbo and their non-Igbo neighbors. In line with the nonlinear and modeling approach to this study, and as further detailed in the next chapter, cross-cultural exchanges in southeastern Nigeria began several millennia ago with the Bantu migrations, and there are Pan-Igbo/Pan-Bantu cultural forms that bind. Further studies could reveal richness in subcultural variations. Also, what Afigbo and Onwu failed to acknowledge is that all the various communities that are identified by their use of the Igbo language today did not move into their present homeland at the same time. While some have been here since prehistory, as the Igbo Ukwu culture proves, other groups are relatively new to the Igbo area.[71] There is no single or monolithic culture found anywhere in the world, and the Igbo specifically have discernible subgroups based on cultural differences and geographical locations. The use of masks and masquerades as social control mechanisms reveals the direction of a society as people struggle to survive in their ecosystems.

The foregoing reveals that the proto-Bantu people comprising the Igbo and their Ibibio, Èfik, and Ijọ neighbors constructed their masks and masquerade institution by upholding, protecting, and deepening the utilitarian values and functions of masquerades in the religious, political, and socioeconomic domains.[72] Working with the masses, the indigenous elite, whom Steve Feierman in a study on Tanzania identified as "the peasant intellectuals,"[73] accomplished the intended goals of the institution through diverse ways as summarized in the cosmological/philosophical and the entertainment domains. In both domains, the critical strategy was to mobilize the masses to invest deeply in the institution nurtured with the traditional religious belief system as cultivated with powerful and gripping ideologies of myth making, secrecy, and ritual observances. For continuity, the family traditions and socialization processes were supported with rites of passage that introduced new members of the society into a plethora of village-based age-grade associations, secret societies, masquerade cults, and prestigious social clubs such as the *ọzọ* (or Ágbálánze). The *ọzọ* institution is for individuals committed to live within high moral standards, and they share with the lineage heads and elders the responsibility for ordering society. The *ọzọ* titleholder is a priest, a high-ranking member of the community's judicial system, and an aristocrat whose respect is derived mostly from his sacred position as a bearer of truth and social order. Given that the rite of initiation is very expensive, often people can only gain entrance at a ripe old age. Afigho correctly observes:

> Not only had they an interest in the peaceful ordering of society, but as successful farmers, they had the expert knowledge needed in settling what must have the mainly farming disputes and affrays which arose around them. Their success also enabled them to build up fairly large followings in form of large households, which supplied the labor that kept them on top of society. They were also respected by their less successful neighbors who needed their patronage and protection or simply admired them and sought, or hoped to be like them.[74]

Within these agencies, members were schooled to uphold the myths and legends constructed and offered as the authentic history of the people.

Altogether, the precolonial civil association networks—masquerades, secret societies, age-grade associations, and social clubs—created multiple centers of power and authority. As Afigbo sums it up, "many were the foci of authority and so complex the checks and balances that the [Igbo chief] was barely little more than a titular official except in a [few border] communities," where centuries of interaction with non-Igbo elements had led to the development of monarchical structures that are substantially ceremonial. A few examples of these communities include Ásábá, Onitsha, and Ogutá.[75] Although some other African societies did not have the same form of sociopolitical heritage like the Igbo, Èfik, Ibibio, Ijọ, and Igálá of modern Nigeria, many of those located along the Bantu migratory routes have a heritage of similar cultural practices.

To summarize, the fundamentals of religio-cultural and sociopolitical traditions found in the original Bantu/Bight of Biafra hinterlands, particularly in the Igbo area, have been used to illustrate why and how the tradition of masks and masquerades came about and over time became deeply entrenched in society. Next, we discussed how the genre of masquerading invented in the original Bantu hinterland began to travel everywhere as an imperial force of culture. It has been further explained that religion not only suffused the worldview and sacralized the indigenous agents of socialization in Africa, but it was also used to restrict or dissuade individuals from flouting sacred values. Mythologies and folktales moralized on how the spirits and departed ancestors could punish offenders and reward honesty, patience, parsimony, reverence for elders, and modesty. During moonlight activities, children were raised with stories, songs, and choruses that inculcated the desired values, mores, and taboos that were meant to restrain individual behavior.

CHAPTER 3

Bantu Migrations and Cultural Transnationalism in the Ancient Global Age, c. 2500 BCE–1400 CE

NO DISCUSSION ON LANDSCAPES and waterscapes as conduits of diffusion in global history would be comprehensive without due attention to the Bantu/Biafra hinterlands, a small corner of the world in West Africa. For several centuries, this region bordering southeastern Nigeria and western Cameroon has served as an influential channel of cross-cultural fertilization on the global stage. Connecting the origin and global journey of the masquerade culture to the Bantu migrations offers two rare opportunities to test the processes of cultural globalization or diffusion evolving from the Igbo/Èfìk/ Ibibio/Ijọ hinterlands and the formation of identities in Africa and the New World. From about 2500 BCE, the so-called proto-Bantu people began to leave the region in small numbers organized around family units.[1] This migration appears to test the strength, so to speak, of their adaptability among the alien communities located along their chosen migratory routes. As they sojourned through West, Central, East, and Southern Africa, the Bantu exchanged some cultural ideas with their host communities, including religious and philosophical ideologies, family and kinship customs, age-grade and secret society associations, and the mask and masquerade art form.

The second opportunity that lends itself to this test on the export of cultures across regional lines is the processes of expansion of masquerade carnivals to the Americas. This dynamic came about in the second half of the fifteenth century following the European voyages of discovery and rise of the transatlantic slave trade. In this chapter, we make a full treatment of this history in light of the Bight of Biafra hinterland's role in the mass transportation of millions of Africans to the New World and of how the victims of this trade injected elements of African-styled masquerade carnivals in the Americas.

In the meantime, the primary focus at hand is the historical forces related to the Bantu borderlands and how the proto-Bantu and succeeding generations

affected the African world's culturescape, with a focus on the masquerade institution. No study has fully articulated this history of cultural diffusion with
the seriousness it richly deserves, given what I have identified as the rise of the
Ancient Global Age, c. 2500 BCE –1650 CE. Among other things, the Bantu
migration and its continent-wide scope explain the harmonization of African
cultures across all regions. As Yi Wang has argued, globalization enhances cultural identity: "At the source of culture, there is social agency: a group of people
with freedom and creativity. Creative persons can contribute to the change and
development of a culture. People are not mere objects of cultural influences, but
subjects who can sift various influences and reject or integrate them. Sometimes,
advocates of anti-globalization overlook the power of people's subjectivity."[2]

Wang's scholarship reinforces Ralph Linton's threefold paradigm of the processes through which diffusion occurs: presentation of new cultural elements to
the society, acceptance by society, and integration of the accepted elements into
the preexisting culture.[3] In other words, Linton sees diffusion as involving active
subjects and not mere consumers of alien ideas as the early twentieth-century
British and German-Austrian Diffusion Schools of cultural diffusion promoted.

Culture Diffusion Theories

Culture diffusion theory emerged at the turn of the twentieth century as a response to the theory of evolution of cultures, which proposed that human cultures are subject to similar changes to biological/genetic evolutionary processes.[4]
In advancing the argument that there are centers from which traits of culture
disperse to other areas, exponents of cultural diffusion challenged the separate
stages of sociocultural evolution outlined by the evolutionists. Though the various diffusionist schools are in consensus on the basic premise of diffusion as an
explanation for the spread of cultural traits, they tend, however, to disagree on
what explains similarities among cultures even when cultures may be separated
by long distances.

For instance, the British School of Diffusion led by William Perry, W. H. R.
Rivers, and others, hypothesizes with diverse shades of emphasis that cultures
emanate from one point and then spread to other areas. In their extreme position, the British School believes that Egypt was the fountainhead of world cultures and that other regions were inhabited by mere "Natural Man," incapable
of cultural inventions and only consuming culture traits produced in Egypt.[5]
While the British School promotes the diffusion of culture traits in their singular capacity, the German-Austrian School of Diffusion led by Frederick Ratzel,

Leo Frobenius, Fritz Graebner, and others puts forward multiple centers of creativity and "culture complexes"—that is, a combination of traits such as beliefs and practices associated with a phenomenon.[6] In other words, the German-Austrian School holds that culture complexes diffuse in their entirety through the migration of people. Along with this line, Wilhelm Schmidt points out that with migration, peoples and cultures came into contact and mutually influenced one another. According to Schmidt, "this mutual influence has been exercised to a greater extent than had hitherto been admitted," which explains the dynamics of "new creations and modifications of culture, and wherever positively established it makes the assumption of independent origin untenable and superfluous."[7]

To their credit, the functionalist and methodological approach introduced by the German-Austrian School has been acknowledged by Hornayun Sidky, John V. Ferreira, and others who also named them variously the "Cultural Historical School," the "Culture-Circle School," or "historical ethnology."[8] However, one of the major criticisms leveled against the German-Austrian School of diffusion is its overemphasis on "trait complex." It has not been fully explained how the fundamental complexes of diffusion are established as historical realities. Yet, proponents tend to exclude the possibility of independent origins of at least some elements of the complex whole. Rather, as Annemarie Malefijt has noted, the German-Austrian School has tried, although unsuccessfully, to accommodate the complications surrounding the theory with such categorization as primitive, secondary, and tertiary circles (*kreis*) of cultures; each of the three demarcated circles (*kulturkreis*) has subcircles. Those that did not fall within the categories were either a marginal, peripheral or an overlapping element.[9]

Like the British School, the German-Austrian School did not offer much to desire in arguing that every cultural practice in human society today came either from one source or only a few centers. Both schools tend to be arbitrary in their association of certain elements of culture circles and deny agency to those receptive to alien cultural traits. This brings us to the alternative perspective the American School of Diffusion advanced by Franz Boas, the father of American ethnology, who although associated with the German-Austrian School insisted on the significance of cultural rudiments in the context of sequence of events and space.[10]

The American School of Diffusion holds the view that people tend to learn and acquire practices from cultures they encounter along the way. The reasoning is that the more the contact persists, the more chances both cultures in contact will lend and borrow from each other. For instance, Melville Herskovits, a student of Boas, argues that cultures in an area are inclined to creating clusters that are "sufficiently homogenous that regions on which they occur can be delimited on a map."[11] In light of this, Nita Mathar defines culture area as "the geographical space in which similar cultures are found."[12] The American diffusionists believe that by drawing geographical spread of specific traits (i.e., culture areas) the chances exists to describe the parallels or divergences between cultures, including the culture of Native Americans. Meanwhile, the genesis of the idea of culture areas in American ethnography goes back to 1895, when Otis T. Mason first used the term "culture area."[13] Building on this, other scholars have since expanded the theory by correlating dominant cultural traits with geographical areas.[14] Clark Wissler provides a conceptual and methodological approach to the study of culture areas when he stated that if "we take all traits into simultaneous consideration and shift our point of view to the social or tribal units, we are able to form fairly definite groups. This will give us culture areas, or a classification, of social groups according to their culture traits."[15]

The following discussion is located within the American Diffusion School with emphasis on the dynamics of culture areas, which corresponds to the overall essence of the Bantu migrations. After laying out the geographical moorings of the historic population movements using the linguistic evidence provided by anthropologists and linguists, attention is shifted to the patterns of culture the Bantus fostered, with a focus on religion and its masquerade agency. The approach is to map out the locations of some of the known Bantu peoples on the continent and then discuss how some of their cultural traditions compare with those found among the Igbo/Ibibio/Èfik/Ijọ using the religion, age-grade, secret society, and masks and masquerade matrix.

The Geographical Spread

The Bantu expansions represent one of the greatest migrations in human history in terms of the huge number of people involved, and more important, its extensive, continent-wide impacts. Oral, linguistic, and archaeological sources show that the proto-Bantu group lived somewhere in Central Africa—precisely in the areas bordering parts of the Benue-Cross River Basin of southeastern Nigeria, and western Cameroon.[16] It is believed that the first Bantu migrants left this area around 2500 BCE on what would become an endless and intermittent relay-journey involving hundreds of generations of descendants spreading across different regions of the African continent. There is no clear evidence that the movements involved a mass horde of people leaving simultaneously in the

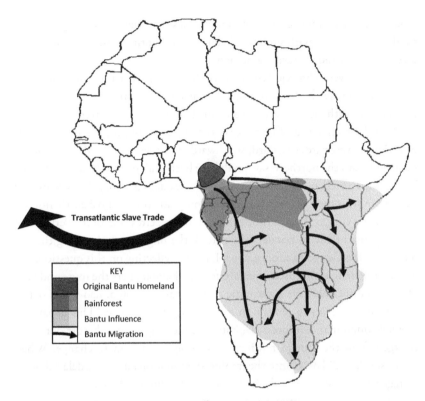

FIGURE 3.1. Bantu migrations

manner, for example, of the chaotic exodus of the enslaved Israelites out of Egypt (c. 1450 BCE) or the recent arrival of refugees in Europe or those illegally crossing the southern border of the United States. Besides, Bantu migrations and resettlements were not accomplished through wars and conquests.

In retrospect, it was mostly a willful and peaceful migration, and the population resettlements spanned over a long chunk of history. In the ancient era, much of the African continent was open to such massive demographic changes. The extensive spread of the migrants affected all regions of sub-Saharan Africa with the expansion and separation of Bantu cultural institutions, including the emergence of secondary languages from its parent stock. Today, most groups commonly identified as Bantu-speakers are found in modern Democratic Republic of the Congo (DRC), Republic of the Congo, Uganda, Kenya, Tanzania, Zimbabwe, Swaziland, and Malawi. It is not by coincidence that most of these modern African countries harbor communities that share some profound cultural characteristics with groups inhabiting the Bantu ancestral homeland in eastern Nigeria and western Cameroon.

Roland Oliver, who rejected the early hypothesis that the Bantu subdued their host societies by force of arms, has asserted that the Bantu migrations commenced with neither a predetermined direction nor pattern.[17] While a southward direction was often the case, the migration of people was in multiple directions—westward, eastward, southward, and even backward. In addition, incursions into the northern savannah have been underscored by a recent study by Thembi Russell and co-scientists using the modeling theory.[18] It is estimated that those who took the eastward direction gradually established themselves north of the Congo River on the savannah fringe, circa 500 BCE. Perhaps we should pause briefly to ponder why it took the migrants such a long time to break into the Congo rainforest zone. Directly reflecting on this question, Rebecca Grollemuna and coscientists argue that "habitat alters the route and pace of human dispersal." The Bantu, the authors further noted, had swept out of West-Central Africa to resettle in a vast geographical area: "This expansion avoided unfamiliar rainforest habitats by following savannah corridors that emerged from the Congo rainforest, probably from climate change. When Bantu speakers did move into the rainforest, migration rates were delayed by on average 300 [years] compared with similar movements on the savannah. Despite unmatched abilities to produce innovations culturally, unfamiliar habitats significantly alter the route and pace of human dispersals."[19]

The Bantu entered the new areas with the accouterments of material and nonmaterial cultural hybridization, including language development and other new formations lasting several centuries. In both the savannah and the rainforest regions, the proto-Bantu or UrBantu language continued to acquire new dialects, splitting into several sub-Bantu languages in a process that could be qualified as split and compare.[20] The most prominent of the new tongues became the proto-western and proto-eastern Bantus. The process of differentiation was more or less complete by the beginning of the fourth century CE. Afterward, the various subgroups began to migrate again in opposite directions. In the northern Congo, the proto-western Bantu settled the forest and swamp areas between Sangha and Ubangi (Oubangi) Rivers. From here they ascended the Congo-Lualaba River, settling the woodland area of southwestern Zaire, and then moved southward into the grasslands of Angola and Namibia. The proto-eastern Bantu expanded from their settlement in the equatorial rainforests to the Zambezi River. A northward advance from here saw the migrants passing slowly through Mozambique, to the Mount Kilimanjaro area of Tanzania. From there, they moved upward into the Great Lakes areas of Central Africa embracing modern Rwanda, Burundi, and Uganda.

Meanwhile, Bantu expansions into the Central and Southern African regions are fresh in mind today because succeeding generations of the proto-Bantu and semi-Bantu-speakers began to move into them roughly between 500 and 1000 CE. It is believed that Bantu population movements were coming to an end by the mid-seventeenth century when the Ngoni and other sub-Bantu groups reached the Cape of Good Hope—that is, the southern tip of the continent. At the cape, the Bantu population movements involving the Ngoni, Sotho, Shona, Rozwi, and Zulu of the Southern Africa region came to a halt when in the 1650s Africans were confronted by the Dutch Frontier Boers near the Great Fish River.[21] This contact would later precipitate a cycle of bloody wars between the Africans and the Europeans (Dutch and later British settlers) along the Eastern Cape, which did not end until the nineteenth century. By 1820, theoretically, the more than five millennia of Bantu population movements concluded.

The Language Evidence

In the contemporary period, the word "Bantu" may resonate with the "Bantustans" or Black homelands officially passed into law in 1963 by the segregationist apartheid rulers of South Africa. But Bantu as a marker of identity does not denote a distinct ethnic group or a race, as some scholars like Harry H. Johnston had tried to assert in 1886.[22] It denotes rather several linguistic groups in a culture zone as identified in this study, with a population estimated at 100–150 million. In this study, the term Bantu applies to the ancient people in motion and the culture they nurtured, modeled, and spread across the African continent. The Bantu-speakers represent a dominant part of the parent stock, the larger Niger-Congo language family, comprising around 450 African languages. The parent family accounts for nearly 85 percent of the population of sub-Saharan Africa, thus constituting the largest language bloc among the continent's four major language groups. The other three are Afro-Asiatic, Nilo-Saharan, and Khoisan.

However, there are conflicting arguments as to whether the Niger-Congo family includes a subfamily called Benue-Congo.[23] The Benue-Congo, as postulated by German linguist Wilhelm Heinrich Immanuel Bleek (1827–1875) in 1862, are mostly identified as part of a common source in which, for example, the singular word *ntu* means "person," and its plural usage with the prefix *Ba* as in

BaKongo or Baganda, means "persons" or "people."[24] A few examples of words and languages identified as part of the Bantu subdivision with similar or approximate syntax and words for "people" or "person" includes *watu* as in Swahili or Kiswahili (the lingua franca widely dominant on the east coast of the continent), and *vantu* as in Shona language found in South Africa. Early on, the Portuguese had, in the course of their initial contacts with the Africans beginning in the late fifteenth century, noticed this shared linguistic heritage among different ethnicities. But it was Martin Affonso (1500–1564), as recorded in the *Journal of the First Voyage of Vasco da Gama*, who began to examine the unique syntax of the Bantu while residing for some time in the ancient Kingdom of Kongo.[25] From this initial inquiry would develop the first publication of a few grammars in an African language. Later studies led to the idea of an African family of languages named the "Niger-Congo" by Joseph Greenberg in 1947.[26]

By the late 1800s, the curiosity of Europeans about African languages had expanded to include the languages spoken in the areas stretching from the old Kingdom of Kongo (modern Angola and some parts of Namibia) to the central, eastern, and southern parts of Africa including Mozambique in the southeastern part. The logical thought emerged that there must be an explanation as to why these speakers share certain words in common. Further investigations (although often considered insufficient) have now shown that what explains the puzzle is one of the results of a historical process of the Bantu migrations. While much remains unknown about Bantu movements, scholars investigating oral sources along with results of studies by archaeologists and linguists have unraveled some pieces of information on the Bantu and their influences on the development of African traditions.

While it is uncertain how many African languages belong to the original Bantu and its outliers, studies by Sir Harry Hamilton Johnston (1858–1927), Malcolm Guthrie, and others have identified scores of languages they *think* belong to the original Bantu and semi-Bantu family groups.[27] They are: (1) the *Cameroon-Cross River* comprising Èkọi, Manyan, Bali-Bamum, Ndob, Nsom, and others; (2) the *Cross River-Calabar* comprising Olulomo, Èfik, Akunakuna, among others; (3) the *Benue* made up of Munshin, Boritsu, and Afudu; (4) the *Bauchi* found in Jarawa; (5) the *Central Nigeria* of the Kaduna Basin; (7) the *Togoland* including Lefana, Bale, and Kedea; and (8) the *Senegambia or Guinea*, comprising Temne and its dialects of Landoma and Baga, Bulom, Biafada, Pajade, Bola, Pepel, Sarar, Dyola, and Konyagi. If these are accepted as the core Bantu language speakers, then we can identify the semi-Bantu or variants of Bantu speakers, including: Ganda (or Luganda) speakers of Uganda; Tumbuka (or ChiTumbuka) speakers of Malawi; Kako, Ngumba, and Basaa speakers of Cameroon; Kikuyu (or Gikuyu) speakers of Kenya; and Zulu, Shona, Sotho, Ndebele (Matabele), Xhosa, and Tswana (or Setswana) speakers of South Africa.[28]

To proceed, it is crucial to note that there is at best skeletal evidence to help put all the pieces of the language puzzle together. This illuminates several lacunae surrounding Bantu studies. The linguistic evidence around which the bulk of Bantu migration history is built is prone to serious errors. For instance, in regard to the Igbo, the idiom *madu bu ntụ* ("We are nothing but ash") is a common saying among the people, which the initial classification of African languages by Johnston, Malcolm Guthrie, and others did not take into proper account; hence the Igbo language was erroneously excluded from the Bantu subgroup and rather placed in the Kwa subgroup of the Niger-Congo family. It is also curious that the word *Njọku* or *Ahịajọku* connected with farming and agricultural festivals in Igboland of southeastern Nigeria is also found among the Mbere of the Embu District of Kenya dominated by the Kikuyu, a Bantu group.[29] Yet, Guthrie and others separated the Igbo and the Kikuyu in their classifications of African languages. Discussions with the Kikuyus of Kenya have also led to the questions whether the Igbo word for "child," *nwá*, has a connection to the Tsonga and Venda word *nwáná*, which also means "child." In Igbo, *nwáná* means literally "father's child," while the Zulu word for child is *(um)twáná*, literally "little person." The use of the prefix *umu* as in *umu-ntu* (human beings) in Zulu is akin to the use of Igbo *umu mmádu* (human beings). Add this to the Igbo word *ọkukọ* (chicken), which is equivalent to the Bantu word *nkukhu* (chicken) and *ngunku* in Kikuyu, and one is left without doubt that these similarities are not just mere coincidences.[30]

Further, it is neither clear why the Pigmies included as Bantu-speakers appear so physically different from their other Bantu neighbors, nor why the Igbo-speakers who share very close language and cultural characteristics with their Ibibio, Èfik, Èkọi, and Ijọ neighbors (as elaborated in the preceding chapter) are classified separately in most of the Bantu language studies.[31] Hence Joseph Greenberg warns, with the hindsight from his study on the influence of Kanuri on Hausa, that there are several "limitations of one particular type of historical influences that can be drawn from language, namely the study of words borrowed from one language into another."[32] More daunting is the length of time dating the beginning of the first Bantu population movements and, given the paucity of sources on African prehistory, what is known about the Bantu migrations is replete with some glaring factual disjunctures and inconsistencies. Generally, a historian of the African precolonial era is often confronted with overwhelming challenges of authentic sourcing of information and therefore must be very careful in order not to fall into wild idealism or erroneous speculations. There are numerous subjects in Africa, such as disease, racial or ethnic characteristics, medical knowledge, education, as well as migration about which information is imperfect and opinion divided.

The point of departure for the present study is the corrective that the Cross River Igbo and their southeastern Nigerian neighbors (Ibibio, Èfik, Èkọi, and Ijọ) belong to the same language family whatever this is called. This assertion is based on the strong evidence of their close geographical, cultural, marital, and linguistic linkages. In his ethnographic fieldwork, the current researcher visited the separate Azumini, Áfikpo, Arọchukwu, and Unwáná Igbo-speaking communities bordering the Cross River confluence. Their brand of Igbo language is, in fact, closer to the Èfik and Ibibio languages than to the Igbo dialect spoken in central Igbo areas of Owerri, Mbáno, Orlu, and Mbieri. This implicates the definition of culture area by Ogbu Kalu and Ogun U. Kalu, which bears a direct relevance to this study: According to Kalu and Kalu, "A culture area is defined as a geographical delimitation of an area that has the same dominant and significant culture traits, complexes, and patterns." The authors further provide a fuller geographical spread of the communities that belong to the Cross River area:

> Cross-River Igbo communities ranged along the left bank of the Cross River constitute such an identifiable unit. In the north are communities within the Ezza, Ikwo and Ezzikwo group; the middle section of the river bank is inhibited by Áfikpo, Uburu, Okposi, Unwáná, Èddá, Nkporo, Ábiribá, and Igbèrè. Further downstream are a number of communities whose myths of origin are closely intertwined: the Ọháfiá, Ábám, and Ihe who trace their origin to a common ancestry. The Ututu and Isu share some traits with Ọháfiá but relate more to the Arọ who are at the boundary of the Cross-River Igboland. Most of the Cross-River Igbo communities (Ábiribá, Igbèrè, Èddá, lhe, Ututu, and Arọ) allege non-Igbo origins or admixtures of [the] non-Igbo group."[33]

The eminent Igbo historian Adiele E. Afigbo has made a similar point. Among other things, of particular interest in Afigbo's study is the observation that some Igbo communities such as "the Ezza, Izzi, and the Ikwo have been treated [in the previous studies] as a language different from Igbo" [sic].[34] The renowned Ijọ Niger Delta historian E. J. Alagoa has further observed that Greenberg's classifications with regard to the Benue-Congo and Kwa subfamilies were seriously flawed.[35] More important, Greenberg himself has "raised several doubts when he suggested that the affiliation of Kru and Ịjọ to the Kwa group should be considered tentative and that Kwa and Benue-Congo are quite close to each other. He even goes so far as to say that there is legitimate doubt as to whether or not the two should be separated at all."[36] Guthrie has further warned about what he calls "speculative hypotheses," which can lead to the danger of using language "material of this kind in such a way that the results cannot be verified."[37] Addressing this issue, Vansina highlights the complexities of internal relations in the Benue-Cross/Lower Niger, which poses a problem as to what precisely the term Bantu is. Jan Vansina has observed that Greenberg's Bantu is more inclusive than Guthrie's while others like Patrick Bennett and Jan Sterk have reorganized associations within Niger-Congo family. For Bennett and Sterk, Kwa and Benue-Cross form a single unit, within which some "Semi-Bantu" languages are grouped, as well as a few "Bantu" languages, while the bulk of Bantu joined by some "Semi-Bantu" languages form another subdivision. In light of these complexities, Vansina warns that "any historian using linguistic arguments would be wise to check them carefully before proceeding very far with his inferences."[38]

As if directly speaking to the concerns explicated by Greenberg, Guthrie, Afigbo, Alagoa, and others, Grollemuna and coauthors captured the imperative of the present study in relation to the Bantu migrations when they stated that "humans are uniquely capable of using cultural innovations to occupy a range of environments, raising the intriguing question of whether historical human migrations have followed familiar habitats or moved relatively independently of them."[39] This highlights a couple of the basic flaws inherent in the earlier culture diffusion discourse—namely, the arbitrary demarcation of culture areas including language families and daughter-tongues. The other is the wrong notion that diffusion of culture traits—whether we are talking about agriculture, language, or masquerades—flows freely from one area to the other. These ideas do not properly take into consideration the symbiotic relationships among cultures in a common geographical zone. As Schmidt explains, "new creations and modifications of culture" occur within this symbiotic context and thus make "the assumption of independent origin untenable and superfluous."[40]

Among other things, while the Bantu phenomenon explains the peopling of the continent, in addition it demonstrates how human interaction can facilitate the rise of cultures. It also highlights the mythological notion of a "pure" human race or an exclusive ethnic identity composed of a single bloodline or with one progenitor. This corroborates the theory of cultural divergence and the nonlinear theorem basis of this entire work. Cultural divergence points to the role of networks and the centrality of peoples and cultural productions at different times. As evidence regarding the Bantu migrations, the period between 2500 BCE and 1650 CE witnessed one of the most extraordinary eras in human history, when people took the center stage in forging networks of exchanges and cultural connections in different parts of the African world. Again, it is reiterated that this challenges both imposition of chronological readings and the tyranny of language classification without incontrovertible supporting evidence. Scholars are therefore urged to think spatially instead—that is, in a pattern that points to position, the size of specific area, and other local and outside factors. More important, cultural imperialism or expansion does not follow one directional movement. There is also a backflow—which has the potency to contaminate the taste and color of the original. This corroborates the theoretical postulation by Clark Wissler with the hindsight of the Native American culture that caution should be applied in accepting the basic premise of culture traits or else categories may have misinterpretation repercussions.[41]

Indeed, no civilization has developed in isolation of others—hence racial and ethnic identities, as manifested today, are culturally constructed around commonly shared values, norms, and practices that might have been drawn from diverse racial and ethnic divides. Above all, the Bantu population movements explain an important connection between different regions of African societies as a "distinct" cultural zone. Movement in history means displacement, alterity of habitats, the influx of new ideas, and cultural reordering. And migration, a very important factor in precolonial Africa, brought about the spread of religions and ritual practices, family and kinship customs, development of vocabularies and new syntax that are found in different languages, political institutions, technology, agriculture and dietary habits, and so on.

The Bantu migrations further support the view that all human societies evolved in a process of continuous change by way of adaptation and hybridization between internal and external cultural dynamics. As a historical phenomenon, the migrations further debunk the formerly held idea that Africa was culturally and historically static before the arrival of the Europeans or even the Arabs. We now understand that there were several channels for the cross-fertilization of ideas and knowledge several centuries before the first European visitors set foot on the continent in the fifteenth century. A detailed understanding of this will begin with identifying the reasons why the Bantu migrations occurred.

Several reasons have been advanced as to why some of the dwellers of the Benue-Cross River Valley decided to leave their original homeland. As in all migrations, people move for various reasons: population growth, search for new opportunities due to unavailability or lack of resources and fauna that support populations in certain locations, changes in climatic conditions, and attempts to escape common threats to life.[42] The results of Merrick Posnansky's archaeological studies in Kenya, Uganda, and Ghana suggest that the proto-Bantu were undergoing a period of transformation from a precarious hunting and food gathering economy to a more settled life marked by improved agriculture. This, in turn, led to a significant increase in population, forcing some people to move outward in order to create living space for themselves and for those who remained behind. Posnansky corroborates the common view that the early population movement did not involve a mass emigration of people and that instead the Bantu population expansion was slow and involved small family and kinship groups covering only short distances over a period of time.[43] One may understand the Bantu expansion as a process of "split and fusion"—meaning that the movement of a group of families or individuals into a new settlement was followed by a split that would see a part of them melt into the host society while the other part moved on to another settlement. Nita Mathur has argued "sometimes culture contact leads to the rise of compound cultures constituted of fusion of several cultures."[44] In other words, sometimes the migrants joined an existing community while at other times they founded an entirely new settlement within the larger host community.

Those who moved may have been forced to escape problems of drought and search for better farmlands. For populations that relied heavily on subsistence agriculture and livestock grazing (in this case, goat, sheep, and chickens), drought and famine apparently posed a serious threat to their survival. Perhaps this may partly explain why Bantu activities were not very pronounced in the northernmost parts of West Africa following the beginning of the desertification of the Sahara region beginning around 1000 BCE. Prior to this period, the Sahara region was marked by grasses and low shrubs as showed by fossilized pollen, and there is ample evidence supporting the fact that agricultural communities lived here. Between February 1350 and December 1351when he visited Mali, Ibn Battuta observed that "The road has many trees which are tall and of great girth: a caravan can find shade in the shadow of one tree; . . . There are trees that bear fruits like cucumber. . . . The calabashes in the land of blacks become big and from them, they made wooden dishes."[45] What this eyewitness account tells us is that as of the fourteenth century—that is four millennia after the Bantu migration began—the Sahel region of West Africa was still capable of sustaining a viable agriculture. This may debunk the initial hypothesis that the Bantu migration and its impacts did not embrace northwest Africa.[46] There has always been the tendency for people to move away from areas of drought and

famine to more arable lands with pasture for their livestock, but there also can
be other factors and considerations that come first before ecological reasons. For
instance, wars and epidemics also necessitate the emigration of people to areas
of peace and hospitable environment. The outbreak of diseases poses a threat to
both humans and livestock.[47]

In general, those who migrated considered their comfort and survival as paramount. Bantu migrants may have also thought about the challenges and risks
involved in venturing into unfamiliar territories and living among alien groups.
This has led to the speculation by scholars like Christopher Wrigley that the
proto-Bantu possessed iron-working ability, which enabled them to make better
tools with which they dominated the environment and peoples they came in
contact with in the areas where they chose to resettle.[48] This assumption should
not be taken uncritically, for various Bantu families and groups may have been
forced to move in an attempt to evade harm from their opponents bearing superior weapons and implements.

The most crucial and pertinent question, then, is to show the impact of the
Bantu population movements on the evolution of new cultural ideas in the regions they settled. How do we know whether these cultural institutions were
indeed invented by the Bantu or the migrants were instead assimilated into them
by their host communities? What specific cultural ideas are we looking at to
help us assert this claim of Bantu culture modeling in Africa, and how do we
connect them to the other locations they settled in, not least in Central Africa?
The approach is to seek evidence of cultural institutions associated with the
Bantu homeland in eastern Nigeria and western Cameroon that are also found
in those separate locations the Bantu settled. It is difficult to make these connections without errors, as scholars have pointed out in the past. To control the
variables and thus limit the probability of errors, the areas of focus are limited
to those institutions that helped define and enabled the operationalization of
masks and masquerade custom as encountered in the indigenous religion that
recognizes the role of ancestors and spirits in human affairs. As fully explained
in the preceding chapter, the masquerade culture was legitimized within the
realms of the indigenous cosmology, religious philosophy, and the sacralization
of familial agents of socialization—the age-grade associations, secret societies,
and of course political institutions.

Religion, Indigenous Politics, and the Masquerade Culture

The task now is to systematically link items of culture highlighted in the Bantu homeland with those found in Bantu satellite communities scattered across the continent. This is examined through the prism of indigenous religion, politics, and the accouterments of indigenous civil society institutions—age-grades, secret societies, and masquerade cults. The most identifiable Bantu-speakers are found in about twenty-seven African countries today: Angola, Botswana, Burundi, Cameroon, Central African Republic (CAR), Comoros, Congo, DRC, Equatorial Guinea, Gabon, Kenya, Lesotho, Madagascar, Malawi, Mayotte, Mozambique, Namibia, Nigeria, Rwanda, Somalia, South Africa, Sudan, Swaziland, Tanzania, Uganda, Zambia, and Zimbabwe. The culture and traditions of some of the Bantu groups found in these countries are highlighted in a comparative context, starting with the religion question.

Starting with worldview matters because it falls into the heart of what Colin A. Palmer has described as "the core beliefs and practices at the heart of a people's consciousness and identity." According to Palmer, people do not easily discard those cultural ideas that are at the heart of their very existence, and "this must be distinguished from others that are secondary and can be changed without considerable consequences for their cosmologies, behavior, and self-definition."[49] The mask and masquerade traditions and political cultures of the Igbo, Ibibio, Èfik, and Ijọ peoples were deeply rooted in an indigenous cosmology that recognized the Supreme God (Chukwu) as the Creator God (Chinéké), while the lesser divinities were conceived as intermediaries in a universe in which humans, deities, and ancestral spirits share the earthly space. As resonating in the concepts of Katonda (among the Buganda of Uganda), Bumba (Bushoong of Central Africa), Imana (Banyarwanda, Rwanda), Ngai (Kenya), Ukulunkulu (Zulu, South Africa), Mwari (Zimbabwe), and so on, the belief in a Supreme God who is also the Creator God remains central in the indigenous religions of the various Bantu groups found across the continent. For example, the Abaluhya, a Bantu people of modern western Kenya, believe that the earth was created by Wele Xakaba (Creator God), who is also described as the granter and giver of all things.[50] As the Ijọ of southeastern Nigeria believe that Woyengi, a female deity, descended from heaven to physically create humans, so do the various Bantu groups—the Efe of Central Africa, and the Zulu of South Africa—respectively believe that Muungu or Ukulunkulu was the creator and provider of all things. At the same time, notions of the existence of ancestral spirits, smaller divinities, water spirits, and deities are strong and used as tools in the ordering of the socioeconomic and political practices. For instance, in the traditional Luhya religion that featured animism and spirits, funeral rites are held in high regard as a custom to please and honor ancestral spirits.[51]

Thus, through the course of their migration, marriage connections, and trading contacts, the Bantu and their various host communities fashioned out diverse but similar belief systems commonly identified today as African traditional religions. Though there are a variety of mythologies peculiar to every community, African traditional religions resemble one another in the basic beliefs in a Supreme Being, the existence of ancestral spirits, and the dualism of worlds inhabited by man and ancestors. It is believed that the ancestors and other divinities control the human world and often impose their wills when things are not going well. This entrenched belief system left a lasting impact on the various African societies, and its effects are still strong even though alien religions like Islam and Christianity have infiltrated and brought about some far-reaching changes to the resilient indigenous order.

Among the Bantu groups, the pervading belief in God Almighty, deities, and ancestral spirits brought the need for the sacralization of all rites of passage, including marriage, birth, coming of manhood or womanhood, memberships in age-grades, secret societies, social clubs, and end of life as a transition into the world of the spirits. This ideology necessitated the elaborate religious idioms that mark every stage in life starting from birth. Among the initiation ceremonies associated with the Kuria found in the Nyanza Province of Kenya is circumcision, which, as practiced among the Igbo, Èfik, Ijo, and Ibibio people, marks the identity of an individual within the community and defines a person in relation to the extended family, lineage, descent group, and ethnic group. A day before a female child undergoes circumcision rites, relatives are invited to the public square (*okorea obosamba*) to sing praises and provide support to the girl who should not demonstrate fear or weep during the ceremony.[52]

Also outstanding is the marriage tradition of the Kuria, which has a striking relationship with the customs associated with the people who inhabit the original Bantu homelands today. Like the Cross River Igbo, Ibibio, Èkoi, Èfik, and Ijo of eastern Nigeria, the Kuria girls and their chaperones are involved in elaborate marriage arrangements that may last for months from the moment a go-between, a friend of the groom, introduces the couple to each other. The Bantu tradition dictates that a man is to marry a woman in his ethnic group but not from his village or clan, a transgression of which is considered a serious taboo and sanctioned with serious punishment. After the introduction, bride price negotiations begin between the families of the groom and the bride until they come to an agreeable settlement. Once the bride price is paid, the groom takes the bride home. The same marriage protocols are observed among the Igbo, Ibibio, Èfik, and Ijǫ. Writing on bridewealth in among the Igbo, Uche Isiugo-Abanihe stated that it "was a symbolic token in form of services, goods or money, given to bride's parents by the prospective groom."[53]

In the sphere of political culture, it has been further noted that across the continent, Bantu expansions gave rise to mixed political systems. These are the brand of indigenous, village-based republicanism found among the Igbo and Ibibio peoples of southeastern Nigeria, as well as the development of states with centralized forms of authority as encountered among the Èfik and Ijǫ. In both the decentralized and centralized systems, it has been revealed that the idea of ancestors as political actors remained strong and masquerade cults functioned as ancestral spirits, occasionally visiting the human world for various purposes. Most of the Bantu people of northern Tanganyika, Uganda, and Ruanda-Urundi by tradition had political systems of the centralized state form. State formation in Africa (and elsewhere in the world)—whether in the stateless or centralized societies—could not have been easy without some measure of a shared religious ideology among the constituent units. Shared religious symbolisms provide legitimacy for political power and exercise of authority.

In some parts of East Africa, the Bantu presence influenced political organizations incorporating age-grades or age-set associations. For instance, Getahun Benti reminds us that among the highly democratic people of Oromo (Galla) of southern Ethiopia, before their conquest under the Amharic imperial expansions, the Oromo societies of the South had fashioned a democratic political economy undergirded by the *gada* system. The gada system was based on a rotational eight-year cycle in which age-grades took control of the economic, social, and political life of the community as a corporate entity. Ceremonies that marked the end of a gada cycle were conducted at elaborate gada centers that evolved into towns.[54] Remnants of a similar sociopolitical organization based on the age-grade systems still exist today among the Ibibio, Èfik, and some Igbo communities of eastern Nigeria. The age-grade system, synonymous with the so-called stateless societies of Africa, defined the social organization of the Cushitic and Nilotic speakers of central Sudan and Great Lakes areas like the Konjo, Amba, Kiga, and Gishu. In these Bantu communities that had no centralized system of authority before the colonial order, secret societies and guilds permeated the entire fabric of village life. The process of decision making followed the principles of democratic procedures. Decisions reached by the village councils comprising all adult males and elders of the land were enforced by the appropriate age-grades and secret societies as endorsed by the elders.[55]

With regard to masquerade culture within African cross-migrations, ethnographic and anthropological fieldwork associated with this study indicates that the Ágábá and Okoroshá masquerade festivals of the various Igbo communities like Abágáná, Ifákálá, Umunneohá, Mbieri, Ọgwá, and Ubomiri are similar to the masks and masquerade dances of the Bamanan, Bozo, and Sòmonò groups of Mali.[56] For example, Sogo Bo or youth association puppet masquerade theater found among the three communities of south-central Mali reminds one of similar age-grade associations' operating the Okoroshá and Kéléké stilt masquerades among the Mbáitoli communities of Imo State, Nigeria.[57] Again this goes back to the imperfect state of Bantu studies.

Meanwhile, among the Luvale, Chokwe, Luchazi, and Mbunda of the Vaka Chiyama Cha Mukwamayi peoples of Zambia, the Makishi masquerade is performed at the end of an annual initiation ritual known as *mukándá*. This initiation is for boys between eight and twelve years old. The ritual starts from the onset of the dry season with the young boys leaving their homes to take up temporary residence in an isolated bush camp. The temporary separation from the outside world, which may last from one to three months, "marks their symbolic death as children."[58] The mukándá observance, which reminds one of the Ègbélé societies of the Áfikpo and Unwáná and the Erusi-Èddá of the Èddá communities of Igboland, involves the circumcision of the initiates. As with the Ègbélé, mukándá is also invoked as a test of courage and manhood. Therefore, it is a period when the young males are schooled on their future role as men and husbands.

During the period that the mukándá ceremony lasted, each initiate is assigned a specific masked character that remains with him the entire duration of the process. Among the various characters that the masquerades portray are Chisaluke, a powerful and wealthy man with spiritual influence; Mupala, presented as the "lord" of the mukándá and protective spirit with supernatural abilities; Pwevo, a female character (played by a masked male performer) representing the ideal woman and account for the music and dances that go with the rituals. Another masked character is Makishi, portraying the essence of a late forebear who comes back to the community to support the young boys. Like the Erusi-Èddá of Igboland, by the time the *mukándá* observances had run its course, the initiate had undergone a life-changing experience with the people's most powerful gods.

After the mukándá rituals, a graduation ceremony, is held in honor of the initiates. It was necessary that everyone in the village attend the Makishi dance and satirical performance that follow, until the graduates reemerge from the camp to reintegrate with their communities as adult men. As a means of socialization and societal belongingness, the mukándá festival helps in "transmitting practical survival-skills as well as knowledge about nature, sexuality, religious beliefs, and the social values of the community."[59] Initially, the entire festival and the masquerade appearance lasted for several months and represented the raison d'être of the Makishi masquerade. In contemporary times, many changes have come to the tradition in accordance with modernity. In relation to the school calendar, for instance, the festival is now condensed to one to three months to put up with the Western educational calendar. As the Makishi masquerade dance maintains its popularity at social gatherings and party rallies, the original purpose of its ritual observance might be compromised.

Iron Working, Agriculture, Pottery, and Rituals

It will be proper to end this section with a short discussion on iron working, agriculture, and pottery in relation to the Bantu migration and cultural diffusion in Africa. In addition to food cultivation and the spread of many cultural practices, iron smelting and pottery are linked with Bantus in several studies. For instance, Russell et al. have applied the modeling theory in a recent study of the Bantu, whom they describe as modeling agents of agriculture and horticulture in sub-Saharan Africa.[60] The connection among metallurgy, agriculture, and pottery is that tools and implements fashioned from iron enhance the ability of farmers in tilling the soil as well as in fitting and beautifying pottery objects employed in precolonial times for various uses. While scholars like Wrigley postulate that the Bantu migrants must have learned the skills of iron working before they left their original homeland in the Benue-Cross River Basin, others hypothesize that this skill was not acquired until about 600 BCE when some Bantu groups began to make their way across the Central African region into the Upper Nile from the ancient Kingdom of Meroe located in the area now known as Sudan. From here it is held that with their acquisition of iron technology the Bantu moved southward, and those early Iron Age settlements of Bantu speakers were dotted across much of Africa south of the Sahara.[61]

Based on the limited evidence available to historians, it is tricky to assert a definite conclusion in regard to the origins and points of dispersal of iron technology in Africa. Again this implicates the problem with seeking an exact chronological order in a period when we should instead think thematically. Archaeological research in a new region or in a new time span inevitably poses

more questions than answers. Therefore, it is difficult for anyone to be entirely
objective in making archaeological interpretations. For instance, archaeological
studies by D. D. Hartle and others have proved that knowledge of iron working was known to the Igbo-Ukwu culture earlier than 500 BCE and that this
culture may or may not have any link with the Meroitic civilization.[62] Adiele E.
Afigbo, an authority on Igbo history, citing archaeological excavations carried
out by Thurstan Shaw, suggests that the Igbo of southeastern Nigeria may have
entered their present homeland from somewhere around the Jos Plateau close
to where the first evidence of iron metallurgy, the Nok culture (c. 500 BCE),
is recorded.[63] If this is confirmed, it will be hard to sustain the notion that the
Bantu migrants acquired their knowledge of iron from the Nile Valley region of
Meroe and from there carried this knowledge southwards. What is true, however, is that different societies transited from Stone Age to Iron Age culture at
different times and places and applied their knowledge of the new technology
to practical tasks in industry, study, mastery, and using agricultural and artistic
traditions, and mechanical and industrial materials. Ironworkers produced tools
and weapons far superior to those made of copper and bronze. Iron tools and
weapons facilitated the Bantu expansion by enabling them to master diverse ecological zones. The waste products of smelting like slag (from ore) and charcoal
used in making furnaces constitute some of the most useful materials for dating
the earliest sites of human settlement.

Pottery is another form of evidence that has helped archaeologists and historians determine aspects of precolonial African history with the used of radiocar-
bon dating and other scientific methods. Both agricultural and pastoral communities use pots for preparing food, and carrying and storing farm harvests, water,
milk, and other liquids. Iron Age cultivators became skilled makers of baked-clay
pottery. Their craftsmanship was so much esteemed that they adorned their pots
with carefully shaped grooves and regular stamped patterns. While motivated
by aesthetics, the intricate patterns and designs they made were dictated by local
customs and symbols drawn from religious and ritual practices, architecture, art,
music and dance, and technology. In the sphere of music and dance, iron gongs,
horns, rattles, and other musical instruments were fashioned. These musical instruments have been used in the Bantu cradle for several millennia in religious
worship and the music and dances that accompany masquerade festivities. As a
result, groups who shared similar cultural institutions used identical patterns
and methods of pottery decoration. Potsherds found in different locations have,
to a great extent, helped archeologists and historians differentiate the Bantu

Culture Area from those of their neighbors. The pieces of evidence have also helped us gain some insight on the antiquity of the Neolithic (or Agricultural) Revolution in Africa. While the most recognized Neolithic sites are found in Egypt and the Middle East, it is ahistorical to assume that the various African peoples who lived in prehistoric times did not consider putting back seedlings and fruits into the earth.

As the Bantu expanded in different directions, it is not clear either how those they encountered reacted toward them or how they reacted toward their host communities. The mere possession of iron weapons may not necessarily mean having the capability and logistics to fight and subdue the numerous autochthonous societies they came in contact with in diverse locations. This is especially true in consideration of the fact that the population movements were sporadic and small scale. Undoubtedly, if the Bantu expanded to other territories as colonizers, it is most improbable this was displayed in the same asymmetric might-is-right approach with which the Europeans colonized the world. It is, therefore, reasonable to assert that there was extensive absorption, assimilation, and displacement of other peoples during the long period of migrations. There were also significant social interactions through trade and intermarriage. In the indigenous system, marriage served as a diplomatic strategy for initiating and cementing social relationships across cultures.

So far, Bantu population movements have been used to demonstrate the connection between different regions of sub-Saharan Africa with regards to human settlements, the evolution and modeling of cultural practices, statehood and political organization, ritual and family practices, technology, linguistic traditions, and more. This history, among other things, teaches how the cultures in Africa can be similar even though they appear somehow different. Across the centuries, the Bantu, it seems, proved themselves successful at adaptation to their new environments. In a sense, we may see the Bantu population movements as a process that involved individuals and groups in the choice of habitats most suitable to their lifestyles and temperaments. Through this process, the Bantu migrations helped in facilitating the creation of human settlements across the sub-Saharan African region and they facilitated and modeled the evolution and development of what we commonly refer to today as "African culture." Marching across diverse cultural terrains, the Bantu offered to and borrowed from their host communities some elements of rituals and religious ideas, patrimonial kingship and political organizations, and masquerade cults. Considering the several millennia of human activities involved, the Bantu migration is not by any means a story about a group's adventure or heroism. It is rather about the peopling of Africa and the establishment of culturescapes and the linkages that have come to define the totality of African heritage. The intricacies and implications of the movements are extensive and far-reaching. No one can claim absolute knowledge of all strands of the history in all its ramifications and the complexities that surround the various lacunae highlighted in this chapter. But for sure, we can conclude that there is a bit of Bantu blood in every person of African descent. At least, a preliminary scientific study based on mitochondrial (mtDNA) has recently confirmed the genetic legacy of the western direction of Bantu migrations.[64]

By the beginning of the transatlantic slave trade in the late fifteenth century, the culture of masking (like the spread of agricultural cultivation, pottery, family traditions, age-grade associations, secret societies, social institutions, and metallurgy) had completed its Africa-wide journey, thus making it one of the most important forms of social control, religious expression, and identity formation, as well as a mode of artistic/intellectual tradition that the African victims of the transatlantic human cargo trade carried with them across the Atlantic. The centuries of the transatlantic slavery (c. 1480–1840s) provided the impetus for the overseas expansion of the African masking tradition, the modeling trajectories it imposed, and the specific forms it assumed in the African Diaspora. Taking into consideration the totality of this history and the implications of cultural inventions, including arts and mode of expressions, the argument is reiterated that the African cultural artifacts that were transferred to the Americas during the transatlantic slave trade are not Igbo, Èfik, Ibibio, or Ijọ. They were all of these and more. They must be seen as a conglomerate of Bantu-African ethnic cultures in motion. This corroborates the position of the American School of thought on cultural diffusion, which posits that over time, the cultures found in an area tended to form clusters that are "sufficiently homogenous in that region on which they occur can be delimited on a map."[65]

Bight of Biafra, Slavery, and Diasporic Africa in the Modern Global Age, 1400–1800

T HE BIGHT OF BIAFRA delineates parts of the West African coastline from the Niger Delta creeks where the Niger River discharges into Cape Lopez, a thirty-four-mile-long peninsula in modern Gabon. This historic and key trading emporium traversed by the fifteenth-century European visitors covers coastal shores in four West African countries: Nigeria, Cameroon, Equatorial Guinea, and Northern Gabon. During the transatlantic slave trade, the most important trading cities in the Bight included Kálábári, Bonny, Old Calabar (Ákwá Ákpá), and New Calabar.[1] From this region, an estimated 1.54 million Africans were bundled into slave ships to the New World.[2] Over a period of four hundred years, the Bight's hinterlands, from where the majority of the slaves were captured, increasingly merged with the wider global economy and cultures as the transatlantic slave trade—led by the inhabitants of the original Bantu homeland and their African diaspora—redefined the Modern Global Age, 1400–1800.

Scholars have speculated on the etymology of the word *Biafra* and how it entered the European lexicon.[3] One idea is that Biafra may or may not have a tie with Igbo words *bịá* (come) and *fárá* (take up or pick up as in a knife suspended in a rafter), which combined means "come and take."[4] Alternatively, the word could be an Ibibio derivation, a combination of *bi-a* (yam) and *áfárá* (a yard; also meaning shoulder); thus Ibibio *biáfárá* (yam-yard), Europeanized as "Biafra" (the "Bight of Yam").[5] This invention reflects the historical tendency of early European visitors to name coasts in Atlantic Africa after its main products: the coasts of rice, pepper (Malagueta), ivory, gold, slaves, though in this case appropriating an African-language term for the coast. It is further possible that the Europeans got this biáfárá word from Bini (Benin), Itsekiri, or western Ijo, with whom the Portuguese first traded in a 1485 expedition led by Joao Afonso de Aveiro.

Early modern maps of Africa made by Portuguese cartographers reveal that the Europeans used the word *Biafara* to describe the entire region sprawling from east of the Niger River and running down to the Cameroon Mountains. Also included in this early European depiction are large swaths of lands in Gabon, the Gambia, and Guinea. Therefore, it is not surprising that there are diverse interpretations of Biafra from one location in West Africa to another. In fact, the closest idea about the origin of Biafra is connected to the Biafar (Biafada) people of the Tenda, an ethnic Bantu group found primarily in modern Guinea-Bissau. Manuel Álvares (1526–1583), a Portuguese Jesuit missionary and educator, in his book *Ethiopia Minor and a Geographical Account of the Province of Sierra Leone*, writes about the "Biafar heathen," in reference to the indigenous people and their traditional religious practices: "the lands inhabited by the Biafares belong to the patrimony of the Bijago [Bijango] people" of Guinea.[6] Despite Álvares's displeasure with the native religion, he was highly impressed with what he witnessed among the Africans when he wrote: "Nothing affords a more lively proof of the benignity or otherwise of a locality than the nature, good or bad, of its inhabitants. If this principle, revealed to us by philosophical truth, is correct, then the province of the Biafar heathen is in no respect inferior to the very best of localities."[7]

While the derivation of Biafra remains unclear, the main concern is to illuminate another great migration in world history, the transatlantic slave trade in which the people within the delineated Bantu Culture Area were principal actors. Biafra's hinterlands' role in the trade and the consequent demographic changes that resulted altered the tapestry of cultures in the Atlantic world. In the course of the four centuries of the transatlantic slave exchanges, the various African groups comprising the Igbo, Èfik, Ibibio, and Ijọ along with other African groups took the masquerade culture to various locations in the Americas as the incorporation of West Africa into the capitalist world system expanded. Similar to Donald Wright's study of Niumi, an enclave on the northern coast of the Gambia River bay in West Africa, the aim here is to highlight the incidents of historical forces emanating from the Bight's hinterlands and their monumental impacts on world history.[8] No one has fully articulated this history with the seriousness it deserves.[9] Unlike Wright's treatment of Niumi with more emphasis on the economic integration of the indigenous society, here, following the arguments of Immanuel Wallerstein's *The Modern World-System*, the intent is to demonstrate how the centrality of people at different times in human history and in different parts of the world, indeed, contributed to global history.[10] First, a quick look at the slave trade census figures reminds us of the huge number of people taken into slavery from the Bight's hinterland. The statistics further reveal the Igbo role in the exchanges and some of the slaves' New World destinations. Wherever they ended up in the New World, Africans helped reinvent different shades of masquerade carnivals with the accompanying idioms of music, dance, and civic actions.

The Transatlantic Slave Trade Census and the Biafra Hinterlands

Several studies have put to rest the contentious debate over the number of Africans sold into slavery across the Atlantic as popularized by the various studies by Philip D. Curtin, F. D. Fage, and others.[11] The cutting-edge works by Joseph Miller, Joseph E. Inikori, David Eltis, Paul E. Lovejoy, G. Ugo Nwokeji, and others together rested the population argument.[12] What is more central here is to briefly refresh our memory about the sheer volume of the trade and number of people who were shipped from the Bight of Biafra's embarkation ports, and their various destinations in the New World. Understanding this with a focus on the Igbo will enable us better situate the ethnic origins of masquerade carnival plays that sprouted in the African Diaspora.

As the data shows, from 1651 to 1850, about 11.3 million Africans were sold into slavery. This represents almost 15.2 percent of the entire population of sub-Saharan Africa estimated at 74.2 million in 1820.[13] West Central Africa—encompassing the Kongo, Cameroons, Gabon, Rwanda, Chad, Equatorial Guinea, Sao Tome and Principe, and the Central African Republic—accounted for 4.8 million (42.8 percent) of the slave departures. The Bight of Benin shipped 1.9 million (17.2 percent), while the Bight of Biafra came in the third position with 1.54 million (13.7 percent) over the same period.[14] Although the Bight of Biafra entered the overseas trade relatively late, several studies have focused on the significant role of the Arọchukwu (Arọ) people in the export trade that fed on the densely populated Igbo hinterland, mainly in the eighteenth and nineteenth centuries.[15]

The Arọ of the Igbo/Ibibio/Èfik/Ijọ/Èkọi borderlands holds the key to a proper grasp of the intricate story of the Igbo in the transatlantic slave trade emanating from the Bight from about 1650.[16] Adiele E. Afigbo's authoritative works remind us of the complex aspects of the trade and the dynamics in which the Arọ emerged as key players. One of the trades, preceding the transatlantic slave trade by several centuries, was primordial or local and involved exchanges in local products (agricultural, crafts, and specialized professions like medicinal and oracular services, and so on). The second, which is our priority here, was

TABLE 4.1. Africa Departures by Region

	Senegambia	Sierra Leone	Windward Coast	Gold Coast	Bight of Benin	Bight of Biafra	West Central Africa	SE Africa	Totals
1651–1675	27,741	906	351	30,806	52,768	80,780	278,079	16,633	488,064
1676–1700	54,141	4,565	999	75,377	207,436	69,080	293,340	14,737	719,674
1701–1725	55,944	6,585	8,878	229,239	378,101	66,833	331,183	12,146	1,088,909
1726–1750	87,028	16,637	37,672	231,418	356,760	182,066	556,981	3,162	1,471,725
1751–1775	135,294	84,069	169,094	268,228	288,587	319,709	654,984	5,348	1,925,314
1776–1800	84,920	94,694	73,938	285,643	261,137	336,008	822,056	50,274	2,008,670
1801–1825	91,225	89,326	37,322	80,895	201,054	264,834	929,999	182,338	1,876,993
1826–1850	17,717	84,416	6,131	5,219	209,742	230,328	989,908	227,518	1,770,979
Totals	554,010	381,199	334,386	1,206,824	1,955,585	1,549,638	4,856,528	512,157	11,350,328
Percent	4.9	3.4	2.9	10.6	17.2	13.7	42.8	4.5	

SOURCE: Voyages: The Trans-Atlantic Slave Trade Database (www.slavevoyages.org/).

the overseas slave trade, with a domestic precedent that Susanne Miers and Igor Kopytoff described as a benighted "process of integration and marginality."[17] The avalanche of the controversy triggered by Miers and Kopytoff has been covered elsewhere. For now, perhaps one may ask if the Arọ dominance traversed both the local and external trade and whether the Arọ supremacy in the Bight faded with the abolition of the transatlantic slave in 1807. The short answer to the latter question is that as the transatlantic slave trade unraveled, the Arọ adapted the internal slave trade in response to the labor demands of the legitimate commerce.[18] The internal slave trade would linger on for the next four decades until in the 1850s.

Thus, a full appreciation of the Arọ factor in the trade of the Bight begins with a clarification of the geographical, ethnocultural, and economic contexts along with the mechanics and infrastructure of Arọ involvement.[19] Located in the frontier zones between the Kwa-speaking and Benue-Congo-speaking peoples, the linguistic and cultural evidence show that the Arọ are mainly an Igbo group with considerable dilutions of Benue-Congo population, culture, and language. As the eminent colonial British scholars Daryll Forde and G. I. Jones explained, the Arọ belong to the Cross River Igbo subculture zone.[20] This means that the Benue-Congo neighboring peoples—namely, Ibibio of the middle Cross River, the Èfik of the Cross River Delta, and the Èkọi of the upper Cross River—all of whom the Arọ people have shared centuries of intermarriage, trade, military, and oracular contacts—deeply influenced and altered the Arọ ethnic composition and vice versa. The Arọ experience is not unique; their story parallels that of most precolonial African communities, not least the rest of the Igbo communities going back several centuries.

Some of the literature produced during the colonial and early postcolonial eras erroneously claimed that the Arọ evolved as a distinct group around 1650, which implies according to the now discredited Hamitic hypothesis that everything of material and spiritual value found in Africa has a connection with the European or Asian presence. For example, Frank Hives, British district commissioner of Bende and later resident commissioner of Owerri, Nigeria, wrote in 1905: "The Arọ were quite a different racial type from the indigenous inhabitants of the I[g]bo country."[21] Consequently, Kenneth O. Dike and Felicia Ekejiuba erred along this line in their accounts of the Arọ history.[22] As Afigbo explains in *Ropes of Sands*, the Arọ ancestors belong to the Isu Amá (or "diasporic") Igbos who migrated from the Orlu highlands centuries prior to the appearance of the first Europeans on the Bight. The dynamism that led to the Arọ emigration was similar to that behind the rise and making of the Nri civilization, which Elizabeth

A. Isichei believes was founded in 900 CE.[23] In the borderlands between the
Kwa and the Benue-Congo, the course of the Arọ migration ran into some violent opposition, forcing the migrants to move northeastward. From this conflict
emerged the Arọ, Áfikpo, Ọháfiá, Ábám, Èddá, and other kindred border Igbo
peoples with recognizable evidence of Benue-Congo (which some studies equate
with Bantu) impact.[24]

Taking a moment to provide a rough outline of the geographical context of
the trade of the Bight is vital for a deeper understanding of the trade and the Arọ
role. The setting is predominantly the southeastern part of modern Nigeria, bordered in the north by the Benue Valley and in the east by the Cross River. In the
south are the deltas of the Niger River and the Cross River. To the west resides
the Lower Niger from where it empties into the Atlantic Ocean to the point of
contact with the Benue River.[25] With the service of the canoe, which the study
by Robert Smith shows emerged early during the Neolithic Revolution in West
Africa as a vital means of transportation,[26] the Bight's river system provided a
crucial network of communications to the various groups within the Bight's
riverbanks and rivulets.[27] Essentially, we are looking at the eastern corner of
the tropical forestlands of West Africa endowed with crops and economic trees
such as the obeche, mahogany, iroko, oil palm, bamboo, rubber, and raffia palm,
among others that provided vital raw materials for the many arts and crafts produced by the people of this region. In terms of the vegetation—whether we are
looking at the swampy mangrove forest or the succeeding lush secondary forests
or the savannah grasslands, which tapers as one moves away northward toward
the Tropic of Cancer, a wide range of economic opportunities are available for
intergroup and regional exchanges. If we consider the area's vast deposits of iron
ore in the highlands running north to south, we begin to see why many guilds
of artisans and smiths in different parts of this area leveraged their opportunities
for trade, influence, and other purposes.

It will be helpful to add a few words about the core peoples of the Bight's economic commonwealth and their socioeconomic strengths. The autochthonous
Ijọ people of the Niger Delta, whose language is several millennia old, somewhat serve as a bridge between the Kwa and Benue-Congo languages groups.[28]
Like their neighbors—the Èfik, Ibibio, Igbo, and Ogojá peoples—the ancient Ijọ
began with a segmented lineage and fragmented political system, but they later
developed a centralized city-state system as their economy made the transition to
a mainly salt-boiling, fishing, and trading economy.[29] Thus, one can necessarily
equate their political system with the Igbo and Ibibio, as this study has consis-
tently indicated it is not a mistake in comparative discourse but a corrective to

assert that these groups belong to the same culture area with membership in the same language subfamily.

Like the Ijọ, the Benue-Congo-speaking Èfik of the Cross River Delta were fishermen, traders, and salt producers. Over time, they also made the political transition from a segmentary lineage system to centralized city-states. To the north of the Èfik are found another Benue-Congo-speaking group, the Ibibio, with a culture of a segmented political system that bears a striking resemblance to the Igbo. Unlike their Èfik neighbors, agriculture and handicrafts define their specialties. To the north of the Ibibio are the multifarious Benue-Congo-speaking peoples of Ogojá, among whom the most prominent is the Èkọi. These peoples also traded in agricultural products and seafood such as crayfish, periwinkle, and smoked meat. The Igbo-speaking peoples, who dominate the Bight in terms of population, are bordered to the north by the Igálá and the Idomá Kwa-speaking peoples of the Benue Basin and the Benue-Congo-speaking Tiv people. While all these groups flourish with agriculture, they were also famous for their variety of crafts and trading activities. Additionally, the Idomá and the Tiv occupy an area of salt-bearing lakes and thus produced and marketed salt. The Igálá, who controlled the trade of the lower Niger down to the city-states of Abọh to the south, evolved a centralized state that exerted cultural influence on the northern borders of Igboland. Across the Niger River from Onitsha and to the west of the Igbo are the Edo speakers who founded the once-glorious Benin Empire. The Edo brought immense political and cultural influence to the Onitsha and Niger western Igboland.

Before proceeding with a discussion of the trade proper, it is pertinent to summarize the ethnocultural and economic landscapes in which both internal and external trades functioned. Located at the center is the Igbo Cultural Area. To the south of this is the Niger Delta Cultural Area. Then we have the Lower Niger Cultural Area, the Cross River Cultural Area, and the Benue Basin Cultural Area. Despite their unique cultural and economic strengths, all the people who formed these areas were invested in the Bight of Biafra's commonwealth by trade and other means of cultural interactions—marriage, religion, ritual observances, war, diplomacy, secret societies, titles taking, and age-grade associations.

The Bight of Biafra was an area of ancient human settlements. In the Nsukka area, for instance, settlement of Neolithic communities has been reported for as far back as the third millennium BCE.[30] Thus, by several centuries, the Bight's primordial trade in local products such as food, crafts, healing herbs and roots, and so on preceded the transatlantic slave trade (in which the Arọ played the central part). Apparently the internal trade was organized in a kind of relay fashion in which surplus goods and services moved from a community to the one immediately adjoining it, until it developed into a full-blown regional trade by the ninth century CE.[31] The energy derived from the economy helped the people build up the political and socioeconomic system. Alagoa explains that by the late fourteenth and early fifteenth centuries, the Ịjọ of the Niger Delta had started developing their centralized village-states on the same economy, and their distant trade linked them to the reaches of the Biafra interior.[32] Also prior to the transatlantic slave trade, an ongoing internal slave trade served part of the labor needs of an agriculture-based economy that supported slavocracies in Africa and some parts of the Arab world. In the Bight of Biafra prior to the 1650s, the indigenous elite of the Bight's commonwealth monopolized this trade, while the trade in the other products of the area was generally open for every class and all genders. Eventually, the transatlantic slave trade arrived and began to quickly suck in the Bight's coastal peoples in the course of the fifteenth century.

It remains unclear how the overseas impetus for the slave trade got to the Igbo and the Ibibio of the Bight of Biafra interior. What is less doubtful is that by the end of the sixteenth century the impact of the trade was already being felt in many parts of the interior through the activities of the Niger Delta traders plying the Niger River and up to the creeks and rivers between the Nun estuary of the Niger and the Cross River. Under early commercial pressure from the European traders on the Bight, Niger Delta businessmen started establishing contacts with allies in the Igbo and Ibibio hinterland areas, cajoling them to source the victims of the transatlantic slave through kidnappings.[33]

U. Ugo Nwokeji has made the overall point that, contrary to common assumptions, the Arọ initiated neither the internal trade nor the overseas slave trade that they came to be associated with from the seventeenth century.[34] Rather, they entered the slave trade through working first as agents of their oracle, the Ibiniukpabi—an oracle the Arọ oral tradition claims was seized from the Èkọi, their Benue-Congo neighbors. Like communities in other parts of the world, the people of the Bight's interior always had groups of victims and social outcasts who because of either unacceptable behavior or accidents of birth earned themselves the wrath of their communities. This category of people considered by their communities as deplorable formed the initial victims of the transatlantic slave trade in the Bight's hinterland areas.[35]

The picture that unfolds is that the Arọ emerged as top competitors in a transatlantic slave trade that was initially introduced into the Bight by the Niger Delta middlemen and which, during this early stage, involved diverse individuals, speculators, and groups vying to profit from the lucrative trade. The explanation for Arọ slaving ascendance may be found in their ability to leverage their institutions and practices as aids in the business. Among these institutions were the exploitation of occult arts and institutions—fortune telling, the practice of herbal and other medicines, oracles—which they leveraged for power, privilege, and profit. According to Richard O. Igwebe, these tangibles offered the Arọ opportunities for unhindered external travel, for settling in remote communities to promote and practice one's business, and thus to worm oneself into the confidence of customers whom one could then serve and exploit as much as possible.[36]

Other factors that promoted Arọ ascendancy were the establishment of Arọ satellite towns across the entire Igboland region and beyond. These satellite communities served as intelligence-gathering points and helped them avoid internal rivalry and friction, which could lead to revealing whatever business secrets they may have to their competitors. Additionally, the Arọ forged an armed alliance with the Ọháfiá, Ábám, Èddá, and related peoples—all of whom Afigbo has described as "the professional merchants of bloody violence in the interior of the Bight—the headhunters of which the Arọ used to teach business associates who turned coat that such action did not pay."[37] In a previous study, I have reiterated that the Arọ-led alliance was formidable.

> [Just as] the U.S. today controls the world with superior technology and military muscle, [so did] the Arọ employed the use of their all-powerful oracle, known as the Ibinukpabia (Long Juju), and their military alliance with the Ọháfiá, Ábám, and Èddá as instruments of fear and domination. The Arọ-Ọháfiá-Ábám-Èddá military alliance, like the U.S.-led North Atlantic Treaty Organization (NATO), accorded the Arọ the military muscle to threaten and often raid other communities who were opposed to their commercial and religious interests.[38]

All these intricate networks were put together with the practice of blood-oath (*igbandu*), which created fictitious blood links and thus confidence and trust between the Arọ and their trade associates), and the Arọ "brilliant talent for diplomacy"; as underscored by Elizabeth Isichei, one could see why the Arọ elite were able to sustain their dubious slaveholding monopoly in the Bight of Biafra's hinterland for over two centuries.[39]

This was the economic structure operated by the Arọ that sent over 1.54 million Bight of Biafra hinterland people, primarily the Igbo, as slaves to the New World. Among the estimated 1.54 million that left the Bight's embarkation port, about 1.3 million either arrived in the Americas or were rescued off slave ships and resettled in Sierra Leone. The Bight's slaves were especially prominent in the British colonies in North America, and they were an active and sizeable community in Cuba in the nineteenth century, as reflected in the importance of Abakuá, a secret society cloned from its Èkpé precedence from Calabar and other communities in Bight of Biafra's interior.[40] It must be stated that while the Arǫ had contact with the Ijǫ, and the Èfik of the coast obviously had some influence over them through their oracle, they never attempted to upstage them or tried to wrestle the direct contact with the visiting Europeans. In other words, the Arǫ trading autarchy was limited to the coastal headwaters of Itu on the Cross River, Ázumiri on the Imo River, and Ogutá on the Uráshị River. At these collection points, the Arǫ met with the delta intermediaries and exchanged European goods such as clothes, guns, glasses, mirror, cigarettes, and so on for Igbo slaves. Arǫ dominance was oligarchic, a secured circle in which non-Arǫs were barred unless they first subjected themselves to an extended immersion in Arǫ culture.[41]

The transatlantic slave trade exports from the Bight of Biafra became more intense from the eighteenth century to the first decades of the nineteenth century. As may be recalled, it was in the early nineteenth century that the abolition debate began in the British Parliament, and soon after the slave trade was banned in the British Empire in 1807, the Bight of Biafra became a target of British anti-slave-trade campaigns.[42] The Bight of Biafra's departures represented just fewer than 14 percent of total departures from Africa between 1651 and 1850 (see table 4.1). The numbers increased dramatically in the early eighteenth century. With about 265,000 in the first quarter of the nineteenth century and 230,000 in the period from 1826 to 1850, the Bight of Biafra emerged as a leading region of departure from 1725 to 1840. Merchants from the coasts sent commercial expeditions inland to Igbo markets where Arǫ merchants held supreme control.[43]

But where did the slaves who boarded the ships from the Bight of Biafra end up in the Americas? Knowing this helps connect the masquerade culture associated with the Bantu Culture Area with its reinvention in the African Diaspora. The figures in table 4.2 reveal that those slaves who departed from the Bight initially landed in at least thirty-four overseas locations. Among them, Sierra Leone, Gold Coast, and Senegambia in West Africa provided refuge for the more fortunate slaves rescued from smugglers' clutches on the Atlantic after the abolition of the British slave trade in 1807. Meanwhile, the disembarkation point for about 79,168 slaves is unknown.

Wherever the slaves who departed from the Bight of Biafra landed, they seemed to have found a way to either permeate the preexisting masquerade plays of their host societies or reinvent and blend them into the existing culture with the inherited traditions they brought along. Separate studies by Robert Nicholls and others have established credible linkages between Bantu/Igbo traditional practices and the evolution of Creole culture in the African Diaspora, particularly in Jamaica, the United States, Cuba, and the Virgin Islands.[44] In the context of Atlantic history, one may talk about the Igbo masquerades based on certain observed characteristics that compare favorably with the African Diaspora versions. However, it is important to recognize the important caveat that the purported features of Igbo culture found in the African Diaspora—whether we are looking at Jamaica, the Virgin Islands, Saint Thomas, Cuba, Brazil, or elsewhere—also contain dilutions of traditions found among the Èfik, Èkọi, Ijọ, Ibibio, and other ethnic groups in Africa.

A closer look at the Bamboula dances of Saint Thomas, the Virgin Islands, where 13,167 Igbo/Biafra slaves ended up is educative. Referring to the Bamboula, an editorial of the Saint Thomas *Tidende* newspaper of December 28, 1872, strongly renounced the party as a celebration of "a remnant of barbaric Ebo [Igbo] drum." In other words, the editorial categorically saw the Bamboula as an Igbo invention. But the evidence shows that the Bamboula was not originally from the Igbo homeland and therefore not an Igbo invention. Although the Bamboula prototype is associated with the Kongo of Central Africa, the truth of the matter, which the *Tidende* editorial failed to acknowledge, is that the African Diaspora genre is a diffusion of traditions from West and Central Africa, with perhaps more doses of Igbo imputations—a consequence of the sheer number of Igbo slaves on the island. The same pattern of cultural diffusion explains the reinvention of the "Jonkonnu" in Jamaica and the Bahamas and the evolution of the Cuban Abakuá, which is a reinvention of the original Èkpé masquerade of the Èfik, Èfut, and Qua Ejagham groups of Calabar, and the allied Èkpé of Arọchukwu, Ngwá, Ábám, Áfikpo, and Ábịrịbá communities of the Igbo.[45]

The point is that our study of African cultural practices in the New World must be pursued in culture areas in order to better capture both the specific and transnational contexts. To reiterate, the African cultural trends that emerged in the African Diaspora are dilutions of the originals emanating from several parts of Africa. The sociopolitical and historical contexts and constraints in which migrants in the African Diaspora attempted to reconstitute aspects of their inherited traditions, and the symbols and meanings they assigned to these ideas, must be properly explained. Here is where the question of memory comes alive in relation to performance and discourses, history and emergence of cultural forms in alien lands, and the strings of identity it conjures. One of the most pertinent questions becomes, how do we know who was Igbo and who was not in the context of the transatlantic slave disembarkations and resettlements? Slave cargoes departing from the Bight of Biafra in West Africa contained captives from diverse ethnic origins, although the bulk of them came from the Igbo region. Additionally, how do we know that traditional genres of masquerades recreated in the African Diaspora were Igbo, Ibibio, Èfik, or something else?

Igbo in the Atlantic World

The availability of records of slave ships departing the Bight's embarkation port and recent studies are now helping scholars to identify specific destinations of the African captives in the New World. Some of the earliest mentions of the Igbo in the Caribbean list them among various enslaved African groups. They are either identified explicitly or implied by the stated origins of shipments, for example, Bight of Biafra. Occasionally the Igbo are mixed up with Ibibio, Èfik, Ijọ, Èkọi, and other neighboring groups from the Bight's point of embarkation—that is, the Nigerian-Cameroonian borderlands.[46] One of the many dramatic arrivals of African slaves was observed in the Windward Islands by Sir William Bart Young, colonial governor of Tobago, on December 16, 1791: "The ships came from distinct districts and with people of different nations on board: The Pilgrim of Bristol, with 370 Eboes [Igbos] from Bonny. The Colus of Liverpool with 300 Windward Negroes from Baffa [sic]. The Anne of Liverpool, with 210 Gold Coast Negroes from Whydah."[47] Here, Governor Young explicitly acknowledged the arrival of 370 Igbo slaves and another 300 from "Baffa," which apparently refers to the Biafra of the West African Bight the missionary Manuel Álvares talked about in his *Ethiopian Minor*.[48] This would mean a mixture of Igbo and other ethnic Africans from that West African region identified as the Bight of Biafra. Again, it is crucial not to ignore the obvious fact that in the early literature ethnic identifications are often unclear, as Colin A. Palmer and others have underscored.[49] Writing about the Virgin Islands, where 13,167 Igbo people landed (as documented in table 4.2), the Moravian missionary Christian G. A. Oldendorp, who was a pioneer in the field of ethnological description of Africa and the Caribbean, identified some African groups in the island as follows: the Ibo (Igbo), Karabari [Kálábári], Mokko [sic] (Nigeria), Fula (Fuláni), Mandango [Mándinká] (Upper Guinea), Akkran [Akán], Fante (Ghana), and so on. Oldendorp correctly noted "the I[g]bo, friends of the Karabari [Kálábári], possess a vast land which lies in the interior of Africa. The Mokko also share a border with

TABLE 4.2. The Bight of Biafra Embarkation and Principal Port of Disembarkation, 1601–1800

Region	Number	Percent of total	Percent less unspecified
Jamaica	218,007	28.70	32.00
Not specified	79,158	10.40	—
Dominica	57,353	7.54	8.42
Barbados	51,982	6.84	7.63
Grenada	38,254	5.03	5.62
St. Kitts	35,923	4.73	5.62
Cuba	35,552	4.73	5.22
St. Dominique	30,436	4.00	4.47
Sierra Leone	29,937	3.94	4.40
Virginia	22,520	2.94	3.31
Antigua	21,569	2.84	3.17
Martinique	19,556	2.57	2.87
St. Vincent	18,692	2.46	2.74
Guianas	17,300	2.28	2.54
Virgin Islands (St. Thomas)	13,167	1.73	1.93
Carolinas	10,766	1.42	1.58
Trinidad	10,408	1.37	1.53
Guadeloupe	10,399	1.37	1.54
South-east Brazil	9,189	1.21	1.35
Bahia	6,485	0.85	0.95
Nevis	4,288	0.56	0.63
St. Lucia	3,670	0.48	0.54
Rio de la Plata	3,010	0.40	0.44
Tobago	2,994	0.39	0.44
Puerto Rico	2,865	0.38	0.42
Spanish America (main)	1,717	0.23	0.25
Bahamas	1,199	0.16	0.18
Dutch Caribbean	1,061	0.14	0.16
Northeast Brazil	816	0.11	0.12
Pernambuco	676	0.09	0.10
Montserrat	528	0.07	0.08
Maryland	310	0.04	0.05
Off-shore Atlantic	232	0.03	0.03
Gold Coast	144	0.02	0.02
Senegambia	81	0.01	0.01

SOURCE: Voyages: The Trans-Atlantic Slave Trade Database (www.slavevoyages.org/).

Karabari."[50] First, we see that Oldendorp appears to have a good geographical
knowledge of this part of Africa. While the Igbo and Kálábári are related, the
Mokko is supposed to be found somewhere among the Ịjọ of the Niger Delta and
the Igboland, but no one can say precisely where this group is located today.[51]
This raises concerns as to the accuracy of these ethnic names and categories in
an era when the orthographies of African languages were seriously convoluted.

Moving on to Jamaica where about 218,007 Biafra/Igbo slaves landed overall, the British slaveholder and planter Bryan Edwards, who assessed African
ethnicities in Jamaica in 1794 for their productivity, temperament, and music
traditions, wrote that "the Eboes" had a tendency to commit suicide rather than
suffer in abject slavery. Edwards added that the Igbo were "timid," and had a
"desponding temper." But in another breath, Edwards expressed more compli-
mentary views about the Igbo, this time regarding their traditional music styles.
As he noted the "gentle Igbo music" was in contrast to fiery Asante (Koromante/
Cromanti) music, Edwards further asserts that "their [Asante] tunes in general
are characteristic of their national manners; those of the Eboes being soft and
languishing; of the Koromantyns heroick and martial [sic]."[52] This musical depiction by Edwards reminds us of A. M. Jones's 1959 notion of Igbo music as that
which provides gentle and reflective musical sequences.[53] Or what Meki Nzenwi
and coauthors have characterized as "the Igbo Concept of Mother Musician-
ship."[54] Early on in 1790, J. B. Moreton had documented the text of a chorus recorded in the African languages by the African slaves in Jamaica with references
to the Ebo [Igbo].

> If we want for go in a Ebo
> Me can't go there!
> Since dem tief [thieve] me from a Guinea
> Me can't go there! (1790).[55]

Lorna McDaniel, who studied slave culture in Carriacou—the island immediately to the north of Grenada, where 38,254 Biafra/Igbo slaves disembarked—
highlights a mid-nineteenth century patois song collected by Andrew Pearse in
1955.[56] McDaniel noted that the slaves often expressed the belief in the existence
of spirits and that at their death, their spirits will definitely return to Africa.[57]
Robert Nicholls asserts that this belief "suggests the longing for homeland and
the ultimate form of rebellion [in that suicide became a route to freedom] often
realized by the Igbo."[58] There is copious literature linking Igbo slaves with the
propensity for suicide, among them McDaniel arguing that "Igbos, coming

from a highly individualistic society, were probably extremely perplexed at their condition under slavery, and being assured that they would consummate their existential notion of the inseparability of their culturally essential brotherhood, could not conceive of not rejoining their families at death."[59] However, it is important to point out that in Igbo indigenous society, suicide was very rare because it was associated with a religious taboo, and those who commit the act are traditionally buried in the evil forest (*ájọ ọfiá*). The Igbo believe that those who commit suicide as a way of escape from life's many vicissitudes bring shame to both their living kin and departed ancestors and therefore will not reincarnate into the world of the living. Therefore, the suicide chatter related with the Igbo slaves should be made with caution, for it is a deviation for individuals from a culture that prohibits suicide to engage in the practice at the level emphasized by the extant African Diaspora literature.[60]

Meanwhile, corroborating the Igbo-Grenada connections, a 2001 *Tombstone Feast* music album of Carriacou contains a track entitled "Igbo ginade-o" (Granadian Igbo). In corrupted English, the song's refrain, documented by Lorna McDaniel, goes as follows: "Ba t'ni mama; ba t'ni papa," (I have no mother; I have no father). While this may remind one of the typical lamentations of enslaved people, a song of loneliness and hopelessness of people in bondage,[61] the word "Ba t'ni" sounds more Yoruba than Igbo. The Igbo equivalent is more like *Ewe m* as in "I have no. . . ." This corrective sheds a new light on Bryan Edward's 1794 description of the "Eboes" [Igbo] as a "soft and languishing" people.[62] Many of the ideas and practices arbitrarily assigned to a particular ethnic group from Africa must be reexamined with critical eyes.

Many African ethnic groups continued their musical traditions in the New World with impoverished musical instruments and dancing paraphernalia that have African ancestry. One of the instruments identified in the seventeenth century purportedly has parallels in Igboland. In 1688, Hans A. Sloane saw dancers in Jamaica adorned with leg and wrist rattles that were shaken in time with an instrument that seems like a kind of idiophonic pot drum. Sloane states that the musician "makes a sound on the mouth of an empty Gourd or jar with his hand."[63] This musical style was known as "Jenkoving" in Jamaica and "Jinkgouing" in Barbados, and is described as involving clapping of hands on the mouth of two jars.[64] Sloane's description reminds us of a combination of the Igbo aerophone musical pot (*údú*) molded in clay like a spherical gourd and rattles (*ọyọ*), which comes in different forms. The latter is an idiophone, while the former is beaten with either the open palm or a padded slapper. Among the

Ibibio, the musical pot is called *kimkim*.[65] These musical instruments—the clay pot, the spherical gourd or calabash, and rattles—are also known to the Ibibio, Èfik, and Ijọ.

Besides the use of cultural similarities like music as identifiers, another critical approach that has assisted scholars in the arduous task of tracking down the ethnic origins of migrating slaves is the information from the slaving ships' manifests. In June 1793, for instance, the slave ship *Jupiter* left the Bight's Bonny port to Jamaica with 359 captives. The Igbo cargo that disembarked at Martha Brae comprised sixty-one adolescents, eighty-three children, and an infant—all the victims of kidnappers who sold them off to John Goodrich, the ship's captain.[66] The *Jupiter*'s manifest and Goodrich's comments corroborate that many children were forcibly transported from the African ports, with a good number of them from the Igbo area.[67] Re-echoing a parallel feeling, Captain Forsyth, a slave merchant, regretfully told his employer that he was unable to acquire additional male captives at Old Calabar because the captives were "through the cuntry [*sic*] for the Camaroo [*sic*] where they receive a greater price for them."[68] If Captain Forsyth got his story right, it means that some of the slaves were sent to the market in Cameroon from the hinterland for maximum profit. But it cannot be assumed that these people were only Igbo. African slave dealers respected neither ethnic boundaries nor distance.

Audra Diptee has argued persuasively that from the eighteenth to the early nineteenth century when the transatlantic slave trade was outlawed by the British government, higher numbers of Igbo children were transported on British ships than children of other ethnic groups, and the vast majority of them ended up in the Caribbean. Again it is tricky to draw such sweeping conclusions based on ethnicity. What is more pertinent, as Diptee rightly stated, is that the ways in which these young African captives in the New World reacted to their conditions were influenced not only by the challenges they met in the New World but also by their individual experiences in Igboland and of course those of their peers from the Bight of Biafra—the Ibibio, Ijọ, Èfik, Èkọi and others.[69] Once more, we must emphasize that these ethnic categories or labels are problematic in an era when the individuals concerned did not fully self-identify as Igbo, Èfik, Ijọ, Èkọi, or Ibibio. Scholarly opinions are divided on whether there was a concept of the "Igbo" as a cohesive and "self-conscious" group in the precolonial era. This controversy gained popularity following the influential work of colonial anthropologists Daryll Forde and G. I. Jones, who concluded that the precolonial Igbo, who lived in independent villages, are a single people in the sense that they speak a number of related dialects but on the other hand lacked political

TABLE 4.3. Percentage of Enslaved Children Sold to British Slave Traders at the Bight of Biafra

Year	Children from Bight of Biafra (%)
1701–1725	18.5
1726–1750	19.8
1751–1775	30.4
1776–1800	18.4
1801–1808	14.0

centralization. And based on this, Forde and Jones assert that the Igbo hardly perceived themselves as a nation in the modern sense.[70]

Extending this view, James Coleman argued that there was no preexisting pan-Igbo identity and that this instead evolved in the colonial setting, acquiring an innovative dimension by the mid-1930s when Dr. Akanu Ibiam, the first Igbo missionary doctor, completed his medical program in Scotland and returned home to join the leadership of the nascent Igbo State Union in Lagos.[71] The inaugural meeting of the pan-Igbo Union was formally launched in Lagos in June 1936, and similar associations were founded in other major cities in Nigeria.[72] The declared main purpose of the union was to move forward the Igbo people chiefly in the field of education.[73] Coleman's work is important because it identified the colonial urban center, in a sense a diaspora social milieu, as a platform for ethnic inventions in colonial Nigeria. In her magisterial study of the Igbo in 1976, Elizabeth Isichei reaffirmed the previous studies with the assertion that Igbo ethnic identity was first articulated by the Igbo Diaspora. "A sense of Pan-Igbo identity came only when its people left Igboland—an experience first imposed by the slave trade or when colonial conquest and rule violently extended the categories through which the Igbo perceived their world."[74]

Indeed, the ample evidence of the autobiography of Igbo-born ex-slave Olaudah Equiano's *The Interesting Narrative of the Life of Olaudah Equiano*, first published in 1789, provides historians with the earliest attempt in the modern era to articulate and contest a sense of Igbo identity as opposed to the "Other"—or what Equiano qualified as "primitive Europe."[75] Equiano's graphics and prideful description of his "Eboe" (Igbo) life and customs in the eighteenth century mirrors similar accounts by Archibald Monteath, an Igbo-born "Anaso"

enslaved in Jamaica from around 1802.[76] Similar mentions of the Igbo, Ebo, or
Heebo (as it appeared in the early slave trade) as a cultural group exist in the documented memoirs of early European visitors to the Bight of Benin and Biafra.
Both Duarte Pacheco Pereira, a fifteenth-century Portuguese sea captain and
geographer, and John Grazilhier, who made a voyage to Old Calabar in 1699,
wrote about the "Hakbous [Igbo] Blacks" in their separate memoirs.[77] Thus,
we understand the origins of Pan-Igbo ethnic identity, like Pan-Africanism, as
an ideology that gained relevance in the diaspora and gradually infiltrated the
ancestral homeland.

Thus, it is important to reiterate Carolyn Brown and Paul Lovejoy's advice
that these groups we see as separate today were in contact for centuries and had
"porous conceptual boundaries." Although those forcibly abducted to the New
World from the Bight of Biafra were part of a "cultural amalgamation that was
heavily Igbo,"[78] it is obvious also that it is impossible to determine the actual
number of Igbo sent across the Atlantic with precision, given the paucity of relevant records, not least of them the problematic ways in which captive Africans
were ethnically labeled.[79] Using the information on population densities and
slaving patterns, David Northrup estimates that the percentage of people from
Igboland leaving that port could have been as high as 60 percent over the course
of a century starting in 1730.[80] There are records for at least six slave ships in
which children made up more than 50 percent.[81] Table 4.3 shows the percentage
of young people from the Bight of Biafra's hinterlands sold into the British slave
trade from 1701 to 1808. Added together, 93 percent of these young people disembarked from the slave ships in the various Caribbean islands. A breakdown
shows that Jamaica received 39 percent of them, Dominica (10 percent), Barbados (8 percent), Grenada (6.5 percent), and Saint Kitts (6 percent).[82]

In the late eighteenth century, the evidence shows that White planters in the
Caribbean were open to acquiring African youths in general, and Igbo youths
in particular. Antiguan merchant James Maud advised that "Windw[ard] Coast
Negroes" were preferred, but "should they be Eboes," he advised that the traders should avoid grown men and should preferably "let the majority be young
Women, with girls and boys in proportion."[83] In August 1789, Jamaican merchant Francis Grant explicitly requested for captives from the Gold Coast, but
if that was not possible, he asked his business associates in Bristol to send one of
his "best Ebo Cargoes." A couple of months later, Grant turned 180 degrees by
modifying his preferences for "an Eboe Cargo to a Gold Coast one" noting that
those captives from Bonny "are the sort most runs upon among us."[84]

Again, it is judicious to question the accuracy with which the Caribbean merchants and planters could distinguish the precise ethnic origins of the captives from different ethnic backgrounds. In a business where morality and honesty were the least concerns for those involved in the trade, there was nothing stopping the merchants and their associates in Africa from labeling captives with fake ethnicities. This is especially true considering that Africans were signified only by their port of embarkation. Writing from Dominica, for example, merchants Francis and Robert Smyth advised that captives from Old Calabar do "not answer so well, as those from new C[alabar] & Bonny."[85] But the reality is that whether the captives came from Old or New Calabar, most of the captives were procured from the Bight's interior.

Agency and Igbo Youth in the Caribbean

In her pioneering work on enslaved African children in the New World, Colleen Vasconcellos argues that definitions of childhood were a point of contestation and planters' attitudes toward enslaved African children in Jamaica changed significantly after the abolition of the British slave trade. More recently, Cecily Jones has explored the ways in which enslaved youth often exercised agency and found ways to resist their enslavement. Other studies focusing on children look at a range of issues including health, labor conditions, and child socialization under slavery.[86] Audre Diptee has contended that the historical experiences of captive African children must be appropriately contextualized within the broader context of childhood.[87]

The first point of consideration is that Africans brought their own ideas about childhood and child labor to the Caribbean, and given that most children transported to the Caribbean on British ships were, in fact, Igbo children, this raises important questions about the ways in which Igbo conceptions and cultural transfers shaped childhood experiences under slavery. According to the Jamaican plantation owner Bryan Edwards who reportedly once witnessed the branding of twenty young boys, ten of whom were Igbo (the oldest among them about thirteen years), the other ten were from the Gold Coast. In his description, the first Igbo boy that was branded "screamed dreadfully" and the other Igbo boys "manifested strong emotions of sympathetic terror." However, Edwards tells us that the boys from the Gold Coast laughed aloud, "offered their bosoms undauntedly" when they were to be branded, and received the mark without so much as flinching.[88] One must be cautious in reading Edwards's account if he was assigning ethnic identities based on individual responses to crude and cruel acts of branding. Gloria Chuku explains that the bulk of "evidence from different parts of the Igbo region . . . points to the fact that *ichi* facial markings were not only a mark of transition to a new status but also a symbol of authority and a badge of protection. The visible marks gave their wearers considerable immunity to travel from place to place especially within Igbo areas without molestation or being subjected to kidnapping or enslavement. It was not a test of courage."[89]

In addition, Paul Lovejoy and David Trotman among others have long seen past the manner of ethnic stereotyping peddled by the likes of Edwards. The authors advise that scholars involved in the study of Africa and the African Diaspora should rather focus on historical specificities in Africa to explain the behavior of captives on the other side of the Atlantic.[90] In light of this, we must take note of the fact that most Igbo children made the transition to slavery in the Caribbean without parents or other relatives, and so they had to draw on their Igbo-oriented child's view of the world to make sense of slavery systems and cultural ideas in the Americas. This point mitigates the notion of cultural transfers as original of Igbo or African parent traditions for what these young people were able to remember or re-create, as inherited African traditions were altogether limited by their "expertise" in these cultural traits and therefore grossly flawed. Some Igbo children, if they were old enough to remember them and fully comprehend them, would have relied heavily on proverbs and stories they were told by parents, relatives, and community elders. Oral traditions were, after all, an important mechanism used in child socialization among the Igbo (as with other ethnic groups).[91] It is also crucial to keep in mind that the very circumstances in which Igbo youth were welcomed into the slaveholding societies, to a great extent, molded their overall experiences. Kristen Mann has rightly exhorted scholars to shift emphasis from who the slaves were to how specific circumstances encountered in the Americas "helped or hindered" the Africans in their efforts to reconstruct a world that drew on African cultural beliefs and practices.[92]

In general, from at least 1750, Igbo youth transported to the Caribbean entered a world in which children playing adult roles were commonplace in the local landscape. Additionally, there was an increasing number of enslaved children born in the Caribbean; hence Michael Craton contends that the importation of captive Africans should not be seen solely as a function of natural increase or decrease among the enslaved. As he points out, the slave trade to the British West Indies served "to 'top up' the numbers depleted through natural decrease."[93] In other words, the issue of reproduction aside, slave acquisition was also linked to expanding frontiers and subsequent increased agricultural production. This explains why Barbados, which had no space for further expansion by the early eighteenth century, was the only sugar colony to have a self-reproducing enslaved population in 1807.[94] It also explains why, on islands such as Jamaica, which did not reach its "saturation point" for enslaved laborers even by the end of slavery in 1838, there were many established plantations for which generalizations about high mortality and low fertility are not applicable.

In this chapter, we discussed another milestone in migration history—the transatlantic slave departures led by the hinterland people from the Bight of Biafra. The overall population of the victims of the trade numbering nearly 12 million people included at least 1.54 million from the Bight. Africans, whom I have characterized as modeling agents, reshaped the intensity of cross-regional migration and cross-cultural fertilization in First Global Age, 1400–1800. With the intent to highlight Pan-African transatlantic migrations and the patterns of culture the migrants brought to the New World, the slave census statistics were revisited. With this data, we delineated some of the major locations where the Igbo elements ended up in the New World—principal among them Jamaica, the U.S. Virgin Islands, Cuba, Barbados, and others. In these locations, the Igbo and their other African cohorts participated in diverse genres of religious, masquerade, music, and dance cultures that were often modeled after the African ones.

Overall, the main contention here is that given the sheer numerical dominance of the Igbo among those African slaves brought to the Caribbean, it is obvious that the Igbo among them had more opportunities in the Caribbean for continued exposure to Biafra hinterland traditions. Slave owner Bryan Edwards observed that it was common, at least among the slaves he owned, for "old-established Negroes" to request permission to take in newly arrived "young people" and "for their sons to take to themselves wives from their own nation."[95] While caution is called for regarding Edwards's propensity for exaggeration as a slavery apologist, this pattern of transitional preference in modeling provided room for the attempt to re-create old symbols and was a sort of compensation for their peers left behind in Africa or lost by death through the notorious Middle Passage. However, we know that human memories are feeble and prone to forgetfulness. Under the mentorship of their fellow ethnic Igbos, the newly arriving Igbo youth in the Caribbean during this period may have been exposed to only the forms of the Igbo cultural complex that memory could recollect, including religious and masquerade traditions. Yet, it must be clearly

stated that not all Igbo children had ready access to Igbo adults and the consequent cultural reinforcements that such interactions engender. These children
and their mentors did not constitute an island unto themselves. They lived and
socialized with other children from Africa, Europe, the Americas, and other
parts of the world.

CHAPTER 5

Igbo Masquerade Dances in the African Diasporas

Symbols and Meanings

I N 1995, COLIN A. PALMER produced a compelling piece on the bond among African-born slaves in Mexico, thereby triggering a rebirth in studies assert-ing one-to-one cultural connections between specific ethnic groups in Africa with their African Diaspora genres. Using a sample of the surviving marriage licenses issued to African-born slaves, Palmer showed how ethnicity informed the spousal choices by African-born slaves who were married in the Roman Catholic Church in Mexico City between 1590 and 1640. Over this period, the greatest proportions of the slaves, as the study reveals, were shipped from West-Central Africa, particularly Angola.[1] Among the subsequent similar stud-ies, of particular interest are Linda Heywood's edited volume and Kwasi Kona-du's work. While Heywood and co-contributors highlight the Kongo-"Angola culture area" and their traits in the New World, Konadu focuses on the Akán in the African Diaspora.[2]

In the area of masquerade studies, Ivor Miller—building on earlier works by Fernandez Ortiz, Melville J. Herskovits, and Rafael Núñez Cedeño (all of the Culture Transfer School)—remains one of the leading scholars in this field of Black Atlantic cultural history. Miller's research has focused on the Abakuá of Cuba, modeled after the Ékpè secret/masquerade society of the Èfìk, as Cedeño's and Miller's separate studies reveal, Abakuá, founded in Havana, Cuba, in 1836 by enslaved leaders of Cross River villages, started off as a multiethnic mutual aid society. Over time, it strengthened to become a distinguishing feature of the wider Cuban cultural identity. Abakuá ceremonies consist of drumming, danc-ing, and chanting activities using the esoteric Abakuá language.[3] However, Ivor's and other accounts either overlooked or omitted a crucial fact: the Èfìk along with Ibibio, Arọ, and Ngwá communities of southeastern Nigeria; the Èkọi and

Úgbè societies of Ejághám of southwestern Cameroon; and others also have
Ékpè masquerade lodges, and hundreds of enslaved Africans from these ethnic groups in Cuba also participated in the Abakuá. This reality problematizes
the allure of assigning ethnic colors to African cultural artifacts in the Americas; hence the argument to better focus on Bantu Culture Area than forcing
one-to-one culture transfers. Neither Robert W. Nicholls's more nuanced work
focusing on Igbo cultural traits (specifically masquerades, music, and dance)
and their African Diaspora descendants in the U.S. Virgin Islands, nor that by
Heywood and coauthors in the Congo-Angola region transcended the test of
multivalent susceptibility.[4] Multivalent or visually complex work, as invoked in
this study, refers to a concept that is susceptible to many interpretations, applications, meanings, and values. Like in medicine where a multivalent antigen draws
multiple sites through which attachment may occur, properly understanding the
very complex nature of colonial American society in which enslaved Africans
were inserted holds the key to a better grasp of the new cultural frontiers they
produced in the New World.

     This understanding begins with revisiting Lucie Pradel who studied African
beliefs in the African Diaspora. Pradel reminds us that the Caribbean world is
like a kaleidoscope that portrays the vibrant colors of its diversity. From four
continents, diverse ethnic groups brought their customs and beliefs to the region.[5] Much of the literature has not fully acknowledged the fact that prior to
the transatlantic slave trade, African culture was not static; it was changing by
incorporating regional varieties while adapting to Arab and European ones. In
fact, it is crucial to remember that before slaves started arriving in the Americas,
the mixing of European and African cultures following the Portuguese presence in Angola had started reshaping the contours of religious practices.[6] Yet,
no single African group operated in isolation, either on the continent or in the
Americas. In the New World, enslaved Africans lived among host communities
that harbored other ethnicities and races—among them Whites and Native Indians. These non-African groups in the Americas also had their own versions
of the very customs and traditions (religion, music, masking, carnival dances,
languages, and so on) the enslaved migrants shared.

     In the British West Indies, the Afro-Creole model of masquerading, like the
Creole language, emerged at the outset of the plantation economy. Corroborating this view, Cedeño reaffirms that "the slaves not only influenced each other
interculturally but they transformed the culture and lifestyle of their masters as
well."[7] Another complexity of one-on-one cultural connections is encountered
in ethnic self-identification among the enslaved people. African slaves often

drew on multiple ethnic identities to suit certain circumstances. In a different but related study, I have shown how African elements in Cuba including the Igbo sometimes claimed Yoruba ancestry in order to partake in the Cuban Orisá religion and rituals.[8] In Jamaica on February 5, 1816, a jailor noted that a runaway slave named Bessy first claimed to be Igbo and later changed her story. "BESSY, formerly said she was an Eboe, but now found out to be a salt-water creole (in this context meaning someone born during the Middle Passage or someone who was an infant when enslaved) and that she belonged to a gentleman at Black Water, since dead, but does not know his name, marked with *WB* on left shoulder, she came in on her own and has no owner."[9] The inclination to claiming multiple identities makes it tricky to pinpoint who was truly Igbo and who was not.

Added to this is the fact that the Igbo and Èfik slaves were not even among the earliest groups of Africans in the New World. Although a sprinkling of them was found here and there, between 1526 and 1640 African slaves disembarking in the Caribbean came primarily from Senegambia, Guinea-Bissau, Sierra Leone, Cameroon, Congo, and Angola.[10] Then from 1655 to 1807, there was a steady inflow of slaves into the Caribbean from the Akán of the Gold Coast. But from 1776, when the Arǫ-directed Bight of Biafra slave trade was in top gear, the Gold Coast slave supply line declined to a second position in terms of numbers.[11]

With the eighteenth-century increase in demands, Crahan and Knight explain, the Caribbean experienced an influx of "ethnic and culturally cohesive cohorts and allowed for the establishment of certain societal norms to which later arrivals, regardless of their customs, would have to conform."[12] In other words, the early arrivals such as the Mandinka, Mende, and groups from Upper Guinea and Congo/Angola created the background on which the Bight of Biafra Igbo, Ibibio, Éfik, and Ijǫ slaves adapted to and ultimately tried to insert their own ethnic styles. Like the Igbo, all the early batches of African groups arriving in the Caribbean, with the exception of the Akán, are of Bantu ancestry. If we further consider the fact that the Bantu ancestors had left their West African cradle several millennia back, modeling and indigenizing cultures across sub-Saharan Africa, then we have rock-solid evidence of how not to see the African culture and traditions in the Americas from narrow ethnic lenses. Those traditions were well prepared in Pan-African garb for their global migration.

The use of the term *Bantu*, as in relation to Cross River Igbo, needs a little more clarification here in relation to other Africans. René A. Bravmann has argued that the Akán contributed meaningfully to the evolution of Caribbean Creole culture but not much to masquerading because "masquerades are not now, and probably were never, products of Akán societies."[13] However, Douglas

Fraser, who studied the symbols of Ashanti kingship, reminds us that the Akán have a rich tradition of artistic artworks in diverse media, and Bravmann adds that the Akán was further subject to diffusions from the Ashanti imperial authority.[14] In contrast, the Igbo, Ibibio, Èfik, Èkọi, and Ijọ migrants inherited a flourishing masquerade tradition from their ancestral homelands in southeastern Nigeria, and their subsequent entrance in the New World culturescape reinvigorated preexisting dance and masquerade styles there. Hans Sloane, who visited the Caribbean in the 1680s, observed masquerading in Jamaica, and African-styled masking conceivably goes back to the beginning of slavery in Antigua, Barbados, Montserrat, and Saint Kitts-Nevis, from where the first batch of European planters and African slaves were transferred to Jamaica.[15] Procurement, reselling, and relocation of slaves from one region in the Americas to another lend credence to the culture modeling and reinvention argument rather than the culture transfer paradigm often encountered in the previous studies.

In light of the foregoing, the plan here is to combine both the big picture (Pan-African/Pan-Bantu) and case study (Igbo) approach to demonstrate the inherent difficulty in pushing the specific ethnic culture transfer monologue when the bulk of evidence points to a multicultural diaspora dialogue that resulted in the rise of new cultures in the Americas. Collections of American colonial-era primary sources preserved in forms of newspaper articles, personal memoirs, travel journals, and ethnographic and anthropological writings have not only privileged the Igbo activities in the wider resonance of masquerade discourses but also suggest one-on-one African and African Diaspora linkages.[16] Some of these sources are hard to refute or ignore. The point is not to merely dispute the credibility of some pointers to specific Igbo or Èfik ideas or those from the other thousands of ethnicities found in Africa. However, taking the accounts on face value accentuates the tendency to promote a single story in a globalizing world of culture and metanarratives. It is, therefore, incumbent to explore the Igbo-centric perspectives along with their southeastern Nigeria neighbors (Èfik, Ibibio, and Ijọ) within the wider resonance of Bantu/African connections. We thus reiterate that the notion of Igbo/African identities in New World societies crisscrossed multiple cultural, ethnic, geographical, and even racial boundaries.

On the strength of their sheer numbers, the enslaved Igbo indeed played a significant role in the flowering of the New World music, dance, and masquerading in those places where they were concentrated in huge numbers.[17] But we are not dealing with a mathematical question in which elements in a range of functions correspond to exactly one element of the domain. Crahan and Knight have made a relevant point that although new arrivals usually identified with members of their ethnic group, a wholesale cultural transfer of any specific ethnic group in the New World slaveholding societies was practically impossible because the Africans involved were not "free individuals in families, but with slaves in slavery."[18] This is why the concept of modeling—both in its sociocultural and natural science interpretations—is apt in a study of this nature. Perhaps by putting the family in purview, Crahan and Knight want to remind us about the central role of kinship in socialization and sociocultural mobilization.[19]

However, the African family institution and the values it inculcates were seriously fractured in the Americas. Again the risk of forgetting this is high if scholars fall victim to sterile romanticism in a field of inquiry where the bulk of available evidence points to cultural hybridity rather than to wholesale transference of traditions and practices. It is more rewarding, therefore, to emphasize congenital forms of life in specific culture areas as templates from which the enslaved Africans drew in an attempt to cope with their conditions of servitude in the Americas.[20] Along with this line, a Bantu Culture Area is invoked as already delineated in the previous chapters, and the term is employed as more descriptive of the wider African culture milieu reflecting the centuries of cross-cultural fertilization involving all the Bantus and their host societies across the continent. This approach allows for a fuller exploration of the role of diffusion in the development of New World masks and masquerading performances. The Afro-Caribbean examples are analyzed in the light of possible precedents in West and Central Africa, along with possible Western European and Native American practices. How then do we know who was Igbo and who was not? Or which masquerade traditions were Igbo and which were not?

The Burden of Evidence

Ivor Miller made a pertinent point that because most of what we have as sources were created by White planters and administrators, "A great obstacle to our understanding of the cultural dimensions of the African diaspora in the Americas is the paucity of written documentation left by those who were sold and transported as slaves, that is, by those who experienced the worst forms of oppression."[21] The available sources indicate that toward the end of the nineteenth century, noisy Christmastime and New Year masquerade celebrations in the former Dutch Virgin Islands (now U.S. owned)[22] were common among African slaves, for whom the festivities provided some respite from relentless and oppressive plantation servitude. It is therefore no surprise that the celebrations were sometimes elevated to a point where they constituted a social nuisance in the opinion of the island's established elite, who blamed it on the "Eboe [Igbo] of Dinka or Corromantee [Ashanti/Akán] of West Africa." The complaint published in Danish in *The St. Croix Avis* of January 3, 1901, expressed frustration with what the author described as "the noisy rites of human sacrifice and cannibal feasts to the fetish of Eboe."[23]

While one must be wise enough not to take the words of an angry letter writer on face value, the allegations reveal a number of ideas that may illuminate the character of Igbo presence in the New World in general. That the Igbo were singled out as culprits tells us that they were numerically visible as an African ethnic bloc: 18,692 Igbo slaves landed on Saint Croix Island alone. Standing on their own, however, numerical indices do not always translate to action or active participation in a sociocultural movement. Rather, something unique pushed the Igbo to the center stage of the Caribbean culturescape. In the canon of anthropological and social science literature, the Igbo of southeastern Nigeria, among other things, have been described as receptive, democratically minded, clannish, daring, ambitious, intelligent, colonialist, and sometimes uppity.[24] Among their Ijọ neighbors, the Igbo personality appeared in the late nineteenth-century masquerade satires as "impulsive" and "mischievous." In a Kalabari song invoked during its annual Ekine masquerade festival: "His mother sent him to buy red dye; He went and bought yellow. O, Igbo, son of a chief! O, Igbo, son of a chief! His mother sent him to buy red dye; He went and bought a woman's vagina. O, Igbo, son of a chief! O, Igbo, son of a chief!"[25] In this song, the Igbo is portrayed as a willful, lustful young man, whose craving for women has reached the point of obsession if not madness.

Appraising these collections of stereotypes known in Nigeria political discourses as "the Igbo Problem," Chinua Achebe admits that Igbo proclivity for adaptation under European colonial oppression and their record of success in postcolonial Nigeria has engendered a general dislike of them among their fellow Nigerians. According to Achebe, "Nigerians of all other ethnic groups will probably reach consensus on no other matter than their common resentment of the Igbo. They would describe them as aggressive, arrogant, and clannish. Most would add grasping and greedy."[26] Ultimately, it was colonial scholar Robin Horton who noted that the familial basis of decentralized and segmentary societies like the Igbo and Ibibio often produce individuals with a great deal of personal autonomy.[27] Drawing from a contemporary reality, we have seen to what degree democracy and freedom have elevated the American citizen of today into near Igbo-like being: outspoken, fearless, self-opinioned, if not loud and arrogant.[28]

In the Americas during the period of slavery (c. 1500s–1888), the Igbo village personality manifested in certain ways they responded to slavery and oppression. The enslaved Igbo were stereotyped in the Americas as "bad" slaves. Sometimes they resorted to rebellion, poisoning, or exit by way of either suicide or running away to join the so-called Maroons in isolated locations.[29] At other times, the Igbo engaged in satires and raucous activities like the Bamboula fiesta characterized by loud drumming, singing, and dancing. In South Carolina, other slaves saw the Igbo as "rascals" and "rogues." They would tease about one another's African ethnicities, especially the "Guli (Gullah, i.e., Angolans) and Iba (Igbo)." James Barclay recorded that "the one will say to the other, 'You are Gulli Niga [Gullah Nigger], what be the use of you, you be good for nothing.' The other will reply, 'You be Iba Niga [Igbo Nigger]; Iba Niga great 'askal [rascal].'"[30] Carefully interpreted, one can surmise by this that on occasions where the "good" slaves would normally exercise caution and discretion, the "bad" slaves comprising Igbo (and non-Igbo) individuals targeted the calamity of bondage and human carnage that New World plantation slavery perpetrated.[31] The average Igbo, like every other enslaved person, seemed to have no aspiration to be seen as the "good slave," for there was nothing good in a life of servitude.

Having explained the context in which the Igbo became agent provocateurs, it is now time to closely examine examples of masquerade/dance festivities often associated with them. Among these are the Bamboula, Jonkunnu, and Mocko Jumbies. It has been established in the historical literature that the Bamboula was a popular ritual dance linked to the ancestor spirits native to the Kongo of Central Africa. There are thousands of sacred cults that used music as a mode of religious worship in Africa. The Bamboula in the Americas, with its accompaniment of music and dance, was first adopted in Louisiana and is marked by a special drumming at which the Igbo and other Bantu groups such as those in Central Africa are adept. R. J. Damm reminds us that the Bamboula drum, rhythm, and dance is central to the story of African slaves and their descendants in Louisiana and New Orleans who gathered in a place called Congo Square (now Louis Armstrong Park) during the eighteenth and early nineteenth centuries to partake in their traditional music on Sunday afternoons.[32]

Some of the enslaved Africans for whom this dance served as a form of coping strategy arrived in Louisiana directly from Africa; others were resold from Haiti and Cuba in the Caribbean.[33] Narrating his experience with the dance celebrations, Midge Burnett—from Raleigh, North Carolina, who was under ownership of one "Master Williams"—recalled that "We had square dances dat last all night on holidays an' we had a Christmas tree and an Easter egg hunt an' all dat, case Marse William intended ter make us a civilized bunch of blacks."[34] Many slaves like Burnett saw Congo Square as a "home," a meeting place, and a place where identity expression meant taking a short reprieve from the drudgery of slavery. Hence, Ted Widmer emblematically describes Congo Square "as a place of the mind as much as it was a real location."[35] In the context of this pattern of culture modeling and cross-breeding in the New World, Bamboula, from which ballet evolved, connotes a metaphor for racial solidarity and survival, a genre of African (rather than a Kongo or Igbo) dance and its associated rhythms. The particular drum on which it is played, thus, became the objectified emblem for those who partook in the dance.[36]

Contrary to what the early records left by White planters often claim, neither in Africa nor in the Americas were the Igbo originators of the Bamboula; rather, they identified with and adapted to the dance, in which dancers established circle formations and an additional ring of onlookers is formed around the dancers. The adaptation occurred in two meaningful ways (among others). At the level of material culture, the adaptation occurred through the use of the transverse "Ebo [Igbo] drum." At the philosophical level, it was related to the Igbo through the adaptive *ọzọ* title culture in which, for a citizen to attain the status of ancestors, a transparent life as implied in the moral code (*ọfọ ná ogu*) was mandatory.[37] In traditional Igbo, Ibibio, Èfìk, Èkọi, and Ijọ societies, one of the methods of social control was to call out the individual who defiled the moral laws of the land in public squares where the offenders are shamed in satires.[38] In his *Igbo Philosophy of Law*, F. U. Okafor explains that once a decision has been acclaimed, "it is given a ritual binder" and propitiation was observed.[39]

Putting the place of African drum in context, Roberto Nadal reminds us:

> It is well known that Africans have drum languages, by which news is transmitted to great distances. These languages were used by the slaves in Cuba from earliest times. The restless workers on coffee and sugar plantations kept in contact that way, to such an extent that the authorities had to forbid it. In Cuba, blacks who are acquainted with the music and liturgy of their African religions say that certain drums "speak" on given occasions, even though they are played without any vocal accompaniment"[40]

How much the Europeans understood the widespread use of drums and its rituals, whether as sacred or profane symbols, is open to speculations. In 1836, Michael Scott observed a procession of "a negro funeral" along a street in Kingston, Jamaica, and left us with a description of the African drums as "made out of

FIGURE 5.1. A slave dance in Surinam, 1830. Used with permission
from the Rijksmuseum, Amsterdam.

pieces of hollow trees, about six feet long, with skins braced over them, each carried by a man, while another beats it with open hands."[41] The drum so described
is common in the Igbo/Bight of Biafra Culture Area. The same source from 1836
observed a typical Bamboula Negro carnival in Kingston: "This day was the first
of the Negro Carnival, or Christmas holidays, at the distance of two miles from
Kingston, the sound of the negro drums and horns, the barbarous music, and
yelling of the different African tribes, and the more mellow singing of the Set
Girls, came off upon the breeze loud and strong."[42]

The opponents of the Bamboula and similar wild African-themed Christmas merrymaking in Jamaica, the Virgin Islands, Louisiana, or elsewhere in the
Americas were particularly irked not just by the boisterous drumming, singing,
and dancing; the part that got to their heads most was the effrontery with which
the African performers called out oppressive plantation owners and corrupt administrators in songs throughout the Christmas and New Year festivities. As if
to emphasize that the Christmas festivities were simply a temporary inversion of
social distinctions, Joseph Tuckerman in a letter of 1837 addressed to Dr. John C.

Warren of Boston somberly described the Christmas observances in Saint Croix:
"The noise of the music, which was of drums and kettle drums, made it quite
impossible that the voice should be heard. But their liberty expired with the
day. They slept, and were again *slaves*."[43] Additionally, Dirks maintains that the
annual revelry constituted "a symbolic representation of the slaves' worldview
. . . [which] gave voice to an illiterate and therefore historically mute folk."[44]
Although the masquerading and Christmas songs were often viewed simply as a
spectacular form of entertainment, through parody and satire, they served as a
vehicle for social commentary and protest.

It was particularly the dire consequences of exposing the transgressions of the
elite that drove their strong objection to the Bamboula. An editorial published
in the semiweekly *Saint Thomas Tidende* Danish newspaper on December 28,
1872, strongly repudiated the Bamboula dance as a "remnant of barbarism" that
should only be practiced in Africa.[45] In a similar tone, the same newspaper in
another editorial of November 22, 1890, kicked against the Bamboula as a detest-
able form of amusement. It advocated that the music and dance that accompany
it should be completely censored because it is "used mainly as a channel of open
lampoonery."[46] These and similar complaints predictably led to the Bamboula's
loss of attractiveness early in the twentieth century. The less confrontational
African cultural exhibitions with purported Igbo influences received lesser negative reaction in a White-controlled multiethnic/multiracial Caribbean society.

A genre of Caribbean masquerade plays often associated with Igbo slaves is the
Jonkunnu. Indeed, whether we are looking at masquerading or music, cultural
trends in Caribbean society as we see it today emerged from colonial times as
a hybrid of styles. Some early nineteenth-century writers observed striking features between African-style masquerading and European-themed masquerades.
The evolution of Jamaica's Jonkunnu provides a compelling illustration of how
the "Western" and the "African" merged into a unique art form in a colonial/
slaveholding American setting. The origin of the word *Jonkunnu* has remained
a contested subject. The exponents of its "European" connotations claim that
it represents the name of a folk hero named John Canoe, a supposedly British
figure.[47] A related European-based account has it that Jonkunnu is derived from
the French phrase *gens inconnus* or "unknown people," as carousers use masks to
hide their identities.[48] Other competing views suggest that Jonkunnu is either
connected to the Yoruba Egungun masquerade festival or the Igbo Ahịajọku or
Njọku Ji (New Yam) festival. Along with this line, Douglas B. Chambers suggests that Jonkunnu may be a corrupted version of Ọkọnkọ masquerade, which
appears during the New Yam festival among the Ngwá people of Igboland.[49]

However, a more plausible explanation is that it is linked to the Akán people of Gold Coast (modern Ghana). A number of indicators may support the fact: First, the Jonkunnu dance first took root in the Bahamas, where many Akán people were enslaved prior to the Igbo arrivals in that island.[50] More important, Edward Long, a planter historian who watched the masquerade in 1774, informs us that "Jolm Conny [possibly John Canoe or "Kenu"] was a celebrated Cabacero at Tres Puntas, in Axim, on the Guiney [Guinea] coast, who flourished about the year 1720. He bore great authority among the Negroes of the district."[51] The true identity of the king and hero that once ruled Axim in the Gold Coast or modern Ghana from 1683 to 1720 is still shrouded in mystery; incidentally, this was the same period that the Jonkunnu festival, also observed in South Carolina, was established in the Caribbean. Jonkunnu is prominent in the Bahamas, from where it possibly entered Jamaica. It is also popular in the U.S. Virgin Islands.[52]

It is not the intent here to resolve the question of the origins of Jonkunnu in the Caribbean or in America. In broad terms, what is more pertinent is that the debate reflects the multiple ethnocultural matrixes in which the Jonkunnu festival was established. On a more specific level, the closer association of Jonkunnu with the Igbo once again mirrors the Bight of Biafra slaves' active participation in and adaptation of the culture they met on arrival. The Igbo and their Calabar River Valley neighbors (Èfik, Ibibio, Èkọi, and Ijọ) brought new vigor and style to the Jonkunnu festivities. This is what Palmer has described as "cultural accretion": "practices or ideas borrowed from other people that elaborate but do not alter or modify the existing core beliefs in any significant way."[53] Long, alluded to this dynamic in 1769 when he observed that "several new masks appeared, the Ebos [Igbos], the Pawpaws [one of the Ewe group in Ghana] & co having their respective Connus, male and female, who were dressed in a very laughable style."[54]

A historian cannot ignore the word "new" or the costumes associated with the popular masked characters that featured in the Jonkunnu plays of the eighteenth and nineteenth centuries as a site of cultural syncretism. While the "new" here connotes injection of new features, the masks are drawn from a variety of racial and ethnic divides. In his resourceful journal kept during his period of residence in the island of Jamaica (1816–1818), Matthew Gregory Lewis, the English novelist and dramatist (who died at sea on the voyage back to England in 1818), wrote on January 1, 1816: "The John-Canoe is a Merry-Andrew dressed in a striped doublet, and bearing upon his head a kind of pasteboard house-boat, filled with puppets, representing, some sailors, others soldiers, others again slaves at work on a plantation. The negroes are allowed three days for holidays at Christmas, and also New-year's day."[55]

Corroborating Lewis, Michael Scott in his 1836 *Tom Cringle's Log* gave an even more elaborate eye-witness account of what he described as the "Butcher's John Canoe Party" by a band of Negro performers in Kingston, Jamaica. According to Scott, different streets were crowded with

blackmoors,[56] men, women, and children, dancing, singing and shouting, and all rigged out in their best [dresses]. . . . The Butcher John canoe party [was] a curious exhibition, it unquestionably was. The prominent character was, as usual the John Canoe or Jack Pudding. He was a light, active, clean-made young creole negroe [*sic*] without shoes or stockings; he wore a pair of light jean, small clothes, all too wide, but confined to the knee, elbow and above, by bands of red tape, after the manner that Malvalio would have called cross-gartering . . . he had an enormous cocked-hat on, to which appended in front a white false-face or mask, of a most method-istical [*sic*] expression, while Janus-like, there was another face behind, of the most quizzical description, a sort of living Antithesis, both being garnished and overtopped with one coarse wig, made of hairs of bullocks' tils on which the *Chapeau* was stripped down with a broad band of gold lace.[57]

The emerging picturesque reveals juxtapositions of African and European costuming traditions and other paraphernalia of carnival dances/plays in the Caribbean slave-holding society. For instance, because it was difficult to re-create the traditional British greenery in Jamaica at this time, Isaac Belisario noted in an illustration drawn in 1836 that the "Jack-in-the-Green performance impoverished the British greenery with palm fronds."[58] A similar admixture of Afro-European traits was observed during Christmas in 1839 by Joseph Gurney who reported witnessing "a merry-andrew" during a "negro Saturnalia" in Saint Thomas.[59] These corroborate Robert W. Nicholls's summation that cultural evolution in the Caribbean is a sort of "sliding scale between African and European poles, with Quadrille gravitating towards the European end while the Mocko Jumbie [stilt masquerade dancing] is closer to the African end of the continuum." The European tradition, Nicholls continues, is also associated with the folk play "Maypole and in hero-combat Mummer's plays such as King George and the Dragon, or David and Goliath . . . where European influences have been incorporated, African aesthetic sensibilities have been applied."[60]

The preceding account implicates one of the several strands of academic debates converging on the interface between African and African Diaspora culture traits. Richard Burton contends that the early Jonkunnu with bullhorns "is clearly a neo-African or indigenized, rather than creolized, cultural form."[61] But Kenneth Bilby counters with the view that within the initial process of creolization, "blending occurred not only between European and African traditions, but also within the varied traditions of a multitude of African ethnic groups."[62] Illustrating his position, with the call-and-response singing genre, polymeter, and other African musical complexes in the Caribbean, Bilby notes that while these neo-African traditions remain "essentially African in every respect," they are at the same time mixed. The African models in the New World are "hardly traceable to any specific region or ethnic group in Africa," in whole, except for a few exemptions.[63] Nothing could be closer to the truth. A deeper treatment of the Caribbean masquerade societies at the level of costuming and symbols will help deepen insights about how they portray multiple ethnic and racial hybridized colors.

Symbols, Costumes, and African Masquerade Dances

The Jonkunnu is perhaps the most popular masquerade dance in the Caribbean. It is noteworthy that the Jonkunnu mask usually had two prominent adornments, a spreading ox horn headdress and boar tusks around the mouth. Masks with real or carved animal horns are common in traditional African masks/ performance art forms. In connection with masquerade dancing (which is the theatrical performance of the mask art form), real animal horns are less frequent and carved wooden horns are more common. In other words, the use of headdresses with a pair of real horns is generally limited to some groups but common among the Igbo, as illustrated by G. I. Jones in a 1939 study in Bende Division entitled "Ifogu Nkporo."[64] For instance, cattle horns feature in the masked initiation rituals of various Mande people in the Upper Guinea region, including the Bámáná of Mali and the Mandinka and Jola of Senegambia.[65] The Toussian, a small group found in the southwestern area of Burkina Faso, has a genre of masks with horns used in initiation ceremonies. The Toussian masks, made by blacksmiths, have two diagonals indicated with incrusted red seeds. On top of the mask is "the head of a big bird (the *calao*) or horns that symbolize the spirit of the clan/totem of the initiated boy."[66]

Some of the Bantu West and Central African groups arrived in the Caribbean early in the slavery era. In the literature, the horns appended to the masks are often emphasized more than the tusks. Elliot Picket's study reveals that the use of actual horns is the prerogative of hunter societies such as found in Sudan,

Bambara, and other parts of the savannah where animal husbandry is predominant.[67] Carved horns are also encountered in the various Bambara headdresses known as the Chi-Wara or Tji Wara. In Bambara tradition, the horn and the curved motif depict a source of artistic inspiration: a symbol of a magical being often visualized as part man, part antelope, who brought to man the concept of soil cultivation. This is part of the cosmology that dwells on increase—whether it is an increase in agricultural productivity or childbirth and children. A rather interesting substyle of the Tji Wara masks is found in the rare headdresses primarily from the Bámáná and Bambara of Mali.[68] In the modern Congo, the Tsonga are among the most noted users of animal horns. Among the Luba of the Congo, the animal horn was often attached to a carved figure as in the Bwoom headdresses, which are one of the royal masquerades in the Kuba Kingdom of Zaire: "They are regarded as 'friends of the king' in the dual sense that they are actually worn by the ruler and they represent a spirit or *ngesh*. Used in festivals and initiations, the dance of bwoom conveys qualities of youthful vigor and pride."[69] Some of the Tusyâ masks, called Loniakê, found in Upper Guinea, are surmounted by an animal head or horns, which symbolize the totem of the clan.[70]

Elsewhere, a particularly interesting use of animal horns in Yoruba ritual material is connected with the Alagida doll, related to the cult of Eshu and to an increase in childbirth and children.[71] Among the Igbo, horns are emblematic of aggression as associated with hunting guilds or warrior groups. For instance, the Ọháfiá, Èddá, and Ábám military allies of the Arọ blow the horns to herald the alliance's historic war-themed dances.[72] Within other masking genres in Igboland, there are several types of masks with specific appearance, costume, dance, drum rhythms, music, and rules of behavior.[73] Carved or real horns are sometimes used to decorate certain kinds of Igbo masks such as the Okoroshá and Ojịọnu. The Okoroshá masquerades from Mbáitoli sometimes hold real animal horns in their hands, which they use to collect gifts from their accolades. In Arọndizuọgu, the Mgbérédike masquerade, described by Richard Igwebe as aggressive and fearless, wear the skull and horns of a bull instead of a face mask when they appear during the New Yam festivities.[74] The Ọgáráchi masquerade of the Unmuezearoli of Onitsha has a pair of animal horns. In Umuezukwe, Umuọwá of Orlu, and Isu Njábá communities of Igboland, during the Ọkọnkọ masquerade (which has *Ngbárá* as its secret symbol festivals), the accompanying procession of musicians includes a group thumping horns with sticks as percussion instruments.[75] Nicholls has concluded, however, that unlike with the horned masks of the Jola of Gambia and Mande of West Africa, there is no historical evidence indicating the antiquity of the Igbo horned masks.[76] While further research is required on this, what is pertinent is that one cannot make any valid claim that horned masquerades were introduced into the New World by the enslaved Igbo, Èfik, Ibibio, Ịọ, Luba, Bámáná, and so on during the eighteenth century. All these groups contributed to shaping the Caribbean Bull. Once again the record of evidence indicates adaptive Caribbean genre with the Igbo elements involved in an existing cultural trend.

Beside horns, there are other features, styles, and paraphernalia associated with African masks and masquerade performances. A description of the Jonkunnu in Jamaica in 1797 by an anonymous observer is pertinent: "The Negroes have their droll, which, however it may be dressed is always called a John Canoe; a whimsical character.... Sometimes they wear two faces ... usually they have but one, which is often rendered hideous by beards and boar's tusks."[77] A related description in 1836 by Scott described the Jonkunnu as having "Janus-like" features: "there was another face, behind, of the most quizzical description.[78] These accounts suggest Janus masks and a description of a bearded mouth embellished, yet again, with boar's tusks. The tusks may or not indicate an Igbo influence as already underscored. However, certain kinds of Igbo masks, such as the Okoroshá of the Ummuneọhá, Isuámá, and Mbieri areas come with double faces. Also, specific categories of Ibibio and Boki masks are decked with double faces, as with the Dan of Liberia and Ivory Coast that feature tumors and other disfigurements; masks rendered hideous by tusks are unusual in West Africa.[79] Masks with tumors are encountered among the Èfik and Ibibio, as studies by Donald Simmons reveal:

> Masks of Efik and Ibibio, and some I[g]bo, groups in Calabar Province, Nigeria, frequently portray a noseless human face either in realistic representation or stylized form. Natives assert that these masks depict a disease which ulcerates the soft parts of the nasal membranes, eventually resulting in complete extirpation of the nose, and aver that the disease is portrayed on the masks to inspire fear in the beholder. Oron and some Ibibio denominate this disease *ọdọk*, while Èfik name it *ọnọk*; English-speaking natives usually translate the term as no-nose.[80]

Other Igbo examples of masks and masquerades with ugly and terrifying facial appearance include the Ágábá masks of the Mbáise, Owerri, and Umuáhiá communities. These masks are designed with warped human teeth and animal tusks with the intent to invoke fear to the onlookers. Some categories of Okoroshá called *oriukpọrọ*, *ákárákposhá*, and *nwánnekọrọshe* are found among

FIGURE 5.2. Àgábá masquerade of Umunneǫhá Mbáitoli

the various communities in Mbáitoli and Ikeduru.[81] In connection with the Jonkunnu embellished with tusks and other features, what the record of evidence reveals is that the African-styled Caribbean masquerades emerged out of an ensemble of ideas and material cultures put together by people of African descent in the American cultural theater.

Worthy of some attention here is the timing of the Caribbean and African masquerade festivals. The Caribbean Jonkunnu, Bamboula, and other masquerade celebrations like the Mocko Jumbie, which will be further explored, are usually observed during the Christmas and New Year celebrations. But in precolonial Africa, most of the masquerade celebrations were held during the harvest season. For example, the New Yam festival among the Igbo comes in August during the time of harvest. It is the equivalent of U.S. Thanksgiving celebrations. During the festivals, the Igbo thank the Áhịájọku or Njọku deities for blessing their agricultural harvests.[82] The Igbo, like their Ibibio, Ijọ, Èfik, Igédé, and other neighbors in southern Nigeria, customarily celebrate the annual agro-cultural festivals with music, dance, food, and masquerading. These are enacted to "foster productivity of both fields and women."[83] The village communities such as Ummuneọhá that perform the Okoroshá masquerades, for instance, believe that the spirits that dwell in the masks purify the community and remove all evil and negativity from the village so that the next year begins fresh and clean. The Okoroshá masquerades, just like some genres of Ibibio and Ogoni masquerades of the Niger Delta, featured both sexes and dark and white colors.[84] Although the masquerades are performed by men only, the white or light-colored Ekpo, Mmụọ, and Okoroshá masks represent female spirits, while the dark masks embody the male spirits. With these, a parity of obligation is accorded to both sexes of spirits. This is in line with the Igbo understanding of the world as a function of dualism, or what Chike Aniakor identifies as "the inseparable unities of Igbo cosmology (*Ihe kwụrụ, ihe ákwụdebe yá*)—that is 'when something stands, the opposite joins it.'"[85]

In his study of northern Igbo masquerades, J. S. Boston explains that Mmụọ masquerades of the Nri-Ákwá with female counterparts "represent traditional I[g]bo ideas of beauty and feminine character."[86] Nicholls adds that these classes of "white face masks" or "maiden spirit masks," are known in Onitsha and Okwée Uwáni Ngwo of Udi Division as *ágbọghọ mmwánu* (young or unmarried maiden spirits).[87] However, the light-colored masks also have an extra historical symbolism: they tell of the African people's encounter with the Europeans. Artistic representation of white or light-faced masks did not enter into the Igbo pantheon of spirits until between the late sixteenth and early seventeenth centuries, when the

FIGURE 5.3. Female counterpart of Achi Mbieri Okoroshá masquerade

first modern Europeans began to appear in the coastal enclaves of Africa, including the Niger Delta and the Bight of Biafra. Besides their appearance during the New Yam festivals, this genre of African masks can also perform at funerals of members of the masquerade cults or in connection with male initiation. Nicholls has observed that almost all the Igbo neighbors—Èfik, Ibibio, Ijọ, and so on—have their own versions of the light/dark, beauty/beast masks.[88]

To an extent, the dark beast masks of the Bight of Biafra area could be compared with the tusked Jonkunnu mask in the New World, while the light Igbo masks can be compared to the wire mesh masks, which are painted in light colors and are ubiquitous throughout the Caribbean. Within the Poro society in West Africa, some artistic representations of masked spirits are further conceived in

FIGURE 5.4. Achi Mbieri Okoroshá masquerade

white colors. This is seen among the Dan in Liberia and Ivory Coast and Temne of Sierra Leone, who paint the initiates with white clay to symbolize that they are temporarily dead.[89] Modeled along with this pattern, it is fascinating to observe that in the Virgin Islands, some of the Creole masks were purposely painted pink with blue eyes as a means of subtly satirizing the White population.[90] The crucial lesson is that the Caribbean art forms are eclectic—they represent derivations of ideas from various Bantu Culture Areas.

Another New World masquerade dance that reflects some degree of similarities with the Bantu Culture Area precedents is the Mocko Jumbie stilt-dancing masquerades. In West Africa, several stilt walking/dancing masquerades are common. Among the Igbo, the Kéléké (or Èkéléké) masquerade of the Ubomiri community is a spectacle in stilt-dancing/walking as with the Chákábá found in Senegal, Gambia, and Guinea.[91] Kariamu Welsh Asante, who personally observed Chákábá in Guinea in the 1950s and 1960s, noted, "These towering figures were called gods of the sacred forest and actually frightened some of the younger people in the audience." Asante explains that the Guinea Ballet and their cohorts found in West Africa perform a special function in African folklore: "Because of their heights, they act as mediators between the living and the spiritual world of the ancestors and are able to ask for special favors such as rain to save their crops from the drought. It is also said that they mediate disputes among the living when all else have failed."[92] The tallness and costumes of the stilt-masquerades include items like fauna (animal), flora (plant), mineral (earth), water (fresh water, the sea), and gendered attire such as men's trousers and women's wrappers and skirts. Together, these items remind the community that a healthy world must strive to be in balance with nature for peace, continuity, and order.

In the New World in general and the Caribbean in particular, one of the most popular stilt-dancing masquerades remains the Mocko Jumbie, which appeared in the Caribbean as early as the 1770s.[93] Widely celebrated in Trinidad and Tobago, and the U.S. Virgin Islands (including Saint Croix, Saint Vincent, and Saint Thomas), the term *Mocko Jumbie* is believed to be a combination of "Moko" (also Moco or Mocho), which some believe is of Malian Mandinka derivation; and "Jumbi," a West Indian word for spirits or ghosts. Robert Nicholls asserts that while "Jumbie" is commonly understood by Virgin Islanders to refer to a ghost or spirit, it is probably coined from the term "Ekpo" (ghost) associated with the Ibibio of Nigeria and/or "zumbi" (departed spirit) linked with the Kimbundu people of the Congo. "Mocko," on the other hand, appears to be a compound term with multiple meanings, including its reference to Ibibio slaves.[94] However, the first appearance of the word in the Americas was in 1627 when Alonso de Sandoval referred to the "Moco" as a group of Calabarians (Calabar people), thereby linking the Mocko to the Old Calabar country.[95] In 1777, C. G. A. Oldendorp, a missionary in Sierra Leone, identified the location of the "Moko" (Ibibio) near the Ijọ of New Calabar and differentiated them from both the Igbo and Èfik.[96] The truth of the matter is that the etymology of the word Moko is from the Ibibio words *Mokop* (I hear) and *Omokop* (Do you hear?). According to Edet Udo, during the early period of the transatlantic slave trade in the Bight, "Slaves were asked if they heard what white slave traders were saying ("Do you hear?"). In reply, they said *Mokop* ("I hear")."[97] From these words, the Europeans who obviously could not comprehend the Èfik language took *Mokop* (variously Moco, Mocko, or Moko in Diaspora literature) to mean an ethnic affirmation.

What all of these sources reveal is that the Caribbean Mocko Jumbie was constructed from different ethnic and racial lines. What it looked like in the early days of slavery is not clear. The play has, over the years, passed through different stages, including the idea of the masquerade as a "sham jumbie" and "derider of jumbies" as encountered in most of the Virgin Islands. Also, such idioms as the Jumbie as "sorcerer" and "bogey man" are commonplace. A couple of eighteenth-and nineteenth-century records on stilt masquerades in the Caribbean focus on Saint Vincent, in the Windward Islands. While the first report by William Young informs us that the "Moco-Jumbo" is of Mandinka heritage, the second identifies the performer as an Igbo who is assisted by some of the Igbo soldiers of a "negro regiment."[98] Again, we see a combination of cultural ideas and imageries drawn from Western and Central Africa giving birth to a new tradition in Caribbean society.

A character of the Mocko Jumbie masquerade portrayed in the Young report, which was related to the 1791 Christmas festivities, stated that a stilt dancer called "Moco-Jumbo" wore a "false head" [mask] and, accompanied by musicians and swordsmen, roaming the streets assuming the "antic terrible" and entertaining passersby.[99] Another account by Edwards the planter identifies the masquerade with the "Mumbo Jumbo of the Mendengoes [Mandinkas]." He is probably correct in this assumption because Young concluded the Christmas season with a feast and was entertained by visiting slaves who danced to the music of a "balafo [*sic*]." A *balafon* is a wooden xylophone used by Mandinka and neighboring people.[100] Dirks also saw the Mocko Jumbie as "a Mandingo import."[101] Additionally, Charles Williams Day's report published in 1852 describes an Igbo stilt dancer whose costume was a mixture of African and European features (i.e., cowrie shells and a grenadier's cap). The stilt dancer was referred to as a "De Jumpsa-man brought out of a negro hut on the shoulders of the soldiers and being upon stilts six feet high."[102] However, Day does explain that "'De jumbee' was of course an imitation of the genuine." Nonetheless, Day included in his report a story of an African who expressed serious fear of the Jumbies: "I feared of the Jumbee in the crane sar [sir] (The African devil and evil spirit)."[103]

Although there are many different stilt masquerades in the Caribbean, the U.S. Virgin Islands has two potential, disparate prototypes of the Mocko Jumbie. These are the Laniboy masquerade play among the Toma, Guerzé, and Kissien communities of Guinea and the similar Dan of Liberia masquerade; versus the Ėbili (a type of animal masquerade from Ihiálá division) and Kéléké masquerade

of the Mbáitoli of the central Igbo, the Urhobo of Niger Delta, and the Kwale
of western Nigeria.[104] Thus, Nicholls suggests that a provenance for the Mocko
Jumbie in the Upper Guinea region seems more plausible than an origin in
southeastern Nigeria.[105] This conclusion appears to be drawn based on Day's
1852 report that describes the Virgin Island Jumbie masquerade he witnessed
as wearing striped trousers, as was common among the stilt masquerades of the
Upper Guinea region.[106] In Upper Guinea, this genre of masquerades is believed
to expel sorcery and witchcraft. Similarly, it is believed among the Creoles in the
Caribbean that the Mocko Jumbie combats wicked spirits and is associated with
good luck or divine blessings.[107] The Upper Guinea origin hypothesis might as
well be the case, but on the strength of available evidence, it is evident that the
Mocko Jumbie masquerade emerged as a collection of Bantu-wide /Pan-African
culture (Ibibio, Igbo, Upper Guinea, and so on).

How can one, then, rationalize the overemphasis on the Igbo connection
with the various masquerade dances encountered in the colonial and antebellum
Americas as alluded to by the bulk of early European planters, administrators,
and travelers?[108] One explanation remains that the Igbo readiness to adopt and
adapt a tradition, culture, skill set, or institution and attempt to dominate it by
turning it into an Igbo village affair is a crucial factor. Thus, culture, adaptation,
and continuity seem to be the practice as the record of evidence indicates. The
enslaved Igbo habitually combined their inherited knowledge of the Kéléké masquerade stilt-dancing with the Mandinka style, in a similar way they adapted to
the Jonkunnu of the Upper Guinea region and Bamboula of the Kongo. In other
words, the Igbo partook in established masquerades they met in the Americas
and injected into them some doses of their Igbo village characters. How much
their contributions made them owners of these cultural artifacts is not clear.
What emerged as the New World masquerade culturescape is not and should
not be seen as either Igbo or Guinean or Èfik or Kongo or Mande or Akán or
any one ethnic group's culture. They were all these and more in the context of
Bantu culture in transition in a new sociopolitical milieu.

While the tone and visual presentations of African Diaspora cultural inventions and ethnic identifications may suggest close linkages with those found in
Africa, the American progenies are products of totally different sociopolitical
and historical milieus. In Africa, the triad of music, dance, and masquerading
serves a central role in the indigenous politics, including social control functions.
In Igbo and Ibibio segmentary societies where political decisions were attained
by consensus, masquerades such as the Ulágá, Okoroshá, and Ojiọnu among the
Igbo and Ekpo among the Ibibio were famous for their fearless commentaries on

social ills that affected everyone in their communities.[109] That is why the Igbo often assert that "if a king refuses to behave like a king the ordinary man will talk to him adorned in the Ulágá mask." In Achi Mbieri, the Nkwá Love group appropriates this form of powers in a forum for social criticism as performers' satire observed antisocial behaviors while drumming and dancing to the entertainment of the onlookers.[110] This corroborates Visona et al.'s observation that the regulatory roles of masquerades include providing "models of ideals" and "satirizing unacceptable behavior."[111]

In the New World, African masquerades tried to re-create similar sociopolitical roles but with minimal success because of the colonial sociopolitical structure. It must be added that through the device of satire and shaming, enslaved Africans aimed to instigate change. Michael Scott noted in 1836: "The John Canoe, who was the workhouse driver, was dressed up in lawyer's cast-off gown and bands, black silk breeches, no stockings or shoes, but with sandals of bullock's hide strapped on his . . . feet, a small cocked hat on his head, to which was appended a large cauliflower wig, and the usual white false face, bearing a very laughable resemblance to Chief-Justice S_____, with whom I happened to be personally acquainted."[112] It is evident that the intent may have been the same but the Caribbean model was dissimilar to the African homeland. While the African genre was empowered to the point that no individual could transcend its authority and tongue lashing, the Caribbean progeny did not enjoy the benefit of such empowerment. The Caribbean masquerades had to guard against negative repercussions from Caribbean planters and administrators. Thus, rather than name specific persons, messages were usually encoded in metaphor; using such codes, masquerades indirectly poked fun at the establishment and lampooned figures of authority.

It is essential to add that it was not only the African traditions that the Caribbean masquerades imitated. In Antigua, at Christmas, the John Bull masquerade modeled the Old World European regulatory functions when he would visit various houses and be told to "run" any child who had been naughty, a bed-wetter being a prime target. William Richardson says that when he performed as a Mocko Jumbie in Saint Kitts-Nevis, parents would sometimes ask him to chase a naughty child, and often adults would run as well as children. Visby-Petersen in her report of a Mocko Jumbie in Saint Thomas in 1892 describes the masquerade as a "bogeyman" who performed "an insane dance on tall stilts."[113] Her use of the word "bogeyman" is significant because, unlike its mysterious function of fighting off evil spirits and attracting good ones, bogeyman refers to the more pragmatic function of social control. This reminds us about the masked

Krampus of Styria, in Eastern Austria, which goes around the village at Christmas with the legendary Saint Nicholas. He has been described in the literature as "shaggy, has a goat mask and horns, cloven hooves and a long tail, rattles his chains, and brandishes a bundle of birch twigs . . . to punish naughty children."[114] In Malmö, Sweden, a decree of 1695 banned the "Julbuck," the Christmas buck, from performing because it "frightened children and caused pregnant women to lose their babies."[115]

The fierceness of some Caribbean masquerades is also implied in Thora Visby-Petersen's description of horned masquerades in a Saint Thomas Christmas parade in 1892. Of particular relevance is the extra effort made by the performers to restrain the masquerades from attacking people. "A strong rope, held by a muscular negro, is fastened to the waist of each devil so that he will not endanger the crowd."[116] Yet, no matter how one reads this piece of information, the fact is that the New World African masquerades had no actual authority to discipline social miscreants. But among the precolonial Igbo, Èkọi, Èfik, Ijọ, and Ibibio, the spirit-regarding classes of masquerades performed sociopolitical functions.[117]

It must be reiterated that the African Diaspora masquerade genres evolved out of what some scholars have identified as a two-dimensional ethnography— that is, a linkage between a particular cultural form with obvious African roots and an equally unique political community with a more Western foundation. The nature of the relationship between the two forces explains the characteristics African-themed masquerades have assumed in the African Diaspora.[118] Joyce Jackson and Fehintola Mosadomi have pinpointed the origins of the Black Mardi Gras Indian carnival tradition from the colonial encounters "between black and red men, the Afro-Caribbean ties to Trinidad, Cuba, and Haiti, the links to West African dance and musical forms, the social hypothesis stressing fraternal African-American bonds in the face of oppression."[119] L. M. Fraser, a colonial anthropologist, has provided an instructive illustration of this ethnographic dualism and the history surrounding it. Writing in a memo in 1881, Fraser captured the dynamism of the slave status of the enslaved Africans and the origin of Trinidad masquerade carnivals: "In the days of slavery, wherever fire broke out upon an estate, the slaves on the surrounding properties were immediately required to actively put the fire out. They were summoned by the sounds of horns and shells and marched to the spot, their drivers cracking their whips and urging them on. After emancipation, the Negroes began to represent this scene as a kind of commemoration of the change in their condition."[120] Thus, every year in commemoration of the day of emancipation, on August 1, ex-slaves remembered their history with a carnival procession as a vehicle of political mobilization under communal leadership.

Altogether, the majority of incidents of masks and carnival performances in the African Diaspora were generally conceived and deployed as a model of marital or ceremonial protestation against the exploitative nature of master/slave, elite/subaltern relationships characterized by systemic corruption, racial discrimination, and economic marginalization in a White-dominated society. While masquerading is reminiscent of the communal sociopolitical structures in precolonial Africa, the African Diaspora masked carnivals challenged the political powers and interests of the dominant White elite. In this regard, performance arts were intended to function as an alternative medium of social control—this time an agitation by the downtrodden for a new social order of equal rights, social justice, fair redistribution of national resources, minority empowerment, and the preservation of historical memory especially in the post-abolition Americas.[121] Jackson and Mosadomi have further noted: "The Mardi Gras Indian tradition is a way for blacks to come together without being exploited by the white community. It is a refusal to conform to the white carnival and it is very important to the Indians and it is a characteristic that they are very proud of."[122] Carol Flake adds, "In a sense, the history of carnival in New Orleans can be viewed as an evolving pattern of order and disorder, of exclusion and expansion—of drawing circles and dancing around the limit."[123] At times Black carnival performances have involved some erotic or obscene displays, as often seen with the New Orleans Mardi Gras Indians and Jamaican dancehalls and soca music. Yet, this form of carnival display, which is also expressive of resentment of conditions of sociopolitical and economic domination, has today become perhaps one of the most dominant attractions of the carnival festivities.

It is clear that the mask and masquerades of Africa are a continuing art form that is original and peculiar to all people of African descent. The original concept is spirit bound, but as the art tradition traveled around the globe it has adapted to other purposes without a total loss of its African ancestry. While diverse manners of African-themed masquerades are found in the New World, the relationship between these and the African prototypes are striking: what transpired in the New World is a conglomeration of Bantu/African genres fusing into a unique Caribbean style with some European flavor. As European colonists held political power, Jonkunnu became a generic name for a widely dispersed assortment of masquerades in Jamaica, Tortola, Belize, Bahamas, and even North Carolina during the antebellum era.

CHAPTER 6

Unmasking the Masquerade

Counterideologies and Contemporary Practices

T HE DYNAMIC SYMBOLS AND meanings of African masks and masquerades and their evolution from a transcendental undertone to a more secular and popular carnival of today deserve a detailed treatment. Since African masquerades were originally embedded in indigenous religious ideology and served as a tool of sociopolitical control, they have been a target of assaults by alien ideologies. Crossing the Arabian Sea into Sudan in the seventh century, the Arabs launched Islam's imperialistic push into the continent. Eleven centuries later, Europeans brought a new wave of Christian evangelism in sharp conflict with the indigenous African belief systems.[1] Soon, the late nineteenth-century missionary push, initially centered on African coastal cities, secured an alliance with colonial conquest, and the entire apparatus of indigenous traditions configured on religious idioms came under vicious attacks.

Three overlapping historical milestones are demarcated in the developments that unmasked the African masquerading traditions. The first is what may be called the Afro-Arab Muslim Cultural Interface, starting from about 642 CE and continuing to the present. Islam began its assault on African culture from the northeast as exemplified by the cultural transformations the religion brought upon the Berbers of North Africa, who also had a masking tradition. The Berber encounter with the Arabs and their religion was just the beginning of a long-lasting encounter involving nearly a half of the African societies in general and the inhabitants of the West and East Africa in particular. West Africa increasingly became more prominent as Islam and trade grew exponentially, drawing the region into a wider circuit of global commerce through the trans-Saharan trade networks.

The second stage of the process that has led to the demystification of the rituals, secrecy, and aura surrounding the spirit-regarding African masquerade institution mirrors Africa's meeting with Western modernity. Specifically, this is connected with the counterideologies that came with the transatlantic slave trade, Christian evangelism, and colonialism proper. This stage of cultural subversion starting from about 1500s has two related dimensions. One aspect of it is centered on the discovery of the New World and the transatlantic slave trade that took African captives as laborers to the Americas. Under conditions of servitude and colonial oppression, the enslaved Africans tried to reinvent their masquerade culture, with varied success. However, given all the odds they had to contend with in the Americas, the chances of re-creating authentic African versions of their religious-sanctioned masquerade culture were imperiled on arrival. The other dimension of the African-European cultural confrontation took place on African soil with the rise of Christian evangelical missions in the nineteenth century. This development was also accompanied by colonial overtures. Christianity and colonialism, therefore, defined the contours of the unmasking processes that crisscrossed between Africa and the Atlantic world, as manifested in several steps: the use of masks in Africa and the African Diaspora as an instrument of resistance and mobilization against slavery, colonialism, and oppression; and the resilience of masquerading in the face of a brutal campaign waged by slave owners and colonial administrators on both sides of the Atlantic.

Emerging from these dialectics of control, conflict, and resistance was the eventual acceptance of—or should we say the triumph of—masquerade carnivals as a popular culture in the New World societies. On the African continent, masquerades fought through a sustained campaign by colonial administrators, and Christian evangelists and their new African converts, to break the power, secrecy, and ritual observances with which the masquerades were associated with in precolonial and colonial Africa. Coming out of these struggles, the brand of masquerade carnivals that survived on both sides of the Atlantic did not follow the original intents for which the institution was invented among the Igbo, Ibibio, Èfik, Èkọi and Ijọ peoples of the Bantu/Biafra homeland in southeastern Nigeria and western Cameroon. In other words, one of the important parts of this discussion is the long processes of Islamization and Christianization of the African masquerades both in Africa and in the African Diaspora. This is followed by the (re)-secularization of the masquerade institutions in the postcolonial setting.

In precolonial and most of colonial Africa, memberships in the masquerade societies were exclusively reserved for the initiates in the various age-grade associations and secret societies that owned and operated the masquerade cults. Since the alien religions permeated the African continent, particularly since the postcolonial era, membership and participation in the masquerade plays have become flexible and in some places open to all and sundry. If one accepts modernity, as articulated by Jürgen Habermas, to connote the aspiration for cognitive rationality, moral autonomy, and sociopolitical self-determination, then we may begin to see the intrusion of Arab and Western ideas on Africa as part of the wider modernism project gone bad.[2]

Fred Dallmayr has noted correctly that one of the chief merits of Habermas's work remains "the treatment of modernity not as a platform or doctrine but as a discourse or conversation—a conversation made up of different protagonists or voices and stretching over successive historical periods."[3] This observation is central in the unfolding discourse because the seventeenth-century roots of the Renaissance and Reformation movements in Europe coincided with the European voyages of discoveries that resulted in the colonization of the "New World." The so-called Age of Enlightenment ushered in an implicit break from the classical and medieval past. As the discussion proceeds, one sees the intersections of modernity, globalization, and new cultural imputations unfolding on the global stage as technology and cross-cultural exchanges expand the horizons of cultures including the masquerade tradition. In other words, in the contemporary masquerade and carnival dances—from the Igboland rainforest village communities of the Bight of Biafra to the cosmopolitan cities of Bahia, Toronto, London, New York, New Orleans, Kingston, and Mona, Jamaica—one encounters the functions of masquerade carnivals as an instrument of mobilization, human rights campaign, quest for freedom of expression, and identity formation for diverse communities, not least the African communities.

Thus, O. P. Fingesi finds it critical to remind everyone that in the African (precolonial) world, ancestors had well-defined ideas of nature, human life, existence, social relations, as well as man himself.[4] On the basis of these time-honored ideas, Africans developed meaning in their distinct civilization. Similarly, the Black West Indians in England, as Cohen noted, would quickly claim, "Carnival is our culture, our identity here in Britain. . . . It is our heritage. . . . It teaches our children who we are."[5] While this idiom of identity compares favorably with its continental African connotations, the Caribbean versions are products of a totally different sociopolitical and historical milieu—an environment of a "two-dimensional ethnography"[6]—that is a linkage between a particular cultural form with obvious African roots and an equally unique oppressive political community with a more Western foundation. The nature of the relationship between the two unequal forces (the Western foundations and the African roots) explains the characteristics Black masquerade dances have assumed in the African Diaspora today. In order to impose some measure of order on the ensuing discussions, a chronological approach is important.

Encounter with Islam in Northern/Western Africa

Prior to the Arab invasion, North Africa shared common historical, economic, and sociocultural ties with the rest of the continent. A visitor to the region now mostly populated by people of Arab descent would be struck by its marked peculiarity—that is, a seemingly distinct Muslim culture zone in the north versus a more "authentic" African culture zone south of the Sahara. The marked differences emerged as a result of a battery of developments dating back several millennia. Archaeological evidence suggests that somewhere between 40,000 and 25,000 BCE an advanced Paleolithic culture or Old Stone Age cave-dwelling people had developed in the Mediterranean Basin. The Mediterranean is a strategic crossroad embracing portions of Africa, Europe, and Asia. This region was host to the late Pleistocene epoch (a period of world glaciations) now dated about 1.8 million to 10,000 years ago. The end of the Pleistocene era coincided with the end of the late Paleolithic Age. In other words, the aquatic region has been continuously inhabited by humans for more than a million years. In their accounts between 3000 and 30 BCE, Egyptians, Phoenicians, Greeks, and later Romans had recognized the presence of the Berbers as the earliest known inhabitants of North Africa.[7]

Historians still speculate on the racial ancestry of the Berbers, who were known as "Libyans" by the ancient Greeks but who called themselves the Imazighen (singular Amazigh). Writing in 1600 CE, Arab scholars like Leo Africanus claimed that Imazighen connotes "free people" in the Moroccan parlance or "noble people" in the Tuareg dialect.[8] That the Berbers were well acknowledged by their neighbors on the other sides of the Mediterranean in ancient times is a pointer to the long history of land-borne/water-borne cross-regional interactions between the Africans on the one hand, and the Semites, Europeans, and Arabs on the other. A small number of Phoenicians, a seafaring people from modern Lebanon who spoke one of the Semitic dialects, started arriving in North Africa in about 1200 BCE. By 814 BCE they had effectively colonized a prosperous commercial nerve center called Carthage or "New City" (now modern Tunis). The Greeks joined the Phoenicians (also called Carthaginians) in North Africa, seizing Egypt as a colony in 332 BCE. In the following centuries, both powers dominated the entire Mediterranean Basin. Their influence resonated beyond Carthage and Egypt, and across the Maghrib.

When the Romans became the next global power, they first ended Phoenician influence in North Africa in 146 BCE after a series of battles known as the Punic Wars. A century later, the Romans dislodged the Greeks from Egypt in 30 BCE. In 429 CE, the Vandals (a Germanic group) overthrew the Romans, assuming control of North Africa until Muslim Arabs arrived about two centuries later. These diverse groups of people that traversed the region at different historical periods routinely exchanged material and ideological cultural items with the indigenous people. Through this manner of exchange, they left their cultural prints on the development of Berber identity in particular and North African history in general.

The transformations that defined modern North Africa assumed a more radical dimension from the late seventh century CE when the jihadists from the Arabian Peninsula invaded the region. Over time, the invaders, filled with a new religion called Islam, subdued the Berbers through combinations of warfare, diplomacy, and religious and prestige persuasions. The Berber land covers the entire Maghrib (from the westernmost point in Morocco to the Niger River to the Siwa Oasis of western Egypt to the east). The Berber population today is currently estimated at thirty to forty million and they are mostly found in the modern countries of Western Sahara, Morocco, Algeria, Mauritania, Tunisia, and Libya. The Berber people speak different dialects belonging to the Afro-Asiatic (or Afro-Mediterranean) language family, which some linguists believe "was spoken at least 15,000 years ago in northeastern Africa, probably by ancestral Afro-Mediterranean peoples."[9] In the past, most of these sublanguage groups primarily found in Morocco and Algeria were independent and self-sufficient. The ideology of Pan-Islamism would change the ethnic and cultural landscape as the Arabs introduced new religious and commercial impetuses. While underscoring the changes that resulted to African culture following the encounter with the Arabs, African agency is more important in connection with masks and masquerade plays.

The Berbers (Amazigh/Imazighen) and the Arab Factor

Like all imperial religions, Islam frowns at any alien traditions and cultural practices that contradict its five core pillars: (1) *Shahadah*, a profession of the belief that Allah is the one and only God and Muhammad was his last messenger; (2) *Salat*, praying five times a day; (3) *Zaqat*, almsgiving; (4) *Sawm*, abstinence from sex, food, and water from sunrise to sunset during the month of Ramadan, which comes in the ninth month in the lunar calendar year; and (5) the *Hajj*, making a pilgrimage to the Holy Land in Mecca (located in Saudi Arabia) at least once in one's lifetime.[10] Among these core principles of Islam, the one that is most critical to the belief system remains Shahadah, profession of the belief that Allah is the one and only God, and Muhammad was his last messenger. Muslim purists, therefore, usually found it extremely vexing and intolerable for any individual or agent of a counterideology or cultural practices like the masquerade tradition to suggest the existence of other gods than Allah. Related to this is the belief in the existence of spirits or deities.[11] In the field of arts and artistic production and representations, Islam strongly abhors any artwork or mode of theatrical plays imaging God (Allah), or his Holy Prophet Mohammed. Additionally, the Islamic belief system also censors images created in the likeness of man or woman, including abstractions.

Given that masking and masquerade traditions are rooted in all that Islam forbids—belief in the multiplicity of gods, existence and veneration of ancestors, representation of these deities in artistic forms and theatrical performances— the ground was prepared for a perfect storm. Thus, following the arrival of Arabs in the seventh century, part of the conversion was the blighting of every semblance of traditional practices that contradict Islam's foremost belief—no God but Allah. This is the story of North Africa and some parts of East and West Africa where the Islamic religion has taken firm root.

But cultures hardly go into complete extinction; instead, they mutate into new species over time. Colin A. Palmer has underscored this point in his study of the African Diaspora in Mexico in the early colonial era. According to Palmer, primary cultures, as opposed to secondary cultures, die slowly because they are at the core of the people's existence.[12] Thanks to the anthropological works of Edvard Westermarck, who studied the Berber indigenous culture in the late nineteenth century, we know that the Berbers had a rich tradition of masks and masquerade dances that survived the Muslim onslaught. In other words, over a millennium following the Arab conquest of North Africa, the autochthonous Berbers have somehow retained some of their indigenous African traditional roots. We may be reminded that several millennia prior to the trans-Saharan trade exchanges, the Sahara area was more conducive for human habitation with lush fauna and savannah grassland. The environment and climate enabled people in the north and south of the region to engage in constant trade and cultural relationships. The most populous of the several Berber subgroups who were in a closer relationship with the peoples of western Sudan included the Ruffians, Chleuhs, Jebala, and the Soussi of Morocco; the Chaoui, Mozabite, and Kabyle of Algeria; and the Tuareg and Zenata found in several parts of the Maghrib.

Within the local community, the Berber derives primary social identity from membership in specific linguistic dialects such as the Tarifit spoken near Al Hocema; the Tachelhi predominant in the southwestern region near Agadir, northeast of Marrakech and east of the Draa Valley; and Tamazight spoken in the Central Atlas region. Before the arrival of the Arab Muslims in the seventh century, the various Berber dialects were the dominant languages spoken across the entire Maghrib.

Languages are the vehicles of culture. The various Berber tongues are now mostly consigned to the mountainous and arid countryside since Arabic, English, and French have occupied the center stage as international languages. Without a well-developed writing culture until orthography was developed from the Phoenician, Berber identity could be easily lost because of lack of the cohesion a written vernacular can help create. This perhaps explains why today ethnic and cultural boundaries are becoming less salient with centuries of miscegenation and the predominance of Arabic as the language of power and identity. Berber or Arab identity has rather become more of a reflection of personal behavior than of membership in a distinct and delimited social unit.

According to Westermarck, among the Berbers of the Rif Valley, "Masquerades or carnivals take place on various occasions with Muhammadan [Islamic or Muslim] feasts, but sometimes at certain periods of the solar year. We have previously noticed those held at ăsūra. Others are reported to occur in a few districts at the mūlūd and in the Rif, at the Little Feasts."[13] With this, what immediately comes to mind is the survival of the indigenous art forms and practices connected with the pre-Islamic religious beliefs and cosmology. This is despite centuries of Islamization in the region. More important, we see that the Berbers have successfully adapted these forms of African-style carnivals into Islamic holy days and observances. It was not only the Berbers of Morocco who have held on to their masquerade dances. Westermarck further noted that similar masquerade carnivals are held in Algeria. "Masquerading at New Year's tide (Old Style) at two places in Algeria. Carnivals are known to be held between the end of February and middle of March. And among the At Zīhri (Zkăra) in the neighborhood of Ujda, there is said to be a little masquerade, called sūna, about the middle of May, the persons taking part in it representing a Jew, his wife 'Azzuna, and a Christian."[14] A number of ideas are revealed from Westermarck's report—among them the Africanization or rather Berberization of the North African brand of Islam. It is also striking that the Berbers used the masquerade forum to satirize Jews and Christians in North Africa, as the precolonial Igbos in southeastern Nigeria used occasions of masquerading to satirize social miscreants. In the New World, African performers used African-styled Christmas and New Year masquerade parades to ridicule White planters, slave owners, and administrators in the Americas.[15]

As in societies in other regions of the world, North African cross-cultural interaction, among other things, also involved trade. The nature and volume of any trading relations are usually structured by the utility of goods produced locally, the tastes of the peoples involved, the available modes of transportation, the nature of governments that regulate the trade, and their capacity to provide security for lives and properties. These tangibles also determined the origins, scope, and growth of the trans-Saharan trade exchanges between North and West Africans. Medieval-era trade moved the frontiers of Islam deep into the western Sudan. By the eleventh century, it was no longer only Muslim Berber merchants who regularly made the journey to West Africa. Muslim Arab merchants started to navigate their ways through the desert dunes and into the Sahelian parts of West Africa—that is, the area of grassland south of the Sahara. As merchants, scholars, artists, architects, and ordinary travelers, the visitors from the north talked about Prophet Muhammad and Islam to those open enough to listen. Among the initial audience were the Muslims' local business associates, often city dwellers. Later on, ordinary people would be exposed to the beacons of the new faith, and over time such contacts began to create some converts. The results manifested in the blending of local and Muslim practices as revealed in local politics, religion, family traditions, medicine, language, architecture, art, music, and so on. The emergent hybrid of cultures blurred lines of distinction between what was classified as "indigenous" or "alien." With dilutions from Arabs, Berbers, Soninke, Mande, and Fulani, the peoples of western Sudan took advantage of innovations such as the Arabic scripts originally from India, to connect business and cultural linkages with the outside world. The trading world that was created brought West Africa, North Africa, the Middle East, and the Indian Ocean in a commercial commonwealth.

As the coastal contours of European colonial influence in Africa reveal, the countryside is often shielded from massive or wholesale alien enculturation. The same dynamics were true for North Africa in the initial period of the Arab conquest. While some of the Berbers who encountered the Arabs had quickly joined forces with them against Spain, others, particularly those in the countryside, would likely not have seen an Arab, let alone speak Arabic. They did not easily give up their time-honored modes of worship. Even Egypt, which was a less complex entity to deal with and which capitulated to the Arabs early on, did not fully adhere to the tenets of the new faith until a couple of centuries later.

Actually, Berber encounters with the Arab army were not anything entirely different from previous waves of foreign adventurers and occupiers going back to the ninth century BCE—namely, the Phoenicians, Greeks, Romans, Vandals, and Byzantine (Eastern Roman Empire) forces. The Arab presence was certainly another chapter in the long history of invasions from outside.

For another reason, the new Muslim overlords in North Africa seemed satisfied with the exercise of political control without forcing the religious conversion project too far. As was later the policy of the Ottoman rulers in most of their conquered territories including the Balkans, insistence on strict religious compliance for the conquered people would translate to loss of revenues accruable from *jizya*—a poll tax paid only by non-Muslims. What this tells us is that lasting Islamic influence in Africa or elsewhere did not necessarily come with military coercion despite the spates of jihads that shocked the peace of West Africa at the beginning of the nineteenth century. Rather, Islamic practices gradually permeated into the fabric of African societies over the course of many generations by way of prestige suggestions. Among the actors behind this transformation were the first Berber Muslim traders who frequented the trading centers; clerics who sought peaceful conversion by extolling the divine works of Prophet Muhammad and his message to mankind; and scholars whose erudite knowledge of the Quran (Koran), the Holy Book of Islam, placed them in a position of influence among the faithful. As evident in both West Africa and the Swahili coast of East Africa, these players came first through the trade routes. After they had successfully carved out a niche in the trading terminuses and cities, their next target became penetrating the countryside, the last bastion of African life.

As a matter of tradition, Muslim merchants were accorded hospitality in the western Sudan—as was extended to the early European visitors to the region. The degree of hospitality provided by the Soninke, Mande, Doula, Wolof, Tukulor, and other Sahelian groups was even more generous.[16] Because it was considered an act of cowardice, it was not in the habit of Africans to attack defenseless strangers or visitors in their midst. Rather, to this day strangers are often welcomed with a child-like embrace. The guest is offered a seat, water to quench his thirst, and a bath to soothe his journey-trodden body. Soon afterward the family head or an elder invites the stranger to the table. Salutations are offered with cheerful faces, and after meals, proverbs, travel tales, legends, and riddles are used to enliven the occasion until the stranger is ready to retire to bed. On the one hand, traditional hospitality proved more crucial at first when the Muslims arrived in the western Sudan in their small numbers. On the other hand, these Muslim merchants, who strived to lead by a good example, realized early that their survival and protection among their host societies was invariably dependent on their good manners and orderly business conduct. Such a realization, more than anything else, guaranteed the survival of the visitors, their extended families, and close business associates.

Additionally, the Islamic ethos of social egalitarianism, simplicity, and adaptability as implied in the Quran made the merchants from the north easily approachable to the poor and the marginalized. In principle, matters of race, geography, ethnicity, and language did not prejudice social interaction among Muslims. Yet, the use of non-Muslims as slaves was allowed—a contradiction to the principle of moral piety and norms of egalitarianism. The victims of the Arab slave trade were taken from the western Sudan to different destinations in North Africa, Southern Arabia, Persia (modern Iran), India, and China. In these places, they were often employed as concubines, entertainers, personal guards, artisans, and domestic servants. The greater majority of slaves sold to the Arab world were women.

But Africans who accepted Islam tended to gravitate toward syncretism—a mixture of the alien faith with indigenous practices or, even more so, Africanization of the new faith. For example, Africans saw a similarity between concepts of one God in Islam and Supreme God in the indigenous religion. Over time, however, reformers would demand strict compliance with Islamic practices. Their goal was to stamp out what they considered syncretism, polytheism, and spiritual corruption. Such dogmatic rules periodically led to violent ethnic/ideological conflicts. As the Muslims gradually won the attention of the indigenous population, they extended existing networks, and Islam increasingly became a permanent part of the life of the ordinary people, even as state builders attempted to build new spheres of authority or consolidate existing ones.

The Islamic Impact

Much of our residual knowledge of premodern Africa is derived from archeological remains (e.g., buildings, sculpture, tapestry, clothing, jewelry), and discernible ideas preserved in forms of music, song, dance, cuisine, and dressing habits. The surviving written accounts of the period were mostly recorded by Muslims—whether as court officials, travelers, or chroniclers like Abu Ubaydallah Al Bakri of Spain; Ibn Battuta of Morocco; Mahmud al-Kati, a chronicler of late fifteenth-century West Africa; and Ibn Khaldūn of Tunis. In fact, the various works of Ibn Battuta (1304–1368) and Ibn Khaldūn (1332–1406) provide historians with eyewitness accounts of life in the West African kingdom of Mali.[17] Even with their biases, these books are important because they offer the reader very rare insights on West African society at a time when Islam was a strong cementing force binding much of the Eastern Hemisphere.

Building on local traditions, such as surviving indigenous oral histories, Africans enhanced Arab Muslim folktales, just as the visitors enriched indigenous culture with alien practices. Although this is not often emphasized, it was during the period of the trans-Saharan trade that elements of African music and dance genres took root among the Berbers. For example, the music and dance of the Gnawas (or Gnaouas) of the Great Atlas region is a combination of Black African and Arab traditions. It is a typical trance music employed by members of the Sufi brotherhood to attain mystical ecstasy. Members of the group who claim descent from Sidi Bilal, the ex-slave from Ethiopia who became a highly respected caller to prayers (*muezzin*) in Islam, comprise master musicians, drummers, eye-catching women, mediums, and other participants who long ago established their historical home in Marrakech and other places in the Sahara regions. The West African slaves who arrived in North Africa in the sixteenth century brought with them this genre of music; hence there are several components of Senegalese, Guinean, and Malian traditions in the lyrics. Such instruments like the lute (Arabic *qsbah*) with a long neck of African origin called *gimbri*, double iron cymbals (*qaraqab*), and a double-headed cylindrical drum (*tbel* or *ganga*) played with curved sticks are common instruments of the Gnawa music. Members of the brotherhood observe a nocturnal rite of a ceremonious possession (*deiceba*), during which participants practice the dances of possession and trance called *derdeba*.[18]

Other visible forms of innovations ranged from architecture to clothing and dietary habits to Muslim observances absorbed into traditional festivals. Cultural borrowings are a two-way traffic. The African cult of departed ancestors, juju culture, and incantations permeated Muslim traditions of wearing amulets or talismans for protection. For instance, being of descent from Fatima (Muhammad's daughter) and Ali (his son-in-law)—or claiming descent to some other forms of noble ancestry—all became new arenas of identity construction. While most of these claims and counterclaims were often invented, they, however, point to the blurring of cultural lines between the "indigenous" and the "alien." The deep impacts of the Muslims' activities were most visible on the rise and fall of the western Sudanese empires of the medieval era.

From 1590 when Al Mansur and his sect, the Almoravids, attacked the Songhai Empire leading to its eventual collapse in 1591, the problem of syncretism in West African Islam has remained a flashpoint up to the present.[19] Ibn

Battuta noted in the mid-fourteenth century that there was concrete evidence of attempts to stamp out Bozo fishing and hunting rituals involving masks and figurative sculptures.[20] But Al Bakri dismissed outright the Soninke/Mande traditional belief system as "paganism and worship of idols."[21] The legendary medieval Berber Arab traveler Ibn Battuta had a similar view of Mande culture but acknowledged the music and details that often accompanied the official duties of the king of Mali when he stated: "When he [the king of Mali] sits down, they [the people of Mali] beat the drums, blow the bugles and the horns."[22] These are part of the indigenous Mande and Bambara masquerade dance traditions. As Conrad further noted, in Mande traditional society,

> the most important of the traditional religious objects were (and still are) material representations of various gods and spirits. The objects were not worshiped as idols, the way foreign observers have often mistakenly thought. Masks were worn by dancers in musical rituals as a means of communicating with the spirits they represent and to include those spirits in community affairs. Statuettes served the same purpose when they received ritual offerings such as kola nuts, dègè (sweet millet balls or porridge), chickens, and other kinds of food. Many of these religious objects, including masks and statuettes, whether ugly or beautiful, are regarded as fine works of art and can be found in important museums in Europe and the United States. Al-Bakri said only the priests were allowed to enter the sacred.[23]

Recent studies on the Islamized Mande of northeast Cote d'Ivoire and west-central Ghana by Rene A. Bravmann show that from these early encounters, the arts have been neglected following the quest to deepen the Islamic religion in West Africa. However, those aspects of masking that are used to combat witchcraft have persisted because the locals consider it more efficacious than Islam in dealing with those problems.[24] In his *The Great Empires of the Past*, David C. Conrad stated: "Some of the religious objects of the Soninke [a Mande group] traditional religion do look intimidating and dangerous because they were meant to cause fear and respect when seen." Then Conrad adds: "But there are also many masks and small statues of wood, terracotta (clay), and materials that are beautiful."[25] It is out of this sociopolitical milieu in which indigenous practices were engaged with the Muslim religion that certain aspects of the masquerade, music, and dance traditions of the Mande and other groups transformed. As fully treated in the preceding chapter, the emergent brands of Mande and other African ethnic cultures migrated with the enslaved Africans to the

New World destinations during the era of transatlantic slavery. The implication is that the enslaved people modeling these cultural traits overseas were not likely to replicate the exact indigenous pre-Islamic African prototypes. The African culture we refer to was not and had not been static. It was already changing and absorbing alien influences prior to the transatlantic slave trade.

Colonialism, Christianity, and African Masks and Masquerades

Colonialism, which accompanied Christian evangelical missions to Africa and the Americas, was the biggest force that unmasked the secrecy with which the masquerade cults operate. Nwando Achebe's biography of Ahebi Ugbabe, the prostitute turned female king of colonial Nigeria, provides the most pugnacious devaluation of the masquerade tradition in the then Enugu area of Igboland. Empowered by the colonial system, Ahebi founded her own "Ekpe Ahebi Masquerade" as a rival institution, to the outrage of the Enugu community. This development was a stark defilement of the age-honored tradition that excluded women from membership in masquerade cults.[26] Many instances of other patterns of devaluation are documented in the African colonial literature.[27] Perhaps the best known of the literary accounts remains Chinua Achebe's description of the Egwugwu and Ọtákágu masquerades of Nnewi, and Imo, which fought with the Christian converts in colonial Igboland.[28] The incident involved one Enoch, a fanatical new convert, who unmasked an Egwugwu masquerade (seen as an ancestral spirit) in public. By this act of sacrilege, "Enoch had killed an ancestral spirit and the Umuofia [village] was thrown into confusion." Consequently, the act of abomination attracted the gathering of other masquerades from far and near. "On the next day, all the masked *egwugwu* of Umuofia assembled in the market-place. They came from all the quarters of the clan and even from the neighboring villages. The dreaded Ọtákágu came from Imo, and Èkwénsu, dangling a white cock, arrived from Uli. It was a terrible gathering."[29] Among other things, it should be noted that it was a very serious occasion and involved the presence of the spirit-regarding masquerades in contestation of power and authority with a rival ideology, as represented by the Church and the new African Christian converts. One realizes that in matters like this when the spirit-regarding masquerades take center stage, what transpires is not for entertainment, and neither women nor children were involved.

But much of the masquerade carnivals encountered in the African Diaspora diverged from this course for reasons already outlined, chief among them the structure of power in the Americas. Although the enslaved Africans strongly objected to their conditions of servitude, many of them accepted Christianity (sometimes reluctantly), the religion of their owners, even when most times this acceptance was superficial. As Robert Hinton, a former slave from Raleigh, North Carolina, recalled: "We had prayer meetin' in our houses when we got ready, but dere were no churches for niggers on de plantation. We had dances and other socials durin' Christmas times. Dey give us de Christmas holidays."[30] This fact reminds us of the origins of the popular Afro-Cuban "Day of the Kings" festival, which Fernando Ortiz identifies with the early days of slavery following the arrival of slaves from Old Calabar, which goes back in time to 1573 and the later abolition movement. According to Ortiz: "In 1573, the Havana City Council or *Cabildo* . . . ordered all emancipated Negroes to aid in the Corpus Christi procession with their 'inventions and games,' as tailors, carpenters, cobblers, blacksmiths and caulkers. . . . Up until the law of abolition of slavery, that is, until 1880, there was one day, January 6 of each year, when both the free and the slave Afro-Cuban Negroes celebrated their festival." This celebration was soon made part of the Catholic Church festivities of "Epiphany, the Adoration of the Three Magi, commonly called Dia de Reyes, 'Day of the Kings.'"[31]

In the Caribbean, the enslaved people's Christmas revels were described as "Bacchanalia" or "Saturnalia." The Saturnalia we might recall was originally an ancient Roman agricultural festival that was held during the month of December. During its limited duration, it was characterized by a symbolic reversal of power relations, whereby the meek appeared mighty and the mighty appeared meek. Joseph Tuckerman writing in 1837 described the Christmas and New Year's activities of Saint Croix, Virgin Islands, as a "complete Saturnalia." He states: "The houses of the proprietors of slaves are thrown open and long processions of slaves decked in silks and in showy white muslins, and with banners and music, enter at will the habitations to which they determine to go, obtain undisputed possession, are served with cakes and wine by their owners, or by others upon whom they may call, and dance till they may be disposed to depart."[32] In *Black Saturnalia*, Robert Dirks notes: "Christmas meant setting aside the very premise of inequality upon which relations normally rested and replacing it with a cordial and sportive, if at times somewhat tense, egalitarianism."[33] He further states, "If those who ran the estates were not fully committed to the spirit of the bacchanal, at least they were aware of having to deal with an 'overheated boiler' and were prepared to bend every effort toward making sure it did not explode."[34]

The African-themed American masquerades embraced both genders. Indeed, what is not often asserted in the Africa-focused literature is that the encounter between colonialism and unmasking of African masquerades did not begin on

the African continent; it started in the African Diaspora. The description of
the Jonkunnu mask by planter-historian Edward Long in 1774 proves the point:

> In the towns, during the Christmas holidays, they have several tall or ro-
> bust fellows, dressed up in grotesque habits, and a pair of ox-horns on their
> head, sprouting from the top of a horrid sort of visor, or mask, which about
> the mouth is rendered very terrific with large boar tusks. The masquerader,
> carrying a wooden sword in his hand, is followed with a numerous crowd of
> drunken women, who refresh him frequently with a cup of aniseed-water,
> whilst he dances at every door, bellowing out John Connu.[35]

This picturesque description allows one to immediately see that right from
its reinvention in the New World, African masquerades were open to corruption. In fact, the structure of power in the New World slaveholding societies
ensured that the African slaves were not going to have it their way. While certain genres of masquerades in Africa—the human-regarding type—were for
entertainment and could allow for women and children's participation (not as
masquerade dancer but) as onlookers, the spirit-regarding kind was never open
to well-behaved ordinary men, women, and children, no less for "a crowd of
drunken women." Describing the Bamboula over half a century later, William
Young observed that the dancers were "dressed in the highest beauism, with
muslin frills, high capes, and white hats." The women wore "handkerchiefs
folded tastefully about their heads and gold ear-rings and necklaces." In due
course, "about a dozen girls, began a curious and most lascivious dance, with
much grace as well as action; of the last plenty in truth."[36] Again we see a pattern
of corruption that was evolving in the African Diaspora in terms of costuming,
participation, purpose, power, and political meaning.

In another account, William Young informs us that rather than being "dressed
down" and disguised in rough attire like an animal masquerade, dancers enhanced themselves and wanted to be seen. The gombay dancers' costumes show
that they were "dressed up" and adopting metropolitan and mainstream styles:

> They were all dressed in their best; some of the men in long-tailed coats,
> one of the gombayers in old regimentals; the women in muslins and cam-
> brics with colored handkerchiefs tastefully disposed round their heads, and
> ear-rings, necklaces, and bracelets of all sorts in profusion. The entertain-
> ment was kept up until nine or ten o'clock in the evening, and during the
> time they were regaled with punch and santa in abundance; they came
> occasionally and asked for porter and wine.[37]

Henry Breen's 1844 account of a Bamboula dance in Saint Lucia is similar to those of William Young and others. The performers' extravagant dresses were once again noted. The male dress is comparable to "that commonly worn by gentlemen in England or France." The females wore a striped skirt of silk or satin, and an "embroidered bodice trimmed with gold and silver tinsel." The headdress is comprised of a "madras handkerchief, erected in a pyramid or a castle." Gold earrings are worn and there is similarly a profusion of necklaces, bracelets, and bouquets.[38] Comparatively, the attire and order described above do not appear to be similar to the order and idioms of masquerade processions obtained in Africa at this period, but the occasion was in a distant land and under colonial America.

Additionally, slavery that preceded colonial rule in Africa brought about a moment of extensive social reordering on both sides of the Atlantic. It might be recalled that not all the Igbo slaves that were captured from the Bight of Biafra hinterlands embarked on the journey across the Middle Passage. Many of them ended up in the coastal towns of Calabar, Bonny, Kálábári, and so on. Their presence deeply altered sociopolitical institutions and preexisting mores. In the delta, especially among the Degema, Bonny, Ubáni, Ndọki, Diobu, Ẹfik, and Ibibio societies, the Igbo language had started to infiltrate popular vocabularies as early as the fifteenth century and even supplanted the indigenous languages in some places like Bonny and Creek Town in Old Calabar. By the mid-nineteenth century, Elizabeth Isichei observes, many Ijọ families had Igbo blood in their veins, and in the Degema (New Calabar) area, many of them spoke Igbo as a second language: "In Bonny, Ubani was almost replaced by Igbo, and most foreign observers assumed the state was Igbo in origin."[39] In Andoni, Ogoni, and Bonny, in the nineteenth and early twentieth centuries, the Igbo language served as a lingua franca.[40]

The impact of these changes was felt on the indigenous Ékpè secret and masquerade society in the nineteenth century postabolition period. While the Ékpè remained the elitist club with some of the accouterments of its old powers intact, the big difference was that wealthy people of slave descent were now allowed to buy a membership in the fraternity. Some of the members achieved success through the new avenues and opportunities opened by the presence of the Europeans—trade, a cash economy, mission schools, and new ideas. Similar changes occurred with the Ékpè institution among the Arọ people.[41] By and large, the transformations of the nineteenth century in Calabar ensured that the Ékpè could no longer exercise acts of oppression without the knowledge of the new members of slave descent who had, by the 1840s, become some of the wealthiest elements in society.[42]

The Ijǫ society adopted a more pragmatic approach in response to social changes. Through the mask-dancing secret society Ekine or Sekiápu (also known as Opomá in Bonny), the Kálábári cultural elite attempted to preserve elements of their culture while also incorporating some new developments. As an agency of acculturation, Ekine masquerades, believed to be representing the water spirits (*owu*), demanded members "to speak Kalabari language or be killed."[43] In Bonny, Nembe, and Igbáni the strangers were allowed freedom of language. In Kálábári, a "recruit to the community who became a member of the Ekine and publicly performed in its dances was a socially accepted individual." Also, the Koronogbo or "the association of the strong," a militant vigilante group, while patrolling the streets at night also derided and penalized the poorly acculturated. As Robin Horton asserts, the adoption of such an aggressive culture-consciousness was aimed to avoid being overwhelmed by the culture brought to it by its slaves.[44]

However, Kálábári retained a prominent place for the Igbo in its value system embodied in the notion of the aristocratic ideal. For Kálábári the notion of nobility implied notions of "youthfulness" and "flamboyance" (*ásá*), preparedness, and dignity (*bu bimi*).[45] It is in these expectations that the Igbo was despised and admired at the same time.

Bonny's exclusionist response to the revolutionary developments of the nineteenth century amounted to a failure. The reasons for this are not far-fetched. Besides its predominant Igbo population, the greater part of the wealth of Bonny remained in the hands of its people of slave origin. This situation demanded a new social and political order, which the reactionary elite of freemen failed to consider. As the wealth of members of the royal house diminished, so did their authority. Early on, Opubu the Great (r. 1792–1830) of Bonny had led his kingdom to attain the apogee of its greatness. His death in 1830 brought Madu, one of his most trusted Igbo slaves, to power as regent. The king's son William Dappa Pepple was still a minor then. Madu's own son, Alali, succeeded him as regent at his death in 1833. Finally, Dappa Pepple, son of Opubu the Great, came of age and assumed kingship in 1835.[46] The new king resented the prominent position occupied by individuals of slave ancestry and was anxious to secure full powers for himself. Thus, between 1853 and 1866 when Dappa Pepple died, there were a series of conflicts involving the new king, the former members of his father's house, and their European counterparts.[47]

With the eventual introduction of colonial administration proper in 1900 came Christianity, Western education, a cash economy, modern cities and urban lifestyles, improved communication systems and other infrastructures; African/

Igbo indigenous institutions were exposed to unavoidable but very complex changes that changed the grand pattern of the narrative.[48] As the Igbo say, "The progress of human societies follows a very diverse pattern and pace" (*Uwá ánághị ágá otu mgbá ná ihu*). While the Igbo communities lying within the boundaries of the major colonial townships like Onitsha, Umuahia, Enugu, Okigwe, Owerri, Port Harcourt, Aba, and Ábákiliki came under a more extensive European influence, hundreds of other Igbo villages like some parts of Mbano, and Mbáise, Ugbomiri, Mbieri, Arọndizuọgu, among others, hardly came into any direct dealing with White people. In these villages, life continued as in the old days, while the harbingers of sociopolitical and economic changes—schools, native courts, Christianity, social amenities, zinc houses, and others—filtered in slowly but steadily through the urban dwellers who maintained home bases in their African villages. In essence, the lineage-based social clubs, age-grades associations, and secret societies that operated the various masquerade cults continued to serve as important arms of village government as well as agencies of socialization and change.

Even in the communities where the European presence was visible, the Ékpè in Arọchukwu and Bende, and Ọkọnkọ in Ngwá, Uzọákọlị, and Mbáise, retained some of their positions in the village government, albeit in a modified form that now had both the educated and noneducated, and Christians and non-Christians as members. The Ékpè in Arọchukwu, like the Ékpè in Èfik and the Èkpo in Ibibioland, was an exclusive club for those who had made material achievements, and this status was maintained in the colonial era.[49] Conceivably the difference in the colonial era was that individuals achieved success through new avenues and opportunities opened by the European colonial presence. Some of these avenues included educational attainment, colonial service, and success in new business opportunities. Now membership in the Ékpè society comprised lawyers, politicians, teachers, businessmen, prominent native doctors, former slaves who had proved their worth, and other professionals. In essence, the secrecies that marked Ékpè activities in precolonial times were no longer what they used to be. Even colonial administrators and other officials tried to join the secret societies in order to understand its secrecies.

There were numerous reports throughout the colonial period against the Ékpè and other secret and masquerade societies in eastern Nigeria as they wrestled with the colonial authorities over the exercise of executive power and influence. For instance, a report of 1946–1947 over alleged killings by the club members branded the society "executive murderers."[50] Then from 1948 to 1956 there were numerous court cases filed against the Ékpè in what the authorities described as a rising incidence of atrocities against civilians.[51] These arbitrations reflect the incidence of the power struggle between the old ways and the entrance of the new forces of social change ushered in by colonial rule. It was within this context that the new Christian converts challenged the aura of invincibility surrounding the Ékpè and the authority it wielded. In Áfikpo and Unwáná Igbo communities in the Cross River Valley, members of the Ègbélé or Ogo secret societies engaged in periodic violent clashes, which often resulted in the burning of members' homes and buildings belonging to the Church. With each of these incidences, the new converts challenged the authority of the masquerade/secret societies to operate in their midst. Thus, the unmasking of a secret society became a reality as its authority could not rise above those of the colonial powers and their supporters, the new Christian converts.

Also under the colonial order, as the Igbo young men and women moved from their villages in search of new opportunities in the colonial townships, they started re-creating their village patterns of civil society networks, including the masquerade dances, in urban settings. Igbo lineage and improvement unions materialized as one of the several means through which the Igbo tried to adjust to colonial urban life. With the emergence of new elite cadres—teachers, colonial police, interpreters, clerks, catechists, and so on—appeared new forms of nonstate associations, social movements, and voluntary agencies that adapted some preexisting patterns of civil society networks, especially their modes of mobilization.[52] The new developments were witnessed in the form of the popular lineage and village unions that sprouted up in all the major colonial Nigerian cities and townships. G. O. Olusanya has observed that funerals, births, marriages, and title coronations—among others—were some of the most usual occasions for this new kind of "togetherness."[53] During each of these occasions, masquerade dances were performed in line with the community's traditions. The Igbo unions provided avenues for cultural interaction in the anonymous urban environments. Some associations like the Mbieri, Abiribá, Owerri, and Onitsha groups constructed multipurpose halls in the cities where meetings, marriages, births, dances, fun fairs, feasts, deaths, and farewell and reception ceremonies were held. The Igbo State Union leaders proclaimed an "Igbo Day" when activities were held as a day of cultural celebration and jubilation. Each Igbo improvement union or lineage group presented its dance and masquerades at this festival in broad daylight. Individual celebrants were honored with awards for their contributions toward community development. Such cultural programs helped the Igbo maintain their cultural heritage and reduce the pressures of urban life.[54] However, the order and conduct of these masquerade plays and dances grossly diverged from its modus operandi in the village settings. The point here is that once the masquerades left their village soils, they were no longer the mystifying, grotesque ancestral spirits their performers once claimed them to be. Rather than chasing people and taking the laws into their hands as they once did in the villages, the masquerade performers were also aware that they had to maintain civil peace so that the police would not have to jail those who breached the peace in the townships.

Having been raised in small villages, the migrant Igbos found apparent attractions in the unfamiliar urban settings. The distant and diverse city life rather freed the migrants who were mainly young people from the intricate rituals of kinship relations, as well as exposed them to other Africans and non-Africans with alien cultural orientations and ideas.[55] Thus, the need for adjustment to reestablish reciprocal social networks in the face of immense sociopolitical and economic challenges of the new environment brought about the lineage and village organization, and the town unions, which were gradually transformed into formal patriotic and improvement unions, and subsequently into the Igbo State Union and onward to political parties.[56]

Among other things, the associations like the Mbieri Development Union (MDU) founded in Aba in the 1920s and the Owerri Improvement Union founded in Port Harcourt in 1916 served as "a forum for getting to know the people from the same village and clan, and to help the new arrivals in town to secure employment or settle down to business and trading," and their mission was primarily to cater for the welfare of their members.[57] Ideally, membership in these organizations was voluntary, but in truth, those who turned down memberships in their lineage or village associations were considered as unpatriotic. For instance, the Áfikpo Association explicitly informed its members that their "membership shall only be terminated by death, permanent insanity or expulsion."[58]

Throughout the colonial period, the Igbo unions maintained close contact with the home branches. The Áfikpo Union was modeled after the village age-grades association. As Njoku has noted, this adaptation helped reinforce the connection between union branches abroad and at home.[59] Most often, the new elite used their memberships in the age-grades, social clubs, and secret societies for reaching out to their local cultural milieu. Despite the campaign put forth by the Church to wipe out these societies, they held their weight as some influential chiefs and nationalists tried to revitalize them in Igboland.[60] Nevertheless, by the late 1940s most of these societies had lost their old secretive character as men and children freely joined their membership merely as nonsecret "social clubs."[61]

Also, the fraternities continued to serve as forums for political socialization at the local levels.[62] The various lineage and progressive associations maintained a very close relationship with their respective family villages. During important events and festivals such as burials, marriages, new yam festivities, Easter, and Christmas, some of these associations organized trips home. It was so crucial that members participate in such trips that often fines were levied on members who failed to join their members on the journey home.[63]

The overall aim of this extended discussion is to underscore the dynamics that have seen to the unmasking of the African masks and masquerade tradition. By *unmasking* I specifically mean the drastically diminished spiritual undertones and secretive culture that shrouded the institution once widely believed to be a manifestation of the ancestral spirits on a visit to the human world. It has been argued that the unmasking process has been ongoing since medieval times following the arrival of the Arabs in the seventh century. Given Islam's cardinal principle of "no God but Allah," it is predictable that it would not coexist with a counterideology that is centered on polytheism and multiplicity of spirits. However, while the alien religion was undermining the efficacy of masquerades as instruments of sociopolitical control, the indigenous art form and all it stood for mutated into a forum for public entertainment through a process of Islamization.

A similar outcome is the case with the encounter with Christianity and European notions of modernism. From colonial Americas back to the African continent, the ideologies of Christianity and Western education as agencies of socialization together with the entire gamut of Western modernism dealt a devastating blow to the secrecy and rituals of the African masquerade institution and the art form it carries. The truth of the matter, as Bryan D. Palmer pointed out, is that slavery was the child of imperialism. And the euphemism "Dark Continent," with which the Western world branded Africa, in the words of Palmer, "was born in the night of empire's material need."[64] If we briefly revisit Jürgen Habermas's idiom of "the wider modernism project gone badly"[65] along with Fred Dallmayr's treatment of modernity as "a conversation made up of different protagonists or voices and stretching over successive historical periods,"[66] then we may begin to understand that the fight between the "Western" modernity and "African" cultures with regards to the masquerade tradition is not yet over. In September 2015 during a Christ Apostolic Church meeting to "exorcise the devil" in the small town of Epinmi, Akoko, in the southeast area of Ondo State, Nigeria, a group of masquerades invaded the church, beat up the pastor and some members of the congregation, and quoted the Bible to justify their actions.

This was similar to what transpired on August 31, 2015, when a group comprising four masquerades disrupted a church service and also flogged worshippers and the pastor in Akure, Nigeria. More recently, pandemonium was reported in Ikun-Ekiti in Ondo State, Nigeria, where Muslims and masquerades locked horns in a bitter fight. These are just a few examples of the continuing incidence of conflict on the broader modernity project.[67] These attacks are reminiscent of similar incidences of fighting between the Ọkọnkọ masquerade society and the Faith Tabernacle Church in 1950s.[68] The timing of these attacks that left some women and children dead in the entire Áfárá clan (Okwulaga Isiama, and Ohokobe na umuokeyi), and which lasted from 1950–1951 was part of the African cultural nationalist movements that accompanied the anticolonial struggles in Africa. However, the villagers of the Áfárá clan claimed that the Ọkọnkọ was flogging people and forcing them to go into the newly erected Gothic-style building. The building was partly destroyed and some of the victims and their descendants who were on the side of the Church during the conflict are still suffering from the effects today.[69]

In the African Diaspora, the process of unmasking the masquerade was predicated on the structures of power and the sociopolitical milieu inherent in the master-slave relationships, constructed by the White planter/slaveowner elite and the colonial administrators. In the African continent, the divisive factors were Christianity and Western education, which inserted an alien ideology in the hearts and heads of the new African converts, among which the first converts were the slaves, orphans, outcasts, women, and other oppressed groups in the old society. In a different study, this author has argued that through time-honored acts of rituals and values, the elders made the appearance of masks and masquerades accepted as the visitation of the gods and ancestors in physical forms. This belief system and its practices were crucial for social control and harmony. Thus, the attempt by missionaries to superimpose their alien ideology on the indigenous order was simply a direct attack on the social fabric that held the African society together.[70] As Achebe aptly captured it, the new ideology turned heads and hearts in diverse directions: "The white man is very clever. He came quietly with his religion. We were amused at his foolishness and allowed him to stay. Now he has won our brothers, and our clan can no longer act like one. He has put a knife on the things that held us together and we have fallen apart.[71]

What has emerged from the ruins of crisis associated with the African masquerades' encounters with Islam, Christianity, and colonialism on both sides of the Atlantic is a mutated and more secular masquerade carnivals of African and the African Diaspora. In the new order, everyone is a player, a dancer, and

a masker. It is a forum for all, the Christian and non-Christian; the African
and the non-African; for men and women, old and young; and for all those in
search of an escape from the presentment that sanity and order often imposes.
For such people, the fun and special entertainment abundantly provided during
the Caribbean carnivals represents a quality vacation. Expectedly, the symbols
and meaning of masks and masquerades have changed tremendously over time in
response to the changing social locations and memberships of the participants.
In the precolonial era, the peculiar masks and masquerades of Africa served as
a mode of cultural communication for centuries. Today, it is a symbol, a metaphor, of the modern and the ancient; of freedom and bondage; and of cultures
in motion.

At a casual glance, it may appear as if what is left today as vestiges of the
indigenous African masks and masquerades are more sacred and the carnivals
of the diaspora more secular in their modes of exhibition. However, on closer
examination, both cultural art forms have been part of the discourses on the
fundamental issues of religion, power, authority, history, poetry, aesthetics,
dance, and entertainment, and the overall existence of all peoples of African descent. Although Western and other cultures have brought many changes to bear
through migration, colonialism, the infiltration of Christianity, new technology,
and ideas, the masks and masquerades have retained some aspects of their indigenous utility.[72] The performance art forms of Africa have spread beyond the
continent as utilitarian art forms, encountered in interior decoration, advertise-
ments, promotions, and fashions. The aspect of the masquerade tradition that
has been substantially lost in both the African Diaspora and on the continent is
its creative powers and ritual mode for social sanctions and control. As the world
now seems eager to explore and adapt to some of the cultures of "primitive" peoples of Africa, the future holds promise for African masks and Black carnivals
to travel even farther as the most popular world culture.[73]

African masking carnivals will continue to provide recreation and leisure for
the performers as well as the onlookers. The Jamaican Jonkunnu festival has
been popularized with soca music and its intricate dance steps. The free-flowing
expressions and performances of both the Jonkunnu and soca dancers are manifestations of rare literary and performing art forms, which have won them both
wide popularity and condemnation.[74] Similar to the Ojiọnu and Èkpo masquerades of Igbo, Ibibio, and Èfik, soca music today provides revelers with both
vocal and instrumental rhythms to which they respond with intricate dance
steps and acrobatic displays, coupled with dramatizations and floorshows. Some
of the indigenous musical instruments including metal and wooden gongs, skin

drums, flutes, rattles, and sound-pots, have been replaced with modern metal and brass bands, xylophone, and piano. The music generally goes with beautiful rhythm but fast tempo. Sometimes there is a lead instrument that directs the movements. For the onlooker, there is a general consciousness of the aesthetic appearance of the masquerades and of the entire crew. There is a display of bold colors, varied shapes, and graceful but rapid movement. The dancers and other members of the crew try to decorate their bodies and wear colorful things like multicolored feathers, headdresses, and raffia waistbands. As John Nunley and Judith Bettelheim explained, "Feathers on masks in Kongo are medicine . . . whereas casual outsiders in New Orleans, for example, might see only fun and fantasy in the brilliantly plumed costumes of Black Indian groups."[75]

Economically, the Black carnivals have become a popular tourist attraction where they exist. Hill observes that carnival performances generate about $300 million annually in Canada, and the carnivals of Trinidad and Tobago generate 20 to 30 million Pounds Sterling annually from tourists.[76] Uko Akpade has made a curious observation in the way African masks are used, which also applies to the carnivals of the diaspora: "Eating houses, hotels and bars and many public buildings are decorated with masks. The elite houses are not fully furnished without masks on the walls, here and there; there are masks of one type or the other."[77] Masks have become lucrative and decorative objects in Africa and all over the world. Artists are now commissioned to produce extra-large masks mainly for decorative purposes. Such gigantic masks are placed conspicuously in the lobbies of high-class hotels, educational institutions, museums, banks, and concert halls, with some colored electric bulbs (usually red) throwing light out of the eyes and mouths of the masks—thereby elevating the aesthetics of the place. In addition, the various artworks, handicrafts, and designs on textiles or fabrics originating from Africa and the Caribbean have become popular around the world.[78] A lot of metal and other materials for pendants and body attachments used as rattle and tambourine sounds are equally becoming parts of common wardrobes worldwide. In the Caribbean, the fabrics and the attachments are finished in bright colors that radiate a flashy, majestic, and interesting appearance. The raffia appendages, which give African masquerades a spirit-like impression, are mostly left out in the African diaspora masquerade carnivals.

Overall, the facts emerging from this treatment of the dynamic symbols and meanings of African masks and masquerades, and their evolution from a transcendental undertone to a more secular and popular carnival of today, demands a further treatment of religion, music, and dance as intricate components of African art forms and their changes in a global context.

CHAPTER 7

Idioms of Religion, Music, Dance, and African Art Forms

> Musical training is a more potent instrument than any other, because rhythm and harmony find their way into the inward places of the soul, on which they mightily fasten, imparting grace, and making the soul of him who is rightly educated graceful, or of him who is ill-educated ungraceful.
> — Plato, *The Republic*[1]

AT MANY LEVELS, PLATO'S thoughts on music education resonate with this study of African masks and masquerades in translational context. The ancient sage enables us to appreciate music and dance as a theatrical art form intimately associated with African life. Music and dance bring life to religious worship, rites of passage, moments of relaxation, reflection, happiness or celebrations, exertion, and loss or sadness. Without music, which edified the ancestors by heralding the season of spirit-regarding masquerade celebrations and ritual ceremonies, the feature of public theatre that it conjured and that united the performer and the onlooker would be at best perfunctory and boring. Also, music in the African world served and continues to serve as a reservoir of historical knowledge passed down from one generation to another. It is not an exaggeration that music is one of Africa's most important gifts to humanity. About 98 percent of all genres of world music have roots in Africa.[2] It is noteworthy that after the four basic needs of life—air, food, water, and shelter—music comes next.

As a potent tool for socialization, music casts insightful lights on the condition of the human mind. Music and dance, as Plato noted, cultivate the educated and liberated spirit. Because of its appealing power, music may also accentuate the potency of imperialism without the physical and mental pains and mutations that colonialism brings on the colonized.[3] The following words from Plato underscore the point: "Any musical innovation is full of danger to the whole state, and ought to be prohibited . . . when modes of music change,

160

the fundamental laws of the state always change with them."⁴ This tells us that music can disempower the powerful and to empower the powerless. Examples of this dynamic have been witnessed in the United States during the civil rights struggle⁵ and in South Africa during the antiapartheid movements. In his study of music as an instrument of opposition against apartheid, Michael Vershbow notes: "Throughout every stage of the struggle, the 'liberation music' both fueled and united the movement. The song was a communal act of expression that shed light on the injustices of apartheid, therefore playing a major role in the eventual reform of the South African government."⁶

In the African Diaspora during both the colonial and antebellum eras, music and dance provided and has continued to provide a compelling voice to the silenced voices of the subaltern; empowered the enslaved and oppressed Africans, and disquieted the dominant White plantation/slave owners. Aristotle and Plato both acknowledged that music and poetry "formed a prominent education of every well-born" by nurturing the human soul while physical exercises shape the body.⁷ More than anything else, these avowals demonstrate the distinct power of the liberal arts in cultivating the human genius. Aware of the liberty and freedom that comes with liberal arts education, religious fanatics around the world have been prosecuting a war of attrition against cultural landmarks in Egypt, Iraq, Syria, Nigeria, Mali, Afghanistan, India, and other places in order to stifle liberal thoughts and knowledge systems.

Aristotle, Plato's esteemed student, also believed that music has cathartic/purifying or liberating powers. His deep interest in music led to Aristotle's three classes of music—ethical music, the music of action, and passionate or inspirational music. Aristotle concluded that music was to be studied with a view to education; purgation (that is, purification, therapy, or catharsis); and for enjoyment, relaxation, and recreation after exertion—we understand this to also include intellectual engagement. In the Aristotelian model, ethical melodies were to be used for educational purposes and music of action and concerts where other people performed. Aristotle provides a rich flavor of humanism in music when he talks about how it reveals emotions—enthusiasm, fear, pity—which may exist strongly in some souls but influence every human. "Some persons fall into a religious frenzy, whom we see as a result of the sacred melodies—when they have used the melodies that excite the soul to mystic frenzy—restored as though they had found healing and purgation. . . . The melodies of purification give an innocent pleasure to mankind."⁸ The preceding provides a background, a context for a better understanding of the role of music and dance that accompany African and African Diaspora masquerade carnival performances.

Utilities of African Music and Dances

We can use the three models of music delineated by Aristotle, slightly amended, to highlight the utilities of music in the African world where music and dance are intimately associated with almost everything including religion, masquerade plays, and carnivals. It was Olaudah Equiano who in 1789 captured the essence of Igbo/African fascination with music and dance when he noted: "We are almost a nation of dancers, musicians, and poets" in reference to his Igbo people. Equiano goes on to elaborate that every major occasion and event that is a good cause of public joy, public dances are held, which are accompanied by songs and music.[9] The Aristotelian classifications (education, purgation, and enjoyment) are not set in rigid compartments. Rather, they are crosscutting: one genre of music could easily fit in two or more categories. For instance, a colonial report from 1920 on native music and dances noted that the Ákupá, involving little girls from Achállá in Awká Division, "dressed in kilts and castanets on their antlers . . . takes place on the occasion of a big feast, or for the funeral of a girl, just like the male version of the dance was danced at feats and for the funeral of a young boy."[10] This means that one music genre could fit into multiple purposes. The classificatory models are therefore used only to impose some measure of order in a field of inquiry that is extensively diversified and difficult to categorize.

The central argument is that music and dance constitute legitimate spheres of intellectual production. Ichie Ezikeojiaku has underscored the need to collect, document, classify, and analyze texts, particularly of Igbo oral poetry.[11] They mirror the totality of African episteme or what Lewis Gordon has identified as "the notion of ontological blackness."[12] Victor Anderson explains the concept of "ontological blackness" to connote the collapse of Black identity into an essentialized being, whereby Black existence is foreclosed by narratives of necessity, homogeneity, and totalization.[13] The elder who legitimized the masquerade or other time-honored traditions, the artist who carved the mask, the designer who costumed the masquerade, the chief priest who infused the art object with sacred powers, the singer and instrumentalist who composed the songs, rhythms, riddles, incantation, and poems for the festivities under observance, and the dancer whose body responds to the rhythms of the occasion—all must be understood as producers of *texts*. Their studied philosophical ideas deserve more than casual attention; a more insightful interpretation is necessary in order to appreciate the unique wisdom and value constructs packaged in the idioms of music and dance that accompany every mask and masquerade celebration. This highlights an apparent affinity to the Foucauldian concept of poststructuralism in which orders of knowledge are diverse and manifest in metanarrative (a post-modernist literary theory) context across different ages.[14] Here, some examples of songs, incantations, and poetics of Ékpè, Okoroshá, Ojiǫnu, Èkpo, and Ágábá are interpreted as part of the corpus of Africa's heritage of intellectual expressions also encountered in other genres of words of wisdom, puzzles, poetries, proverbs, histories, songs, stories, and folklore.

Education/Intellectual Endeavors

Among the genres of African music related to education or socialization of the young are those linked with historical preservation. In precolonial times, the contents of African history were primarily geared toward teaching laws, customs, values, and political institutions of the society. Education is broadly conceived in the context of this study to include equipping the learner with skills and values for everyday living—that is, to function as a useful citizen of his or her community. The exploits of indigenous professional historians or bards known as griots (*jeli* or *jali*) in Mande/Malinke society have been well documented in West African history.[15] With flutes, balafon, drums, lutes, kora, and their trained voices, the Mande *jeli* of modern Senegal, Guinea, Mali, and Gambia recounted and edified the exploits of powerful rulers and patrons. The Sundiata Epic (1217–1255 CE) remains one of their most recognizable intellectual landmarks in the medieval period.[16] The griots and the music that often accompanied their trade, as a genre of sociohistorical construct, "became all the more profoundly ideological" when Sékou Touré, the first postcolonial president of Guinea, "called for the creation of Fodéba Keita's Ballets Africains," a singing and dancing troupe that came to represent the face of Guinean nationalism in 1958.[17]

In his study of the griots, Nick Nesbitt noted that the "very existence of an independent caste of jeli as musician-poet-historians was itself dependent upon a fundamental partitioning of Mande society." According to Nesbitt, the Mande caste system that evolved "allowed for the appearance and reproduction of fundamentally conservative bards who could devote their entire existence to the tour de force of musical, poetic, and mnemonic expression that is the Sundiata Epic."[18] But Thomas Hale and others have strongly disputed this idea of social stratification that depicts the *jeli* as a special caste as nothing but "a destruction of social structure in the region."[19] Although more salient in centralized societies, social stratification has been a common order in most societies—with or without centralized authority systems. Therefore, Mande society is no exception.

Its endogamous practices structured a parasitical relationship between the free-born nobles (Horonnu) and the Nyamakalalu artisan class (including the jeli) who were at the service of the kings and nobles.[20] Today, the jeli, like other classes of professionals and intellectuals—poets, musicians, artists, teachers, and writers—have established an outlet in the global market where they have found a more appreciative and broader audience for their talents. Hitherto, the hierarchical structure of the indigenous Mande society, like its traditional military culture, "has repeatedly threatened to eclipse the imaginative, utopian quality of Mande musical expression."[21] In folktales or storytelling brands, Africans indulged in music to entertain and rehearse the ups and downs that characterize everyday living in all regions of the world. Depending on your brand of music, the implicit philosophical imports of the rhythms always serve to relax the soul and gladden the heart; remind the audience about the values of good moral, civilized attitudes and behaviors; and open the eyes of the people to the issues confronting them in this world.[22]

Like the griots, as a tradition, African musicians promoted social values, laws, and etiquette in songs. Music and dance serve as mnemonic devices; they teach, test, and store information; relay history and local news; instill pride and solidarity; provide a platform for thoughtful and innovative ideas, and critique local action and personages. As Charles O. Aluede observes, "Music is one of the fine arts which is concerned with the combination of sounds with a view of beauty, of form and the expression of thought or feeling."[23]

Singing and dancing go together, and not many songs are performed in a sedentary position. Under colonial rule, singing and dancing, especially when they involved a masquerade procession or women's protests, was approached by the colonial authorities with utmost caution. This is because they were not often sure about the hidden motivations or cause of such musical activities. Traditionally, during performances, singers often appropriate exclusive rights for social commentary. In his study of the musical traditions of Igede women of Idoma, Benue state, Nigeria, Ode Ogede observed that the spoken words and dancing histories speak to social ills without fear. Traditionally, the Igede or Ọkékwé dance was "performed at the funeral of big title men [sic]. Only those who have killed anybody on pre-government [precolonial] days may dance it. The drums are made with human hide . . . and the dance is performed around this drum."[24] From this colonial report, the fact emerges that the women adapted and modified the original men's dance to serve a new function. The women could reward those individuals who support the society with praises and tongue-lash social miscreants in the same breath.[25]

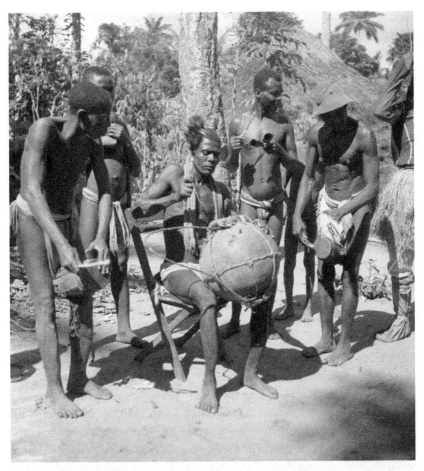

FIGURE 7.1. Band playing for Mmáu masquerade, Amuda Village, Isu Ochi.
This image is copyright. Reproduced by permission of University of Cambridge
Museum of Archaeology & Anthropology (N.13242.GIJ)

The Igede example is not in any way unique to West Africa; instead, public
shaming in songs is common in societies that tolerated freedom of speech in
songs and artistic performances as a sphere of the liberal arts forms. Among the
twenty villages that make up Mbieri town, the annual Nkwá Love, a coed singing and dancing group, remains the classic forum for calling out and shaming
those who indulge in serious antisocial behaviors. The group performs songs
primarily composed for ugly or outrageous incidents that occurred throughout
the year, with a view to moderate those unpleasant human behaviors that may

threaten the peace of the land.[26] What is unique about the Achi community's Nkwá Love dance is that members who flouted the laws of the land during the year are not spared the vicissitude of public shaming. In 1988 for instance, one of the female officials and "chief dancer" of the group was at the center of a marriage scandal. The issue involved a relationship with a well-known criminal in the community from one of the kindreds with which members of the offending woman's own kindred were not supposed to have conjugal relations. Therefore, the relationship that provoked an outcry was not only an incestuous taboo but also an act of defiance to age-honored tradition. Additionally, the dubious lifestyle of the man at the center of the story made the entire episode more scandalous. During a primetime performance, the talking drums, iron gongs, bells, flutes, and poetic voices addressed the scandal in a manner the onlookers had never seen before. Perhaps a fascinating part of the performance of the day was the gleeful manner with which the chief dancer herself, Mrs. Ákụgbọ Oguzié, responded gracefully to the occasion. As she gyrated to the beats of the drums and flutes, the appreciative audience roared and clapped.[27] Throughout the Christmas and New Year festivities, every tongue repeated the rhythm at the marketplaces, dinner tables, village squares, and moonlight times. Not many individuals would have survived this tradition of public satire; the risk of being ridiculed at the village square has been a potent means of compelling conformity to established social norms in Africa.

In the Americas, enslaved Africans tried to reenact a similar form of musical culture in their host societies. In the United States, the Caribbean, and other places, the annual Christmas festivities and New Year celebrations often provided opportunities for dances and songs that focused on local news, trending social ills, and scandals. According to Kenneth M. Bilby, such a musical practice "relying for its effect on such devices as double entendre, irony, and veiled allusions, is a Caribbean specialty.[28] In 1794, Bryan Edwards recorded that enslaved Africans in Jamaica possessed oratorical gifts, a "talent of ridicule and derision, which is exercised not only against each other but also, not infrequently, at the expense of their owner or employer; but most parts of their songs at these places are fraught with obscene ribaldry, and accompanied with dances in the highest degree of licentious and wanton."[29] Deploying symbols and idioms of expression fashioned on slave plantations, the Africans spoke to matters of a touchy nature in public. They disguised the true meanings of their words in proverbs and phrases the outsider could not construe. To say the least, Christmas festivities became a period when many Europeans and elites of society found themselves either cajoled or flattered in songs. These events were sources of great anxiety that often distressed the souls of their targets rather than gladdened them.

Purgation/Purification

Most of the songs in this cluster are connected with religion, collaborative labor, funeral rites, initiation into secret societies, age-grade associations, puberty rites, marriage celebrations, and so on. However, this collection of songs and music could also fit well in the educational cadre as music plays diverse functions depending on the specific context, mode, and occasion of its performance. Every religion uses worship songs to arouse the adherent to the point of voicing their faith to the deity or object of their worship. Religious hymns serve as an expression of restitution, request for a favor (petitions), and/or articulation of gratitude (thanksgiving). All religious hymns aim to communicate good morals, the importance of piety and good deeds, and the dangers of immoral behaviors. Toward this end, African singers such as Chinedu Nwadike talk about "Wave of Miracles," using the lyrics of the indigenous Bongo music style to delve into the philosophy of existentialism enhanced by virtues of patience and strong faith in divine interventions in the face of life's challenges and happenstances.[30]

Andrew Pearse has noted that in colonial Trinidadian society, Bongo music featured "in the houses of the dead at wakes." The description of a scene and the performers he witnessed is very remarkable in the sense that it was "an old Trinidadian, son of a Congo" who remembered "a group of old Africans who would sit in the house of the dead at wakes, playing the 'banja' (*sanza*) and singing about the dead while the younger people danced the Bongo outside."[31] This is reminiscent of a wake this author witnessed in Achi Mbieri in 1972, two years after the end of the Nigerian Civil War. The deceased, simply known as "Tanker," was a Bongo king, a celebrated drummer, a one-man band, bandleader, and Okoroshá masquerade chief. For two weeks, the entire village stood still as Bongo musicians and Okoroshá masquerade cult members from all the neighboring villages in Mbieri, Ubomiri, Umunneọhá, and Ọgwá took turns to honor their hero. The ode of the last day of mourning still reverberates in the heads of many who witnessed the event: "Tanker! Tanker! Tanker! Tanker le! Oh o! Oh o! Onye ámumá!" (Tanker! Tanker! Tanker! Tanker! Oh o! Oh o! Prophet!). The centrality of religious songs in Igbo culture is best represented by the golden voice of one of the Owerri community's Bongo music maestros, Eke Chima. In his epic 2003 album *Ọbáráézé*, Eke Chima emphatically stated,

"One day all of us will go to heaven to receive the rewards of our earthly lives."[32] Eke Chima, a favorite performer at weddings, naming ceremonies, and funerals, always uses his songs to reiterate his Igbo/African religious beliefs and practices, which according to Ade-Adegbola include the desire "for group solidarity in the collective experiences, common sense and conscience of the individual, the influence of proverbs, wise sayings, folktales and stories, some of which may be based on custom and experience."[33] One of the cardinal aspects of African traditional music, as Celestine Mbaegbu has noted, is that it is never bereft of moral instructions. African traditional music frequently "extols, exonerates or justifies some good qualities, condemns or blames the bad. In some cases, it makes value judgments, stipulates or pinpoints moral evil and injustices in various regions of Africa."[34]

It is notable that although the musician may not be living by example as a person, yet, in his or her professional capacity, it remains the musician's responsibility to defend the moral laws of the land. These laws share a symbiotic relationship with religion, and thus music is a vehicle for moral preaching as well as a means to connect with ancestral spirits whose abode is the great beyond.[35] The indigenous worldview motivates the folk musician to make a conscious attempt to use his brand of music to influence good behaviors. Writing about the music of Fela Ransome Kuti (1938–1997)—the Afrobeat maestro who was an exception to the rule on moral education through music—Carlos Moore referred to his defiance as a "bitch of life" in a world where music creates change as a weapon.[36] However, there is no denying the fact that Kuti did not allow his reckless lifestyle to affect his status as a champion of the people. Speaking in defense of his cousin, Nobel laureate Wole Soyinka described Kuti as someone who "loves to buck the system." According to Soyinka, "His music, to many, was both salvation and echo of their anguish, frustration, and suppressed aggression."[37]

Across the African Diaspora, the tradition of music and dance performances intended to denounce bad behaviors was reenacted to some degree. Once again it is important to recall that the sociopolitical milieu in which the African Diaspora performers existed was remarkably different from that of their counterparts in Africa. However, the philippic—a public act of denouncing, characterized by harsh and often insulting language—was practiced in both regions. As with the Gombay dance in Jamaica, in 1820, Cynric Williams observed that "the merriment became rather boisterous as the punch operated, and the slaves sang satirical philippics against their master, communicating a little free advice now and then."[38] In 1826, Cynthia Oliver further noted that the chantwells or prima donnas of the Virgin Islands had dual roles: they were entertainers and they were also the voices of the people.[39] Bill La Motta observed that following "the beat of the Bamboula drums a story-teller would evoke a chant, improvising lyrics based on a given topic. . . . The drumhead [Bamboula] functioned as the eyes and ears of the community. It was a means of communication, comment, and criticism, a local scandal-sheet taken off the tongues of the masses. . . . They were . . . dusted with scorn and ridicule.[40] Robert Nicholls has noted that in the Virgin Islands, women "Cariso" singers were paramount dispensers of commentary in song, but as Christmas approached, men such as Ciple who accompanied his songs on a tin can or Albert Halliday in his various get-ups, would recount the local scandals of the preceding year in songs and speeches. Furthermore, most, but not all, Calypsonians are male. Both before and after Emancipation, Afro-Creole music and dance facilitated nonverbal and verbal communication between various classes and ethnic groups and served as vehicles for intergroup communication and negotiation.[41]

All the emphasis on morality and religion in African music points to the condition of the human soul after death. While the African Christians in the Judeo-Christian tradition believe that there is life after death in paradise, the indigenous religious system was not about heaven or hell. It was about promoting interhuman and intersocial relations. The implicit idea was that those who lived the good life will transition from this human life to the higher rank of the ancestral world of spirits and divinities. The belief was that from the spirit world, ancestors watched their progenies and over time, enjoy the reward of reincarnation that allows them to reenter the human world as newborn babies. Those who did not live the good life will die and their spirits will continue roaming around in frustration and anguish. Neither accepted as an ancestor in the dynamic world of the dead nor enjoying the reward of reincarnation as a newborn child, the evil spirit roams the universe until it ends up in the bosom of a tree or even transmutes into an animal. Because of the importance placed on death and reincarnation, the rites of passage after death were important ceremonies observed with all the trappings of ritual, music, dance, and masquerade festivities. "Among the Igbo, when a man dies, the Ikoro ('a portion of a tree hollowed out so as to allow a narrow slit') or big wooden drum bellows in the announcement of the death. The Ikoro also announces war or when the very unusual thing happened in the town."[42] The signaling type of music from the Ikolo drum "serves the role of disseminating information in most African societies."[43]

Walter Rucker argues that a widespread set of African-derived beliefs in spiritual forces and ideas about death, the afterlife, and transmigration proved crucial in the development of slave resistance and revolt in the United States.[44] Religion strengthened the community ethic of resistance that made large-scale slave rebellion possible. This was the motivation for Nat Turner, the slave preacher turned rebel who, in 1831, organized one of the largest slave insurrections after receiving what he called a divine command. Bryan Edwards witnessed a funeral ceremony in Jamaica in 1806 and noted that the Africans "exhibited a sort of *Pyrrhic* or warlike dance, in which their bodies are strongly agitated by running, leaping, and jumping, with many violent and frantic gestures and contortion."[45] With this description, what immediately comes to mind is the Ábịrịbá-Arọ-Ọháfiá-Ábám-Èddá culture area where the traditional war dance (although primarily performed after vanquishing an opposing village) is also featured at funerals for important individuals and those considered as heroes in these societies. The Ábịrịbá war dance, known as *ikperikpe ọgụ* in the local dialect, is usually accompanied by songs with aggressive tones.[46] The percussion is produced with bamboo slat instruments (*ákwátánkwá*), antelope horns (*opi*), and drums (*udu*, also *ọgwé* in some dialects). The drum calls forth:

> Everyone shout come forth!
> Those in the bush come out!
> Those on the road come out!
> The day is charged![47]

Interestingly, the planter Bryan Edwards shared his perception of the Negro funeral songs as "all of the heroic or marital cast; affording some color to the prevalent notion, that the negro consider death not as a welcome and happy release from the calamities of their condition, but also as a passport to the place of their nativity."[48] Yet, Edwards recorded a funeral poem, which he described as "sympathetic effusion of fanciful or too credulous an imagination." The ode goes as follows:

> Mahali dies! O'er yonder plain
> His bier is borne: The sable train
> By youthful virgin's led
> Daughters of inju'd Afric,[sic] say,
> Why raise ye thus th' heroic lay,
> Why triumph o'er the dead?
> No tear bedews their fixed eye
> 'Tis now the hero lives they cry; –
> Releas'd from slavery chain:

FIGURE 7.2. Ohafia war dancer with headboard (Ọyáyá). This image
is copyright. Reproduced by permission of University of Cambridge Museum
of Archaeology & Anthropology (N.13025.GIJ)

> Beyond the billowy surge he flies
> And joyful views bowers again.[49]

Among the African masquerade literature encountered in forms of songs, idioms, proverbs, and riddles are a genre of intellectual heritage. The Ọzụbụlụ
Ezeigboezue masquerade of the Igbo offers the audience loads of oral literature
words to think about:

> Instead of a man to be inconsequential
> Let him like the *ugá* grow fast and depart.
> To have no money is bad for a man
> It is indeed very bad.
> Holders of money please pardon me
> To beget an idiot is the same thing to lose a child

It happens that when humans assemble for a meeting
It is agreed that it would hold at cock crow
Humans, some have cocks, some have none.
Those killed by small-pox who mourned them?
Those who accumulate wealth without enjoying it
Who mourned them?
Man dissolves.[50]

These poetic performances—whether enacted as a religious song, funeral parade, or correctional syllabi—in Africa or in the African Diaspora—served the same functions for which the communities created them. The songs liberated and purified the performers as individuals and as a group. They addressed the corruptive and dehumanizing impacts of injustices, deviant behaviors, and social misconduct. The singers talked about corruption and leadership failures and frowned at other practices of social injustices with a view to bringing a change. Mbaegbu was apt in his contention that in the "political life of the African, music is not relegated to the background. There are praise songs and music to get the better part of the leaders of various communities and various state governors including any constituted authority. Wealthy men and craftsmen not excluded."[51]

Relaxation/Entertainment

Across the world, the primary role of music appears to be for entertainment, relaxation, and recreation. This explains why performers and their audiences indulge in dancing. On January 9, 1920, the district officer of Awka sent a memo to a resident of Onitsha Province describing different types of dances he has observed in Igboland. These included those rendered during marriage, childbirth, initiation, war, masquerade dances, funerals, and graduation.[52] At each of these occasions, the music and dance define the ebb and flow of the celebration and how it will be remembered in the future. It is the kind of music played and the number of people who stood up in joyful response that makes such an event memorable. Moonlight tales are an important part of African life. These tales, put together by the organic intellectuals to educate and entertain, are always accompanied by music and songs. They teach the rewards of the good life; virtues; obedience; respect for parents, elders, and authority; hard work; and so on. The Anansi series focus a corpus of West African intellectual traditions that was easily adopted in the African Diaspora. In Jamaica, for instance, folktales collected by Martha Warren Beckwith and transcribed by Helen Roberts include a trove of riddles, folktales, and folk music, all annotated with similar traditions from other places. Anansi the trickster, known in the tradition as a spider from West Africa, plays the role of an ancestral spirit. This strange but wise creature that belongs to the family of arachnids lives on in these tales. The figure, popular among the African Diaspora, is prominent in folktales dating back to about 1816. The storytellers and their audiences stayed awake late at night to listen to the exploits of this culture hero of the Gold Coast, similar to the turtle and hare in the Bantu folklores.

Beckwith explains that Anansi embodies the spirit of rebellion for the Africans. He has the ability to upend the social order, create wealth out of nothing, contract the king's daughter in marriage, confuse the devil, and even cheat death. When Anansi loses in one story, he usually comes back victorious in another. For a race under the worst form of subjugation, Anansi bore a generational message of hope: freedom and dignity are nonnegotiable.[53] Like in the West African tradition, each of the African Diaspora folklores, riddles, and jokes are packaged with songs. The music helps the listener internalize the story and its intended lessons. In this context, music becomes the soul and custodian of the narrative across generations.

In the field of human psychology, Sigmund Freud perceived folktales as something emanating from unconscious needs and frustrations of life that revealed themselves through a person's dreams. According to Freud, symbolic images that disguise painful material make the dream more acceptable even to the sleeping person.[54] On the other hand, C. G. Jung proposed that folktales emerge from our "collective unconscious"—that is, a racial or ethnic group or kindred experience embedded in the human psyche.[55] The stories emerging from those experiences are common in all societies. The psychological approach to understanding folktales enables the interpreter to analyze the mindset and sensibilities behind the storyteller's creative process, including the memorization or recollection of old tales, or analysis/interpretation of the motivation of the characters in the story.[56]

Meanwhile, the sociological interest in folktales is twofold. One is the idea of storytelling itself—that is, the assembling of an audience for the purpose of hearing stories, the process of collecting stories for publication, and decisions to make changes in the stories. The second part involves the sociology (that is, how the story addresses a social problem of the function of a society) inherent in folktales. The story and its contents or lessons are appropriated when these texts are used for studying social relationships. Although the folktales feature individual characters rather than groups of people, social organizations are implied in the background. Religion also permeates folktales in which storytellers are quick to ridicule unworthy priests and target hypocrisy.[57]

Also, music and dance for marriage and certain kinds of initiations such as naming ceremonies and puberty rites are composed to entertain while serving ritual purposes at the same time. During such occasions, libations are poured as the presiding elders or priests pray to the health of the couple, initiates, and their parents. In the African Diaspora, this ritual form survived until the nineteenth century at least, as observed by Cynric Williams, who recorded a slave celebration of Christmas and Boxing Day on a Jamaican estate in December 1823. The description includes Igbo and African-style libation rituals: One of the Africans "poured a few drops [of drink] on the ground, and drank off the rest to the health of his master and mistress." It was not only on this occasion that libation was poured. Williams further informs us that usually "the negroes have a custom of performing libations when they drink, a kind of first-fruit offering."[58] Williams continues, "When the old runaway thief of a watchman reconciled himself to his master, he received a glass of grog in token of forgiveness. . . . On receiving the glass of grog, he poured a few drops on the ground, and drank off the rest of the health of master and mistress." Libation rituals marked several festivities the Africans were involved with, including the Jonkonnu masquerade dances on Boxing Day, Christmas, and New Year festivities. For these and other occasions, the performer "dressed up in a mask with a grey beard and long flowing hair, who carried the model of a house on his head." As noted by Williams, the Jonkonnus were always "chosen for his superior activity in dancing."[59] The performers divided themselves into parties to dance, "some before the gombays, in a ring, to perform a bolero or a sort of love dance." Others performed a sort of pyrrhic [war dance] before the ebo drummer, beginning gently and quickly quickening their motions, until they seemed agitated by the furies.[60] In a related depiction of a Negro festival witnessed in Saint Lucia in the 1840s, Henry Hegart Breen mentioned the use of the tam-tam—one of the species of African drums, which Robert Nicholls said indicates resemblance to the Igbo drum.[61] Breen continued to explain that the song texts were delivered in a call-and-response style: "The chanterelle, placing herself in front of the orchestra, gives the signal with a flourish of her castanet. She then repeats a verse of the belair: the dancers take up the *refrain*; the *tamtams* and timbrels strike in unison; and the scene is enlivened by a succession of songs and dances, to the delight and amusement of the assembled multitude."[62] The call-and-response music and dance art form are very common in West African masquerade dances, religious worship, and other social events.

Music and dance also help to mobilize and energize laborers. In the indigenous culture, it is fully realized that work requires some exertion that takes a toll on the human mind and body. That is why early in life, part of the socialization process involves exposing the child to the values and dignity of labor. Richard Igwebe explains that in his Arọndizuọgu society of the precolonial era, children were exposed to labor training as early as four to six years of age.[63] According to Ghanaian ethnomusicologist J. H. K. Nketia, labor songs were so much a part of raising children that "when children assist in the economic activities of their parents or are given special responsibilities, such as looking after flocks, they may be encouraged to play flutes for their own enjoyment, for giving signals to their companions, or for guiding their flock."[64]

Among the Igbo, the saying goes *Áká ájájá kpátárá ọnu nmánu nmánu* (The busy man can never lack). The flip side of it is "no food for the lazy." One of the favorite songs of my grandfather, who was a farmer, goes like this: *Onye gbuwé áchárá onye gbuwé; onyé ákpọlá ibeyá onye ikoli*. (Let every hand get busy in labor; no one is a prisoner). The intent of this song was to encourage everyone in the family or community to embrace the exertions of farming as something that is both desirable and dignifying. This philosophical song reminds the historian about the popular eighteenth-century King George III (1760–1820) of Britain and Ireland—aka "Farmer George," whose exemplary support for agriculture marked the turning point for the Agricultural Revolution in Great Britain.[65] One of the most popular Igbo songs for labor remains the "elephant song," *Nzọgbu, enyi mbá enyi*. The depiction of labor with the metaphor *enyi* (elephant) shows the projection of strength, respect, and greatness that comes from successful and positive self-exertion. *Enyi Biafra*, therefore, became a symbol of collective strength in the Igbo culture. A correspondent of *Time*, reporting on the Nigerian civil conflict (1967–1970) in 1968, noted that the threat to the existence of the Biafran people by northern Nigerians led to the solemn invocation of the ancient power of enyi mbá enyi, a rallying cry of Igbo brotherhood.[66] Indeed, the elephant song in Igboland certainly calls for unity and collective effort to overcome any challenge. It is not commonly sung except when there is a challenge that requires communal effort. Kenneth Omeje, an expert in peace studies, describes Nzọgbu, enyi mbá enyi as an "idiom of optimism and faith in people's ability to defeat any adversary."[67] Arild Bergh and John Slobodan's argument about using music to mobilize the "cause" fits into the labor songs of the Igbo.[68]

African slaves carried the culture of using songs for motivation and coping in the face of exertion to the Americas. During interludes in their work routines, it was usual for enslaved Africans in the Caribbean, United States, and other parts of the Americas to congregate to sing and dance, and this provided a spectacle for the onlookers. It was from the blood, tears, ashes, and sorrows accompanying these labor songs that jazz music sprang to life among the African American singers of the early twentieth century. Nick Nesbitt reminds us: "Jazz is the realization of an intensive labor that is at once autonomous, freely chosen by and for that musical subject, and an objective product existing within a community of others consisting of both musicians and listeners. African music is itself utopian precisely insofar as it poses an aesthetic counterpoint to the violence of society; as such, it undertakes the determinate negation of totalitarian practice."[69]

In 1890, H. Carrington Bolton provides a description of a "Gomby parade" on the island of Bermuda, in a letter to the editor published in the *Saint Croix Avis*. It is particularly striking that the letter talked about "the laboring populations," who "go in bands along the street with the Gumbee."[70] Olaudah Equiano, the most celebrated Igbo ex-slave, documented a fête he purportedly witnessed in Jamaica in which "different nations of Africa meet and dance after the nature of their own country."[71] Thomas Thistlewood, the Englishman who was in Kingston, Jamaica, in 1750, saw "Negro Diversions—odd Music, Motions, etc. The Negroes of Each Nation by themselves."[72] These ethnic dances continued across the Caribbean until the slave population began to obviously lose memories of their inherited African tradition. However, among the Carriacouans, the tradition of work songs continued uninterrupted. In August 1962, folklorist Alan Lomax and his daughter, Anna, arrived in the Carriacou, a small island of the eastern Caribbean nation Grenada inhabited by the so-called maroons (or runaway slaves), to make a detailed study of African origins of music on the island. Among the recordings that Lomax collected were the songs and music performed by Carriacouans to pass the time at work. "These include solo sea chanties sung by seamen to coordinate physical work, alleviate boredom, and express the homesickness that was often felt by sailors. Lomax also documented the music that Carriacouans performed to entertain themselves and each other, including 'pass play' songs—a social music and dance performed by unmarried young men and women—waltzes, polkas, calypsos, and other string-band tunes, and he captured the stunning polyrhythmic music played for quadrille dancing by solo violinists and accompanied by often virtuoso percussionists."[73] Robert Nicholls, who has made a study of the Carriacou, informs us that two out of the six African nation tracks on the *Carriacou Calaloo* album are Igbo. "Igbo Le Le" is performed by a female lead vocalist with a "chac-chac" shaker, accompanied by a female chorus and three male drummers. "Igbo Le Le, Oh, le, wo yo," a repetitive call-and-response refrain, is primeval to West and Central Africa.[74]

In his *Achievement as Value in Igbo African Identity*, Vernantius Ndukaihe observed that among the Africans, there are genres of music that summon people to action, "music fosters solidarity."[75] Under colonial rule, Igbo women used music and dance as a mode of solidarity and social protest against policies they often considered oppressive and marginalizing. For instance, between 1925 and 1926, several reports surfaced on the "activities of bands of dancing women in Owerri, Onitsha and Ogoja Provinces . . . as a matter worth investigation."[76] This was a sequel to a memorandum dated November 9, 1925, from the senior resident of Onitsha Province to the district officer, "with reference to some towns in the Ajalli district being visited by bands of women dancers preaching their own ideas of desirable reforms."[77] In his response dated December 14, 1925, to the inquiries from the senior resident officer, the district officer of Awká reported that the name of the dance was Nwábálá or Ogbánjili, which he confirmed was "some kind of new dance." The report also stated that the women came from Ákokwá, Okigwi (Okigwe), Abuofu, and Eziámá and that "it was a bad dance," and that "something was sung in the dance about a return to old custom. That was why he considered it a bad dance."[78] But what these dances were all about is that the women were fed up with the nature of the colonial administration that marginalized their gender. As the world would later learn, it was just a dress rehearsal to the explosive Aba Women's Riot of 1928/9 in the entire eastern region of Nigeria.[79]

According to Vernantius Ndukaihe, whatever the intention of the music— entertainment, ritual or religious services—music and dance bring "the community together to forge a social aesthetic or mystical links among its members and to unite emotional responses around defined rhythmic waves and melodies."[80] When people are united, they are motivated to action, to speak with one voice, and to engage in reciprocal actions. Under the worst forms of slavery in the New World, Africans re-created their dances as forums for solidarity and community engagement. In places such as New Orleans, which was purchased from the French by the United States in 1803, semblances of African traditions including music traditions survived longer than elsewhere in the United States. As narrated in the preceding chapter, from the late eighteenth and early half of the nineteenth centuries, every Sunday the Africans brought to the Americas held eye-catching dance festivals at the famous Congo Square in New Orleans.[81] Here, hundreds of Africans danced in circles while hundreds of spectators watched. In 1879, the *Daily Picayune* reported that the Congo Square dances involved diverse clusters of onlookers, musicians, and dancers, "each nation taking their place in different parts of the square": the Hiboas (Igbos), Fulas, Minahs, Kongos, Mandringos (Mandingos), Gangas, and so on.[82]

In 1819, Benjamin Latrobe published a report on two orchestras he observed: one had a square membrane drum (*igbá*), the typical Gombay drum that was later imported into Sierra Leone and Ghana from the Caribbean. The second was a wooden instrument like the slit-drum common among forest peoples of Kongo and Igbo.[83] Historical evidence shows that the native Taino people who inhabited some Caribbean islands in pre-Columbian times used a hollow log slit-drum.[84] Ethnic identification among the Africans remained in Jamaica until the 1830s. James Kelly observed that at Christmas, "the Mangolas, the Mandingoes, the Eboes, the Congoes, etc., formed into exclusive groups" and performed separate music and songs "peculiar to their country."[85]

Musical Instruments—The African Gift to Humanity

Before ending this chapter, it is essential to discuss the musical instruments invented by the Africans. This is important because, in a world where technology has come to define the state of development or underdevelopment of a people, it is easy to forget the rudiments of technology that the Africans accomplished in the music industry. These achievements range from idiophones, aerophones, and chordophones to membranophones.

The idiophones are mainly musical instruments made of natural sonorous materials. They do not usually require extra tension in preparation, as in the case of the drum for example. In his expert study of the traditional and contemporary music of Africa, Alexander Agordoh explains that there are two classes of idiophone instruments—primary and secondary idiophones. The primary instruments consist of bells, metal rattles of gourds, beaded or enmeshed rattles, metal castanets, and percussion sticks. Others included in this class are stamping tubes in the form of stamps of bamboos, sansas, and xylophones (*ngédélégwu* in Igbo). Meanwhile the difference between the primary and secondary idiophones is that the latter is an adornment, usually around the legs, waist, wrist, or ankles; attached to the top of the drums; or attached to the top of the mask in order to accomplish both desired aesthetic effects of the performance as well as the preferred rhythms accentuated by the body movements of the performers.[86] Indications abound that both the mbira (also called lamellaphone) and marimba, two examples of early xylophones found in the Americas are all native to Africa. While mbira is widely used among the Shona, a Bantu group in South Africa, the marimba is associated with Central Africa. The enslaved Africans in the Americas introduced these instruments in the early sixteenth century—that is, soon after the Spanish conquest of the region. The idea of its early introduction came about following the absorption and indigenization of the marimba in the various Spanish dominions in the Americas: Costa Rica, Mexico, Guatemala, Colombia, Ecuador, and others.[87] Dona Epstein has further documented the playing of *balafo* (a similar type of xylophone) by the enslaved Africans in Barbados (1656), Virginia (1775), French Antilles (1776), Saint Vincent (1781), and Jamaica (1823).[88] Meanwhile, the mbira, a larger version of the plucked idiophone, is also widely used in many Caribbean islands where it is commonly known as *marimbula* in Puerto Rico, Haiti, Jamaica, Trinidad, Cuba, Dominican Republic, and Curacao. In New Orleans, it was called *sanzas* and *marimba brett* in Brazil.[89]

The aerophones are wind instruments that come in different forms and categories such as pipes, flutes, horns, and trumpets. They are usually made from iron, animal bones, horns, bamboo, sticks, wood, and so on. Aerophones are common to West and Central Africa and are often employed as background music for traditional dances, rites of passage, and ceremonies. Trumpets are usually made out of animal horns, elephant tusks (*ọdụ*), or wood. Flutes are often carved out of materials with natural hollow spaces such as bamboo or plants with a removable pith. In relation to masquerade dances, it is common that over a long period, some instrumentation becomes the hallmark of particular performances. For instance, the hollow metal gong (*ogélé* or *ọgéné*) weaves intricate and distinctive tunes with other instruments to distinguish Ágábá masquerade instrumentation. Describing the "Juju or Nmánwu dance" among the Igbo in a memo to the resident of Onitsha Province in 1920, the divisional officer for Awká stated, "All dances are accompanied by a band consisting of drums, flutes and sometimes pieces of metal. These bands travel around from town to town."[90] The ọgéné, which chief priests often use to arouse their deities, controls the mask in the absence of the flutist, initiating and dictating various dance steps and activities.[91]

Chordophones are instruments made with strings and include different kinds of harps, lutes, zithers, and lyres, ranging from the one-stringed fiddle (*ubọ ákwálá*) to eight or more strings. They are played with the hand, a pin, or a bow (*une*).[92] The vibrations that pass through the strings produce the sound. In his excellent study of "Music and Migration," John H. Cowley noted, "Of string instruments known to have evolved in the New World, the basic design of the *Creole bania* (a brand of the banjo)" lute chordophone instrument "almost certainly originated in West Africa."[93] In her 1791 description of music and dance among the Timmany (Temne) of Sierra Leone, Anna Maria Falconbridge noted: "Sometimes I have seen an instrument resembling our guitar, the country name of which is *bangeon* (banjo). The company frequently applauds or upbraids the performer, with bursts of laughter, or some odd disagreeable noise; if it is moonshine, and they have spirits to drink, these dances probably continue until the moon goes down, or until daylight. The *Timmany* dialect is commonly spoken here, though the nation so called is some distance to the northward."[94]

The solid evidence proving that the banjo came from Africa rested in the discovery of the oldest banjo relic made by John Gabriel Stedman who stumbled onto a piece of a Creole *bania* during the revolt of the Negroes of Surinam from 1772 to 1777.[95] In fact, various "forensic" studies of the prototypes from Senegambia by Dena J. Epstein and Michael Coolen have all proved consistent with the theory that the version existing in Surinam and other models of banjo in the Americas were designed after the African archetype.[96]

The membranophones are all drums covered with parchment heads or membranes usually made from animal skins. The sounds they produce come from the membranes stretched over an opening. Materials used may include gourd, metal, clay, or wood. The drum could be single-headed or double-headed, and they come in different sizes, shapes (rectangle, gourd, bottle, cylindrical, hourglass, or conical), colors, tones (dull, muted, or sonorous), and pitches. Among the most popular of this class of musical instruments is the talking drum, an hourglass instrument native to West Africa. These drums are played solo or in a group; while standing or sitting; carried on the head or suspended on the back, depending on the desired effect.[97] In some *mmánwu* masquerade performances, membranous drums (*igba*), slit wooden pieces (*ékwé*), metal gongs (*ogéné*), and horns (*shofar*) are combined to create the distant and haunting music that is synonymous with this performance. In some performances, instrumentation enhances such participation activities as singing and clapping.[98] Writing about the Timmany (Temne) of Sierra Leone in 1791, Anna Maria Falconbridge reported: "Their chief amusement is dancing: in the evening, men and women assemble in the most open part of the town, where they form a circle, which one at a time enters, and shows his skill and agility, by a number of wild comical motions. Their music is made by clapping of hands, and a harsh sounding drum or two, made out of hollowed wood covered with the skin of a goat."[99]

According to John Crowley, the drum is the "most obvious instrument identified as African in the historical and contemporary literature on black music in the Americas."[100] Mainly because of its function as an instrument of summoning solidarity among the slaves, the European elite in the Caribbean and elsewhere dreaded the drum and often tried to brand it a nuisance to society. The early Christians in the Caribbean also described it as the "devil's instrument of worship and violent disorder." The truth of the matter is that these stereotypes stemmed from elites' fears for the potency of the drum to summon people of African descent as a community in the face of oppression. For there were diverse uses of the drum that also came in different shapes and sizes. Crowley notes, "in one respect, however, the potency of the drum as a signal for African integrity was sustained alongside these variations—its use for the sacred ceremony."[101]

Indeed, drums serve in both sacred and secular observances in both Africa and the African Diaspora. Robert Nicholls has affirmed aptly that a discussion of drums provides a segue from masquerades depicted as vehicles of behavior modification to song texts that serve a similar function. Just as the Igbo have been identified with male Caribbean masquerades, the inclusion of the Igbo drum in Gombay identifies the Igbo with mixed-gender drum dances such as Bamboula and Gombay that feature satirical songs. References to the "Igbo drum" appear prominently in the Caribbean literature. In 1826 for instance, Cynric Williams left us with a vivid description when he attempted to distinguish between a "gombay" drum and an "ebo [Igbo] drum" and describes dancers performing "a sort of pyrrhic [war dance] before the ebo drummer."[102]

Historically, given that the drum is closely associated with the culture of forest people of West and Central Africa, it is believed that it may have spread from the Bantu Cradle and then to the various locations in Central Africa—the Kongo, Rwanda, and Burundi. The biggest musical drum and most skillful drummers are found in Burundi today. Joy Lo-Bamijoko has noted, "the drum is the broadcast of the town hall, the instrument of summons, and everybody on hearing its sound would halt and listen to its heart searching message as it glides through the air."[103] Williams noted that the "ebo drum [is] made out of a hollowed tree with a piece of sheepskin stretched over it."[104] Early on in 1794, Edwards described the "Goombay" as "a rustic drum; being formed of the trunk of a hollow tree, one end of which is covered with a sheepskin." Thus, both descriptions point to an interchangeability of "Gombay" and "Igbo" drums to mean the same. Lewis in 1834 narrates a dance group whose drums "consisted of Gambys (Eboe drums), Shaky-skekies [maracas] and kitty-katties." Although Lewis refers to Gombay drums as Igbo drums, Williams distinguishes between them.

Most often "Gombay drum" refers to a square frame drum (or bench drum) that eventually crossed back over the Atlantic to Sierra Leone in 1800 with repatriated maroons. Subsequently, the drum and the name spread throughout West Africa.[105] Oldendorp provides an early description of frame drums in Antigua, which "consisted of small square boxes over which skins have been stretched."[106]

In a report of Virgin Islands dances in 1831, Johan P. Nissen, however, describes a "Gombee" drum as "a small barrel, the bottom of which is taken out [and] a goat skin is drawn over the rim."[107] Many such descriptions of Caribbean drums exist in the literature and may not seem remarkable. Indeed, the standard drum of southeastern Nigeria is a hollowed log with an animal skin at one end. It is significant, however, because a consideration of the Igbo drum helps to differentiate between masquerades who parade through the streets and Bamboula performers who are based in a fixed location. While the former use European-style drums and sometimes Creole frame drums, the latter use the Igbo drum. The term *Gombay* is treated rather loosely in the literature and sometimes describes a stationary group and sometimes a perambulating group.

In the literature, the drums of the early Jonkonnu are not described in detail, but the portable fife and drum bands based on European military models or their Hausa-Fulani counterparts that invariably accompanied the Bull and other masquerades in the British West Indies were not of the single skin Igbo drum variety, which is beaten with bare hands. Instead, a bass drum and a "kettle" or "kittle" drum, with skins at both ends, were suspended from the neck or waist of the rhythm and lead drummer, respectively. While the bass drum is struck with a padded beater on a stick, conventional drumsticks are used with the kettledrum. The Caribbean kettledrum has no resemblance to the kettledrum used in European orchestras. In today's usage, the term *kettledrum* is often used interchangeably with the *snare drum*, although it lacks the "snare" (cords stretched across one skin to increase reverberation). Belisario's (1838) sketch, "Band of the Jaw-Bone John Canoe," shows a perambulating group that includes two drummers with drums suspended from their necks.[108] One beats a frame drum with his hands, while the other has a large double-ended European drum suspended from his neck that he beats with padded sticks.

On Christmas Eve in 1852, it was a stationary Gombay group that sparked off the confrontation between "Gumbee dancers" and the Militia in Christiansted, Saint Croix, which "led to bloodshed and loss of human life." This, in turn, resulted in the militia being disbanded because of their overreaction. On New Year's Eve of 1852, Governor Birch was prompted to write a letter of explanation to the Danish Colonial Office in which he differentiated between street parades and the stationary Gombay bands:

> The lower part of the population in the towns is accustomed to spend Christmas and New Year's Eve with amusements consisting partly of street parades accompanied with boisterous music and singing; partly in dancing to the sound of an instrument called the Gumbee, a peculiar kind of drum presumed to be of African origin.... On St. Thomas ... the drumming has in recent years been directed to the outskirts of town.[109]

Probably the parades' perambulatory aspect rendered them more transitory and less disturbing than drum dances that remained in one spot. Subsequently, the pressure to quell boisterous music and dancing in the Virgin Islands increased but seems to have been aimed more at African drum dances such as Gombay and Bamboula, with their biting song texts, than it was at masquerading. In contrast to the response to drum dances, the establishment appeared at times to tacitly encourage masquerading. In 1872, Haynes wrote: "The Danish governor ... this year permitted the privilege of masquerading, wisely concluding that this gratification of vanity would prevent the riot ... of former occasions."[110]

African world music, like African religion, art, and oral traditions, provides a looking glass into the civilization and its modes of expressions Africans have bequeathed to humanity. As discussed above, African music and dance is extensive and diverse. The masquerade dance is one of several dances and artistic performances invented by Africans. These dances are produced by different cultural groups and differ accordingly with respect to the value systems, beliefs, norms, recreation, politics, economy, social institutions, and taboos of those societies that produced them. Some aspects of precolonial African music and songs were influenced by internal and external borrowings. One of those is visible with the influence of Islam on North African and some West African music traditions.[111]

The Africans transplanted to the Americas attempted to re-create their music and dance traditions in the African Diaspora, with mixed results. The truth of the matter is that the enslaved Africans imposed their rich indigenous culture on those of the Europeans who settled the New World and those of the Amerindians who were indigenous to the society. The result was the development of new kaleidoscopes of religious, masquerade, musical, and dance performances. In the African continent, these performances were established in specific religious and ritualistic contexts. In the African Diaspora, Christianity, Western education, and structures of power in the political system did not allow for

wholesale reenactment or transfer of the original African practices. What came
to life became new world cultures with African undertones. Additionally, the
cultural dichotomy between African-born slaves and their Creole cohorts created a cultural gap despite the efforts by the Africans to close these differences.

Whether we are concerned with the African-born or Creolized Negros, the
tropes of music and dance they fostered in the Americas remains the master
keys to a proper understanding of the African world and the complex inter-
relationships among memory, reality, and abstractions. Abu Abarry has aptly
noted with his study of the Ga of the southeast of Ghana's *Ga Homowo* (Hunger Hooting) first fruit harvest festival that in all their daily activities, "music,
dance, and drama all contain gems of oral literature, are the main vehicles of
communication. The arrival of the gods is hailed by music and dancing which
also hails their triumphant return to their abode."[112] Songs are rendered in invocation and exultation of the gods, who are also persuaded to descend upon their
mediums through whom their wills and injunctions are expressed. Perhaps it is
this significance of music and dance in African worship as perceived by Nketia
that made him conclude that "African gods are music-loving gods."[113] Abarry
further reminds us that the "secular songs also have their functions; they often
have congratulatory, exhortatory, punitive or reformatory import."[114]

CHAPTER 8

Memory and Masquerade Narratives

The Art of Remembering

Although literature is one thing and morality a quite different
one, at the heart of the aesthetic imperative we discern the moral
imperative.
— Jean-Paul Sartre, *What Is Literature?*

T HIS BOOK HAS ENGAGED with the history, religious idioms, symbols,
and the music, dance, and drama that go with African masks and masquerade and African Diaspora carnivals. Throughout, the central argument remains that we better understand Africans enslaved in the New World as
modelers of African culture and that the traits of traditions they brought with
them need not be exact replicas of those found in Africa. The question arises
about how to best describe the intricate ties between African and African American cultural artifacts and the modifications they have undergone across time
and space without misplacing the inherent Pan-African spirit. This question
has been addressed by situating this investigation within the Igbo masquerade
culture, which brings us to the realization that African-styled masquerade is a
device of representation using narrative to promote identity; propagate, defend
or pursue a cause; and recover or reshape self-consciousness in a continually
changing world. Constant changes marked masquerade displays in Africa, and
its shifting nature continued in the American slaveholding society. In her study
of the carnival culture in Cuba, Judith Bettelheim expressed a similar view:
"Carnival has always been an expression of shifting power negotiations among
aspects of Cuban Society."[1]

As an integral part of masquerading and power negotiations, memory needs
more in-depth treatment. Emmanuel Obiechina's pertinent definition of memory

as "the story of remembering" reminds us that there is a story behind every masquerade display; in the same manner, every work of literature carries a storyline.[2]
Elsewhere, I have defined narrative as "a storied approach to the unfolding of
events," which in poststructuralist thinking explains the world through collaborative story development.[3] Both designations of narrative allow us to properly
situate Africans' perception and responses to everyday occasions, especially the
critical challenges related to slavery and colonialism. Masquerading was one
among other reactions to the European encounter. In the African culture, masquerading is not just a form of entertainment; it is primarily a performative story
of collective remembering and an effective affirmative technique of narrative
engagée. Jean-Paul Sartre may as well be speaking about masquerade narratives
when he tells us that literature has no alternative function more important than
to be engaged and committed to social issues, when he declared that "*la literature
engagée* is worth a fortune in France." According to Sartre, "although literature is
one thing and morality a quite different one, at the heart of the aesthetic imperative we discern the moral imperative."[4] Writing to the *Trinidad Chronicle* in 1881,
an old man who identified himself simply as "Censor" affirms that:

> Canboulay was played (in the streets?) during slavery by many members of
> the middle and in some cases the upper class that it was intended to "take
> off" slave life on a plantation, and hence the driver with a whip pretend-
> ing to drive the people before him to extinguish a night-fire in the cane
> piece, the slaves tramping in time and singing a rude refrain, to a small
> negro-drum and carrying torches to light their way along the road.[5]

Hollis Liverpool, corroborating others such as Selwyn Cudjoe, further asserts
that "Africans, the enslaved as well as the freed participated in Cannes Bruîtes as
part of their masquerading activities on Carnival days; that Whites participated
in the African form of masquerades as well and that African instruments were
used to supply the music."[6] This assertion reinforces the point that despite the
strong campaign by the White elite in the Caribbean to ban African-themed
masquerades, the masquerade narrative engagée continued as an unswerving
mode of dialogue through which the low and the high, the free and bonded, the
rich and the poor fight for a common cause, promote social values, or denounce
vexing sociopolitical issues.[7] This truism is core to grasping the spirit behind the
enslaved Africans' masks and masquerade carnivals in the Americas. Masquerading gave the Africans a platform on which they registered their feelings on
diverse sociopolitical issues affecting their lives.

To clarify, most stories are appropriated in written and oral accounts; others are encountered in nonverbal forms such as mimes, dramatizations, dances, drawings (other forms of artists' designs included), cultural motifs, and artifacts. For the Africans without well-developed writing systems, traditionally memory took the place of archives. From the ellipsis of recollection, Africans created the oral and performative cultural artifacts and modeling skills they enacted on both sides of the Atlantic. On the continent, the Igbo, Èfik, Ibibio, Èkọi, and the Ijọ masquerades combined both verbal and nonverbal modes of expressions in challenge of oppression, criminal and antisocial behaviors, and abuse of power and collective identity. Similarly, as the record of evidence from this and other studies have shown, Africans enslaved in the New World used masquerade carnivals as a forum to protest their plight, represent their African heritage, and request social reforms and freedom as everyday events unfolded.[8] This practice continued long after the Emancipation.

Thus, after Sartre, the language of masquerade, as a genre of narrative engagée, is equated with a literary commitment to a moral cause. It is well known that none of the thousands of African tongues (Igbo, Èfik, Ibibio, Kálábári, and so on) survived in the Americas. For instance, Rafael Cedeño's study of the Carabali (Kálábári) and Abákuá in Cuba reveals that "the Calabali, like other slaves brought forcefully to strange lands, were in the beginning unable to communicate among themselves." Yet, "the slaves not only influenced each other interculturally but they transformed the culture and lifestyle of their masters as well."[9] Along with music and dance, a few of the African languages transmogrified into diverse shades of Creole patois. Gwendolyn Hall reminds us that "the most precise definition of Creole is a person of non-American ancestry," though the term sometimes applies to Native Indians who were born into slavery. According to Hall, "Louisiana creole language was created by the African slaves brought to Louisiana and their creole children."[10] Some other features of African languages fused with ritual art forms, voodoo practices, and the aesthetics that masquerades communicate. For instance, in their separate studies, Harold Courlander and Douglas Chambers have identified Igbo syntax in Haitian voodoo (vodun) culture including Igbo spirits such as "Ibo Foula, Ibo Jérouge, Ibo Mariant or Mariané, Ibo Héquoiké, Ibo Lazile, Ibo lélé, Un Pied Un Main Un Je (One Hand, One Foot, One Eye), Ibo Takwa (who was said to speak an unknown language), and Ibo Ianman, among others."[11] A closer look at these words reveals a hybrid of words from different languages, including French, English, corrupted Yoruba, Ijọ, Ibibio, Rastafarian slang, and Creole Ebonics. The only recognizable Igbo word on the list is "lélé," (as in "look at") which reminds one about Owerri-Igbo common phrase "Àkágbọ lélé."

The relevance of any language (written or otherwise) is to communicate meanings within a social group. In the New World, African languages ultimately became irrelevant primarily because prior African group affiliations along language lines changed radically and instead, music and dance became more effective as a mode of communication. Akin Euba has noted that musical instruments that "talk" serve as an area of cooperation between speech and music. "In a song, the pattern of speech tones of the text would normally be maintained in the melodic line in order that the correct meanings of the words may be indicated."[12] This is the reason Obiechina sees the "use of the journey as a creative metaphor within the narrative mode." Obiechina perceptively contends that as far as the journey exposes individuals to fresh experiences transpiring over space and time, it pragmatically "spans the realm of history and geography, environment and society."[13] In other words, the migration of African music and dance that go along with masquerade displays altered as major parts of the enslaved people's repertoires of memory, remembering, and narrative engagée. In this light, one would better understand why the Congo Society championed by its trustee Joseph Allen, as reported in the *Port of Spain Gazette* of September 12, 1853, "associated themselves together" to purchase "certain premises in Charlotte Street, known as the Congo yard, where three or four nights every week they had public dances, to the music of the banjee drum and shack-shack until the hour of 10 p.m.—and often much later."[14]

As obtained in Africa, the diaspora Africans and their progenies used performative languages and kinesics (the science of body movement as a form of nonverbal communication) to mobilize for cooperative endeavors and narrate those vexing issues pertaining to them as both individuals and groups. Whether displayed as a ritual art form or in a more secular theatrical art form, masquerade narrative, like la littérateur engagée, makes use of a plot or a storyline to represent a message or a cause the performers wanted to bring to the attention of their audience as everyday events unfold. Robert W. Nicholls has noted in his study of masquerade carnivals in the Virgin Islands that in fact, throughout the era of slavery and some part of the postabolition era, the Caribbean African-styled masquerade performers had to guard against negative repercussions from planters and administrators.[15] Rather than name persons, messages were usually encoded in metaphors. Using similes and codes, masquerades indirectly poked fun at the establishment and lampooned figures of authority.

Once the critical point is acknowledged that masquerades were a committed form of narrative expression, students of Africana Studies will be better informed and subsequently avoid the pitfalls of reifying masquerading as a stagnant tradition that was either wholly or partially transferred to the New World. Such ways of thinking in Africana Studies pose a serious problem of anachronism—the tendency to use historical actors who lived in the past to judge those in a different era. As Pieter Van Hensbroek explains, the "historian, in such cases, enters the field with a prior substantial theory of history. Having some a priori knowledge about what this period in history 'really' is about. The historian does not have to ask the historical actors what is at issues. The historian pretends to know beforehand the drama that they were enacting."[16]

The preoccupation with the similarities and differences in African cultural artifacts in the Americas that characterizes the bulk of literature on masquerade carnivals on both sides of the Atlantic is understandable. Bettelheim has noted: "Based on a Herskovitsian retention model, a *retardataire* analysis might stress a continuous historical connection with Africa."[17] Julian Gerstin adds that this approach is a product of the anxiety associated with the search for a lost African ancestry. According to Gerstin: "More recent Caribbean writers—political, literary, scholarly, and popular—tracing their own roots, have often sought the specific African provenance of one or another custom, or have attempted to designate a single neo-African dance as the source of today's welter of styles. This is understandable: the search for origins can easily become a search for a singular, definite beginning; a desire to say, 'this is my ancestry.'"[18] It is therefore incumbent on scholars not to completely ignore the essence of a deeper and more forceful interrogation of memory as a site of remembering for the historical actors and the form of narratology they generated for their specific needs. The prerogative then is to further our appreciation of the effectiveness of masquerade carnivals in structuring narratives that have, across the centuries, attended to and continue to attend to the needs of those groups who fashioned them. Masquerade narratology is not cast in stone. The emphasis or storyline changes as the society transforms. A proper recognition of this dynamism holds the key to savoring the central argument of this study—that African masks and masquerades may be prototypes of the African Diaspora carnivals, but the diasporic antecedents need not be judged as a replica or one-on-one retentions of those found in Africa. This is in the respect that the sociopolitical and economic milieu that shaped the New World masquerades were quite dissimilar to the African ones.

Like all narratives, when the cause or initial target of engagement changes or becomes irrelevant, the focus of masquerade narratives also shifts. The only thing that remains constant with all techniques of narrative engagée is the use of memory or the act of remembering to serve a purpose in the *present*. The phrase "present" in this context is a present that is in constant mutability. The fluid nature and ability to masquerade in response to the needs of the changing times are in tune with the modernization discourse—assuming that the term is conceived as a process of adapting habits, ideas, institutions, and material cultures to more pressing needs of the today. Along this line of reasoning, Joseph LaPalombra has rejected the strict and controversial econometric definition of modernization as "counterproductive"—that is "the ubiquitous urge to industrialization," which hardly resonates with the realities in non-Western societies.[19]

Narratology, Authenticity, and Modernity

Tradition, adaptation, and continuity are synonymous with narratology, authenticity, and modernity. At every epoch in history, a people's traditions or customs are narrated as authentic, but the reality is that every "authentic" culture is an adaptation from something from the past or that already existing somewhere. Adaptations, therefore, are natural responses to needs of the present. To proceed, it is well known in the masquerade studies literature that memory is the key to a group's relationship with their pasts and their consciousness. What is often overlooked is that a people can selectively reinvent who they are by cherry-picking only those symbols and myths supporting the intended goals. The ways in which the past and the present are conceived and repackaged in a narrative, therefore, constitutes the notion of "authenticity" on which identity is supported. This study of African masquerades and carnivals of the African Diaspora vindicates Benedict Anderson's conclusion that identities are imagined, mythologized, and appropriated with inclusive and exclusive ideologies.[20]

As identity constructions are dynamic, so are masquerade arts, which have multiple lives and appropriate the language of socioeconomic and political modernities to reinvent and mutate their consummate nature of the struggle for space and empowerment. This explains why Brian Schiff proposes, "one of the primary functions of narrating is to 'make present' life experience and interpretations of life in a particular time and space."[21] Schiff further contends, "the most salient aspect of narrative is not the arrangement of speech elements into a particular order but the kinds of actions that can be accomplished with narratives. It is an expressive action, something that persons do. Narrating brings experience and interpretations into play, into a field of action, in a specific here and now."[22]

To further illustrate the fact, we may find the Sòmonò masquerade in the riverine areas of Kirango, Mali, a classic story of the "authentic" in a slowly changing society. In 1986, Susan Vogel observed the Sòmonò puppet masquerade festival organized by fishermen in the area.[23] The 1986 Sòmonò parade, as Vogel noted, echoed a similar event recorded over a century ago by Paul Soleillet, a French geographer, who was in a village south of Segou city in December 1885.

> I stopped there . . . to see Guignol! A square tent of white and blue striped fabric is installed in a boat with two paddlers, an ostrich head fixed upon a long neck extends from the front . . . then two marionettes appear suddenly out of the middle of the tent, one clothed in red, the other in blue, and they abandon themselves to some grotesque pantomimes. The drums, placed in a second boat, accompany the spectacle with deafening music.[24]

Along with other masquerades found in Mali, Guinea, and adjacent areas, the Sòmonò masquerade puppet characters remind the communities about the importance of the Niger River as a source of life; hence, the fishermen who own the masquerade are narrated as the originators.[25] At first glance it may appear that this centuries-old tradition is unchanging. It is revealing, however, that even the most seemingly static tradition is strategically revised and adapted to the needs of the time. In realization of the importance of an inclusive culture, the Sòmonò fishermen changed the narrative to accept Bamana blacksmiths (*numu*) as stakeholders who also created the popular wooden masks and rod puppets that feature in the annual festivals.[26]

With the Sòmonò, we see a masquerade narratology that was open to revision, adaptation, and modernization with blacksmiths, hunters, and farmers merged as stakeholders. To further ascribe legitimacy to the masquerade, the timing of the masquerade festival was changed so that all three troupes in Kirango performed their masquerades at the beginning of the dry season in October, which coincides with the harvest and hunting seasons for both fishermen and farmers.[27] By recognizing the most important local professions (fishermen, farmers, hunters, blacksmiths), the masquerade became an inclusive ethnic marker that celebrates the people's history. Vogel and Arnoldi further observe that the greater majority of the young generation in Kirango today "have no memory of the [Boso] Jara [men's] association, but the appearance of the jarawara masquerades in the annual Sòmonò theater may indeed create a special resonance for older fishermen who still attend its public performance."[28] This assertion mirrors Chinua Achebe's emphasis on the centrality of the story to mind: "It is the story that outlives the sound of war-drums and the exploits of brave fighters. . . . The story is our escort: without it we are blind."[29]

In Trinidad and Tobago, the use of masquerade narrative to "make present" is worthy of deeper exploration. The mid-nineteenth century witnessed a fierce anticarnival campaign from the popular press, apparently because of the confrontationist stance of these maskers toward unpopular government policies. However, from the late 1850s, following lesser antigovernment campaigns, there was a change in attitude by the press. For instance, the *Trinidad Sentinel* of February 23, 1860, argued that "the people have a prescriptive right to mask" but at the same time emphasized that it was time to modernize the festival with the inspiration of "civilization."[30] Philip W. Scher's inquiry on carnival, memory, and national culture in this island nation reveals that the way we choose to remember the past and the manner in which it is narrated shapes the nation rather than the other way round. Using the lens of masquerade carnival preservation, Scher elucidates the process of reconstructing a postcolonial Trinidadian national memory. The process sees the Trinidadian state jealously playing a central role in the erection of "authentic Carnival" forms. In this plot, the "Devil," a popular masquerade carnival among enslaved Africans, is embraced as an embodiment of the spirit of resistance and rebellion against oppression, inequality, and human rights abuses.[31] This is, of course, a saleable choice of narrative engagée that enhances the image of Trinidad's national culture and at the same time strikes harmonious chords among the domestic and international communities of political watchdogs, human rights activists, Western donor nations, and prodemocracy campaigners and other stakeholders.

The new focus of the masquerade narrative engagée in Trinidad and Tobago reminds us the "unauthentic" masquerades, as defined and remembered by the nation's authorities, are such obsolete characters as *upissenlit* or bed-wetter. The point should not be lost in thinking that the "Devil" and its past resilient fight against slavery was okay with the White planters and slave owners while the "unrefined" narratives associated with the bed-wetter were unwelcome by the elite in the late nineteenth and early twentieth centuries. The pertinent point is that the times and needs have changed. Today, this story of remembering appropriated with "selective amnesia" has helped Trinidadians establish a solid "national memory that is acceptable, proud, and in keeping with the current agenda of the state and affiliated social classes"—Whites, Creoles, Native Americans, Asians, and other stakeholders. Scher's study allows us to see the bond between the state, masquerade carnival, and a postcolonial consciousness that is alive to the ideals of the global neoliberal economic agenda. In the new self, culture in Trinidad has come to represent notions of state sovereignty (as a basic collective right of a national citizenry), in dialogue with the ideology of freedom, free market, and human rights protection. In this way, "the selection and preservation of culture is a process jealously guarded by local structures of power." But the discourse is carefully recontextualized and prioritized as modernization agenda for the survival of Trinidad's marginal economy within the larger world system.[32]

A similar reconfiguration has been witnessed in Nigeria where the "authentic" masquerade carnivals have been redefined and deployed to address the economic needs of today. Like in Trinidad where the state seized the initiative, in 2004, the then state governor of Cross River State, Donald Duke, leveraged masquerade carnivals to market his state as a hub for tourism and hospitality in Nigeria. Articulated in the context of "modernity" rather than another cultural nationalist scheme that often misses the target, the governor and his planning committee distanced themselves from the old narratives propagated by the Èkpé, Èkpo Onyohò, Ogbom, and other assortments of precolonial masquerade cults found in this region.[33] Rather, the governor introduced new ideas along with modern Caribbean forms by promoting carnival bands like Seagull, Passion, Masta Blasta, Bayside, and Freedom. This pattern of backflow in cultural diffusion between Africa and the African Diaspora is, to borrow an analogy from Michael Gomez, a "reversing sail" in the history of the African Diaspora complex.[34] Now held annually, the highpoint of the 2009 carnival was the "Carnival Cup 2009," a football competition among the carnival bands.[35]

Since 2004, the Calabar carnival has emerged as the fastest growing industry in Cross River State, celebrating Calabar culture as modern. This is what Will Rea has described in relation to his own study of masquerades in Ikoli Ekiti, Yorubaland, as the "penetration of and persistence of cultural and artistic forms into a present defined as 'modern' or modernity."[36] In this framework, through the instrument of modern masquerade carnivals, the state redefines itself as a parsimonious neoliberal entity open to the ideals of liberty, democracy, and inclusiveness. Thus, instead of reifying the masquerade tradition as a static institution that must be harnessed in its "original" forms, the recent trends in Mali, Trinidad, and Nigeria affirm that mask and masquerade carnivals have always served the needs of the present and adapted to the needs of those who created them as the times changed.

In light of the "Tabula Rasa" versus the "Retention" Schools in African and African American culture debates, the emergence of masquerade carnivals today as the cornerstone of Trinidad's and Calabar's modern economies predicated on

tourism and heritage could be captured with the biological theory of translocation, in which nutrients manufactured on leaves of a plant through the process of
photosynthesis move to other tissues of the plant. Here, the masquerade genres
invented in precolonial Africa represent the leaves of a plant. And the process
of photosynthesis in translocation represents the enslaved Africans' migration
to the Americas where they injected and adapted semblances of African-styled
masquerades to address the urgent social issues beleaguering their host societies.
While the nutrients of the culture have, in due time, permeated all fabrics of Caribbean life to the point where it is now both the motif and emblem of identity,
one must not lose sight of the critical fact that the African-themed masquerades
responded to the New World realities the way plants respond to the stimuli of
light in phototropism. As the roots of a plant give life to the entire system, so
the American soil gave life and form to the entire edifice of multiculturalism in
existence in the Americas.

   Thus, whether we are looking at masquerade performances in precolonial
Africa, colonial America, or in the antebellum/postcolonial state, the narrative
of identity and remembering that masquerades espoused has always been a contested arena of space, politics, social change, and mythmaking. Stanley Elkins
and others who forcefully push the view that enslaved Africans who survived the
perilous Middle Passage suffered memory blackout tend to forget that ellipsis of
memory and remembering are not unique to enslaved Africans.[37] Memory loss
and remembering are constants in history. As the saying goes, "He who arrives
at the middle of a story leaves with a disjointed narrative." Many who write on
African Diaspora history without a grounded knowledge of the African background often provide fragmented and disjointed stories. The critical issue is not
essentially that amnesia or forgetfulness might occur; what matters most is what
realities gave the individual or group a full sense of identity or relevance and
making the memory or what we remember to respond to the challenges of life
experiences.

   Olaudah Equiano's *The Interesting Narrative* remains an exemplar in the narrative art of remembering given its strategic response to the needs of his time.
In this literary engagée, Equiano consciously resisted focusing solely on himself as a former slave. Rather, he confronted the more crucial cause of abolition,
using his Igbo/African heritage to narrate Europe as a "primitive" slaveholding
culture in a global context. Comparing slavery in Igboland and in the Western
world, Equiano wrote: "I must acknowledge in honor of those sable destroyers
of human rights, that I never met with any ill-treatment, or saw any offered
to their slaves, except tying them, when necessary, to keep them from running

away."[38] The most critical message of Equiano's narrative is not whether he remembered correctly the nature of slavery and other subjects of interest in his account of Igboland or if actually he was born in Africa, as Vincent Carretta has questioned.[39] The fact is that he used what he committed to memory, or rather what he chose to remember, to advocate change in his eighteenth-century world. This was the prerogative need of "the present" in his time. Equiano's narrative engagée was a powerful modernist dialogue, which is often lost in the search for his true nativity.

In relation to the history of slavery in African American culture, it must be reiterated that memory and forgetfulness are constant parts of the history. One need not cross the Sahara Desert, the Pacific Ocean, or the Atlantic Ocean before amnesia sets in. Because the human mind is susceptible to forgetfulness, Europeans created the archives and Africans used the techniques of mimes and performative languages such as masks and masquerades to preserve, remember, and communicate their pasts for the present needs. Irobi uses the concept "phenomenology" to emphasize, "the engagement in lived experience between the individual consciousness and reality as sensory and mental phenomena."[40] Long before the African encounter with Europeans, it must be appreciated that the entire purpose of African festival and ritual theater—with all its spectacles, costuming, spatial configurations, architecture, music, drum language, dance, songs, choreography, and masking—has always been passed from generation to generation. The mode of passage made use of phenomenological channels and senses through the aptitude of the human body.[41] The discourse of phenomenology provides scholars with space to further explain the somatogenic abilities—the conscious and unconscious capacities of the human body as a site of narrative.

But a useful discussion in this direction must begin with a caveat that, despite the progress recorded so far in the field of kinesics (including sign language and lip reading), it is difficult to interpret the precise meanings of bodily movements to musical notes. A look at modern choreography shows that dancers are trained to move in unison without much attachment to or coherent understanding of the unspoken words. In 2008, I asked the Achi-Mbieri Nkwá Love chief dancer and choreographer, Akugbo Oguzie (whose uncle Athanasius Oguzie once occupied the same position), about the meaning of the group's dancing moves. The chief dancer started off with the comment that "every bird speaks the language of the audience." With those proverbial words, she emphasized the central determinant of language and cultural competence in music appreciation.[42] This assertion corroborates the position held by some scholars that "musical meaning is determined exclusively by cultural convention."[43] Having demarcated the basis for discerning the message hidden in a dance style, Akugbo Oguzie continued with a few examples from her Nkwá Love dance group's presentations during the 2008 Christmas festivities: "Every year, we train secretly for months prior to Christmas, and it is during this period of training that members learn, rehearse, and internalize the songs and choreographs. Waist wriggling in the Love dance represents communal unity and love. When we jump up and make an about turn following a song in progress, it signifies that there should be a turnaround from a social ill under focus in the song to a more acceptable societal behavior."[44] Nkwá Love reminds us of the Abigbo dance of Mbáise people of Igbo. Abigbo dancers also recount social ills and call out wrongdoers as enemies of society while challenging them to turn from their old way for good. Like the Nkwá Love, the Abigbo is both a dance style and a musical ensemble.[45]

The insights provided above affirm the role of cultural competence in dance interpretation. This corroborates Irobi's observation that in Africa and many parts of the African Diaspora, "dance, accompanied by music, represents the supreme art, the art par excellence. This is because dance, as a form of kinesthetic literacy, is the primary medium for coding the perception of our outer and inner worlds, our transcendent worlds, our spiritual history, and the memory of that complex history. The body is the major conduit of artistic expression, whether it is a painting, a dance, a book."[46] The meanings associated with Nkwá Love is different from the Ọháfiá-Èddá-Ábám-Arọ Ikpirikpi-ọgụ (War Dance), which uses aggressive thumping and a shaking of the chest to narrate valor and celebrate accomplishments of the warrior group in local wars. Similarly, an outsider to the Okoroshá masquerade dance of Achi-Mbieri, Umunneọhá, and Umunnáá Ámáụbụrụ Ubomiri will not recognize why the performers usually dance to the music with their thighs flapping in open-and-close movement while surging forward across the open square in the direction of the drummers. That dance style represents the phenomenon of increase and reproduction as in harvest and childbearing.[47] The Ọmụrụ-ọnwá and Ágbáchá-Èkuru ńwá dances for married ladies are a forum for womenfolk, especially new mothers, to exercise their bodies, shed baby fat, and stay healthy through weekly rehearsals. The dancers cuddle a wooden effigy of a baby and move their bodies in different directions such as holding it close to the chest, throwing it up, bathing positions, and so on, as a mother would with a new baby.

Combined together, the waist wriggling and about-turn jumps associated with the Nkwá Love, the lap flapping and surge through the dance arena noted with the Okoroshá masquerade, and the cuddling of wooden effigies and other bodily movements identified with the Ọmụrụ-ọnwá and Ágbáchá-Èkuru ńwá dances all describe several aspects of the Kalenda dance of the African Diaspora as observed by Jean-Baptiste Labat in 1722: "What pleases them most and is their most common dance is the calenda, which comes from the Guinea coast and, from all appearances, from the kingdom of Ardá [in Dahomey]. The Spanish have taken it from the blacks, and dance it in all America in the same manner as the blacks." Labat goes on to provide a vivid account of the dance formations, spectators, singers, and even bodily movements:

> The dancers are arranged in two lines, the one before the other, the men to one side, the women to the other. Those are the ones who dance, and the spectators make a circle around the dancers and drums. The most skilled sings a song that he composes on the spot, on such a subject as he judges appropriate, and the refrain, which is sung by all the spectators, is accompanied by a great beating of hands. As regards the dancers, they hold up their arms a little like those who dance while playing castanets. They jump, they spin, they approach to within three feet of each other, they leap back on the beat, until the sound of the drum tells them to join and they strike their thighs, [the thighs of] some beating against the others, that is, the men's against the women's. To see this, it seems that they beat their bellies together, while it is however only their thighs that support the blows.[48]

As the picturesque reveals, there is no gainsaying that the so-called Kalenda could best be defined as a conglomeration of diverse African dancing styles appropriated in a new culture. It was more a metaphor that embraced everything genre of African-styled dance from the Belair, Bomba, and Bamboula to Okoroshá, Djouba (djuba, juba, Yuba), and guiouba (ghoba), found in different regions of the Americas including Saint Thomas, the Dominican Republic, Puerto Rico, Martinique, Louisiana, and so on.[49]

While the meaning of dance is harnessed in specific cultural context, what distinguishes mass popular culture from indigenous culture are the context and the range of the message it communicates. This insight explains the power of African-themed popular music in the diffusion of global cultures. Blues, for instance, is better understood in light of its historical and transnational development as an offshoot of West African traditional labor or work songs. In Africa, labor songs are not danced like in other songs but harnessed in the manner with which laborers respond to the task before them. The version that would metamorphose into blues was first rendered by enslaved Africans on the American plantations in forms of lamentations, call-and-response, and shouts and hollers.

After the Emancipation, blues was quickly transformed into "classical" or "city blues." The tunes captured widespread emotions and moods of loneliness, confusion, and hardship among the Black population. Today, the sentiments that informed this unique musical genre have been repackaged and commercialized as a force in popular entertainment.

In sum, this study of African masks and masquerade carnivals in transnational context has shown that while the African tradition influenced the African Diaspora masquerade art forms, the proper way to approach their transatlantic journey is within the narrative context. The spectacles associated with African masquerades are both contagious and entertaining; but they are more than fun theater. They combine drama, dance, and music to engage with pressing social issues. Once this lesson is understood, we begin to see the proper historical links between African and African Diaspora masquerade carnivals across time and space. Thus, rather than focusing on the ethnic dimensions that often underestimate the more auspicious purposes masquerades provided enslaved people in the Americas, this work combined the broader African approach with the Igbo case study, in a metanarrative that underscores how tricky it is to assert with certainty which tradition is Igbo, Èfik, Ibibio, Ijǫ or derived from some other African group or regional culture. Just as in the African context, African diaspora masquerades were transnational, bridging the divide between memory and history.

NOTES

Introduction

1 Herskovits, *Cultural Anthropology*, 296. For a critic of this theory see Hernnerz, "Fluxos, Fronteiras, Híbridos," 3.

2 Mathur, "Diffusion of Culture," 13.

3 It is notable that the original application of the theory was in specific reference to Native American cultures.

4 Mason, *Influence of Environment*. Mason's essay appeared first in the Annual Report of the Smithsonian Institution in 1895.

5 Mason demarcated eighteen culture areas in his work. Then, Clark Wissler developed the concept with his study of the indigenous Native American traditions.

6 Wissler, *American Indian*, 220.

7 Herskovits, *Myth of the Negro Past*, 6. Herskovits pioneered this field of study with the objective to restore dignity to the Africans.

8 Elkins, Slavery, 91, 101–2. For an engaging analysis of these ideas, see Young, "African Religions," 1–18.

9 Raboteau, *Slave Religion*, 47. Although Raboteau was specifically speaking about African traditional religious presence in the U.S. South, the entire notion of an individual with a form of cultural/mental erasure is inconceivable. It is devoid of any scientific logic or evidence.

10 For a detailed discussion on the nature/nurture debate, see for instance Barlow, "Nature–Nurture and the Debate," 286–96.

11 For a cursory survey of this, see Cohen, *Masquerade Politics*, *Politics of Elite Culture*, and *Customs and Politics*.

12 Scher, *Carnival*.

13 Stolzoff, *Wake the Town*; Aching, *Masking and Power*.

14 Littlefield, *Contemporary African Art*; Jegede, *Art by Metamorphosis*; Dagan, *Spirit's Image*.

15 Gray, *Black Theater and Performance*.

16 See Miller, *Voices of the Leopard*; Nicholls, *Old-Time Masquerading*; and Falola and Genova, eds., *Orisa*, esp. 143–386. The various chapters of the volume explored the similarities of Yoruba culture with the New Orleans, Cuban, and other African Diaspora identities.

17 Falola and Njoku, eds., *Igbo in the Atlantic World*; Heywood, ed., *Central Africans*; Miller, *Voices of the Leopard*; and Falola and Childs, eds., *Yoruba Diaspora*.

18 See Okere, "Assumption of African Values," 6, 11. Against this background, it is apparent, as we have seen with Western education, soccer, and masquerade carnivals that certain institutions and ideas transcend their initial places of origin. For a further reading on this, see also Njoku, "Originality of African Philosophy," in *African Philosophy*, eds. Oguejieofor and Onah, 104.

19 Bettelheim, "Negotiations of Power in Carnival," 66.

20 Stuckey, "Through the Prism of Folklore," 417–37. See also Stuckey, *Slave Culture*.

21 Louisa Adams, interviewed on June 7, 1937, in *Slave Narratives*, 2.

22 Palmer, "From Africa to the Americas," 223–37.

23 Benjamin, *Atlantic World*.

24 Strogatz, *Nonlinear Dynamics and Chaos*.

25 Just to mention a few of these opposing views, see Perry, *Landscape Transformations* particularly, 22–24; and Russell, Silva, and Steele, "Modelling the Spread of Farming," 1–9.

26 Grow and Bavel, "Introduction," in *Agent-Based Modelling*, eds. Grow and Bavel, 3–27.

27 Bracketed explanations of the four key concepts are mine. Courgeau, Bijak, Franck, Silverman, "Model-Based Demography," in *Agent-Based Modelling*, eds. Grow and Bavel, 29–51.

28 Although Westermarck did not relate his findings on the Berbers to the Bantu, the similarity is striking. See Westermarck, *Ritual and Belief in Morocco*. See also Westermarck, *Marriage Ceremonies in Morocco*.

29 In the United States today, we are seeing the struggle between English and Spanish; in the United Kingdom, the wrestling match between English and Irish continues; and in Belgium, the Flemish and French languages often clash.

30 Keohane, *After Hegemony*, 51. See also Keohane, "International Institutions," 379–96.

31 Battuta, *Ibn Batoutah*; Álvares, *Ethiopia Minor*; Barbot, "Voyage to New Calabar Rivers"; Falconbridge, *Two Voyages to Sierra Leone*; Oldendorp, *History of the Missions*.

32 Sloane, *Voyage to the Islands*; Long, *History of Jamaica*; Barclay, *Voyages and Travels of James Barclay*; Lewis, *Journal of the West Indian Proprietor*; Scott, *Tom Cringle's Log*; Belisario, *Koo or Actor Boy*; Tuckerman, *Letter Respecting Santa Cruz*; Gurney, *Winter in the West Indies*; Day, *Five Years*.

33 Harris, *Rise of Anthropological Theory*, 377. Steward, *Theory of Culture Change*, esp. 83–88.

34 See Nicholls, *Old-Time Masquerading*; Diptee, "A Great Many Boys and Girls," in *Igbo in the Atlantic World*, eds. Falola and Njoku, 112–22; and Chambers, *Murder at Montpelier*.

35 Fyfe, *Africanus Horton 1835–1883*. See also Nwauwa, "Far Ahead of His Time," 107–21.

36 Gomez, *Exchanging Our Country Marks*. Gomez argues that the millions of

Africans brought to America would not have initially thought of themselves as Africans; rather, they were Asante, Yoruba, or Igbo, their lives and characters defined by village or nation.

37 For a similar idea, see the impressive study by Jackson and Mosadomi, "Cultural Continuities," in Falola and Genova, *Orisa*, 143–45. Interestingly, there also is a secret society called "Egungu" (without the second "n") among the Osomari Igbo community. See Nzimiro, *Studies in Ibo Political Systems*, 81.

38 See Lovejoy, "African Diaspora," 2.

39 Echeruo, "Dramatic Limits of Igbo," in *Drama and Theater in Nigeria*, ed. Ogunbiyi, 147.

40 Ukaegbu, "Composite Scene," PhD diss., University of Plymouth, May 1996, 25–26.

41 It is important to note that the mainstream studies on the Bantu may not recognize all these groups, especially the Igbo, as belonging to the proto-Bantu. My personal research based on linguistic, cultural, and geographical evidence indicates otherwise.

42 Cohen, *Masquerade Politics*, 3. See also Crowley, "Traditional Masques of Carnival," 194–223; and Mayer, *Origins, Commodification*, 2.

43 Enweonwu, Keynote Address (FESTAC), 4.

44 I spent the Christmas period of 2008, 2009, and 2010 on fieldwork in eastern Nigeria, observing the masquerade dances of Igbo, Ibibio, and Èfik communities, interviewing the participants, and comparing the data with that obtained from Mali.

45 Miller, "Cuban Abakuá Chants," 23–58; Chambers, *Murder at Montpelier*; Nicholls, "Igbo Influences," in *Igbo in the Atlantic World*, eds. Falola and Njoku, 228–52.

46 See for instance Heywood, "Portuguese into African," in *Central*, ed. Heywood, 105.

47 See Eze-Orji and Nwosu, "Contents of Carnival Calabar," 254–67.

48 Binder, "Crises of Political Development," in *Crisis and Sequences*, eds. Binder and LaPalombra, 40.

Chapter 1

Epigraph: Ezeowu, interview, Monday, June 18, 2008.

1 Woodward, *African Art*, 80. See also Picton, "What Is in a Mask?" in *Performance Arts in Africa*, ed. Harding, 51–53.

2 Lawal, *Gèlèdé Spectacle*, 39–40.

3 Kajobola, personal communication, Tuesday, June 6, 2017. According to Kajobola, in the Yoruba culture, Gélédé could also be used as a blanket name for "masquerades."

4 Abimbola, personal communication, Lagos, Thursday, March 23, 2017. See also Speed and Harper, "Gelede—A Yoruba Masquerade"; and Fantel, "Gelede Mask," 75.

5 Dete, *Wole Soyinka*, 22. See also Babatunde, "New Light on Gelede," 66–70, 94; and Drewal, "Gelede Masquerade," 8, 19, 62–63, 95–96.

6 Gramsci, *Prison Notebooks*, 248, 417. See also Erikson, "Popular Culture," 13–35.

7 See, for instance Johnson, *Venice Incognito*.

8 Glotz and Qerlemans, "European Masks," 14.

9 Carroll, "Carnival Rites," 490.

10 Ibid., 489–90.

11 Ugorji, personal communication, June 27, 2008. Vicky lived in Italy for twenty years and helped put this information in proper perspectives.

12 Schomburg Center for Research in Black Studies (hereafter SCRBS), SCMG 264, Michael Anthony Papers, "People Who Brought Us the Carnival," 1.

13 In another way, this was a plan devised by the Spanish authorities to encourage French nationals from neighboring islands to move to Trinidad in order to help them with managing the island, which the Spaniards could not staff at this time.

14 SCRBS, SCMG 264, Michael Anthony Papers, 2.

15 Ibid.

16 Hill, *Trinidad Carnival*, 11. See also Fraser, "History of Carnival, Colonial Office Original Correspondence, Trinidad" (CO 295), vol. 289, Trinidad No. 6160. Anthony and Carr said that "the Africans began to take part in Carnival after they had attained freedom under the Emancipation Bill of 1833." Anthony and Carr, eds., *David Frost*, 57.

17 Pearse, "Carnival in Nineteenth Century Trinidad," 176–77; Anthony and Carr, *David Frost*; Leon, *Calypso from France to Trinidad*.

18 Chasteen, "Prehistory of Samba," 29–47, 35.

19 I got this insightful proverb from my grandmother Nne Nkáru Njoku, personal communication, October 10, 1973.

20 For the original series, see Udal, "Dorsetshire Folklore," 174–81. See also Alford, *Hobby Horse*, 59.

21 Hole, *Dictionary of British Folk Customs*, 70.

22 Alford, *Hobby Horse*, 116.

23 Nicholls, "Igbo Influences," 228–52.

24 "Magical History of Yule," *HuffPost*, December 22, 2016.

25 Picton, "What's In a Mask?" in *Performance Arts in Africa*, ed. Harding, 52.

26 Baines and Lacovara, "Burial and the Dead in Ancient Egypt," 5–36. See also Ikram and Dodson, *Mummy in Ancient Egypt*.

27 See one of the most authoritative studies by Budge, *Tutankhamen*. For a discussion on Egyptian origin of masks and carnivals, see Liverpool, "Origins of Rituals and Customs?" 24–37.

28 Zarate, *Dia de los Muertos*; Garciagodoy, *Digging the Days of the Dead*.

29 Personal observation of the Aztec mask of the dead, Smithsonian National Museum of American History, Washington, DC, Monday, July 5, 2010.

30 The Manchester Museum in the United Kingdom holds two crucial pieces of art that provide solid evidence of the use of masks in ancient Egypt.

31 See Enzheng, "Magicians, Magic, and Shamanism," 27–73.

32 Khan, "Art Unmasked," *The Tribune*, Chandigarh, India, Sunday, May 28, 2006.

33 See Ukaegbu, "Igbo Mask Theater," 24.

34 Herodotus, *Histories of Herodotus*, trans. Rawlinson, 106–7.

35 See for instance Thompson, "Chaos and Strange Attractors," 128; Gallant, Rossi, and Tauchen, "Nonlinear Dynamic Structures," 871–77.

36 Khaldun, *Muqaddimah*, 1.

37 See for instance, McCann and Yodzis, "Nonlinear Dynamics and Population Disappearances," 873–79.

38 Strogatz, *Nonlinear Dynamics and Chaos*, 309.

39 Aniakor, "Household Objects," in *African Material Culture*, eds. Arnoldi, Geary, and Hardin, 214–42.

40 Ogbechie, *Ben Enweonwu*, 22.

41 Osuagwu, *Truth and Chaos*, 16–20.

42 Igwebe, *Original History of Arondizuogu*, 63.

43 Ibid., 66.

44 Bascom, "Forms of Folklore," 4.

45 Foucault, *Power/Knowledge*.

46 Olasope, "Gender Ambiguity," in Adelugba, Adeyemi, and Oni, eds., *Developments in the Theory and Practice*, 107.

47 Ibid.

48 Kalu, "Under the Eyes of the Gods," http//ahiajoku.igbonet.com/1988/.

49 In their study on Andhra Pradesh, India, Lambert et al. observed that the family, neighbors/neighborhood, and peer pressures are more effective in social control than the court system, police, and correctional facilities. See Lambert, Jiang, Karuppannan, and Pasupuleti, "Correlates of Formal and Informal Social Control," 1–12.

50 Sigler and Aamidor, "From Positive Reinforcement," 249–53.

51 Kalu, "Under the Eyes of the Gods."

52 Almosawa and Gladstone, "In TV Spectacle," *New York Times*, Monday, July 31, 2017.

53 Hamdun and King, *Ibn Battuta in Black Africa*, 43.

54 Asigbo, "Transmutations in Masquerade," 1–13.

55 I have italicized the word "conceptual" in order to contrast it to the word "practical."

56 Nlenanya, *Ahiajoku Lecture*.

57 Eliade, *Cosmos and History*.

58 Aberle, "Note on Relative Deprivation," in *Millennial Dreams in Action*, ed. Thrupp, 209–14.

59 Wallace, "Revitalization Movements," 264–81.

60 Feuerbach, *Essence of Christianity*.

61 Durkheim, *Division of Labor*.

62 Kalu. "Under the Eyes of the Gods."

63 Asigbo, "Transmutations in Masquerade," 2–3.

64 Ibid., 3.

65 Just to be clear, Judas Iscariot had left the flock after his betrayal of Jesus the Christ.

66 Eliade, *Sacred and the Profane*, 11.

67 The exception here is in theatrical plays, which are nothing comparable to the serious spiritual dimension with which the Africans went about their masquerade business.

68 Rotimi, "Through Whom the Spirits Breathe," in *Masquerade in Nigerian History*.

69 Bravmann, "Gyinna," in *Performance Arts in Africa*, ed. Harding, 149–57.

70 Ezikeojiaku, "Igbo Divination Poetry," 38. The author calls for the need for Igbo scholars to collect, classify, and analyze texts, particularly of Igbo oral poetry.

71 Illah, "Performing Arts of the Masquerade," 8.

72 Ogundeji, "Ritual as Theatre," 20–21.

73 Asigbo, "Transmutations in Masquerade," 5.

74 For a detailed read on this, see Horton, *West African Countries*, esp. 19–21.

75 Brown, "Patterns of Authority in West Africa," 261–78.

76 Fortes and Evans-Pritchard, eds., *African Political Systems*, 5–6.

77 Except for the Tallensi of Ghana, remarkably most these societies included in this model operated masquerade institutions.

78 Kenny, "Mutesa's Crime," 595–12.

79 See Packard, *Chiefship and Cosmology*, 4–6, 84; and Packard, *Politics of Ritual Control*.

80 Udo, *Who Are the Ibibio?* 138.

Chapter 2

Epigraph: Aristotle, *Politics*.

1 Falola, *Culture and Customs of Nigeria*, 38.

2 Nigerian National Archives Enugu (NNAE). Colonial anthropologists had a detailed study of the Njoku deity in Igboland. See ABADIST 1046–1/26/588, Njoku Juju at Ohanso Ndoni Areas, Aba Division, 1938.

3 Sieber and Hecht, "Eastern Nigerian Art," 71.

4 Other authors have emphasized this point. See for instance Sieber and Walker, *African Art*. For a detailed read on African cosmology, see the authoritative works of Mbiti, *Introduction to African Religion*, esp. 34–59; and also Mbiti, *African Religion and Philosophy*.

5 Nwanunobi, *African Social Institutions*, 168. This reminds us of Inglehart's argument that economic development, cultural change, and political change go together in intelligible and sometimes discernible patterns. This implies that while certain changes are predictable, some trajectories of socioeconomic change are more likely than others. Once a society starts to industrialize, for example, a whole syndrome of related sociopolitical and economic changes, including new gender roles, tend to emerge. These changes in worldviews seem to reflect changes in the economic and political environment. See Inglehart, *Modernization and Postmodernization*, 3–8.

6 Coulanges, *Family, Kin and City-States*.

7 Oliver, "Bantu Genesis," 245–58. Linguistic and archaeological evidence places the

cradle of Bantu-language speakers in the Nigeria-Cameroon border area. See also Phillipson, *Later Prehistory.*

8 Nze, *Aspects of Edeh Philosophy,* 84. For a similar argument, see Gutema, "Does African Philosophy Have a Contribution?" 63–75.

9 In line with this thinking, see for instance Basden, *Among the Ibos of Nigeria;* Meek, *Law and Authority;* Forde and Jones, *Igbo and Ibibio-Speaking Peoples;* Ilogu, *Christianity and Igbo Culture*

10 Durkheim, *Rules of Sociological Method,* 81; Durkheim, *Division of Labor in Society,* 44–45; and Durkheim, *Education and Society,* 45.

11 For a colonial anthropological report on the Igwe deity, see NNAE, AFDIST C3/50–6/11/3, Igwe Juju, 1909.

12 Nwala, *Igbo Philosophy,* 26.

13 Onwu, *Uzo Ndu Na Ezi Okwu.*

14 Edeh, *Towards an Igbo Metaphysics,* 116–17.

15 For an engaging analysis of the Greek gods, see Kullmann, "Gods and Men," 1–23.

16 See Uzor, "Omabe Masquerade Festivals," *Vanguard,* May 14, 2015.

17 Onwu, "Uzo Ndu Na Ezi Okwu," 5–6.

18 NNAE, ARODIV 3/1/55. Anthropological Report on the Aro Confederation by Matthews and Shankland, 1945.

19 NNAE, ONPROF 8/1/4702. Anthropological Report on Onitsha Province by Meek C. K., 1931.

20 Colonial anthropological reports show that there were thousands of these village-based deities across Igboland: see for instance UMPROF, PC.10/1911–6-1/2, Obonorie Juju, Report by H. R. A. Crawford, 1911; ONPROF OP.363/27–7/14/139, Omaliko Juju at Agbaja, Report on, 1927; and ABADIST 589–1/26/305, Nnechetara Juju, 1933–49. NNAE, AFDIST 13/1/6, Report on the Cult of *Arunsi* Edda, 1934.

21 NNAE, CSE 1/85/4596A, Anthropological Research on Onitsha Province by Jeffreys, M. D. W., 1931.

22 Kalu, *African Pentecostalism,* 4, 200; and "Under the Eyes of the Gods," 15–17.

23 Chidi Osuagwu, personal communication, Owerri, December 9, 2010.

24 Francis O. C. Njoku, personal communication, July 7, 2017.

25 NNAE, NA.106 vol. II AFDIST/13/1/6, Edda Clan—Report on the Cult of Arunsi, 1934. See also OP.21 ONPROF/7/15/8, Edda Tribe—Anthropological Report on the Sacrifices at the Feast of New Yams in Edda Afikpo Division, 1928.

26 NNAE, NA.106 vol. II AFDIST/13/1/6, Edda Clan—Report on the Cult of Arunsi, 1934. See also OP.21 ONPROF/7/15/8, Edda Tribe—Anthropological Report on the Sacrifices at the Feast of New Yams in Edda Afikpo Division, 1928.

27 Kalu, "Under the Eyes of the Gods," 5. Museum of Archaeology and Anthropology (MAA), N.71839.GIJ, "Boys masquerade" (Ibibio style mask), Abiriba Cross River, Southeastern Nigeria by G. I. Jones Photographic Archive, 1932–1939.

28 Onyishi Ngwu Nwa Idoko in an interview with Chinyere Uzor, "Omabe Masquerade Festivals," *Vanguard,* Thursday, May 14, 2015.

29 NNAE, AWDIST AW 80–2/1/56, Dances Harmful or Otherwise Report, 1919–1920—The Divisional Office, January 9, 1920.

30 Enwonwu, Keynote Address (FESTAC).

31 Trowell, *Classical African Sculpture*; Willett, *African Art*, 40. As Willett has argued, the huge variety of African cultural spaces underscores "the dangers of generalization" (9).

32 Kamer, "De l'authenticité des sculptures africaines," 9. See also Rachewiltz, *Introduction to African Art*, 7–91, and Steiner, *African Art in Transit*.

33 Thompson cited in Harn, *African Art*, 2.

34 MacAloon, "Introduction," in *Rite, Drama, Festival, Spectacle*, ed. MacAloon, 1.

35 According to local historians, the Arǫ people conquered the Ibibio people, who were the original inhabitants of the land now occupied by the Arǫ. The story has it that the Ibibio warriors who fought in the war were slain at Oror; hence it became the chieftaincy village.

36 Igwebe, *Original History of Arondizuogu*, 66–67. There have been ideas floating that the Ǫgéné Njimá masquerade club was instituted in 1972 to revitalize the pre-civil war (1966–1970) masking culture of the community. But the evidence of Richard Igwebe's study of Arǫndizuǫgu masquerades before the war shows that Njimá was not even mentioned among such masquerades as Ǫganigwe, Ájikwu, and Onyekurum—all of which the author described as "Night Masquerades," which were the most powerful spirits. According to Igwebe, Onyekurum was "more useful than all other masks," because it characteristically challenged anybody, including the king. "Onyekurum has all rights to abuse anybody when it comes out."

37 Nzekwu, "Masquerade," 188.

38 See Reynolds, *Secret Societies;* and Howard, *Secret Societies*. For a quick read, see Grecian, "The 7 Most Exclusive Secret Societies in History," *HuffPost*, May 28, 2014.

39 Onwuejeogwu, *Evolutionary Trends*, 12.

40 Falola, *Culture and Customs of Nigeria*, 142.

41 NNAE, OP.21 ONPROF/7/15/8, Edda Tribe—Anthropological Report on the Sacrifices at the Feast of New Yams in Edda Afikpo Division, 1928. See also Ottenberg, "Humorous Masks," in Fraser and Cole, eds., *African Art & Leadership*, 100–1.

42 NNAE, OG/670 UNWANA Clan—AFDIST 15/1/37 Report on Social Organization of Afikpo Division, 1930–3. See Nwafo, *Born to Serve*, 13; Johnson, *Of God and Maxim Guns*, 64–65. The present author was not allowed to watch the Egbele festival during his fieldwork in Afikpo and Unwáná in October–November 2001.

43 Duerden, *African Art, an Introduction*, 2.

44 Millington cited in Harn, *African Art*, 2.

45 For a detailed discussion on this with specific reference to other parts of Africa, see the excellent work of the Hurst Gallery, *African Arts of War and Peace*.

46 Eze, personal communication, Umuahia, July 5, 2011. For practice of this in Amobia village in early 1900s, see MAA, N.71635.GIJ. "Ghost Police, Amobia Village by G. I. Jones Photographic Archive, 1932–1939.

47 Collins Utube Umoh, personal communication, Calabar, July 10, 2011.

48 Kalu, "Under the Eyes of the Gods," 5; Falola, *Customs of Nigeria*, 143.

49 Kalu, *Embattled Gods*, 121; and "Under the Eyes of the Gods."

50 Isaac Kanu, personal communication, July 4, 2011. Formerly, it was important for every person of Arọ descent to attend the annual Ikeji festival. In recent times, it has become practically difficult for those far away in Europe, America, or Asia to honor the annual festival.

51 The "Ukwu" suffix to the name "Enugu" is an Igbo adjective meaning "big."

52 For a report on this see NNAE, OG 2138: Abam Society; CSE 18816: Idong Society, Abak District (Abakdist): Petition to Resident Calabar 15/4/41; & TO 2: Abakdist Leopard Society (Ékpo Owo), esp. D. C. Neilland, Notes on the Leopold Society, 13/5/46.

53 For more on the Ijele, see Aniakor, "The Igbo Ijele Mask," 42–47, 95; Henderson and Umunna, "Leadership, Symbolism in Onitsha," 28–37, 94–96; and Boston, "Some Northern Ibo Masquerades," 61–62.

54 See Willett, *African Art*, 188. Emphasizing this point, Ndukaihe reiterates that masquerade is a universal traditional and recreational activity in the Igbo culture that establishes friendship not only within but across ethnic boundaries. See Ndukaihe, *Achievement as a Value in Igbo/African Identity*, 229. See also Tomaselli and Wright, *Africa*, 132.

55 Ukaegbu, "Composite Scene," 34.

56 Nwafor, *Leopards of the Magical Dawn*, 67.

57 Baldwin Anyasodo, an emeritus professor and professional artist, provided this insight; personal communication, July 26, 2008.

58 Jegede, "African Art," in *Africa,* ed. Falola, 285.

59 Today this genre of masquerades also takes advantage of their disguise to extort money from spectators and nonmembers.

60 Nwaka, "Secret Societies and Colonial Change," 188. For a detailed read on this colonial misunderstanding, see NNAE B 1680/15: J. N. Cheetham, "The Revival of Secret Societies," 1915.

61 Steiner, *African Art in Transit*, 101, 104.

62 Ottenberg, "Illusion, Communication, and Psychology," 149–85. See also Falola, ed., *Igbo Art and Culture*, 149. See also MAA, N.71839.GIJ. "Boys masquerade" (Ibibio style mask), Abiriba Cross River, Southeastern Nigeria by G. I. Jones Photographic Archive, 1932–1939.

63 For a similar observation with African arts in other ethnic societies, see Rachewiltz, *Introduction to African Art*, 70–73; 74–80.

64 For an excellent account on this aspect of core versus peripheral Igbo areas, see Afigbo, "Igboland Before 1800," in *Groundwork of Nigerian History*, ed. Ikime, 73–88.

65 Onwu, *Uzo Ndu Na Ezi Okwu*, 12. For a similar assertion, see also Jaja, Erim, and Andah, *Old Calabar Revisited*, 189; Abasiattal, *History of the Cross River*, 7; and Afigbo, *Ground Work of Igbo History*, 301.

66 See OW.Conf.1/13–1/4/1 ABADIST Long Juju of Aro Revival of the worship of

by Aro resident in the Okigwe District, 1913. For the various studies, see Afigbo, "Eclipse of the Aro," 3–24.

67 Dike and Ekejiuba, *Aro of Southeastern Nigeria*, 223–26.

68 NNAE, Ajali-Aro Agreement of August 17, 1911. See also Edeh, *Towards an Igbo Metaphysics*, 11; Nwabara, *Iboland*, 19; Hives, *Juju and Justice*, 248–52.

69 See Afigbo, "Igbo Subculture Areas," for a good summary. See also Talbot, *Peoples of Southern Nigeria*.

70 Just to mention but a few, see reports on Agbe, Njoku, Agaba, Omaliko. NNAE, ONPROF, OP 363/27–7/14/139, Omaiko Juju at Agbaja, Report on, 1927; ABADIST 1046–1/26/588, Njoku Juju at Ohanso Ndoni Areas, Aba Division, 1938; CSE EP 23403—1/85/11255, Agaba Juju, 1949–50; and OW 8102—5/1/128 AHODIST, Agbe Juju, 1949–50.

71 Several studies on the Igbo Ukwu culture have shown that this culture, renowned for its numerous sculptures, vessels, and ornamental objects, was "largely locally evolved." See Sutton, "International Factor at Igbo-Ukwu," 145–60. See also Afigbo, "Anthropology and Historiography," 1–16.

72 Udo, who has studied a plethora of the Ibibio masquerade art forms from inside, also underscores similar dynamics. See Udo, *Who Are the Ibibios?* 138.

73 Feierman, *Peasant Intellectuals*. See also Falola, *Yoruba Guru*.

74 Afigbo, "Among the Igbo of Nigeria," 5–6.

75 Afigbo, *Igbo Enwe Eze*, 13. See also Onwumechili, *"Igbo Enwe Eze?"* 18. See also Afigbo, "The Bini Mirage," 17–24. FIGURE 2.1. Dancing initiation masks, boys' initiation, Cross River. This image is copyright. Reproduced by permission of University of Cambridge Museum of Archaeology & Anthropology (N.13095.GIJ).

Chapter 3

1 Malcolm Guthrie coined the word "proto-Bantu." It is important to point out up front that some scholars put the starting date of the migrations at somewhere between 5000 and 3000 BCE. See for instance the authoritative work of Vansina, "Bantu in the Crystal Ball," 287–333. I have deliberately chosen 2500 BCE as a very conservative estimate. This is approximately when the migrations assumed a more meaningful momentum.

2 Wang, "Globalization Enhances Cultural Identity," 84. Similar views have been emphasized by Labes, "Globalization and Cultural Identity," 88; and Inda and Rosaldo, *World in Motion*.

3 Linton, *Study of Man*.

4 For an in-depth discussion on this, see Ellwood, "Theories of Cultural Evolution," 779–800.

5 Perry, *Children of the Sun*. This is the book in which Perry expressed the belief that culture or civilization flows from Egypt. See also Rivers, *History and Ethnology*. The Egypt-centered approach would later inform Diop and Asante's Afrocentricity theory in African Studies. See Asante, *Cheik Anta Diop*.

6 Ratzel, an ethnogeographer, believes that after diffusion, a culture trait could then undergo adaptation to local conditions. See Erickson and Murphy, *History of Anthropological Theory*, 58. Frobenius, *Vom Kulturreich des Festlandes*, used patterns of geography to explain diffusion. He saw culture as a living organism that is born, develops, and dies. See also Schmidt, "Fritz Graebner," 203–14.

7 Schmidt, *Culture Historical Method of Ethnology*, 25.

8 See Sidky, *Perspectives on Culture*; and Ferreira, "Ethnology and History," 1–11.

9 Malefijt, *Images of Man*, 170. Again, the network of culture traits seemed to be too complex to sort out and understand clearly.

10 One of his very influential works remains Boas, "Methods of Ethnology," 311–21.

11 Herskovits, *Cultural Anthropology*, 296.

12 Mathar, "Diffusion of Culture," 13.

13 Mason, *Influence of Environment*. This work was first published in the Annual Report of the Smithsonian Institution.

14 Ibid. Mason found as many as eighteen culture areas in his study and Clark Wissler subsequently provided systematic treatment of the paradigm following his study of Native American indigenous cultures.

15 Wissler, *American Indian*, 220.

16 Currie, Meade, Guillon and Mace, "Cultural Phylogeography," 1–8. The authors remind us that there is a concession among scholars on the point of the Bantu cradle. However, some other studies have included some parts of the Shaba territory in the Republic of Zaire as part of the original Bantu homeland. See for instance, Kahlheber, Bosteon, and Neumann, "Early Plant Cultivation," 253–72; Amadi, "Northern Factor," 87; and Vansina, "Bantu in the Crystal Ball," 306.

17 Oliver, "Problem of Bantu Expansion," 361–76. In fact, by 1966 when Oliver's essay was published, the cause of Bantu expansion was seen to be the desiccation of the Sahara, a point taken from Clark, "Prehistoric Origins of African Culture," 181–82. In other words, the idea of conquest and invasion propounded by Johnston had been abandoned.

18 Russell, Silva, and Steele, "Modeling the Spread of Farming."

19 Grollemuna et al., "Bantu Migration," 13296–301.

20 Split and compare is different from what Meeusen likened to the peeling of an onion: a few languages evolve from the mass of dialects; later, another few break off; and so on until the core of the onion suddenly fell apart. See Guthrie, "Comparative Bantu: A Preview," 6–18.

21 But more important, we should also remember that the pioneers of Bantu studies for a while concentrated on ethnic groups found in the Southern region of Africa. For an engaging exposé on the Bantu and the southern reaches of Africa, see Vansina, "Bantu in the Crystal Ball," 299–311.

22 In a letter to the editor of *Science Progress* dated May 23, 1922, Sheldon used the word "races" to refer to the Bantu. See Sheldon, "Bantu Races," 303.

23 See for instance Guthrie, "Comparative Bantu: A Preview," 40–45; and *Comparative Bantu*; and Flight, "Malcolm Guthrie and the Reconstruction," 81–118.

24 Bleek, *Comparative Grammar*. Bleek coined the name *Bantu* in the 1850s.

25 Ravenstein, ed. and trans., *Journal of the First Voyage,* 26–40. See also Zwartjes, *Portuguese Missionary Grammars*, 205–41.

26 Greenberg, "Studies in African Linguistic Classification," 309–17.

27 The emphasis on *"think"* is mine to denote the obvious problem of errors of omission and inclusion. Johnston, "Bantu and the Semi-Bantu Languages," 97–110, and *Comparative Study of the Bantu*; Guthrie, *Classification of the Bantu Languages, Bantu Language*, and *Bantu Sentence Structure*. See also Bryan, ed., *Bantu Languages of Africa*.

28 See Werner, "Notes on Clicks in the Bantu Languages," 416–21; "Bantu Element in Swahili," 432–56; and *Myths and Legends of the Bantu*.

29 See for instance the Republic of Kenya, Kenya National Assembly Official Report Second Parliament Inaugurated February 6, 1970, 675–76.

30 Research notes and personal communication with three Kenyan professors, April 2–3, 2008. For a similar work on Bantu words in Zulu, see Werner, "Some Bantu Language Problems," 157.

31 A similar observation concerning other African language classifications has been noted by Vansina, "Bantu in the Crystal Ball," 314.

32 Greenberg, "Linguistic Evidence," 205–9. Greenberg has been described by Vansina as a disciple of Herskovits, who taught him to "look at Africa as a whole" rather than in parts. See Vansina, "Bantu in the Crystal Ball," 290–91.

33 Kalu and Kalu, "Battle of the Gods," 1–18.

34 Afigbo, *Igbo and Her Neighbors*, 47–52.

35 Alagoa and Anozie, *Early History of the Niger Delta*, 66.

36 Alagoa and Anozie, *Early History of the Niger Delta*, 66; Lafleur, *Exploring the Niger-Congo Languages*.

37 Guthrie, "Some Developments in the Prehistory," 273–82.

38 Vansina, "Bantu in the Crystal Ball," 294. See also Bennett and Sterk, "South Central Niger Congo," 241–73.

39 Grollemuna et al., "Bantu Migration," 13296.

40 Schmidt, *Culture Historical Method of Ethnology*, 25.

41 See Wissler, *American Indian*, 142–48. Wissler explored the similarities in poems found among the various groups separated by geography. More important, see his chapter 10 on "Social Grouping."

42 One revelation made by Russell King in relation to this study is that we are not really in the "Age of Migration" as some exponents of globalization assume. With only 3 percent of the global population representing international migrants, the Age of Migration was actually in the Ancient Global Age as demarcated in this study. See King, *Theories and Typologies of Migration*, 5.

43 Posnansky, *Archaeology and Linguistic*.

44 Mathar, "Diffusion of Culture," 9.

45 *Ibn Battuta in Black Africa*, trans. by Hamdun and King, 30–31; *Travels of Ibn Battuta*, trans. by Gibb, 6–7; and Levtzion and Spalding, *Medieval West Africa*, 69.

46 Amadi, "Northern Factor," 80–89, has explored this idea. Further studies are required in this direction.

47 While some of the Bantu may have left to avoid inter-and intragroup conflicts, including family quarrels, nonetheless, love, hate, the quest for freedom from oppression, and the sheer spirit of adventure usually play determinant roles in migrations around the world. If the French, Belgian, and German colonial stranglehold in Africa could serve as an example, the colonized people tried to escape from these Europeans' African dominions as expressions of their objections to excessive imperial taxation, forced and free labor demands, and other forms of oppression. It is well known that the first consequence of the mass movement of populations in history is displacement. Powerful people need living space or what the Germans call *lebensraum*.

48 Wrigley, "Speculations," 189–203.

49 Palmer, "From Africa to the Americas," 225.

50 Kilonzo, "Trajectories of Culture," 61–69.

51 See Pulford, ed., *Peoples of the Ituri*; Turnbull, *Forest People* and *Mbuti Pygmies*. For a similar Igbo culture, see Onyishi et al., "Female Genital Cutting," 1–7.

52 Wanyama and Egesah, "Ethnography and Ethno-music," 6–18.

53 Isiugo-Abanihe, "Bridewealth, Marriage, and Fertility," 151–78. However, this tradition has undergone considerable changes over the years to now involve heavy monetary demands.

54 Benti, *Urban Growth in Ethiopia*.

55 See Turton, "Bantu, Galla, and Somali Migration," 519–37. For more on this, see Njoku, *History of Somalia*, 12–13, 49, 109, 162.

56 I spent parts of 2009, 2010, and 2017 on ethnographic fieldwork in eastern Nigeria observing the masquerade dances of Igbo and Èfik communities, interviewing the participants, and comparing the data with similar data obtained from Mali.

57 For details, see Conteh-Morgan, "Francophone Africa," in *History of Theater in Africa*, ed. Banham, 106–7.

58 See UNESCO, "Makishi Masquerade."

59 Ibid. See also Leo and Jordan, *Makishi Lya Zambia*; and Jordán, "Chokwe!" 18–35.

60 Russell, Silva, and Steele, "Modeling the Spread of Farming."

61 Robertson and Bradley, "New Paradigm," 287–323.

62 See Hartle, "Archaeology in Eastern Nigeria," 13–17.

63 Afigbo, *Igbo History and Society*, esp. 125–42.

64 Beleza, Gusmao, Amorim, Carracedo, and Salas, "Genetic Legacy of Western Bantu," 366–75.

65 Herskovits, *Cultural Anthropology*, 296. A student of Boas, Herskovits remains one of the proponents of this view.

Chapter 4

1 Jones, *The Trading States of the Oil Rivers*, 15–17. See also Oriji, "Oracular Trade," 42. Oriji sees the Kálábári part of the Bight's port as the Dutch sphere, and when the volume of trade shifted to the other ports, "the Arọ trade network was stimulated."

2 I am using data from the UNESCO Slave Trade Project. See Voyages: The Trans-Atlantic Slave Trade Database (www.slavevoyages.org/). Estimates from other studies may vary.

3 The name *Biafra* became controversial when the eastern Nigeria enclave, led by the first republic Igbo politicians, seceded with that name from the Nigerian State in 1967.

4 I gained this insight from Catharine Anosike, personal communication, December 10, 2008. *Fárá* is a local dialect for "pick up" for the Ụbákuru community in Mbieri.

5 I thank Professor Douglas Chambers for drawing my attention to this discussion. See Goldie, *Dictionary of the Efik Language*, xlvi, 5, 25, 49; and *Addenda to the Efik Dictionary*, 8, 13, 24–25. See also Kaufman, *Ibibio Dictionary*, 15, 72.

6 Álvares, *Ethiopia Minor*, chap. 13. See also Johnson, "Visit to Fernando Po." The visit covered Fernando Po, Old Calabar, Bonny, and Opobo in the Niger Delta, as well as Èfik, Benin River, and the interiors—areas the bishop identified as the Bight of Biafra. This article was first published in *Church Missionary Intelligencer and Records* (December 1904): 896.

7 Álvares, *Ethiopia Minor*, 11.

8 Wright, *World and a Very Small Place*.

9 Nicklin in his "Cross River Studies," *African Arts* 24–27, has made a similar point by stating that "research and publication on the peoples and cultures of the Cross River region have never progressed systematically and without interruptions." Not even the resourceful Imbua and coauthors' recent work could deal with the aspect of the historical trends prior to the sixteenth centuries or the masquerade traditions associated with the region as detailed in the preceding chapter. See Imbua, Lovejoy, and Millar, eds., *Calabar on the Cross River*.

10 Wallerstein, *Modern World System*.

11 Curtin, *African Slave Trade*; Fage, "Slavery and the Slave Trade," 393–404; and "Effect of the Slave Trade," in Moss and Rathbone, eds., *Population Factor*, 15–23.

12 These are among the major scholars who helped create the Trans-Atlantic Slave Trade Database (www.slavevoyages.org/).

13 Manning, "African Population Projections, 1850–1960, 8.

14 Eltis and Richardson, "A New Assessment of the Transatlantic Slave Trade," in *Extending the Frontiers*, eds. Eltis and Richardson, 46–47. For an engaging read on the effects of the trans-Atlantic slave commerce on the Bight of Biafra and its hinterlands, see Brown and Lovejoy, eds., *Repercussions of the Atlantic Slave Trade*.

15 As Morgan noted: "High population densities in the Igbo heartland, sustained by a balance between the sexes and good reproductive capacity, meant that large numbers of slaves could be supplied to ships without depleting the demographic stock." Morgan, "Atlantic Slave Trade," in *Igbo in the Atlantic World*, eds. Falola and Njoku, 82.

16 This was the period when the Igbo entered into the slave trade fully. Brown and Lovejoy in *Repercussions of the Atlantic Slave Trade* have provided a good account of this dynamics.

17 Miers and Kopytoff, "African Slavery as an Institution," in *Slavery in Africa*, eds. Miers and Kopytoff, 3–73.

18 Afigbo, "Aro and the Trade," in *Igbo in the Atlantic World*, eds. Falola and Njoku, 71–73.

19 Despite their elaborate story of the Arọ, Dike and Ekejiuba ignored these diverse and multidimensional contexts. See Dike and Ekejiuba, *Aro of South-Eastern Nigeria*.

20 Forde and Jones, *Ibo and Ibibio-Speaking Peoples*.

21 Hives, *Ju-Ju and Justice*, 248–52. See also Nwabara, *Iboland*, 19.

22 Latham, *Old Calabar 1500–1891*, 26–27; Isichei, *History of the Igbo People*, 58–59; Dike and Ekejiuba, *Aro of South-Eastern Nigeria*, chap. 2. The man who initiated this error was H. F. Matthews, government anthropologist, in his "Reports on the Arọ," see the file A. D. 635 on Arọ Subtribes in the Nigerian National Archives, Enugu (NNAE). See also Afigbo, *Ropes of Sand*, chap. 6; and Northrup, *Trade without Rulers*, 34–36.

23 Isichei, *Igbo Worlds*, 10. See also Onwuejeogwu, *An Nri Civilization*.

24 Afigbo, *Ropes of Sand*, 200–23.

25 NNAE, EP1331/07–16/2/608 CALPROF "Cameroon-Nigeria (Cross River) and Cameroons (Yola) Boundary Delimitation, 1907."

26 Smith, "The Canoe in West African History," 515–33.

27 For details on this, see Alagoa, "Long-Distance Trade," 319–29, and *History of the Niger Delta*; Northrup, "Growth of Trade," 217–36, and *Trade without Rulers*, chap. 1; Nadel, "The Kede," in *African Political Systems*, ed. Fortes and Evans-Pritchard; Kolapo, "Canoe in Nineteenth Century," in *Aftermath of Slavery*, eds. Korieh and Kolapo.

28 Nzewunwa, *Niger Delta*, 239.

29 Alagoa, "Development of Institutions," 269–78.

30 Hartle, "Archaeology in Eastern Nigeria," 134–43.

31 This conclusion is drawn based on the evidence presented by the research of Shaw and Onwuejeogwu. See Shaw, *Igbo-Ukwu*; Onwuejeogwu, *Igbo Civilization*.

32 Alagoa, "Long-Distance Trade," 319–29. Alagoa, "The Development of Institutions," 269–78. It is important to remind the reader once again that initially the Ijọ indigenous political system was same as the Ibo Ibibio village-based democratic system, and this blueprint for the sociopolitical organization did not change despite the transition to the centralized system.

33 None bears this story of kidnapping better than the experience of Olaudah Equiano. See Equiano, *Interesting Narrative*, esp. 45–47.

34 Nwokeji, *Slave Trade and Culture in the Bight of Biafra*, esp. 181–87.

35 For more details, see Afigbo, *Abolition of the Slave Trade*, 128.

36 Igwebe, *Original History of Arondizuogu*, 76–81.

37 Afigbo, "Aro and the Trade," 71–81.

38 Njoku, "Neoliberal Globalism in Microcosm," 59.

39 See Isichei, *History of the Igbo People*, 62. On theories of Arǫ success, see Northrup, *Trade without Rulers*, 114.

40 Miller, "Cuban Ábakuá Chants," 23–58 and *Voices of the Leopard*; Joseph Miller, "Secret Society Goes Public," 161–88; Röschenthaler, *Purchasing Culture*; Lovejoy, "Transformation of the Ékpè Masquerade," in *Carnival*, Innes, Rutherford, and Bogar, eds.; Ishemo, "From Africa to Cuba," 253–72.

41 For more on cultural emersion, see Afigbo, *Abolition of the Slave Trade*, 111–12.

42 Lovejoy and Richardson, "Slave Ports of the Bight of Biafra," in *Repercussions of the Atlantic Slave Trade*; Northrup, "Growth of Trade Among the Igbo," 217–36, and *Trade without Rulers*.

43 For the Arǫ, see Nwokeji, *Slave Trade and Culture*; Oriji, "Oracular Trade," 42, and "Slave Trade, Warfare, and Aro Expansion," 151–66; Dike and Ekejiuba, *Aro of South-Eastern Nigeria*, 130–42.

44 Nicholls, *Old-Time Masquerading*; Njoku, "Symbols and Meanings," in *Migrations and Creative Expressions*, eds., Falola, Afolabi, and Adesanya, 257–79.

45 See Eze-Orji and Nwosu, "Contents of Carnival Calabar," 254–67.

46 See Chambers, "Ethnicity in the Diaspora," 2–39.

47 Young, *Tour through the Islands*, 269.

48 Álvares, *Ethiopia Minor*, 11.

49 Palmer, "From Africa to the Americas," 223–37.

50 Oldendorp, *Caribbean Mission*, 167, 173.

51 See Prichard, *Researches into This Physical History*, 210–12.

52 Edwards, *History, Civil and Commercial*, 73–75, 87.

53 Jones, *Africa and Indonesia*, and "Indonesia and Africa," 155–68.

54 Nzewi, Anyahuru, and Ohiaraumunna, *Musical Sense and Musical Meaning*, 33–48.

55 Moreton, *Manners and Customs*, 153; see also Nicholls, "Igbo Influences," 231.

56 See Pearse, "Aspects of Change," 29–35.

57 McDaniel, "Concept of Nation in the Big Drum Dance," in *Musical Repercussions of 1492*, 400–401.

58 Nicholls, "Igbo Influences," 231.

59 McDaniel, "Flying Africans," 32.

60 The most celebrated of these stories is the so-called Igbo landing at Dunbar Creek on Saint Thomas Island, Glynn County, Georgia, where it was reported that a cargo of Igbo slaves disembarked at the port and committed mass suicide by drowning in order to evade slavery. See, for instance Goodwine, *Legacy of Ibo Landing*.

61 McDaniel and Hill, *Tombstone Feast*. See also Nicholls, "Igbo Influences," 231.

62 Edwards, *History, Civil and Commercial*, 11, 85.

63 Sloane, *Voyage to the Islands*, xix.

64 Leslie, *New and Exact Account of Jamaica*, 326; and Spencer, *Crop-Over*, 4.

65 Ames and Gourlay, "Kimkim," 56–64; Ahuwan, "Clay as a Creative Media," in *Diversity of Creativity in Nigeria*, ed. Bolaji Campbell, 143–52.

66 Details of the cargo came from the record of sale and the Trans-Atlantic Slave Trade Database (2008). See National Archives, Kew Gardens [hereafter NAK], C107/59 John Goodrich to James Rogers, December 30, 1792; John Goodrich to James Rogers, January 11, 1793; John Goodrich to James Rogers, January 24, 1793; John Goodrich to James Rogers, June 15, 1793; "Sales of 342 Slaves Imported in the Ship Jupiter," July 3, 1793.

67 See for example Eltis and Engerman, "Was the Slave Trade Dominated by Men?" 237–57.

68 NAK, 1792, C107/13, Captain Forsyth to James Rogers, July 9, 1792. A fact to consider is that the Trans-Atlantic Slave Trade Database shows that the dominant majority of captives shipped across the Atlantic from the Cameroons between 1750 and 1808 were males. See also Donnan, *Documents Illustrative*, 590.

69 Diptee, "'A Great Many Boys and Girls,'" in Falola and Njoku, eds., *Igbo in the Atlantic World*, 82.

70 Forde and Jones, *Ibo and Ibibio-Speaking Peoples*, 4, 10, 28–57. See NNAK, File No. 15911 vol. 1, Tribes of Nigeria (i) Inter-Relations (ii) Arochukwu, Jukun, etc.; and Nigerian National Archives Ibadan (NNAI) CSO 26/240 File No. 29380, Milne Report on Ogboli Group of Nsukka Division (n. d).

71 Coleman, *Nigeria*, 340.

72 NNAE, C 632, RIVPROF 2/1/87, Activities of Village Unions (1947); C 633, RIVPROF 2/1/87, Native Authorities and Clan Unions (1947).

73 NNAE, OP 3029, ONDIST 12/1/2094, Ibo State Union Matters Affecting (1949).

74 Isichei, *History of the Igbo People*, 19–20.

75 Equiano, *Interesting Narrative*, 5, 43.

76 Horsfield, "Archibald John Monteath," edited by Nelson, *Transactions*, 29–51.

77 Pereira, *Esmeraldo de situ orbis*, 72–84, and "Mr. John Grazilhier's Voyage," in Barbot, "Description of the Coasts," in *Collection of Voyages and Travels*, 380–81.

78 See Brown and Lovejoy, eds., "Introduction," in *Repercussions of the Atlantic Slave Trade*.

79 For a discussion of African ethnicities in the Biafra region, see chapter 6 in Hall, *Slavery and African Ethnicities*, 126–43. For a debate on methodological problems of determining the number of Igbo sold into the Atlantic slave trade see: Kolapo, "Igbo and Their Neighbours," in *Slavery and Abolition*, 114–33; Chambers, "'My Own Nation,'" 72–97, and "Significance of Igbo in the Bight," in *Slavery and Abolition*, 101–20; Northrup, "Igbo and Myth Igbo," in *Slavery and Abolition*, 1–20. See also Nwokeji, "Atlantic Slave Trade," 616–55.

80 Northrup, "Igbo and Myth Igbo," 1–20. For a discussion of Bonny, see Lovejoy and Richardson, "'This Horrid Hole,'" 363–92.

81 In total, the Trans-Atlantic Slave Trade Database has records for 254 British ships that documented the number of children leaving the Biafran coast between 1701 and 1808. For sixty-one of these, children accounted for greater than 30 percent. See, http://slavevoyages.org/tast/database/.

82 Approximately 10 percent of Biafran captives on British ships ended up in Martinique, Guadeloupe, and the Spanish, Dutch, and the Danish Caribbean. For the statistics, see the Trans-Atlantic Slave Trade Database, http://slavevoyages.org/tast/database/.

83 NAK C107/9, James Maud to James Rogers, July 30, 1786 (Antigua); and Samuel Richards to James Rogers, June 21, 1788.

84 NAK C107/9, Francis Grant to James Rogers, August 4, 1789; Francis Grant to James Rogers, October 10, 1789.

85 NAK C107/8 Francis Grant and Robert Smyth to James Rogers, February 22, 1788. See also C107/7, Box 2. Reporting on Jamaica, Francis Grant also advised that slaves from Old Calabar were of less estimation in Jamaica than those from the Gold Coast. Francis Grant to James Rogers, December 1788. For another reference to Jamaica, see a note by John Taylor where he noted that slaves from Angola are of less value in Jamaica than slaves from "Eboe." John Taylor Letter to Simon Taylor, August 7, 1793, Taylor/14, Letter book A. In a memo from Grenada, a trade specifically requested for a couple of good Bonny slaves See Munro MacFarlane to James Rogers, September 4, 1792, C107/5.

86 Vasconcellos, "And a Child Shall Lead Them?"; Aird, "Forgotten Ones"; Inniss, "From Slavery to Freedom," 251–60; Teelucksingh, "The 'Invisible Child,'" 237–50; Jones, "'Suffer the Little Children,'" 7–25, and "'If This Be Living I'd Rather Be Dead,'" 92–103.

87 Diptee, "Imperial Ideas," in *Children in Colonial America*, ed. Marten, 48–60.

88 Edwards, *History, Civil and Commercial*, 83–84, 88.

89 Chuku, "Olaudah Equiano," in *Igbo Intellectual Tradition*, 10, 38–39, 42–44. See also Jeffreys, "Winged Solar Disk," 94–101.

90 Lovejoy and Trotman, "Enslaved Africans," in *Questioning Creole*, eds., Shepherd and Richards, 67–91.

91 Uba-Mgbemena, "Role of Ífò in Training the Igbo Child," 57–61; Daniel, Smitherman-Donaldson, and Jeremiah, "Makin' a Way Outa No Way," 482–508.

92 Mann, "Shifting Paradigms," 10.

93 Craton, "Jamaican Slave Mortality," 3. See also Higman, *Slave Populations,* 78.

94 According to Higman, the enslaved population of Barbados "leveled off" after about 1710; see *Slave Populations,* 43.

95 Edwards, *History, Civil and Commercial,* 117, 342.

Chapter 5

1 As one may recall also, Angola has an early history with Portuguese Catholic evangelism. See Palmer, "From Africa to the Americas," 229, 234.

2 Heywood, ed., *Central Africans*; Konadu, *Akan Diaspora in the Americas*.

3 Miller, "Cuban Abakuá Chants," 23–58, and "Relationship between Early Forms of Literacy," in *Calabar on the Cross River*, eds., Mbua, Lovejoy, and Miller, 177–216; Ortiz, Herskovits, and Cedeño, "Abakuá Secret Society in Cuba," 148–54.

4 Nicholls, *Old-Time Masquerading*. One of the strengths of Nicholls's works is that

the complications of ethnic identification in the African Diaspora are acknowledged. See also for instance MacGaffey, "Twins, Simbi Spirits, and Lwas in Congo and Haiti," in *Central Africans*, ed. Heywood, 211–26.

5 Pradel, *African Beliefs in the New World*, vii, 324.

6 Heywood, "Portuguese into Central Africa," *Central Africans*, in Heywood, 91–116. In this essay, Heywood contends, "by the beginning of the eighteenth century, a Creole culture had already emerged in Portuguese Angola and Benguela and was undergoing significant transformation" (91). For a similar argument, see Candido, *An African Slaving Port and the Atlantic World*, 93–94. These studies refute the notion that African cultures were unchanging prior to the colonial era.

7 Ortiz, Herskovits, and Cedeño, "Abakuá Secret Society in Cuba," 149.

8 See Njoku, "Meanings of Igbo Masks and Carnivals of the Black Diaspora," in *Migrations and Creative Expressions*, eds., Falola, Afolabi, and Adesanya, 257–78. For a related observation, see also Lovejoy, "Yoruba Factor," in *Yoruba Diaspora in the Atlantic World*, eds. Falola and Childs, 41.

9 See *Cornwall Chronicle*, St. George Workhouse, February 5, 1816. See also Chambers, *Enslaved Igbo and Ibibio in America*, 13–14. According to May, first-generation slaves taken from Africa rather than Creole were called "saltwater slaves." See May, *Women in Early America*, 144. "On plantations that had both saltwater and Creole slaves, there was often a divide between the two."

10 Heywood, "Introduction," in *Central Africans and Cultural Transformations in the American Diaspora*, ed. Heywood, 1–21.

11 Schuler, "Akán Slave Rebellions in the British Caribbean," 373–86; Sherlock, *West Indian Nations*. It is significant whether a trait has roots in Senegambia or Cameroon because these areas are indicative of wider cultural regions. Upper Guinea groups may possess Sudano-Sahelian influences or inherit the legacy of the ancient empires of Ghana, Mali, and Songhai, while forest groups may be more representative of the locally based, segmentary societies. See Herskovits, *Man and His Works*, 191. In his map of cultural areas of Africa, Herskovits positions Senegambia in the "Western Sudan" region and southeastern Nigeria and the Cameroon in the northwestern "Congo Area," with the "Guinea Coast" area in between.

12 Crahan and Knight, *Africa and the Caribbean*, 11.

13 Bravmann, "Gur and Manding Masquerades in Ghana," 44–51, 98.

14 Fraser, "Symbols of Ashanti Kingship," in *African Art and Leadership*, ed. Fraser and Cole, 137–52; Bravmann, "Diffusion of Ashanti Political Art," in *African Art and Leadership*, ed. Fraser and Cole, 152–72.

15 Hans Sloane has left us with an informed knowledge of the Caribbean island nations and the wide range of cross-cultural borrowing among them. See Sloane, *Voyage to the Islands*.

16 See Chambers, *Enslaved Igbo and Ibibio*.

17 This is despite their relatively late appearance in the trans-Atlantic slave trade exchanges.

18 Crahan and Knight, *Africa and the Caribbean*, 10; Ortiz, Herskovits, and Cedeño, "Abakuá Secret Society in Cuba," 149.

19 For a detailed discussion on this in regard to Igbo family system and socialization, see Njoku, *African Cultural Values*, esp. chaps. 3–5.

20 This is in line with the American Diffusion School championed by Boas, "Methods of Ethnology," 311–21; Herskovits, *Cultural Anthropology*. The Heywood edited volume took a shot at this but the coverage was limited to the Congo-Angola culture area. See Heywood, "Introduction," in *Central Africa*, 1–20.

21 Miller, "A Secret Society Goes Public," 162.

22 The trio of Virgin Islands—Saint Thomas, Saint Croix, and Saint John—was formerly known as the Danish West Indies. But the Virgin Islands were acquired by the United States in 1917. They are now run as an American territory.

23 LCCN 84037526, *The Saint Croix Avis*, "A Watcher Against His Will," Christiansted, Saint Croix [V.I], January 3, 1901. The term *Corromantee* [Koromanti] was originally given to the enslaved Ashanti people in Jamaica by the British slavers. It was later generally applied to the all Akán slaves from the entire Gold Coast.

24 See for instance, Ottenberg, "Ibo Receptivity to Change," in *Continuity and Change*, ed. Bascom and Herskovits, 130–43; LeVine, *Dreams and Deeds*, 92–94; Horowitz, *Ethnic Groups in Conflict*, 154, 169.

25 See Njoku, "Igbo Slaves and the Transformation of the Niger Delta," in *Aftermath of Slavery*, eds. Korieh and Kolapo, 122; Horton, "Igbo: An Ordeal for Aristocrats," 169–70.

26 Achebe, *Trouble with Nigeria*, 45–46. These points were recapped in Achebe, *There Was a Country*. For an engaging analysis on this, see also Fishburn, *Reading Buchi Emecheta*, particularly 139–40.

27 Horton, "Stateless Societies," in *History of West Africa*, 78–119.

28 In an interesting article published by the *Huffington Post*, July 19, 2014, Cohan put forth the rhetorical question "How Much Freedom of Speech Is Too Much?" For a serious read, see Bezanson, *Too Much Free Speech?*

29 One of the best discussions on these diasporic imaginings remains Phillips, *American Negro Slavery*, 43–44; Gomez, *Exchanging Our Country Marks*, 116–19; and Mullin, *Africa in America*, 27.

30 Barclay, *Voyages and Travels of James Barclay*, 26; Chambers, *Enslaved Igbo and Ibibio*, 2; and Isichei, ed., *Igbo Worlds*, 15.

31 Konadu's *Akan Diaspora in the Americas*, 200–201, educates about how the Akán enslaved in the Americas were equally stereotyped as "bad" and "rebellious" slaves.

32 This historic site has been renamed after the jazz maestro Louis Armstrong. See Widmer, "Invention of a Memory," 69–78.

33 Johnson, *Congo Square in New Orleans*, 9–11; Long, *Spiritual Merchants*, 21; Cable, "Dance in Place Congo," 517–32.

34 Midge Burnett, in Hinton, *Slave Narratives*, 156.

35 Widmer, "Invention of a Memory," 70.

36 Nash in "Bamboula to Ballet," 50–51, claims that ballet evolved from Bamboula; see Damm, "Remembering Bamboula," 20–24. See also Widmer, "Invention of a Memory," 69–78; and Gerstin, "Tangled Roots," 5–41.

37 For more on this, see the Ọfọ stick in colonial anthropology reports, NNAE, AW383–2/1/266 AWDIST Ọfọ Sticks, Report on, 1927; and OP179/27–7/14/62 ONPROF Ofo in the Owerri Division, Report on, 1927.

38 See Uchendu, *Igbo of Southeast Nigeria*, 21.

39 Okafor, *Igbo Philosophy of Law*, 7.

40 Nodal, "Social Evolution of the Afro-Cuban Drum," 170.

41 Scott, *Tom Cringle's Log*, 241. See also Scott and Brangwyn, *Tom Cringle's Log*, 196.

42 Scott, *Tom Cringle's Log*, 241; Scott and Brangwyn, *Tom Cringle's Log*, 370; and Howard, *Kingston*, 192.

43 Tuckerman, *Letter Respecting Santa Cruz*, 25. See also Nicholls, *Jumbies' Playing Ground*, 227.

44 Dirks, *Black Saturnalia*, xiii.

45 LCCN sn 83025891, Editorial, *Saint Thomas Tidende*, Danish West Indies, December 28, 1872.

46 Cited in Nicholls, *Old-Time Masquerading*, 84.

47 For an engaging discussion on this, see Clarke, "John Canoe Festival in Jamaica," 72–75; and Bilby, "Surviving Secularization," 179–223.

48 The Bahama Tourist Office (BTO), United Kingdom, "What Is Junkanoo," December 22, 2016.

49 Chambers, *Murder at Montpelier*, 182, and personal communication, July 24, 2017. The subject of discussion was on his current work on the "Igbo Landing." On the Ọkọnkọ, see NNAE, MINLOC 16/1/2301, Ọkọnkọ Club in (1919–1920); and File No. 54 ABADIST 13/4/54, LONG JUJU of ARO and Ọkọnkọ Society Report on, 1920.

50 See Konadu, *Akan Diaspora*, 23; and Rodriguez, *Historical Encyclopedia of World Slavery*, 624.

51 See Long, *History of Jamaica*, 424.

52 Clarke, "John Canoe Festival in Jamaica," 72–75; Reid, "John Canoe Festival," 345–46, 349–70.

53 Palmer, "From Africa to the Americas," 225.

54 Long, *History of Jamaica*, 425. See also Hill, *Trinidadian Carnival*, 230; Bettelheim, *Afro-Jamaican Jonkonnu Festival*, 47. Female Konus were represented by a male dancer. See Richards, "Horned Ancestral Masks," in *African Diaspora*, eds. Okpewho, Davies, and Mazrui, 257–59.

55 Lewis, *Journal of the West Indian Proprietor*, 51. See also Hill, *Trinidadian Carnival*, 270; Bettelheim, *Afro-Jamaican Jonkonnu*, 47; and Richards, "Horned Ancestral Masks," 254–75.

56 Blackamoors were originally people of African descent from North Africa serving in wealthy European households as servants and slaves. See Peter Jackson, "Beneath the Headlines," *Geography* 73, no. 3 (1988): 202–7, esp. 203.

57 Scott, *Tom Cringle's Log*, 241; and Scott and Brangwyn, *Tom Cringle's Log*, 371.

58 Belisario, *Koo Koo or Actor Boy*.

59 Gurney, *A Winter in the West Indies*, 26.

60 Nicholls, *Jumbies' Playing Ground*, 44; and Nicholls, "Igbo Influences," 229–31.

61 Burton, *Afro Creole*, 65. See also Bilby, "Surviving Secularization," 179–223.

62 Bilby, "Caribbean as a Musical Region," in *Caribbean Contours*, ed. Mintz and Price, 183.

63 Bilby, "Caribbean as a Musical Region," 187. The common assumption is that those cultural traits that arrived late in the slavery era were more likely to retain observable African traits than those that came earlier. For example, late-arriving Yoruba slaves reinvented the cult of Orissas in Trinidad and Bahia in Brazil. Fon traditions of voodoo were consolidated in Haiti. The Abakuá masquerade of Cuba is akin to the Ékpé masquerade of the Èfik and Ejághám. See Bettelheim, "Negotiations of Power in Carnival," 66–75; and Miller, "Cuban Abakuá," 23–58.

64 Jones, "Ifogu Nkporo," 119–21. See plate IV of Jone's picture illustrations. MAA, N.13163.GIJ. "Ibibio Mask with a Hinged Jaw by G. I. Jones," Photographic Archive, 1932–1939.

65 Mark, *Wild Bull and the Sacred Forest*.

66 See Schmalenbach, ed., *African Art from the Barbier-Mueller Collection*, 76–77; and Newton, *Sculpture*, 72. The authors explain that the masks are named Sira kono or Mpie. When they were not worn, the masks were sometimes kept outside for public viewing.

67 Picket, "Animal Horns in African Art," 27–53; see also Hart, "Afro-Portuguese Echoes," 77–86.

68 Annotations of the masks at the Montclair Art Museum, New Jersey, state that Tji Wara society members use a headdress depicted in the form of an antelope, the mythical being who taught men how to farm. The word *tji* means "work" and *wara* means "animal," thus "working animal." See also Sims, *Anxious Objects*, 83.

69 As annotated at the Cleveland Museum of Art, 2002; and Vrije University Brussels (VUB) consolidated annotations on African masks.

70 Detailed scholarly information can be found in the chapter on the Tusya in Roy, *Art of the Upper Volta Rivers*, 363. Here one will find a sample of the mask.

71 Picket, "Animal Horns in African Art," 27–53. See also Hart, "Afro-Portuguese Echoes," 77–86; and Fagg and Donne, "In Search of Meaning in African Art," 477–79.

72 See for instance McCall, *Dancing Histories*, 93–96, 124.

73 Nicholls, *Jumbies' Playing Ground*, 154–56.

74 Igwebe, *Original History of Arondizuogu*, 63–64.

75 See Oriji, "Oracular Trade," 45.

76 For the Ogáráchi masquerade of the Unmuezearoli of Onitsha, see Ugonna, "Ezeigboezue," 28; Nicholls, "Igbo Influences," 234–37.

77 Anonymous, "Characteristic Traits of the Creolian," reprint, in Higman, ed., *Characteristic Traits of the Creolian*, 9; and Abrahams and Szwed, eds., *After Africa*, 233.

78 Scott, *Tom Cringle's Log*, 241.

79 Hinckley, *To Dance the Spirit.*

80 Simmons, "Depiction of Gangosa on Efik-Ibibio Masks," 17–20. Gangosa is a dangerous ulcerative illness that attacks the soft and hard palates, spreading to the nostrils and outward to the other parts of the face. It is essentially a manifestation of yaws.

81 Personal observation in various locations during my field trips in Owerri, Mbáise, Aba, Umuáhiá and Ọrọn, December 22, 2011. Robert Opara, an Okoroshá masquerader also provided deeper perspective insights. Robert Opara, interview, Achi Mbieri, December 25, 2008.

82 During my fieldwork among the Achi Mbieri community in 2007 and 2008, it was disclosed that initially Okoroshá masquerade festivals occur when the people had completed the farming season and are now resting from their labors. This was to get the people occupied to avoid being taken by social vices. Field work, "Okoroshá and Nkwá Love Dance among the Achi Mbieri Community," December 28–30, 2007; and Ezeowu Ozzy, interview, Achi, Mbieri, December 24, 2008; and Robert Opara, interview, Achi, Mbieri, December 25, 2008.

83 Harris, Abiodun, Poyner, Cole, and Visona, *History of Art in Africa*, 292.

84 Imperato, "Ibo, Ibibio, and Ogoni Masks," 76.

85 Aniakor, "Household Objects and Igbo Space," in eds., Arnolde, Geary, and Hardin, *African Material Culture*, 229; and Imperato, "Ibo, Ibibio, and Ogoni Masks," 76.

86 Boston, "Some Northern Ibo Masquerades," 54–65; and Imperato, "Ibo, Ibibio, and Ogoni Masks," 76.

87 Ugonna, "Ezeigboezue," 23.

88 Nicholls, "Igbo Influences," 234–37. The various riverine communities were the first to encounter the White man in the coastal cities. See Anderson and Peek, "Ways of the Rivers," 12–25, 93; and Imperato, "Ibo, Ibibio, and Ogoni Masks," 76.

89 Arewa and Hale, "Poro Communications (West Africa)," 78–96; Keefer, "Group Identity, Scarification," 1–26.

90 Nicholls, "Igbo Influences," 234–37.

91 The Ubomiri believe that if the Kéléké mask falls from the stilt, the performer will die on the spot. For more reading on the Chákábá, see Asante, ed., *African Dance*.

92 Green, "Traditional Dance in Africa," in *African Dance*, ed. Asante, 25.

93 See Willard, *Mokolution.*

94 See Pratten, *Man-Leopold Murders*, 53; Chambers, *Enslaved Igbo and Ibibio*, 5; Hair, "An Ethnographic Inventory," 235; Nicholls, "Mocko Jumbie," 48–61, 94–96; "Igbo Influences," 237; and "African Dance," in *African Dance*, 63–78.

95 See Sandoval, *Treaties on Slavery*, 47; Pratten, *Man-Leopold Murders*, 53.

96 Oldendorp, *History of the Missions*; Pratten, *Man-Leopold Murders*, 53.

97 Udo, *Who Are the Ibibios?* 2. See also Northrup, "Precolonial References to the Annang Ibibio," 1–5.

98 For the report on the Igbo, see Day, *Five Years Residence in the West Indies*, 53; for the Mandinka, see Young, *Tour through the Several Islands*, 275.

99 Young, *Tour through the Several Islands*, 258. See also Nicholls, "Mocko Jumbie," 48–61.

100 Young, *Tour through the Several Islands*, 258–59; Nicholls, "Mocko Jumbie," 48–61; Doryk, "Dancing in the Virgin Islands," 216–18.

101 Dirks, *Black Saturnalia*, 5.

102 Day, *Five Years' Residence in the West*, 80, 99–100.

103 Day, *Five Years' Residence in the West Indies*, 80; Nicholls, *Jumbies' Playing Ground*, 39–40.

104 See Ugonna, "Ezeigboezue," 29; Cole and Aniakor, *Igbo Arts*; Foss, "Arts of the Urhobo Peoples"; Peek, "Isoko Arts and Their Audiences," 58–60. See also Nicholls, "Mocko Jumbie," 49–61, 94–95; Appia, "Masques de Guinée," 153–82; Huet, *Dance, Art and Ritual of Africa* 26–27; Thompson, *African Art in Motion*, 166.

105 Nicholls, "Mocko Jumbie," 49–61.

106 See Young, *Tour through the Several Islands*; and Day, *Five Years' Residence in the West Indies*. It is of interest that a 1919 photograph of a Mocko Jumbie wearing a suit with bold vertical stripes in Port of Spain, Trinidad, appears in Nunley and Bettelheim, *Caribbean Festival Arts*, 92.

107 See Nicholls, "Igbo Influences," 238–39. According to Nicholls, stilts are not unique to the Caribbean or Africa. Shepherds in France and hop twiners in Britain wore them, and stilt walkers also appeared in European circuses; Nicholls, "Mocko Jumbie," 58.

108 As with "De Jumbee" in the New World, see Day's 1852 report for instance. Day, *Five Years' Residence in the West Indies*.

109 For an excellent study on the Ekpo, see Offiong, "Functions of the Ekpo Society," 77–92. See also Akpan, "Role of Secret Societies in Ibibioland."

110 Personal communication and real-time observation of the Nkwá Love festivities in Achi Mbieri, December 28, 2008.

111 Visona et al., *History of Art in Africa*, 290.

112 Scott, *Tom Cringle's Log*. See also Dole et al., *International Library of Famous Literature*, 6638; Scott and Brangwyn, *Tom Cringle's Log*, 375.

113 Visby-Petersen, *Saint Thomas Tropeminder Fra De Vestindiske Oer*, 26.

114 Cawte, *Ritual Animal Disguise*, 201.

115 Alford, *Hobby Horse*, 120.

116 Visby-Petersen, *Saint Thomas Tropeminder*, 26.

117 There are also instances where other lower-grade masquerades try to intimidate the onlookers: "the fierce characters had ropes or chains around their waists which were held by burly attendants to prevent them from attacking the crowd"; see Jones, *Art of Eastern Nigeria*, 60.

118 Scher, *Carnival*, 64–65. Cohen, *Masquerade and Politics*, 7.

119 Jackson and Mosadomi, "Cultural Continuities," in *Orisa*, eds. Falola and Genova 145–46.

120 Fraser, "History of Carnivals," in Hill, *Trinidadian Carnival*, 10.

121 For an erudite discussion on this, see Anthony, *Parade of the Carnivals of Trinidad*. See also Benitez-Rojo, *Repeating Island;* and Nunley and Bettelheim, *Caribbean Festival Arts*.

122 Jackson and Mosadomi, "Cultural Continuities," 147.

123 Flake, *New Orleans*, 125.

Chapter 6

1 It must be noted that Africa was one of the earliest cradles of Christianity. The early Christians lived in Alexandria, Egypt, from about 60 CE and played a central role in the early growth of Christianity. It was from Alexandria that Christianity came to the Axumite Empire. Jennifer Woodruff Tait nailed home that fact when she stated, "Africa is the home of many Christian 'firsts.'" Tait, "Christianity in Early Africa," 1. See also Decret, *Early Christianity in North Africa*.

2 Habermas, *Philosophical Discourse of Modernity*.

3 Dallmayr, "Discourse of Modernity," 682–83.

4 Fingesi, *Official Document for Festac 77 No. CS/2*.

5 Cohen, *Masquerade Politics*, 5.

6 Ibid., 6.

7 Herodotus, *Histories of Herodotus*.

8 Africanus, *Geographical Historie of Africa*.

9 Iliffe, *Africans*, 11.

10 However, the injunction on pilgrimage is conditional on the physical and financial ability of the believer to make the journey usually observed in the twelfth month of the lunar calendar.

11 See the Wahhabi doctrine, for instance. Telegraph Reporters, "What Is Wahhabism," *The Telegraph*, May 19, 2017.

12 Palmer, "From Africa to the Americas," 223–37.

13 Westermarck, *Ritual and Belief in Morocco*, 146.

14 Ibid, 147.

15 See, for instance, Moulieras, *Une tribu zénète anti-musulmane*, 102.

16 For details of this account, see the account of Ibn Battuta who visited the Mali Empire in the fourteenth century. Hamdun and King, *Ibn Battuta in Black Africa*, 27, 35.

17 See Battuta, *Travels in Asia and Africa*; Khaldūn, *Muqaddimah*.

18 See Njoku, *Culture and Customs of Morocco*, 132.

19 See for instance Monts, "Islam, Music, and Religious Change in Liberia."

20 Hacket, *Art and Religion in Africa*, 201.

21 Levtzion and Hopkins, eds., *Corpus of Early Arabic Sources*.

22 Hamdun and King, *Ibn Battuta in Black Africa*, 39.

23 Conrad, *Great Empires of the Past*, 80. See also 84, 89, and 94.

24 Bravmann, *Islam and Tribal Arts in West Africa*, 62–87.

25 Conrad, *Great Empires of the Past*, 89.

26 Achebe, *Female King of Colonial Nigeria*, 172–92.

27 See for instance Ekechi, *Missionary Enterprise and Rivalry*; and Anyandele, *Missionary Impact*.

28 Achebe mentioned the Ọtákágu/Christian encounter in his fictional novel, but the account is a true example of the fact. See Achebe's *Arrow of God*. See also Obiechina, *Culture, Tradition, and Society*, 58.

29 Udoye, *Resolving the Prevailing Conflict*, 103–4; Achebe, *Things Fall Apart*, 132; Ogbechie, *Ben Enweonwu*, 113.

30 Robert Hinton, *Slave Narratives*, 438.

31 Ortiz, "Afro-Cuban Festival 'Day of the Kings,'" in Bettelheim, ed., *Cuban Festivals*, 1, 21.

32 Tuckerman, *Letter Respecting Santa Cruz*, 25; See also Nicholls, *Old-Time Masquerading*, 169.

33 Dirks, *Black Saturnalia*, ix.

34 Ibid., 189.

35 Long, *History of Jamaica*, 424.

36 Young, *Tour through the Several Islands*, 259.

37 Ibid., 22.

38 Breen, *Saint Lucia*.

39 Isichei, *Igbo People*, 95; and Dike, *Trade and Politics*, 29–30.

40 N. C. Ejituwu, an Andoni indigene and university history professor, provided this information about the Andoni people at the conference: Nineteenth-Century Post-Abolition Commerce and the Societies of Lower Niger River Basin (Nigeria), held at Imo State University, Owerri, Nigeria, June 11–12, 2004.

41 NNAE, CALPROF. CP2061/2/2/1/1952. Efik, Egbo (Ekpe) secret society, Calabar 1918–41.

42 Ikime, *Fall of Nigeria*, 18. See also Boahen and Webster, *Revolutionary Years*, 189–92.

43 See Alagoa, "Eastern Niger Delta," 272; and Jones, *Trading States*, 67–68.

44 See Horton, "Kalabari Ekine Society, 94–114; and "From Fishing Village to City-State," in Douglas and Kaberry, eds., *Man in Africa*, 54; and Alagoa, "Development of Institutions," 276.

45 Horton, "Ordeal," 180. Although the Kálábári highly admired wealth and power, the culture insisted that the qualities embodied in *ásá*—youthfulness and flamboyance—should never be lost in the hunt for wealth. The society scorned misers and individuals who eschewed the chasing and courtship of women, fine clothes, good food, dancing, conviviality, and other luxuries for the pursuit of money and power. In other words, there was a social expectation that a man should always live with a certain style of affluence, grace, and decorum (or *bu nimi*).

46 NAK, FO 313/1. Huntley to Craig, March 27, 1837.

47 Details of these conflicts over trade and power are documented in NNAE, Cons. 2. King Pepple's Correspondences 1847–1848; NNAE. Cons. 14. Manumission Papers 1856–1878.

48 In my recent studies, I have reiterated that social change is a complex topic that must be approached with caution. See for instance Njoku, "Influence of the Family on the Rise of Igbo State Unionism," in Falola and Salm, eds., *Urbanization and African*

Cultures, 385–404; and "Christian Missions and Social Change in Igboland," in Korieh and Nwokeji, eds., *Religion, History and Politics in Nigeria*, 93–116.

49 Dike and Ekejiuba, *Aro of South-Eastern*, 287.

50 NNAE, CALPROF, 8451/3–7/1/1421 Leopard Society, Executive of Murderers, 1946–1947.

51 NNAE, CALPROF, 345/2–7/1/420 Leopard Society, Court Cases, 1946–54; CALPROF, 3451/4–7/1422 Leopard Society, Investigation of Progress Report, 1948–52.

52 See Tangri, *Politics in Sub-Saharan Africa*, 4–9.

53 Olusanya, "Nationalist Movement in Nigeria," in *Groundwork of Nigerian History*, ed. Ikime, 591.

54 See Njoku, "Rise of Igbo State Unionism," 389; Otuka, "Calling on All Ibos"; Obi, "Address to the Mammoth Assembly"; Ibo State Union, "Ibo Day Celebration and Civic Reception."

55 See Afigbo, *Ropes of Sand*, 344–45; and Isichei, *History of Igbo People*, 205.

56 See Nwabara, *Iboland*, 224–25; Osaghae, *Trends in Migrant Political Organizations in Nigeria*; Isichei, *Igbo*, 191, 217–21; Afigbo, *Ropes of Sand*, 345–46. For a detailed account of the rise of Igbo Ethnic Unions in colonial Nigeria, see Smock, *Ibo Politics*.

57 Nwabara, *Iboland*, 224. See also Henderson, "Generalized Cultures and Evolutionary Adaptability," 365–91. See also Coleman, *Nigeria*, 349; "Calabar Improvement League," *Nigerian Daily Times*, 2; and Smock, "The NCNC and Ethic Unions in Biafra," 24–25.

58 See the *Afikpo Town Welfare Association Constitution*, March 20, 1950, Afikpo, 1952, 14–15. See also Smock, "Ethnic Unions in Biafra," 24.

59 Njoku, "Rise of Igbo State Unionism," 399. See Ottenberg, "Improvement Associations," 1–28.

60 See NNAE. "Societies—Revival of Secret Societies in Igbo-land" (1915), RIVPROF 8.3.261; Nwaka, "Secret Societies and Colonial Change," 187–88, 199–200; and Kalu, "Missionaries, Colonial Government, Secret Societies," 75–91.

61 See Offonry, "Strength of Ibo Clan Feelings II," 489; NNAE. File No. OW 557/20 RIVPROF 8/8/433; OW 8358 UMPROF 5/1/138; and File No. OW 8358 UMPROF 5/1/138.

62 See Smock, "Ethnic Unions in Biafra," 28–34; Nduka, *Western Education and Nigerian Cultural Background*, 97–98.

63 See Njoku, "Rise of Igbo State Unionism," 399; Ahanotu, "Role of Ethnic Unions," in *Studies in Southern Nigerian History*, ed. Obichere, 163–64.

64 Palmer, *Cultures of Darkness*, 173, 180.

65 Habermas, *Philosophical Discourse of Modernity*.

66 Dallmayr, "Discourse of Modernity," 682–83.

67 Johnson, "How Masquerade Quoted the Bible," "Masquerades Invade Church," and Ojomeyda, "Pandemonium as Muslims, Masquerades Lock Horns in Ikun-Etiti."

68 NNAE, AHODIST, OW.8358–5/1/138, Okonko Society, Faith Tabernacle Disturbance, 1950–51.

69 John Nweke, personal correspondence, July 2, 2013. According to Nweke, some

of the young people and women that supported the "White man and his church in the conflict were sanctioned with exile and their family lands auctioned off. They cannot come back wherever they are today."

70 Njoku, "Chinua Achebe and the Development of Igbo/African Studies," in *Igbo Intellectual Tradition,* ed. Chuku255.

71 Achebe, *Things Fall Apart*160.

72 For a pictorial study on the alien influence on the transformation of African art, see Beier, *Art in Nigeria,* esp. 14–16.

73 Rachewiltz, *Introduction to African Art,* 137, has made a similar comment. The author stressed the increasing influence of African art forms on the European or Western counterpart since the nineteenth and twentieth centuries.

74 For a detailed read, see Puri, "Canonized Hybridities" in *Caribbean Romances,* ed. Edmondson, 12–38. See also Stolzoff, *Wake the Town and Tell the People,* 240–46. For a theoretical understanding of a globalizing dimension, see Wolf, *Europe and the People Without History.*

75 Nunley and Bettelheim, *Caribbean Festival Arts,* 19.

76 Hill, "The Masquerade," xxii–xxiv.

77 Akpaide, "Concept of the Mask," 26.

78 Fongué, "Market for Works of Art," 1320–43. See also Throsby, *Economics and Culture,* esp. 111–36; and Trowell and Nevermann, *Africa and Oceanic Art,* 6–19.

Chapter 7

1 Plato, *Republic,* 73.

2 Perhaps except for ballet, which has European origins, every other music genre can be traced back to Africa.

3 Along this line of argument, see Fanon, *Wretched of the Earth.*

4 Plato, *Republic,* 93. See Plato, *Republic of Plato,* trans., 225.

5 For analysis on the role of music in the civil rights movement of the 1940s to1960s, see Cobb, *Most Southern Place on Earth*; Gitlin, *The Sixties*; DeKoven, *The Sixties and the Emergence of the Postmodern*; Clayson, *Beat Merchants.*

6 Vershbow, "Sounds of Resistance," 1–2.

7 Aristotle, *Poetics,* 5b.

8 Aristotle, *Politics,* 117.

9 Equiano, *Interesting Narrative,* 4–5.

10 NNAE, AWDIST AW 80–2/1/56, Dances Harmful or Otherwise Report, 1919–1920—The Divisional Office, January 9, 1920.

11 Ezikeojiaku, "Igbo Divination Poetry," 37.

12 Gordon, *Existentia Africana,* 3. See also Akpabot, "Anthropology of African Music," 2–3.

13 Anderson, *Beyond Ontological Blackness,* 37, 89.

14 For comparison, see the section on the modern episteme in Foucault's *Order of Things*.

15 See for instance Hale, "From the Griots of Roots," 247–78; and Kaschula, "Imbongi and Griot," 55–76.

16 Niani, *Sundiata*.

17 The Fodéba Keita's Ballets Africains is a national dance company or troupe based in Conakry, the capital city of Guinea. In the context of African nationalist movements, Guinea, which gained independence in 1958, mobilized the group, first as a poetry group and then gradually a drumming, storytelling, singing, and dancing theater group. See Touré, *L'Afrique et la Revolution*. For a taste of this group's music, see their recording of 1960, "Les Ballets Africains De Keita Fodeba Vol. 2," produced by Disques Vogue—LDM. Track 2—"Soundiata Lounge A L'Emperor Du Manding," is a vintage example of the historical works.

18 Nesbitt, "African Music," 177.

19 Hale, "From the Griots of Roots," 249. See also Conrad and Frank, eds., *Status and Identity in West Africa*, 4–7.

20 Charry, *Mande Music*, 48–49.

21 Nesbitt, "African Music," 177–78.

22 Mbaegbu, "Effective Power of Music," 180.

23 Aluede, "Music Therapy in Traditional African Societies," 31–35.

24 NNAE, AWDIST AW 80–2/1/56, Dances Harmful or Otherwise Report, 1919–1920—The Divisional Office, January 9, 1920.

25 Ogede, "Counters to Male Domination," 117. See also Ogede, *Art, Society and Performance*; and MAA, N.13242.GIJ, "Band Playing for Mmau Masquerade, Amuda Village, Isu Ochi by G. I. Jones Photographic Archive, 1932–1939."

26 Achi, "Masquerade and Love Dance."

27 Achi Nkwá Love, Christmas Season Dances—"Akugbo Álálá Emmanuel Berele yá ákwá," Tape recording, 1988. The author was an eyewitness to the performances, held at Umuduruzubi Village Square in Achi Mbieri on December 25, 1988.

28 Bilby, *Caribbean as a Musical Region*, 201.

29 Edwards, *History, Civil and Commercial* 293.

30 Nwadike, "Waves of Miracle," mp3 soundtrack, 2014.

31 See Pearse, "Aspects of Change," 34; Warner-Lewis, *Central Africa in the Caribbean*, 258.

32 Eke Chima, "Uwá Nká Self," *Olilányám Ọbáráézé*, New Generation Band, 2003.

33 Ade-Adegbola, *Traditional Religion in West Africa*, 171.

34 Mbaegbu, "Effective Power of Music," 181.

35 See Asigbo, "Re-Inventing the Wisdom of the Ancients," in *Bountiful Harvest*, eds., Chiegboka, Okodo, and Umeanoluue, 690.

36 Moore, *Fela*, 18.

37 Ibid., 13.

38 Williams, *Tour Through the Island*.

39 Oliver, "St. Croix Dancing," 74.

40 Motta, "Bamboula to Soul."

41 Nicholls, "Igbo Influences," in Falola and Njoku, eds., *Igbo in the Atlantic World*, 229–31.

42 NNAE, AWDIST AW 80–2/1/56, Dances Harmful or Otherwise Report, 1919–1920—The Divisional Office, January 9, 1920.

43 See Mbaegbu, "Effective Power of Music."

44 Rucker, *River Flows On*, 1–11, 133–34.

45 Edwards, *History, Civil and Commercial*, 293.

46 NNAE, AWDIST AW 80–2/1/56, Dances Harmful or Otherwise Report, 1919–1920—The Divisional Office, January 9, 1920.

47 See the excellent work of McCall, *Dancing Histories*, 53–54. For a graphic illustration of this in the 1930s, see MAA, N.13025.GIJ. "Boys Masquerade (Ibibio style mask), Abiriba Cross River, Southeastern Nigeria" by G. I. Jones Photographic Archive, 1932–1939.

48 Edwards, *History, Civil and Commercial*, 293–94.

49 See Bent, *Universal Magazine of Knowledge*, 203. See also Edwards, *History, Civil and Commercial*, 293–94

50 Ugonna, "Ezeigboezue," 32–33.

51 Mbaegbu, "Effective Power of Music," 181.

52 NNAE, AWDIST, AW80.2/1/56, Dances Harmful or Otherwise, report on 1919–1920.

53 Beckwith, *Jamaican Anansi Series*, 1–5.

54 Freud, *Interpretation of Dreams*, 76.

55 Jung, *Memories, Dreams, and Reflections*, 140, 392,

56 Ashliman, *Folk and Fairy Tales*, 139. This is an excellent resource material for researching folk and fairy tales.

57 Ibid., 146.

58 Williams, *Tour Through the Island*, 26.

59 Ibid., 26–27.

60 Ibid., 22.

61 See Nicholls, "Igbo Influences," 245.

62 Breen, *Saint Lucia*, 196–97.

63 Igwebe, *Original History of Arondizuogu*, 49–51.

64 Kwabena, *Nketia,* 23.

65 King George III was popularly known as "Farmer George" by satirists. Initially, this was to ridicule his interest in things considered by his critics as mundane rather than those befitting to a king, such as politics. Over time, however, more appreciative Britons contrasted his homely thrift with his son's grandiosity to portray him as a man of the people.

66 *Time*, "Nigeria's Civil War," August 23, 1968.

67 Omeje, "*Enyimba Enyi*," 631.

68 Bergh and Slobodan, "Music and Art in Conflict," 4.

69 Nesbitt, "African Music," 184.

70 Bolton, "Gombay," 222–26.

71 Equiano, *Interesting Narratives*, 209.

72 Hall, *In Miserable Slavery*, 12.

73 Lomax and Lomax, "Music for Work and Play."

74 *Carriacou Calaloo*, recorded by Alan Lomax. Nicholls, "Igbo Influences," 233; and Nicholls, *Old-Time Masquerading*, 141.

75 Ndukaihe, *Achievement as Value in Igbo*, 229.

76 NNAE, No. G. 202/6, W. Buchanan Smith Secretary of Southern Provinces to the Anthropology Office, Enugu, February 5, 1926.

77 NNAE, Memorandum dated November 9, 1925 from the Senior Resident of Onitsha Province to the District Officer (DO), Awka, O.P.391/1925. See also Memorandum No. O.P.391/1925, Anti-Government Propaganda in Abakiliki, March 5, 1925.

78 NNAE, O.P. 62/1925 Divisional Officer, Awka to Senior Resident General, enclosures; AWDIST, AW80.2/1/56 Dances Harmful or Otherwise, Report on 1919–1920; and ONPROF, OP391/25–7/12/92, Bands of Women Dancers Preaching Ideas of Desirable Reforms Movement, 1925–26.

79 See *Report of the Commission of Inquiry Appointed to Inquire into the Disturbances in Calabar and Owerri Provinces*, 24–30.

80 Ndukaihe, *Achievement as a Value in Igbo*, 229.

81 Congo Square was initially a ceremonial ground of the Oumas Indians, located on the same grounds where we have Beauregard Square today.

82 LCCN, 83045372, *Daily Picayune*, Louisiana, October 12, 1879. Brown (1860) listed Congo Square ethnic groups as "Kraels [Creoles], Minahs, Congos and Mandringas, Gangas, Hiboas, and Fulas." This list included savannah groups, Mandinkas and Fulani (Mandringas and Fulas) and forest groups, Kongos and Igbos (Hiboas).

83 Latrobe, *Journal of Latrobe*.

84 Rouse, *Rise and Decline of the People*, 6.

85 Kelly, *Voyage to Jamaica*, 21.

86 Agordah, *African Music*, 58.

87 See Garfias, "Miramba of Mexico," 203–28; Chenoweth, *Marimbas of Guatemala*, 52–77.

88 See the extensive work of Epstein, *Sinful Tunes and Spirituals*, 25–57; and Handler and Frisbie, "Aspects of Slave Life," 18.

89 Crowley, "Music and Migrations," 7–8; Thompson, "Poor Man's Bass Fiddle," 11–12; and Berliner, *Soul of Mbira*, 68–69.

90 NNAE, AWDIST AW 80–2/1/56, Dances Harmful or Otherwise Report, 1919–1920—The Divisional Office, January 9, 1920.

91 Ukaegbu, "Composite Scene," 160.

92 See Ekwueme, "Nigerian Performing Arts," 5.

93 Crowley, "Music and Migrations," 6.

94 Falconbridge, *Two Voyages to Sierra Leone.*

95 See Price and Price, "John Gabriel Stedman's Collections," 131, 138.

96 Epstein, "Folk Banjo" 347–71, and *Sinful Tunes and Spirituals*, 359–62; Coolen, "Senegambian Archetypes," 117–32.

97 Agordah, *African Music*, 58–59.

98 Ukaegbu, "Composite Scene," 160.

99 Falconbridge, *Two Voyages to Sierra Leone.*

100 Crowley, "Music and Migrations," 9.

101 Ibid., 18.

102 Williams, *Tour Through the Island*, 22.

103 Lo-Bamijoko, "Music Education in Nigeria," 41.

104 Williams, *Tour Through the Island*, 22.

105 Collins, "Gumbay Drums of Jamaica."

106 Oldendorp, *Caribbean Mission*, 264.

107 Nissen, *Reminiscences of a 46 Years'*, 164–65.

108 Belisario, *Koo or Actor Boy.*

109 Nicholls, *Old-Time Masquerading*, 77.

110 Haynes, "Danish West Indies," 200–2.

111 Euba, "Music in Traditional Society," 475–80.

112 Abarry, "Ga Homowos," in *African Intellectual Heritage*, eds., Asante and Barry, 254.

113 Nketia, *Music of Africa*, 23.

114 Abarry, "Ga Homowos," 254.

Chapter 8

1 Bettelheim, "Negotiations of Power in Carnival," 66–75, 91–92. Bettelheim's nuanced essay allows us to see that historically, the carnival has been cast in a variety of ways.

2 Obiechina, "Nchetaka," 25.

3 Njoku and Yik, "Onitsha Market Literature," in *Narrative, Identity, and Academic Community*, eds. Atterbery et. al., 31.

4 Sartre, *What Is Literature?* 60, 62; Nadel, *Modernism's Second Act*, 17.

5 Liverpool, "Origins of Rituals and Customs," 231. For a similar comment, see Cowley, *Carnival, Canboulay and Calypso*, 21; Cudjoe, *Beyond Boundaries*, 236; *Trinidad Palladium*, February 4, 1880; and *Fair Play and Trinidad News*, March 6, 1879.

6 Liverpool, "Origins of Rituals and Customs," 231; and Cudjoe, *Beyond Boundaries*, 235–36.

7 Example of this vicious campaign is recorded by Hill, "The Masquerade." In this poetic treaties, Hill called masqueraders "fools" and their acts "folly."

8 One may best understand this idea of narrative *engagée* as a form of "literary commitment" to a cause. In the case of the enslaved people, it was a struggle against

oppression, exploitation, and marginalization. It was a quest for freedom in the face of the worst form of indignity and exploitation.

9 Cedeño, "Abakua Secret Society in Cuba," 148–54.

10 Hall, *Africans in Colonial Louisiana*, 157, 187.

11 Courlander in *Drum and the Hoe*, 48, 84–87, and 328, has provided insights into how a number of chants suggesting Igbo syntax calling out Igbo deities and spirits were appropriated as specialized language skills. See Chambers, *Igbo Diaspora in the Era of the Slave Trade*, 11–13, and also "Igbo Diaspora," in *Igbo in the Atlantic World*, eds. Falola and Njoku, 157. For a cursory preview of Yoruba gods in Cuban literature, see Lima, "Orisha Chango," 33–42.

12 Euba, "Music in Traditional Society," 476.

13 Obiechina, "Nchetaka," 28.

14 *Port of Spain Gazette*, September 12, 1853. See also Cowley, *Carnival, Canboulay and Calypso*, 49.

15 Nicholls, *Old-Time Masquerading* and "Igbo Influences," 229–31.

16 Hensbroek, *Political Discourses in African Thought*, 13–14.

17 Bettelheim, "Negotiations of Power in Carnival," 66.

18 Gerstin, "Tangled Roots," 12.

19 LaPalombara, "Distribution," in *Crises and Sequences*, eds. Binder and Palombara, 241–73. In the same light, Lipset in *The First New Nation*, 46, argues that "to a considerable degree the leaders seek development as part of their more general effort to overcome feelings of national inferiority, particularly vis-a-vis the former metropolitan ruler."

20 This has been the central argument of Anderson's *Imagined Community* 187–206. For pertinent discussions, see chapter 11 on "Memory and Forgetting."

21 Schiff, "Function of Narrative," 33–47.

22 Ibid., 33. See also Popova, *Stories, Meaning, and Experience*, 86–87.

23 Kirango has three ethnic-based youth associations (*kamalen ton*)—the Sòmonò, the Boso (Bozo), and the Bámáná—each group performing a separate puppet masquerade.

24 Soleillet's description is found in his journal, *Voyages et Decouvertes*, 170.

25 One legend holds that Toboji Centa, a Boso fisherman, acquired the masquerade tradition from a jinni (a supernatural creature in Islamic theology) during a journey through the forest in the remote past. From Toboji's village, the legend claims, other fishing villages along the river adopted the masquerade, and by the late nineteenth century, local farmers identified themselves with the festival.

26 Arnoldi, *Playing with Time*, 34–36.

27 In and around Kirango the anglers call their masquerade *do bo* (*gundo bo*), which means "the secrets come forth." The farmers named theirs *sogo bo*, or "the bush animals come forth." Kirango Sòmonò elders recalled that as young men they usually prepared the masquerades outside the village in a solitary area on the bank of the Niger River, and then brought them into the village by boat on the day of the event.

28 Vogel and Arnoldi, "Sòmonò Puppet Masquerades," 72–77. See also Arnoldi, *Playing with Time*, 68 and "Performance, Style," 87–100.

29 Achebe, *Anthills of the Savannah*, 124. In line with Achebe's celebrated line, the Society of Nigerian Artists recently celebrated its jubilee at the University of Nigeria Nsukka with the theme *Nkoli Ka,* which means, "recalling in greatest."

30 *Trinidad Sentinel*, February 23, 1860.

31 Warner-Lewis, "Rebels, Tyrants and Saviours," 88. According to Warner-Lewis, the Devil is portrayed by several masked characters. "Lucifer" wears a red costume and has huge, pointed ears, black beetling eyebrows, a hooked nose, and wings. He carries a large open book in one hand and mimes writing the names of the dead with the other hand. "Princes of Hell" wear smaller costumes of a similar pattern. "The Dragon" is a large, scaly, green beast with lolling red tongue. See also Procope, "Dragon Band or Devil Band," 275–80; and Hill, *Trinidad Carnival*, 88–90.

32 Scher, "Devil and the Bed-Wetter," 107–9. As Scher further observes: "Even the casual observer in a country like Trinidad and Tobago cannot help but notice the public service announcements produced each year during key tourist periods entreating locals to treat visitors well. Each member of the nation becomes an ambassador of goodwill and as such is implicitly charged with carrying on an on-going performance of a nationally sanctioned self."

33 Perhaps the most educative analysis of the Ibibio masquerade functions is Offiong, "Functions of the Ekpo Society," 77–92; Udo, *Who Are the Ibibio?* esp. 136–59; and Nicklin and Salmons, "On Ekkpe, Ekpe, Epo, and Ogbom," 78–79.

34 Gomez, *Reversing Sail.*

35 For details, see National Institute for Cultural Orientation (NICO) Abuja, Nigeria; *Vanguard,* "2016 Calabar Carnival"; *Vanguard,* "Calabar Carnivals Is a Melting-Pot of African Hospitality"; and *Vanguard,* "Calabar Carnivals."

36 Rea, "Making History," 10–25.

37 Elkins, Slavery, 91, 101–2; and Raboteau, *Slave Religion*, 47.

38 Equiano, *Interesting Narrative*, 37.

39 Carretta, "Olaudah Equiano," in *Igbo in the Atlantic World*, eds. Falola and Njoku, 188–98; and Lovejoy, "Olaudah Equiano or Gustavus Vassa," in *Igbo in the Atlantic World*, eds. Falola and Njoku, 199–217.

40 Irobi, "What They Came With," 897; Fortier, *Theater/Theory*, 41.

41 Irobi "What They Came With," 897; Gottchild, *Black Dancing Body*, 15.

42 Akugbo Oguzie, interview, Achi-Mbieri, December 17, 2008.

43 Blackwell and Thompson, "Cross-Cultural Investigation," 44. See also, Walker, "Open Peer Commentary," 103–30.

44 Akugbo Oguzie, interview, Achi-Mbieri, December 17, 2008.

45 Onyeji, "Abigbo Music and Musicians," 52–72.

46 Irobi, "What They Came With," 897.

47 I have watched this masquerade since the 1970s and would not have gained this insight but for Robert Opara, Okoroshá Dancer, interview, December 25, 2008.

48 Labat, *Voyage aux isles*, 401–3.

49 Besides Labat and Saint-Méry's *Description Topographique,* which respectively provide accounts from Martinique and Haiti, Kalenda appeared in in 1881 newspaper

article from Port of Spain, Trinidad, on the pre-emancipation Carnival of the 1830s. See Cowley, "Sample of the Complex Development," 8–9, 17. According to Crowley, Kalenda was mentioned in a 1933 account from Saint Croix (U.S. Virgin Islands). See also Dunham, "Dances of Haiti," 6–7. The anthropologist observed a Kalenda in Trinidad in 1932, describing it as similar to Moreau de Saint-Méry's graceful couple dance. Dances called Old Kalenda and Woman Kalenda are part of Carriacou's contemporary Big Drum ceremony. See McDaniel, "Concept of Nation in the Big Drum," in *Musical Repercussions of 1492*, ed. Robertson, 397. In the United States, Pratz in his *History of Louisiana*, mentioned Kalenda dances in Louisiana.

BIBLIOGRAPHY

Archival Sources

Aztec mask of the dead, Smithsonian National Museum of American History, Washington, DC, Monday, July 5, 2010.

Christa Clarke Collections on "The Art of Africa: A Resource for Educators." The Metropolitan Museum of Art, New York.

Danish Newspapers 1859–1924, Library of Congress (LCCN 83025891, 83045372, 84037526) Washington, DC. (Microfiche). December 28, 1872–January 3, 1901.

Falconbridge, Anna Maria. *Two Voyages to Sierra Leone* during the Years 1791-2-3: in a Series of Letters. 2ed. London Printed for the Author, 1794. New York Public Library, New York.

Jones, G. I. "Photographic Archive, Southern Nigerian Art and Culture." Museum of Archaeology and Anthropology (MAA), Cambridge University, U.K.

Janet Lipkin Collections on "African Mask." The Metropolitan Museum of Art, New York.

John Taylor. Letter to Simon Taylor, August 7, 1793. Smithsonian Libraries, Washington, DC,

Igbo Precolonial Art Collections. Mbari Cultural and Art Center, Owerri, Nigeria

Michael Anthony Papers, Schomburg Center for Research in Black Studies, Harlem, New York.

Nigerian National Archives Enugu (NNAE) General Reports (Administrative and Departmental) 1900–1956.

Nigerian National Archives Enugu (NNAE). Anthropology and Ethnography. Ofo Stick, Title Taking, Juju and Charm, Secret Societies, Chieftaincy.

Nigerian National Archives Enugu (NNAE) Intelligent Reports, 1900–1956.

Anthropological and Ethnological Reports, 1927–1957.

Assessment and Reassessment Reports, 1927–1940.

Organization and Reorganization Reports, 1930–1954.

Nigerian National Archives Ibadan (NNAI) CSO 26/240 File No. 29380 n.d. Milne Report on Ogboli Group of Nsukka Division.

The National Archives Kew Gardens, London (NAK). British Transatlantic Slave Trade Records. Records Relating to the Transportation of Slaves and Goods, 1696–1789.

235

James Rogers. Papers, Chancery Master Senior Exhibits, Personal and Family Papers. July 9, 1792–July 30, 1789.

Foreign Office Archives if Havana Slave Trade Commission. Correspondence 1836-1837 (FO 313 Series). Huntley to Craig, March 27, 1837.

Published Sources

Aba Commission of Inquiry. Notes of Evidence Taken by the Commission of Inquiry Appointed to Inquire into the Disturbances in the Calabar and Owerri Provinces, 4th Witness, Nwanyeruwa (F.A.). December 1929.

Abarry, Abu Shardow. "The Ga Homowos; Hunger-Hooting Cultural Festival." In *The African Intellectual Heritage: A Book of Source*, edited by Molefi Asante and Abu S. Abarry, 254–54. Philadelphia: Temple University Press, 2012.

Abasiattal, Monday B. *A History of the Cross River Region of Nigeria*. Calabar: Harris Publishers, 1990.

Aberle, David F. "A Note on Relative Deprivation Theory as Applied to Millenarian and Other Cult Movements." In *Millennial Dreams in Action: Essays in Comparative Studies, Comparative Studies in Society and History*, edited by Sylvia L. Thrupp. The Hague: Mouton, 1962. 209–14.

Abrahams, Roger D. and John F. Szwed, eds. *After Africa: Extracts from British Travel Accounts and Journals*. . . . New Haven, CT: Yale University Press, 1983.

Achebe, Chinua. *Anthills of the Savannah*. New York: Penguin Books, 1997.

———. *Arrow of God*. London: Heinemann, 1964.

———. *The Trouble with Nigeria*. London: Heinemann, 1984.

———. *There Was a Country: A Personal History of Biafra*. New York: Penguin Books, 2013.

———. *Things Fall Apart*. London: Heinemann, 1958.

Achebe, Nwando. *The Female King of Colonial Nigeria: Ahebi Ugbabe*. Bloomington: Indiana University Press, 2011.

Achi Nkwá Love. Christmas Season Dances—"Akugbo Álálá Emmanuel Berele yá ákwá." Audio Recording, 1988.

Achi, Mbieri. "Masquerade and Love Dance." Working Paper from Field Trip, December 28–30, 2007.

Aching, Gerard. *Masking and Power: Carnival and Popular Culture in the Caribbean*. Minneapolis: University of Minnesota Press, 2002.

Adams, Louisa. Interviewed on June 7, 1937 from Rockingham, North Carolina. In *Slave Narratives: A Folk History of Slavery in the United States from Interviews with Former Slaves*. Washington, DC: Library of Congress, 1941.

Ade-Adegbola, E. A. *Traditional Religion in West Africa*. Ibadan: Daystar, 1983.

Afigbo, Adiele Eberechukwu. "Among the Igbo of Nigeria." *Nigeria Magazine* 146 (1983): 13–23.

———. *Ground Work of Igbo History*. Owerri: Vista Books, 1992.

———. *Igbo Enwe Eze: Beyond Onwumechili and Onwuejeogwu*. Okigwe, Nigeria: Whytem Publishers, 2002.

———. *Igbo History and Society: The Essays of Adiele Afigbo*, edited by Toyin Falola. Trenton, NJ: African World Press, 2005.

———. "Igboland before 1800." In *Groundwork of Nigerian History*, edited by Obaro Ikime, 73-88. Ibadan, Nigeria: Heinemann, 1980.

———. *Ropes of Sand: Studies in Igbo History and Culture*. Nsukka and Oxford: Oxford University Press, 1981.

———. *The Abolition of the Slave Trade in Southeastern Nigeria 1885–1950*. Rochester: University of Rochester Press, 2006.

———. "The Anthropology and Historiography of Central-South Nigeria before and since Igbo-Ukwu." *History in Africa* 2 (1996): 1–16.

———. "The Aro and the Trade of the Bight." In *Igbo in the Atlantic World: African Origins and Diasporic Destinations*, edited by Toyin Falola, and Raphael Chijioke Njoku, 71–81. Bloomington: Indiana University Press, 2016.

———. "The Bini Mirage and the History of South Central Nigeria." *Nigeria Magazine* 137 (1981): 17–24.

———. "The Eclipse of the Aro Slaving Oligarch in South-Eastern Nigeria, 1901–1927." *The Journal of the Nigerian Historical Society* 6, no. 1 (1971): 3–24.

———. *The Igbo and Her Neighbors: Intergroup Relations in Southeastern Nigeria to 1950*. Ibadan: Ibadan University Press, 1987.

Afikpo Town Welfare Association Constitution. March 20, 1950.

Africanus, Leo. *A Geographical Historie of Africa, Written in Arabic and Italian by Iohn Leo a More, borne in Granada and brought up in Barbarie*. Londini: Impensis Georg Bishop, 1600.

———. *The History and Description of Africa and of the Notable Things Therein Contained*. Edited by Dr. Robert Brown and Translated by John Pory. 1526 reprint. London: Hakluyt Society, 1896.

Agordah, Alexander Akorlie. *African Music: Traditional and Contemporary*. New York: Nova Science Publishers, 2005.

Ahanotu, Austin M. "The Role of Ethnic Unions in the Development of Southern Nigeria: 1916–66." In *Studies in Southern Nigerian History*, edited by B. I. Obichere, 152–74. London: Frank Cass, 1982.

Ahuwan, Abashiya Magaji "Clay as a Creative Media: A Survey of the Kimkim Musical Instrument from South Kaduna." In *Diversity of Creativity in Nigeria: A Critical Selection from the Proceedings of the 1st International Conference on the Diversity of Creativity in Nigeria*, edited by Campbell Bolaji, 143–52. Ile-Ife, Nigeria: Department of Fine Arts, Obafemi Awolowo University, 1992.

Aird, Sheila. "The Forgotten Ones: Enslaved Children and the Formation of a Labor Force in the British West Indies." PhD diss., Howard University, 2006.

Akpabot, Samuel. "Anthropology of African Music." *African Journal of the International African Institute* 47, no. 2: (1977): 2–3.

Akpaide, U. Uko. "Concept of the Mask: The Otoro Community Example." *Nigeria Magazine* 141 (1982): 24–39.

Akpan, N. U. "The Role of Secret Societies in Ibibioland." *Nigerian Chronicle* Calabar, Tuesday, December 3, 1973.

Alagoa Ebiegberi Joe. *A History of the Niger Delta.* Ibadan: Ibadan University Press, 1972.

———. "Long-Distance Trade and States in the Niger Delta." *Journal of African History* 11 (1970): 319–29.

———. "The Development of Institutions in the States of the Eastern Niger Delta." *The Journal of African History* 12, no. 2 (1971): 269–78.

Alagoa, Ebiegberi Joe and F. N. Anozie. *The Early History of the Niger Delta.* Hamburg: Helmut Buske Verlag, 1988.

Alford, Violet. *The Hobby Horse and Other Animal Masks.* London: Merlin Press, 1978.

Almosawa, Shuaib and Rich Gladstone. "In TV Spectacle, Man Convicted of Child-Rape Murder Is Executed in Yemen." *The New York Times,* Monday, July 31, 2017.

Aluede, Charles O. "Music Therapy in Traditional African Societies: Origin, Basis and Application in Nigeria." *Journal of Human Ecology* 20, no. 1 (2006): 31–35.

Álvares, Manual. *Ethiopia Minor and a Geographical Account of the Province of Sierra Leone* (c.1615). Translated by Avelino Teixeira Mota, Luís de Matos, Paul Edward, and Hedley Hair, Centro de Estudos de Cartografia Antiga (Portugal), The University of Liverpool, Department of History, 1990.

Amadi, I. R. "The Northern Factor in the History of Sub-Saharan Africa: The Hamitic Hypothesis Revisited." *Transafrican Journal of History* 18 (1989): 80–89.

Ames, D. W. and K. A. Gourlay. "Kimkim: A Women's Musical Pot." *African Arts* 11, no. 2 (1978): 56–98.

Anderson, Benedict. *Imagined Community: Reflections on the Origin and Spread of Nationalism Revised Edition.* London: Verso, 1983.

Anderson, Martha G. and Philip M. Peek. "Ways of the Rivers: Arts and Environment of the Niger Delta." *African Arts* 35, no. 1 (2002): 12–25, 93.

Anderson, Victor. *Beyond Ontological Blackness: An Essay on African American Religious and Cultural Criticism.* New York: Continuum International Publishing, 1995.

Aniakor, Chike C. "Household Objects and the Philosophy of Igbo Social Space." In *African Material Culture,* edited by Mary Jo Arnold, M. Christraud Geary, and Chris L. Hardin, 214–42. Bloomington: Indiana University Press, 1996.

———. "The Igbo Ijele Mask." *African Arts* 11, no. 4 (1978): 42–47, 95.

Annual Report of the Smithsonian Institution Washington, DC, 1895.

Anonymous. "Characteristic Traits of the Creolian and African Negroes in Jamaica." *Colombian Magazine* or Monthly Miscellany, edited by B. W. Higman and D. V. Armstrong, vols. 1–3, April–October, 1797.

Arnoldi, Mary Jo. "Performance, Style, and the Assertion of Identity in Malian Puppet Drama." *Journal of Folklore Research* 25, nos. 1, 2 (1988): 87–100.

Anthony, Michael. *Parade of the Carnivals of Trinidad, 1839–1989.* Port of Spain: Circle Press, 1989.

Anthony, Michael and Andrew Carr, eds. *David Frost Introduces Trinidad and Tobago*. London: Andre Deutsch, 1975.

Anyandele, E. A. *The Missionary Impact on Modern Nigeria: 1842–1914: A Political and Social Analysis*. London: Longmans, 1966.

Appia, Beatrice. "Masques de Guinée: Françoise et de Casamance." [Masks of Guinea: Françoise and the Casamance] *Journal de la Societe des Africanistes* (1943): 153–82.

Arewa, E. Ojo and Everett E. Hale. "Poro Communications (West Africa). A Spiritual Channel Where Men Are the Means of Transmission." *Anthropos* 70, no. 1 & 2 (1975): 78–96.

Aristotle. *Poetics*. Translated by Ingram Bywater with a Preface by Gilbert Murray. Oxford: Clarendon Press, 1920.

———. *Politics*. Translated by Benjamin Jowett. London: The Clarendon Press, 1885.

Arnoldi, Mary Jo. *Playing with Time: Art and Performance in Central Mali*. Bloomington: Indiana University Press, 1975.

Asante, Kariamu Welsh. *African Dance: An Artistic, Historical, and Philosophical Inquiry*. Trenton, NJ: African World Press, 1998.

Asante, Molefi Keke. *Cheik Anta Diop: An Intellectual Portrait*. Los Angeles: University of Sankore Press, 2007.

Ashliman, D. L. *Folk and Fairy Tales: A Handbook*. 1954 reprint. Westport, CT: Greenwood Press, 2004.

Asigbo, Alex A. "Re-Inventing the Wisdom of the Ancients: Moral Signposts in Mike Ejiagh's Akuko N'Egwu." In *A Bountiful Harvest: Festschrift in Honour of Very Rev. Msgr. Prof. J. P. C. Nzomiwu*, edited by A. B. Chiegboka, C. I. Okodo, and Ikenna L. Umeanoluue, 681–90. Nimo, Anambra State: Rex Charles and Patrick, 2012.

———. "Transmutations in Masquerade Costumes and Performances: An Examination of Abuja Carnival 2010." *UJAH: Unizik Journal of Arts and Humanities* 13, no. 1 (2012): 1–13.

Astley, Thomas and John Churchill, eds. *Collection of Voyages and Travels*. London: Printed from the Original Manuscript, 1732.

The Bahama Tourist Office (BTO). United Kingdom, "What Is Junkanoo." December 22, 2018. *The Church Missionary Review*. "A Visit to Fernando Po by the Right Rev. Bishop James Johnson." November/July, 1903/1904.

Baines, John and Peter Lacovara. "Burial and the Dead in Ancient Egypt." *Journal of Social Anthropology* 2, no. 1 (2002): 5–36.

Barbot, John. *A Description of the Coasts of North and South-Guinea; and of Ethiopia Interior, Vulgarly Angola: Being a New and Accurate Account of the Western Maritime Countries of Africa, in Six Books*. London: Churchill, 1732.

———. "A Voyage to New Calabar Rivers in the Year 1699." In *A Collection of Voyages and Travels*. 3rd ed., Vol. 5, edited by Awnsham Churchill and John Churchill. Vol. 5. London: H. Lintor, 1732.

Barclay, James. *The Voyages and Travels of James Barclay, Containing Many Surprising Adventures and Interesting Narratives*. London: Printed for the Author, 1777.

Barlow, George W. "Nature-Nurture and the Debate Surrounding Ethology and Sociology." *American Zoologist* 31, no. 2 (1991): 286–96.

Bascom, Williams. "The Forms of Folklore: Prose Narrative." *The Journal of American Folklore* 76, no. 307 (1965): 3–20.

Basden, Georges Thomas. *Among the Ibos of Nigeria*. 1920; reprint London: Frank Cass, 1966.

Battuta, Ibn. *Ibn Ibn Batoutah.* Translated from the Arabic by C. Defremery and B. R. Sanguinetti. Paris: l'Imprimerie nationale, 1863.

———. *The Travels of Ibn Battuta*. Translated by H. A. R. Gibb. Cambridge: Cambridge University Press, 1958.

———. *Travels in Asia and Africa 1325–1354*. Translated by H. A. R. Gibb. London: Routledge, 1929.

Beckwith, Martha Warren. *Jamaican Anansi Series. Translated by Helen Roberts*. New York: American Folklore Society, 1920.

Beier, Ulli. *Art in Nigeria*. Cambridge: Cambridge University Press, 1960.

Beleza, S. Gusmao, L. Amorim, A. Carracedo, and A. Salas. "The Genetic Legacy of Western Bantu Migrations." *Human Genetics* 117, no. 4 (2005): 366–75.

Belisario, Isaac Mendes. *Koo Koo or Actor Boy: Sketches of Character in Illustration of the Habits, Occupation, and Costumes of the Negro Population in the Island of Jamaica*. Kingston, Jamaica: Published by the Artist at his Residence, 1838.

Benitez-Rojo, Antonio. *The Repeating Island: The Caribbean and Postmodern Perspective*. Translated by James Maraniss. Durham, NC: Duke University Press, 1992.

Benjamin, Thomas. *The Atlantic World: Europeans, Africans, Indians and Their Shared History 1400–1900*. Cambridge, UK: Cambridge University Press, 2009.

Bennett, Patrick R. and Jan P. Sterk. "South Central Niger Congo: A Reclassification." *Studies in African Linguistics* 8, no. 3 (1974): 241–73.

Bent, W. *The Universal Magazine of Knowledge and Pleasure Volume XCIV*. London: Published under His Majesty's Royal License, 1794.

Benti, Getahun. *Urban Growth in Ethiopia, 1887–1874: From the Foundation of Finfinnee to the Demise of the First Imperial Era*. Lanham, MD: Lexington Books, 2017.

Bergh, Arild and John Slobodan. "Music and Art in Conflict Transformation: A Review." *Music and Arts in Action* 2 (2010): 1–16.

Berliner, Paul F. *The Soul of Mbira: Music and Traditions of the Shona People of Zimbabwe*. Berkeley: University of California Press, 1979.

Bettelheim, Judith. *The Afro-Jamaican Jonkonnu Festival: Playing the Forces and Operating the Cloth*, vol. 2. New Haven, CT: Yale University Press, 1979.

———. "Negotiations of Power in Carnival Culture in Santiago de Cuba." *African Arts* 24, no. 2 (1991): 66–75, 91–92.

Bezanson, Randall P. *Too Much Free Speech?* Chicago: University of Illinois Press, 2012.

Bilby, Kenneth M. *The Caribbean as a Musical Region*. Austin: University of Texas, 1985.

———. "Surviving Secularization: Masking the Spirit in the Jankunu (John Canoe) Festivals of the Caribbean." *NWIG: New West Indian Guide / Nieuwe West-Indische Gids* 84, nos. 3, 4 (2010): 179–223.

———. "The Caribbean as a Musical Region." In *Caribbean Contours*, edited by Sidney W. Mintz and Sally Price, 181–217. Baltimore: The Johns Hopkins University Press, 1985.

Binder, Leonard. "Crisis of Political Development." In *Crisis and Sequences in Political Development*, edited by Leonard Binder and Joseph La Palonbara, 3–73. (Princeton: Princeton University Press), 1971.

Blackwell, Laura-Lee and William Forde Thompson. "A Cross-Cultural Investigation of the Perception of Emotion in Music: Psychophysical and Cultural Cues." *Music Perception* 17, no. 1 (1999): 43–64.

Bleek, Wilhelm H. I. *A Comparative Grammar of South African Languages*, 2 vols. Cape Town, South Africa: Trubner, 1962.

Boahen, Albert Adu and James Bertin Webster. *The Revolutionary Years: West Africa since 1800*. London: Longman, 1967.

Boas, Franz. "The Methods of Ethnology." *American Anthropologist* 22, no. 4 (1920): 311–21.

Bolton, H. Carrington. "Gombay, a Festival Rite of Bermudian Negroes." *The Journal of American Folklore* 3, no. 10 (1890): 222–26.

Boston, J. S. "Some Northern Ibo Masquerades." *The Journal of Royal Anthropological Institute of Great Britain and Ireland* 90, no. 1 (1960): 54–65.

Bravmann, René A. "Gyinna Gyinna Making the Djinn Manifest." In *The Performance Arts in Africa: A Reader*, edited by Frances Harding, 149–57. New York: Routledge, 2013.

———. "Gur and Manding Masquerades in Ghana." *African Arts* 13, no. 1 (1974): 44–51, 98.

———. *Islam and Tribal Arts in West Africa*. Cambridge: Cambridge University Press, 1974.

———. "The Diffusion of Ashanti Political Art. In *African Art and Leadership*, edited by Douglas Fraser and Herbert Cole, 152–72. Madison: University of Wisconsin, 2004.

Breen, Henry Hegart. *Saint Lucia: Historical, Statistical, and Descriptive*. London: Longman, 1884.

Brown, Carolyn A. and Paul E. Lovejoy, eds. *Repercussions of the Atlantic Slave Trade: The Interior of the Bight of Biafra and the African Diaspora*. Trenton, NJ: Africa World Press, 2011.

Brown, Paula. "Patterns of Authority in West Africa." *Africa* 21, no. 4 (1951): 261–78.

Bryan, Margaret Arminel, ed. *The Bantu Languages of Africa*. London: Published for the International African Institute by Oxford University Press, 1959.

Budge, Ernest A. Wallis. *Tutankhamen: Amenism, Atenism, and Egyptian Monotheism*. 1923; reprint New York: Bell Publishing Company, 2014.

Burnett, Midge. Eighty Years Old, Interviewed on August 7, 1937 at 1300 S. Bloodworth Street, Raleigh, North Carolina. In *Slave Narratives: A Folk History of Slavery in the United States from Interviews with Former Slaves*, 156. Washington, DC: Library of Congress, 1941.

Cable, George Washington. "The Dance in Place Congo." *Century Magazine* 31 (2004): 517–32.

Candido, Mariana P. *An African Slaving Port and the Atlantic World: Benguela and Its Hinterland*. Cambridge: Cambridge University Press, 2013.

Carretta, Vincent. "Olaudah Equiano and the Forging of Igbo Identity." In *Igbo in the Atlantic World: African Origins and Diasporic Destinations*, edited by Toyin Falola and Raphael Chijioke Njoku, 188–98. Bloomington: Indiana University Press, 2016.

Carroll, Linda L. "Carnival Rites as a Vehicle of Protest in Renaissance Venice." *The Sixteenth Century Journal* 16, no. 4 (1985): 487–502.

Cawte, E. C. *Ritual Animal Disguise*. London: Folklore Society, 1978.

Cedeño, Rafael A. Núñez. "The Abakua Secret Society in Cuba: Language and Culture." *Hispania* 71, no. 1 (1988): 148–54.

Chambers, Douglas B. *Enslaved Igbo and Ibibio in America: Runaway Slaves and Historical Descriptions with a Foreword by Anayo Enechukwu*. Enugu, Nigeria: Jemezie Associates, 2013.

———. "Ethnicity in the Diaspora: The Slave Trade and the Creation of African 'Nations' in the Americas." *Slavery and Abolition* 22, no. 3 (2001): 2–39.

———. *Murder at Montpelier, Igbo African in Virginia*. Jackson: University Press of Mississippi, 2006.

———. "'My Own Nation': Igbo Exiles in the Diaspora." *Slavery and Abolition* 18, no. 1 (1997): 72–97.

———. *The Igbo Diaspora in the Era of the Slave Trade: An Introductory History*. Enugu, Nigeria: Jemezie Associates, 2013.

———. "The Igbo Diaspora in the Era of the Atlantic Slave Trade." In *Igbo in the Atlantic World: African Origins and Diasporic Destinations*, edited by Toyin Falola and Raphael Chijioke Njoku, 156–72. Bloomington: Indiana University Press, 2016.

———. "The Significance of Igbo in the Bight of Biafra Slave-Trade: A Rejoinder to Northrup's 'Myth Igbo.'" *Slavery and Abolition* 23, no. 1 (2002): 101–20.

Charry, Eric. *Mande Music*. Chicago: University of Chicago Press, 2000.

Chasteen, John Charles. "The Prehistory of Samba Carnival Dancing in Rio de Janeiro, 1840–1917." *Journal of Latin American Studies* 28, no. 1 (1996): 29–47.

Chenoweth, Vida. *The Marimbas of Guatemala*. Lexington: University of Kentucky Press, 1964.

Chuku, Gloria. "Olaudah Equiano and the Foundation of Igbo Intellectual Tradition." In *The Igbo Intellectual Tradition: Creative Conflict in Africa and African Diaspora Thought*, edited by Chuku, Gloria, 33–66. New York: Palgrave-Macmillan, 2013.

Church Missionary Intelligencer and Records 1904: 896.

Clark, Desmond J. "The Prehistoric Origins of African Culture." *Journal of African History* 5 no. 2 (1964): 161–83.

Clarke, E. A. "The John Canoe Festival in Jamaica." *Folklore* 38, no. 1 (1927): 72–75.

Clayson, Adam A. *Beat Merchants: The Origins, History, Impact and Rock Legacy of the 1960's British Pop Groups*. London: Blandford Press, 1997.

Cobb, James. *The Most Southern Place on Earth: The Mississippi Delta and the Roots of Regional Identity*. New York: Oxford University Press, 1992.

Cohan, William D. "How Much Freedom of Speech is Too Much?" *HuffPost* July 19, 2014.

Cohen, Abner. *Customs and Politics in Urban Africa*. Berkeley: University of California Press, 1969.

———. *Masquerade Politics: Explorations in the Structure of Urban Cultural Movements*. Berkeley: University of California Press, 1993.

———. *The Politics of Elite Culture: Exploration in Dramaturgy of Power in a Modern African Society*. Berkeley: University of California Press, 1981.

Coleman, James S. *Nigeria: Background to* Nationalism. Berkeley: University of California Press, 1958.

Collins, John. "Gumbay Drums of Jamaica in Sierra Leone." Paper presented at the 12th Triennial Symposium on African Art (ACASA), Marriott Frenchman's Reef Resort, St. Thomas, U.S. Virgin Islands, April 27, 2001.

Conrad, David C. *The Great Empires of the Past: Empires of Medieval West Africa Revised Edition—Ghana, Mali and* Songhai. New York: Chelsea House Publishers, 2010.

Conrad, David C. and Barbara F. Frank, eds. *Status and Identity in West Africa: Nyamakalaw of Mende*. Bloomington: Indiana University Press, 1995.

Conteh-Morgan, John. "Francophone Africa South of the Sahara." In *A History of Theater in Africa*, edited by Martin Banham, 85–137. Cambridge: Cambridge University Press, 2004.

Coolen, Michael Theodore. "Senegambian Archetypes for the American Folk Banjo." *Western Folklore* 34, no. 2 (1984): 117–32.

Cornwall Chronicle. St. George Workhouse, February 5, 1816.

Courlander, Harold. *The Drum and the Hoe: Life and Lore of the Haitian People*. Berkeley: University of California Press, 1960.

Cowley, John. *Carnival, Canboulay and Calypso: Traditions in the Making*. Cambridge: Cambridge University Press, 1996.

———. "A Sample of the Complex Development of African Derived Culture in the Americas." Unpublished Manuscript, undated.

Crahan, Margaret E. and Franklin W. Knight. *Africa and the Caribbean: The Legacies of a Link*. Baltimore: The Johns Hopkins University Press, 1979.

Craton, Michael. "Jamaican Slave Mortality: Fresh Light from Worthy Park, Longville, and the Tharp Estates." *Journal of Caribbean History* 3 (1971): 1–27.

Crowley, John D. "The Traditional Masques of Carnival." *Caribbean Quarterly* nos. 3, 4 (1956): 194–223.

Crowley, John Houlson. "Music and Migrations: Aspects of Black Music in the British Caribbean, the United States, and Britain, before Independence of Jamaica and Trinidad and Tobago." PhD. diss., University of Warwick, 1992.

Cudjoe, Selwyn Reginald. *Beyond Boundaries: The Intellectual Tradition of Trinidad and Tobago in the Nineteenth Century*. Wellesley, MA: Calaloux Publications, 2003.

Currie, Thomas E., Andrew Meade, Myrtille Guillon, and Ruth Mace. "Cultural

Phylogeography of the Bantu Languages of Sub-Saharan Africa." *Proceedings: Biological Sciences* 280, no. 1762 (2013): 1–8.

Curtin, Philip D. *The African Slave Trade: A Census*. Madison: University of Wisconsin, 1972.

Dagan, Easther. *The Spirit's Image: The African Masking Tradition—Evolving Continuity*. Montreal: Galerie Amrad African Art Publications, 1992.

Daily Picayune. Louisiana, Sunday, October 12, 1879.

Dallmayr, Fred. "The Discourse of Modernity: Hegel and Habermas." *The Journal of Philosophy* 84, no. 11 (1987): 682–92.

Damm, R. J. "Remembering Bamboula." *Percussion Notes* 53, no. 3 (2015): 20–24.

Daniel, Jack L. Geneva Smitherman-Donaldson and Milford A. Jeremiah. "Makin' a Way Outa No Way: The Proverb Tradition in the Black Experience." *Journal of Black Studies* 17, no. 4 (1987): 482–508.

David Eltis and Stanley L. Engerman. "Was the Slave Trade Dominated by Men?" *Journal of Interdisciplinary History* 23, no. 2 (1992): 237–57.

Day, Charles William. *Five Years' Residence in the West Indies in Two Volumes*. London: Colburn and Co Publishers, 1852.

Decret, Francois. *Early Christianity in North Africa*. Cambridge: James Clerk and Company, 2009.

DeKoven, Marianne. *The Sixties and the Emergence of the Postmodern*. Durham, NC: Duke University Press, 2004.

De Leon, Rafael. *Calypso from France to Trinidad: 800 Years of History*. Trinidad: General Printers of San Juan, 1986.

Dete, Sachin. *Wole Soyinka: A Ridiculous Dramatist*. Raleigh, NC: Lulu, 2016.

Dike, Kenneth Onwuka and Felicia Ekejiuba. *The Aro of South-Eastern Nigeria 1650–1980*. Ibadan: Ibadan University Press, 1990.

Diptee, Audra A. "A Great Many Boys and Girls." In *Igbo in the Atlantic World: African Origins and Diasporic Destinations*, edited by Toyin Falola and Raphael Chijioke Njoku, 112–22. Bloomington: Indiana University Press, 2016.

———. "Imperial Ideas, Colonial Realities: Enslaved Children in Jamaica, 1775–1834." In *Frontiers: Children in Colonial America*, edited by James Marten, 48–60. New York: New York University Press, 2007.

Dirks, Robert. *The Black Saturnalia: Conflict and Its Ritual Expression on West Indian Slave Plantation*. Gainesville: University of Florida Press, 1987.

Dole, Nathan Haskell, Forrest Morgan, Caroline Ticknor, Donald Grant Mitchell, and Andrew Lang. *The International Library of Famous Literature in Twenty Volumes*. New York: Merrill and Baker Publishers, 1898.

Donnan, Elizabeth. *Documents Illustrative of the History of the Slave Trade to America*, vol. 2. New York: Octagon Books, 1965.

Drewal, Henry John. "Gelede Masquerade: Imagery and Motif." *African Arts* 7, no. 4 (1974): 8, 19, 62–63, 95–96.

Duerden, Dennis. *African Art, an Introduction*. London and New York: Hamlyn, 1968.

Dunham, Katherine. "The Dances of Haiti." *Acta Anthropologica* 2, no. 4 (1947): 6–7.

Durkheim, Emile. *Education and Society*. New York, Free Press, 1956.

———. *The Division of Labor in Society. Edited and with a New Introduction by Steven Lukes*. Translated by W. D. Halls. New York: Free Press, 2014.

———. *The Division of Labor and the Elementary Forms of Religious Life*. Translated by Karen Fields. 1892; reprint New York: Free Press, 1912.

———. *The Rules of Sociological Method and Selected Texts on Sociology and Its Methods*. Edited and with a new introduction by Steven Lukes. Translated by W. D. Halls. New York: Free Press, 2013.

Echeruo, Michael J. C. "The Dramatic Limits of Igbo Rituals." In *Drama and Theater in Nigeria: A Critical Source Book*, edited by Yemi Ogunbiyi, 147–57. Lagos: *Nigeria Magazine*, 1981.

Edeh, Emmanuel M. P. *Towards an Igbo Metaphysics*. Chicago: Loyola University Press, 1985.

Edwards, Bryan. *The History, Civil and Commercial, of the British Colonies in the West Indies*, vol. 2. Philadelphia: Printed and Sold by James Humphreys, 1806.

Ejituwu, N. C. "Andoni People: Nineteenth-century Post-Abolition Commerce and the Societies of Lower Niger River Basin (Nigeria)." Imo State University, Owerri, Nigeria, June 11–12, 2004.

Eke Chima. Track: "Uwá Nká Self." In *Olilányám Ọbáráézé* album, New Generation Band, 2003.

Ekechi, Felix K. *Missionary Enterprise and Rivalry in Igboland, 1867–1914*. London: Frank Cass, 1972.

Ekwueme, L. E. N. "Nigerian Performing Arts, Past, Present, and Future with Particular Reference to the Igbo Practice." *Présence Africaine* 94 (1975): 5195–213.

Eliade, Mircea. *Cosmos and History: The Myth of Eternal Return*. Translated by Willard R. Trask. New York: Harper, 1954.

———. *The Sacred and the Profane: The Nature of Religion*. Translated by Willard R. Trash. New York: Harcourt, Brea, and World Inc., 1959.

Elinor Doryk. "Dancing in the Virgin Islands." *The Journal of Educational Sociology* 24, no. 4 (1950): 216–18.

Elkins, Stanley. *Slavery: A Problem in American Institutional and Intellectual Life*. Chicago: University of Chicago Press, 1959.

Ellwood, Charles A. "Theories of Cultural Evolution." *American Journal of Sociology* 23, no. 6 (1918): 779–800.

Eltis, David and David Richardson. "A New Assessment of the Transatlantic Slave Trade." In *Extending the Frontiers: Essays on the New Transatlantic Slave Trade Database*, edited by David Eltis and David Richardson, 1–62. New Haven, CT: Yale University Press, 2008: 46–47.

Enweonwu, Ben. Keynote Address, at the Festival of African Art and Culture (FESTAC). National Theatre Iganmu, 1977.

Enzheng, Tong. "Magicians, Magic, and Shamanism in Ancient China." *Journal of East Asian Archaeology* 4, no. 1 (2002): 27–73.

Epstein, Dena J. "The Folk Banjo: A Documentary History." *Ethnomusicology* 19, no. 3 (1975): 347–71.

———. *Sinful Tunes and Spirituals*. Urbana: University of Illinois Press, 1978.

Equiano, Olaudah. *The Interesting Narrative of the Life of Olaudah Equiano, or Gustavus Vassa, the African Written by Himself*. Marylebone, Middlesex: 1789.

Erickson, Paul A. and Liam D. Murphy. *A History of Anthropological Theory*, 3rd ed. Toronto: University of Toronto Press, 2008.

Erikson, Neil. "Popular Culture and Revolutionary Theory: Understanding Punk Rock." *Theoretical Review* 18 (1980): 13–35.

Euba, Akin. "Music in Traditional Society." *Nigeria Magazine* 101(1969): 475–80.

Eze-Orji, Bernard and Cajetan A. Nwosu. "Contents of Carnival Calabar: Celebrating Cannibalized Cultures in the Age of Transculturalism. *A Journal of Theater and Media Studies* 1, no. 2 (2016): 254–67.

Ezikeojiaku, Ichie F. A. "Igbo Divination Poetry (Abu Afa): An Introduction." *Nigeria Magazine* 150 (1984): 37–39.

Fage, J. D. "Slavery and the Slave Trade in the Context of African History." *Journal of African History* 10 (1975): 393–404.

———. "The Effect of the Export Slave Trade on African Populations." In *The Population Factor in African Studies*, edited by R. P. Moss and R. J. A. R. Rathbone, 15–23. London: University of London, 1975.

Fagg, William and J. B. Donne. "In Search of Meaning in African Art." *Man* 10, no. 3 (1975): 477–79.

Fair Play and Trinidad News, March 6, 1879.

Falconbridge, Anna Maria. *Two Voyages to Sierra Leone during the Years 1791–2–3 in a Series of Letters Second Edition*. London: Printed for the Author, 1794.

———. *Two Voyages to Sierra Leone*—Letter IV Granville Town dated June 8, 1791.

Falola, Toyin. *The Yoruba Guru: Indigenous Production of Knowledge in Africa*. Trenton, NJ: African World Press, 1998.

———. *Culture and Customs of Nigeria*. Westport, CT: Greenwood, 2001.

———. ed. *Igbo Art and Culture and Other Essays by Simon Ottenberg*. Trenton, N. J.: African World Press, 2006.

Falola, Toyin and Ann Genova, eds. *Orisa: Yoruba Gods and Spiritual Identity in Africa and the Diaspora*. Trenton, NJ: African World Press, 2005.

Falola, Toyin and Matt D. Childs, eds. *The Yoruba Diaspora in the Atlantic World*. Bloomington: Indiana University Press, 2005.

Falola, Toyin and Raphael Chijioke Njoku, eds. *Igbo in the Atlantic World: African Origins and Diasporic Destinations*. Bloomington: Indiana University Press, 2016.

Fanon, Frantz. *The Wretched of the Earth, Translated from the French by Richard Philcox with Commentary by Jean-Paul Sartre*. New York: Grove Books, 1963.

Feierman, Steve J. *Peasant Intellectuals: Anthropology and History in Tanzania*. Madison: University of Wisconsin Press, 1990.

Fernando Ortiz. "The Afro-Cuban Festival 'Day of the Kings." Annotated and Translated by Stubbs, Jean. In *Cuban Festivals: A Century of Afro-Cuban Culture*, Judith Bettelheim, ed., 1–40. Kingston: Ian Randle Publishers, 2001.

Ferreira, John V. "Ethnology and History." *Sociological Bulletin* 13, no. 1 (1964): 1–11.

Feuerbach, Ludwig. *The Essence of Christianity*. 1841; reprint Amherst, NY: Prometheus Books, 2004.

Fingesi, O. P. *Official Document for Festac 77 No. CS/2*. Lagos: National Theatre, 1977.

Fishburn, Katherin. *Reading Buchi Emecheta: Cross-Cultural Conversation*. Westport, CT: Greenwood Press, 1995.

Flake, Carol. *New Orleans: Behind the Masks of America's Most Exotic City*. New York: Grove Press, 1994.

Flight, Colin. "Malcolm Guthrie and the Reconstruction of Bantu Prehistory." *History in Africa*, 7 (1980): 81–118.

Forde, Daryll, Cyril and Jones, G. I. *The Ibo and Ibibio-Speaking Peoples of South-Eastern Nigeria*. London: The International African Institute, 1950.

Fortes, M. and Evans-Pritchard, E. E., eds. *African Political Systems*. London: Oxford University Press, 1940.

Fortier, Mark. *Theater/Theory: An Introduction*. London: Routledge, 2002.

Foss, Wilson Perkins. "The Arts of the Urhobo Peoples of Southern Nigeria." PhD diss., Yale University, 1976.

Foucault, Michael. *Power/Knowledge: Selected Interviews and Other Writings 1972–1977*. 1st American Edition. New York: Vintage Books, 1980.

———. *The Order of Things: An Archaeology of the Human Sciences*. Translated by Alan Sheridan. New York: Vintage, 1973.

Fraser, Douglas. "The Symbols of Ashanti Kingship." In *African Art and Leadership*, edited by Douglas Fraser and Herbert Cole, 137–52. Madison: University of Wisconsin Press, 1972.

Fraser, L. M. "History of Carnivals." Colonial Office Original Correspondence, Trinidad (CO295), vol. 289 Trinidad No. 6460, cited in Hill, *Trinidad Carnival*, 10.

Frobenius, Leo. *Vom Kulturreich des Festlandes. Dokumente zur Kulturphysiognomik*. Volksverband d. Bücherfreunde: Wegweiser Verlag, 1923.

Fustei de Coulanges, Numa D. *Family, Kin and City-States: The Ritual Underpinning of Ancient Greece and Rome*. Edited and revised by J. W. Jamieson. Washington, DC: Scott Townsend, 1999.

Fyfe, Christopher. *Africanus Horton 1835–1883: West African Scientist and Patriot*. New York: Oxford University Press, 1972.

Gallant, A. Robert, Rossi, Peter E. and Tauchen, George. "Nonlinear Dynamic Structures." *Econometrica* 61, no. 4 (1993): 871–907.

Garciagodoy, Juanita. *Digging the Days of the Dead: A Reading of Mexico's Dias de Muertos*. Boulder: University Press of Colorado, 1998.

Garfias, Robert. "The Miramba of Mexico and Central America." *Latin American Music Review* 4, no. 2 (1983): 203–28.

Gerstin, Julian. "Tangled Roots: Kalenda and Other Neo-African Dances in the

Circum-Caribbean." *NWIG: New West Indian Guide / Nieuwe West-Indische Gids* 78, nos. 1, 2 (2004): 5–41.

Gitlin, Todd. *The Sixties: Years of Hope, Days of Rage.* New York: Bantam Books, 1987.

Glotz, Samuel and Qerlemans, Marguerite. "European Masks." *The Drama Review: TDR* 26, no. 4 (1982): 14–18.

Goldie, Hugh (Rev.). *Addenda to the Efik Dictionary.* Edinburgh: United Presbyterian College Buildings, 1886.

———. *Dictionary of the Efik Language in Two Parts.* Glasgow: Dunn & Wright, 1874.

Gomez, Michael A. *Exchanging Our Country Marks: The Transformation of African Identity in the Colonial and Antebellum South, 1526–1830.* Chapel Hill: University of North Carolina Press, 1998.

———. *Reversing Sail: A History of the African Diaspora.* Cambridge: Cambridge University Press, 2004.

Gordon, Lewis R. *Existential Africana: Understanding Africana Existential Thought.* New York: Routledge, 2000.

Gottchild, Brenda Dixon. *The Black Dancing Body: A Geography from Coon to Cool.* New York: Palgrave Macmillan, 2003.

Gramsci, Antonio, *Selections from the Prison Notes of Antonio Gramsci,* ed. Quentin Hoare and Geoffrey Nowell Smith. London: ElecBook, 1999.

Gray, John. *Black Theater and Performance: A Pan African Bibliography.* New York: Greenwood Press, 1990.

Grecian, Alex. "The 7 Most Exclusive Secret Societies in History." *HuffPost,* May 28, 2014.

Green, Doris. "Traditional Dance in Africa." In *African Dance: An Artistic, Historical, and Philosophical Inquiry,* edited by Kariamu Welsh Asante, 13–28. Trenton, NJ: African World Press, 1998.

Greenberg, Joseph H. "Linguistic Evidence for the Influence of Kanuri on Hausa." *Journal of African History* 1, no. 2 (1960): 205–12.

———. "Studies in African Linguistic Classification: III, the Position of Bantu." *Southwestern Journal of Anthropology* 5, no. 4 (1949): 309–17.

Grollemuna, Rebecca, S. Branford, K. Bostoen, A. Meade, C. Venditte, and M. Pagel. "The Bantu Migration Shows that Habitat Alters the Route and Pace of Human Dispersal." *PNAS* 112, no. 43 (2015): 13296–13301.

Grow, Andre and Bavel, Jan Van. "Introduction: Agent-Based Modelling as a Tool to Advance Evolutionary Population Theory." In *Agent-Based Modelling in Population Studies: Concepts, Methods, and Applications,* edited by Andrew Grow and Jan Van Bavel, 3–27. Leuven, Belgium: Center for Sociological Research, 2016.

Gurney, Joseph John. *A Winter in the West Indies: Described in Familiar Letters to Henry Clay, of Kentucky.* London: J. Murray, 1840.

Gutema, Bekele. "Does African Philosophy Have a Contribution to Contemporary Philosophy?" *Topoi: An International Review of Philosophy* 17, no. 1 (1998): 63–75.

Guthrie, Malcolm. *Bantu Sentence Structure*. London: School of Oriental Studies, University of London, 1961.

———. *Comparative Bantu: An Introduction to the Comparative Linguistics and Prehistory of the Bantu Languages*, 4 vols. Farnborough, Gregg Press, 1967–71.

———. "Comparative Bantu: A Preview." *Journal of African Languages* 4 (1965): 40–45.

———. "Some Developments in the Prehistory of the Bantu Languages." *Journal of African History* 3, no. 2 (1962): 273–82.

———. *The Bantu Language of Western Equatorial Africa*. London and New York: Published for the International African Institute by Oxford University Press, 1953.

———. *The Classification of the Bantu Languages*. 1948; reprint London: Published for the International African Institute by Oxford University Press, 1967.

Habermas, Jürgen. *The Philosophical Discourse of Modernity Twelve Lecture*. Translated by Lawrence, Frederick G. Cambridge: MIT Press, 1987.

Hacket, Rosaline I. J. *Art and Religion in Africa*. London: Cassell, 1998.

Hair, P. E. H. "An Ethnographic Inventory of the Lower Guinea Coast before 1700." *African Language Review* 8 (1969): 225–56.

Hale, Thomas. "From the Griots of Roots to the Roots of Griots: A New Look at the Origins of a Controversial African Term of Bard." *Oral Tradition* 12, no. 2 (1997): 247–78.

Hall, Douglas G. *In Miserable Slavery, Thomas Thistlewood in Jamaica, 1750–1786*. New York: Macmillan, 1989.

Hall, Gwendolyn Midlo. *Africans in Colonial Louisiana: The Development of Afro-Creole Culture in the Eighteenth Century*. Baton Rouge: Louisiana State University Press, 1992.

———. *Slavery and African Ethnicities in the Americas: Restoring the Links*. Chapel Hill: University of North Carolina Press, 2005.

Hamdun, Said and King, Noel. *Ibn Battuta in Black Africa*. London: Rex Collins, 1975.

Handler, Jerome S. and Frisbie, Charlotte J. "Aspects of Slave Life in Barbados: Music and Its Cultural Context." *Caribbean Studies* 11, no. 4 (1972): 5–46.

Harn, Samuel P. *African Art: Permutations of Power*. Gainesville: University Press of Florida, 1998.

Harris, Marvin. *The Rise of Anthropological Theory: A History of Theories of Culture*. New York: Crowell, 1968.

Harris, Michael D., Roland Abiodun, Robin Poynor, Herbert M. Cole, and Monica Blackmun Visona. *A History of Art in* Africa. New York: Prentice Hall and Harry N. Abrams, 2001.

Hart, William A. "Afro-Portuguese Echoes in the Art of Upper-Guinea." *RES: Anthropology and Aesthetics* 51 (2007): 77–86.

Hartle, D. D. "Archaeology in Eastern Nigeria. *Nigeria Magazine* 93 (1967): 134–43.

——— "Archaeology in Eastern Nigeria." *The West African Archaeological Newsletter* 5 (1966): 13–17.

Haynes, S. B. "The Danish West Indies." *Harpers New Monthly Magazine* 44 (1872): 200–2.

Heywood, Linda M. "Introduction." In *Central Africans and Cultural Transformations in the American Diaspora*, edited by Linda M. Heywood, 1–21. Cambridge University Press, 2002.

———. "Portuguese into African: The Eighteenth-Century Central African Background to Atlantic Creole Cultures." In *Central Africans and Cultural Transformations in the American Diaspora*, edited by Linda M. Heywood, 91–116. Cambridge: Cambridge University Press, 2002.

———. ed. *Central Africans and Cultural Transformations in the American Diaspora*. Cambridge: Cambridge University Press, 2002.

Henderson, Richard N. "Generalized Cultures and Evolutionary Adaptability: A Comparison of Urban Efik and Ibo in Nigeria." *Ethnology* 5 (1966): 365–91.

Henderson, Richard N. and Ifekandu Umunna. "Leadership, Symbolism in Onitsha Crowns and Ijele." *African Arts* 21, no. 2 (1988): 28–37, 94–96.

Hensbroek, Pieter Boele van. *Political Discourses in African Thought: 1860 to the Present*. Westport, CT: Praeger, 1999.

Hernnerz, Ulf. "Fluxos, Fronteiras, Híbridos: Palavras-chave da Antropologia Transnacional." *Mana* 3, no. 1 (1997): 7–39.

Herodotus, Henry Cary. *The Histories of Herodotus. Translated by George Rawlinson with an Introduction by Rosalind* Thomas. New York: Alfred A. Knopf, 1997.

Herskovits, Melville J. *Cultural Anthropology*. New Delhi: Oxford & IBH Publishing, 1955.

———. *Man and His Works: The Science of Cultural Anthropology*. New York: Alfred A. Knopf, 1995.

———. *The Myth of the Negro Past*. 1941 reprint Boston: Beacon Press, 1958.

Higman, Barry W. *Slave Populations of the British Caribbean, 1807–1834*. Baltimore: The Johns Hopkins University Press, 1984.

———, eds. *Characteristic Traits of the Creolian and African Negroes in Jamaica, c.1797*. Mona, Jamaica: Caldwell Press, 1976.

Hill, Errol. *The Trinidadian Carnival: Mandate for a National Theater*. Austin: University of Texas, 1972.

Hill, R. "The Masquerade." *Trinidad Chronicle*, Saturday, February 14, 1880.

Hinckley, Priscilla. *To Dance the Spirit: Visitors Guide to Exhibition of Liberian Art*. Peabody Museum, Harvard University, 1987.

Hinton, Robert. Interview held in 1937 at 420 Smith Street, Raleigh, North Carolina. In *Slave Narratives: A Folk History of Slavery in the United States from Interviews with Former Slaves,* 438. Washington, DC: Library of Congress, 1941.

Hives, Frank. *Ju-Ju and Justice in Nigeria, Written Down by Gascoigne Lumley*. London: John Lane, 1930.

Hole, Christina. *A Dictionary of British Folk* Customs. London: Paladin Grafton Books, 1978.

Horowitz, Donald L. *Ethnic Groups in Conflict*. Los Angeles: University of California Press, 1962.

Horsfield, Joseph (Reverend). "Archibald John Monteath: Native Helper and Assistant in the Jamaica Mission at New Carmel." Edited by Vernon H. Nelson, *Transactions of the Monrovian Historical Society* 21, no. 1 (1853): 29–51.

Horton, Africanus Beale. *West African Countries, and Peoples, British and Native: With the Requirements Necessary for Establishing that Self-government Recommended by the Committee . . . 1865; and a Vindication of the African Race*. New York: W. J. Johnson, 1868.

Horton, Robin. "From Fishing Village to City-State: A Social History of New Calabar." In *Man in Africa*, edited by Mary Douglas and Phyllis M. Kaberry, 37–58. London: Routledge, 1969.

———. "Igbo: An Ordeal for Aristocrats." *Nigeria Magazine* 90 (1966): 166–83.

———. "Stateless Societies in the History of West Africa." In *History of West Africa*, vol. 1, edited by J. F. A. Ajayi and Michael Crowder, 78–119. London: Longmans, 1971.

———. "The Kalabari Ekine Society: A Borderland of Religion and Art." *Africa: Journal of the International African Institute* 33, no. 2 (1963): 94–114.

Howard, David. *Kingston: A Cultural and Literary History with Foreword by Lorna Goodson*. Oxford: Signal Books, 2005.

Huet, Michael. *The Dance, Art and Ritual of Africa*. New York: Knopf Publishing Group, 1978.

Hurst Gallery. *African Arts of War and Peace*. Cambridge, MA: Hurst Gallery, 1988.

Ibo State Union (mimeo). "Ibo Day Celebration and Civic Reception for His Royal Highness, Enugu." December 7, 1963.

Igwebe, Richard Ohizu. *The Original History of Arondizuogu from 1635–1960*. Aba: The International Press, 1962.

Ikime, Obaro. *The Fall of Nigeria: The British Conquest*. London: Heinemann, 1977.

Ikram, S. and A. Dodson. *The Mummy in Ancient Egypt: Equipping the Dead for Eternity*. London: Thames and Hudson, 1998.

Iliffe, John. *Africans: The History of a Continent*. Cambridge: Cambridge University Press, 1995.

Illah, John Egwugwu. "The Performing Arts of the Masquerade and Its Changing Status in Igala." MA Thesis, Department of English and Drama, Ahmadu Bello University, Zaria, 1983.

Ilogu, Edmund. *Christianity and Igbo Culture: A Study of the Interaction of Christianity in Igbo Culture*. New York: Nok Publishers, 1974.

Imbua, David, Paul E. Lovejoy, and Ivor Miller, eds. *Calabar on the Cross River: Historical and Cultural Studies*. Trenton, NJ: African World Press, 2017.

Imperato, Pascal James. "Ibo, Ibibio, and Ogoni Masks." *African Arts* 8, no. 4 (1975): 76–76.

Inda, Jonathan Xavier and Renato Rosaldo. *A World in Motion: The Anthropology of Globalization*. Malden, MA: Blackwell, 2002.

Inglehart, Ronald. *Modernization and Postmodernization: Cultural, Economic, and Political Change in 43 Societies.* Princeton: Princeton University Press, 1997.

Inniss, Tara. "From Slavery to Freedom: Children's Health in Barbados, 1823–1838." *Slavery and Abolition* 27, no. 2 (2006): 251–60.

Isaac Mendes Belisario. *Koo Koo or Actor Boy: Sketches of Character in Illustration of the Habits, Occupation, and Costumes of the Negro Population in the Island of Jamaica.* Kingston, Jamaica: Published by the Artist at his Residence, 1838.

Ishemo, Shubi. "From Africa to Cuba: An Historical Analysis of the Sociedad Secreta Abakuá (Ñañiguismo)." *Review of African Political Economy* 29, no. 92 (2002): 253–72.

Isichei, Elizabeth Allo. *A History of the Igbo People.* London: Macmillan, 1976.

———ed. *Igbo Worlds: An Anthology of Oral Histories and Historical Descriptions.* London: Macmillan, 1977.

Isiugo-Abanihe, Uche C. "Bridewealth: Marriage and Fertility in the East-Central States of Nigeria." *Genus* 51, nos. 3, 4 (1995): 151–78.

Jackson, Joyce Marie, and Fehintola Mosadomi. "Cultural Continuities: Masking Traditions of the Black Mardi Gras Indians and the Yoruba Egunguns." In *Orisa: Yoruba Gods and Spiritual Identity in Africa and the Diaspora,* edited by Toyin Falola and Ann Genova, 143–45. Trenton, NJ: African World Press, 2006.

Jackson, Peter. "Beneath the Headlines: Racism and Reaction in Contemporary Britain." *Geography* 73, no. 3 (1988): 202–7.

Jaja, S. O., E. O. Erim, and Bassey W. Andah. *Old Calabar Revisited: The Civil Service and the Making of Southern Nigeria, 1900–1906.* Calabar: Harris Publishers, 1990.

Jean-Baptiste, Labat. *Voyage aux isles. Chronique aventureuse des Caraïbes, 1693–1705. Edition établie et présenté par Michel Le Bris. [Travel to the Islands. Adventurous Chronicle of the Caribbean, 1693–1705. Edition established and presented by Michel Le Bris].* Paris: Editions Phébus, 1993.

Jeffreys, M. D. W. "The Winged Solar Disk or Ibo It ΣI Facial Scarification." *Africa* 21, no. 2 (1951): 93–111.

Jegede, Dele. "African Art." In. *Africa: The End of Colonial Rule, Nationalism and Modernization,* vol. 4, edited by Yoyin Falola, 279–89. Durham, NC: Carolina Academic Press, 2002.

———. *Art by Metamorphosis: African Art from Spelman College Collection.* Atlanta: Spelman College, 1988.

Johnson, Dayo. "How Masquerade Quoted the Bible, Before Flogging Church Members." *Vanguard,* Friday, September 18, 2015.

———. "Masquerades Invade Church, Flog Pastors, Worshippers." *Vanguard,* Monday, August 31, 2015.

Johnson, Geoffrey. *Of God and Maxim Guns: Presbyterianism in Nigeria, 1846–1966.* Waterloo, Ontario: C.C.S.R. / Wilfrid Laurier University Press, 1988.

Johnson, James H. *Venice Incognito: Masks in the Serene Republic.* Berkeley: University of California Press, 2011.

Johnson, Jerah. *Congo Square in New Orleans.* New Orleans: Louisiana Landmarks Society, 1995.

Johnston, Harry H. *A Comparative Study of the Bantu and Semi-Bantu Languages, by Sir Harry H. Johnston,* 2 vols. Oxford: Clarendon Press, 1919/1922.

———. "The Bantu and the Semi-Bantu Languages." *Journal of the African Society* 16, no. 62 (1917): 97–110.

Jones, A. M. *Africa and Indonesia: The Evidence of the Xylophone and Other Musical and Cultural Factors.* Leiden, Holland: E. J. Brill, 1971.

———. "Indonesia and Africa: The Xylophone as a Culture-Indicator." *The Journal of the Royal Anthropological Institute of Great Britain and Ireland* 89, no. 2 (1959): 155–68.

Jones, Cecily. "'If This Be Living I'd Rather Be Dead': Enslaved Youth, Agency and Resistance on an Eighteenth Century Jamaican Estate." *The History of the Family* 12 (2007): 92–103.

———. "'Suffer the Little Children': Setting a Research Agenda for the Study of Enslaved Children in the Caribbean Colonial World." *Wadabagei* 9, no. 3 (2006): 7–25.

Jones G. I. "Ifogu Nkporo." *The Nigerian Field* 8, no. 3 (1939): 119–21.

———. *The Art of Eastern Nigeria.* New York: Cambridge University Press, 1984.

———. *The Trading States of the Oil Rivers: A Study of Political Development in Eastern Nigeria.* London: James Currey, 2001.

Jordán, Manuel. "Chokwe!: Art and Initiation among Chokwe and Related Peoples." *African Arts* 32, no. 2 (1999): 18–35.

Joseph H. Greenberg. "Studies in African Linguistic Classification: III, The Position of Bantu."

Southwestern Journal of Anthropology 5, no. 4 (1949): 309–17.

Jung, C. G. *Memories, Dreams, and Reflections Recorded and Edited by Aniela Jaffe and Translated by Richard and Clara Winston* New York: Vintage Books, 1989.

Kahlheber, Stefanie, Koen Bosteon, and Katherina Neumann. "Early Plant Cultivation in the Central African Rain Forest: Millennium BC Pearl Millet from South Cameroon." *Journal of African Archaeology* 7, no. 2 (2009): 253–72.

Kalu, Ogbu U. *African Pentecostalism: An Introduction.* Oxford: Oxford University Press, 2008.

———. *Embattled Gods: Christianization of Igboland, 1841–1991.* Trenton, NJ: African World Press, 1996.

———. "Missionaries, Colonial Government, Secret Societies in South-Eastern Igboland, 1920–1950." *Journal of Historical Society of Nigeria* 9, no. 1 (1977): 75–91.

———. "Under the Eyes of the Gods: Sacralization and Control of Social Order in Igboland." Ahịajioku Lecture Colloquium. Owerri, Nigeria: Published by the Ministry of Information and Culture and Printed by Government Press, 2002.

———. "Under the Eyes of the Gods: Sacralization and Control of Social Order in Igbo Land." Originally published 1988. Accessed on 12/5/2016 via http//Ahajioku.igbonet.com.

Kalu, Ogbu U. and Kalu, Ogun U. "The Battle of the Gods: Christianization of Cross River Igboland, 1903–1950." *Journal of the Historical Society of Nigeria* 10, no. 1 (1979): 1–18.

Kamer, Henri. "De l'authenticité des sculptures africaines" ["The Authenticity of African Sculptures]. *Arts d'Afrique Noire* 12 (1974): 17–40

Kaschula, Russell H. "Imbongi and Griot: Towards a Comparative Analysis of Oral Poetics Southern and Western Africa." *Journal of African Cultural History* 12 no. 1 (1999): 55–76.

Kaufman, Elaine Marlow. *Ibibio Dictionary*. Leiden: African Studies Centre, and Cross River State University and Ibibio Language Board, Nigeria, 1985.

Keefer, Katrina H. B. "Group Identity, Scarification, and Poro among Liberated Africans in Sierra Leone, 1808–1819." *Journal of West African History* 3, no. 1 (2017): 1–26.

Kelly, James. *Voyage to Jamaica*. Belfast: Wilson, 1838.

Kenny, Michael G. "Mutesa's Crime: Hubris and the Control of African Kings." *Comparative Studies in Society and History* 30, no. 4 (1988): 595–612.

Keohane, Robert O. *After Hegemony: Cooperation and Discord in the World Political Economy*. Princeton: Princeton University Press, 1984.

———. "International Institutions: Two Approaches." *International Quarterly* 32, no. 4 (1988): 379–96.

Khaldun Ibn. *Muqaddimah: An Introduction to History*. Translated by Frantz Rosenthal; reprint Princeton: Princeton University Press, 1967.

Khan, K. D. L. "Art Unmasked." *The Tribune*, Chandigarh, India, Sunday, May 28, 2006.

Kilonzo, Susan M. "The Trajectories of Culture, Christianity, and Socioeconomic Development in Vihiga District, Western Kenya." *International Journal of Sociology and Anthropology* 3, no. 2 (2011): 61–69.

King, Russell. *Theories and Typologies of Migration: An Over View and a Primer*, Willy Brandt Series of Working Papers in International Migration and Ethnic Relations 3, no. 12. Malmo, Sweden: Institute for Migration, Diversity and Welfare, 2012.

Kolapo, Femi J. "The Canoe in Nineteenth Century Lower Niger and the Delta." In *The Aftermath of Slavery*, edited by Chima Korieh and Femi J. Kolapo, 75–114. Trenton, NJ: Africa World Press, 2007.

———. "The Igbo and Their Neighbours during the Era of the Atlantic Slave-Trade." *Slavery and Abolition* 25, no. 1 (2004): 114–33.

Konadu, Kwasi. *The Akan Diaspora in the Americas*. Oxford: Oxford University Press, 2010.

Kullmann, Wolfgang. "Gods and Men in the Iliad and the Odyssey." *Harvard Studies in Classical Philology* 89 (1985): 1–23.

La Motta, Bill. "Bamboula to Soul: A Long Musical Journey." *The Daily News*, St. Thomas, USVI, Friday, August 1, 1975.

Labat, Jean-Baptiste and Moreau de Saint-Méry's. *Description Topographique, Hhysique, Civile, Politique et Historique de las Partie Francaise de l'isle Saint-Domingue*. Paris: Dupont, 1798.

Labes, Sebastian Andrei. "Globalization and Cultural Identity Dilemmas. *CES Working Papers* 6, no. 1 (2014): 87–96.

Lafleur, Gwenyth J. "Exploring the Niger-Congo Languages." Unpublished manuscript, accessed November 2, 2017.

Lambert, Eric G., Jaishankar Karuppannan, Shanhe Jiang, and Sudershan Pasupuleti. "Correlates of Formal and Informal Social Control on Crime Prevention: An Exploratory Study among University Students, Andhra Pradesh, India." *Asian Journal of Criminology* 7, 3 (2012): 1–12.

LaPalombara, Joseph. "Distribution: A Crisis of Resource Management." In *Crises and Sequences in Political Development*, edited by Leonard Binder and Joseph LaPalombra, 233–82. Princeton: Princeton University Press, 1971.

Latham, A. J. H. *Old Calabar 1500–1891*. Oxford: Clarendon Press, 1973.

Latrobe, Benjamin. *Journal of Latrobe*. ed. J. H. B. Latrobe, New York: D. Appleton and Co., 1819.

Lawal, Babatunde. "New Light on Gelede." *African Arts* 11, no. 2 (1978): 66–70, 94.

———. *The Gèlèdé Spectacle: Art, Gender, and Social Harmony in an African Culture*. Seattle: University of Washington Press, 1996.

Le Page de Pratz, Antoine Simon. *The History of Louisiana or the Western Part of Virginia and Carolina*. Translated by Le Page du Pratz. London: Printed for T. Becket and P. A. De Hondt, 1763.

Leo, Felix Marc and Manuel Jordan. *Makishi Lya Zambia Mask Characters of the Upper Zambezi Peoples*. Munich: Verlag Fred Jahn, 1998.

Leslie, Charles. *A New and Exact Account of Jamaica*. Edinburgh: Fleming, 1739.

Letter to the Editor of *Science Progress*. May 23, 1922.

LeVine, Robert A. *Dreams and Deeds: Achievement Motivation in Nigeria*. Chicago: University of Chicago Press, 1966.

Levtzion, Nehemiah and J. F. P. Hopkins, eds. *Corpus of Early Arabic Sources for West African History*. Translated by J. R. Hopkins. Cambridge: Cambridge University Press, 1981.

Levtzion, Nehemiah and Jay Spalding. *Medieval West Africa: View from Arab Scholars and Merchants*. Princeton: Markus Wiener Publishers, 2003.

Lewis, Matthew Gregory. *Journal of the West Indian Proprietor*. Entry date January 1, 1816. London: John Murrey, 1834.

Lima, Robert. "The Orisha Chango and other African Deities in Cuban Drama." *Latin American Theater Review* (1990): 33–42.

Linton, Ralph. *The Study of Man: An Introduction*. New York: D. Appleton-Century, 1936.

Lipset, Seymour Martin. *The First New Nation: The United States in Historical and Comparative Perspective*. New York: Basic Books, 1963.

Littlefield, Sidney Kasfir. *Contemporary African Art*. London: Thames and Hudson, 1969.

Liverpool, Hollis Urban. "Origins of Rituals and Customs in the Trinidad Carnival: African or European?" *The Drama Review* 42 no. 3 (1998): 24–37.

Lo-Bamijoko, Joy. "Music Education in Nigeria." *Nigeria Magazine* 150 (1984): 40–47.

Lomax, Alan and Anna Lomax "Music for Work and Play." Carriacou, Grenada. Compiled and Annotated by Rebecca Miller, 1962.

Long, Carolyn Morrow. *Spiritual Merchants: Religion, Magic, and Commerce*. Knoxville: The University of Tennessee Press, 2001.

Long, Edward. *The History of Jamaica Or A General Survey of the Antient [sic] and Modern State of that Island: With Reflections on Its Situation, Settlements, Inhabitants, Climate, Products, Commerce, Laws, and Government Volume 2.* London: Lownudes, 1774.

Lovejoy, Paul E. "Olaudah Equiano or Gustavus Vassa: What Is In a Name?" In *Igbo in the Atlantic World: African Origins and Diasporic Destinations,* edited by Toyin Falola and Raphael Chijioke Njoku, 119–217. Bloomington: Indiana University Press, 2016.

——. "The African Diaspora: Revisionist Interpretations of Ethnicity, Culture and Religion under Slavery Studies." *World History of Slavery, Abolition and Emancipation* 2, no. 1 (1997): 1–23.

——. "The Yoruba Factor in the Trans-Atlantic Slave Trade." In *The Yoruba Diaspora in the Atlantic World,* edited by Toyin Falola and Matt D. Childs, 40–55. Bloomington: Indiana University Press, 2005.

——. "Transformation of the Ékpè Masquerade in the African Diaspora." In *Carnival—Theory and Practice,* edited by Christopher Innes, Annabel Rutherford, Brigitte Bogar, 127–52. Trenton, NJ: Africa World Press, 2013.

Lovejoy, Paul E. and David Richardson. "The Slave Ports of the Bight of Biafra in the Eighteenth Century." In *Repercussion of the Atlantic Slave Trade: The Interior of the Bight of Biafra and the African Diaspora,* edited by Carolyn Brown and Paul E. Lovejoy, 19–56. Trenton, NJ: Africa World Press, 2009.

——. "'This Horrid Hole': Royal Authority, Commerce and Credit at Bonny, 1690–1840." *Journal of African History* 45, no. 3 (2004): 363–92.

Lovejoy, Paul E. and David V. Trotman. "Enslaved Africans and Their Expectations of Slave Life in the Americas: Towards a Reconsideration of Models of 'Creolization.'" In *Questioning Creole: Creolisation Discourses in Caribbean Culture,* edited by Verene A. Shepherd and Glen A. Richards, 67–91. Kingston: Ian Randle Publishers, 2002.

MacAloon, John J. "Introduction: Cultural Performances. Cultural Theory." In *Rite, Drama, Festival, Spectacle: Rehearsals Towards a Theory of Cultural Performance,* edited by John J. MacAloon, 1–15. Philadelphia: Institute for the Study of Human Issues, 1984.

MacGaffey, Wyatt. "Twins, Simbi Spirits, and Laws in Congo and Haiti." In *Central Africans and Cultural Transformations in the American Diaspora,* edited by Linda M. Heywood, 211–26. Cambridge University Press, 2002.

"The Magical History of Yule: The Pagan Winter Solstice Celebration." *HuffPost,* December 22, 2016.

Mann, Kristin. "Shifting Paradigms in the Study of the African Diaspora and of Atlantic History and Culture." *Slavery and Abolition* 22, no. 1 (2001): 3–21.

Manning, Patrick. "African Population Projections, 1850–1960: Methods for New Estimates by Regions." African Economic History Conference, University of Vancouver, BC, April 2, 2010.

Mark, Peter. *The Wild Bull and the Sacred Forest: Form, Meaning and Change in Senegambian Initiation Masks.* New York: Cambridge University Press, 1992.

Marquetta L. Goodwine. *The Legacy of Ibo Landing: Gullah Roots of African American Culture*. Atlanta: Clarity Press, Inc., 1998

Mason, Otis T. *Influence of Environment upon Human Industries or Arts*. Washington, DC: Government Print Office, 1896.

Mathar, Nita. "Diffusion of Culture: British, German-Austrian, and American Schools." Reader in Sociology, Working Paper Indira Gandhi National Open University, New Delhi, n.d.

May, Dorothy A. *Women in Early America: Struggle, Survival, and Freedom in the New World*. Santa Barbara: ABC-CLIO, 2004.

Mayer, Florian. *Origins, Commodification, and Significance of Berlin's Love Parade*. Berlin: Grin Verlad, 2007.

Mbaegbu, Celestine Chukwuemeka. "The Effective Power of Music in Africa." *Open Journal of Philosophy* 5 (2015): 176–83.

Mbiti, John S. *African Religion and Philosophy*. Oxford: Heinemann, 1990.

———. *Introduction to African Religion*. 2nd ed. Oxford: Heinemann, 1991.

McCall, John C. *Dancing Histories: Heuristic Ethnography with the Ohafia Igbo*. Ann Arbor: The University of Michigan Press, 2000.

McCann, Kevin and Peter Yodzis. "Nonlinear Dynamics and Population Disappearances." *American Society of Naturalists* 144, no. 5 (1994): 873–79.

McDaniel, Lorna. "The Concept of Nation in the Big Drum Dance of Carriacou, Grenada." In *Musical Repercussions of 1492: Encounters in Text and Performance*, edited by Carol E. Robertson, 395–411. Washington, DC: Smithsonian Institution, 1992.

———. "The Flying Africans: Extent and Strength of Myth in the Americas." *New West Indian Guide/ Nieuwe West-Indische Gids* 64, nos. 1, 2 (1990): 28–40.

McDaniel, Lorna and R. Hill Donald. *Carriacou Calaloo*. Music CD with liner Rounder Records, Caribbean Voyage. 1661-1727-2, Track 29, 1999.

———. *Tombstone Feast: Funerary Music of Carriacou*. Music CD with liner notes. Rounder Records, Caribbean Voyage, 11661–17272, 2001.

Meek, C. K. *Law and Authority in a Nigerian Tribe: A Study of Indirect Rule*. 1937; reprint New York: Barnes and Noble, 1970.

Meki Nzewi, Israel Anyahuru, and Tom Ohiaraumunna. *Musical Sense and Musical Meaning: An Indigenous Musical Perception*. Amsterdam: Rozenberg Publishers, 2009.

Miers, Susanne and Igor Kopytoff. "African Slavery as an Institution of Marginality." In *Slavery in Africa: Historical and Anthropological Perspectives*, edited by Susanne Miers and Igor Kopytoff, 3–73. Madison: University of Wisconsin Press, 1977.

Miller, Ivor L. "A Secret Society Goes Public: The Relationship between Abakuá and Cuban Popular Culture." *African Studies Review* 43, no. 1 (2000): 161–88.

———. "Cuban Ábakuá Chants: Examining New Evidence for the African Diaspora." *African Studies Review* 48, no. 1 (2005): 23–58.

———. "The Relationship between Early Forms of Literacy in Old Calabar and the Inherited Manuscripts of the Cuban Ábákuá Society." In *Calabar on the Cross River:*

Historical and Cultural Studies, edited by David Mbua, Paul E. Lovejoy, and Ivor Miller, 177–216. Trenton, NJ: African World Press, 2017.

——. *Voices of the Leopard: African Secret Societies in Cuba*. Jackson: University of Mississippi, 2012.

Miller, Joseph. "A Secret Society Goes Public: The Relationship Between Ábakuá and Cuban Popular Culture." *African Studies Review* 43, no. 1 (2000): 161–88.

Monts, Lester. "Islam, Music, and Religious Change in Liberia: A Case Study from Vai Country." Conference on Music in the World of Islam, Assilah, August 8–13, 2007.

Moore, Carlos. *Fela: This Bitch of a Life with an Introduction by Margaret Busby*. London: Alison and Busby, 1982.

Moreton, J. B. *Manners and Customs in the West Indian Islands*. London: Richardson, 1790.

Morgan, Kenneth. "The Atlantic Slave Trade from the Bight of Biafra." In *Igbo in the Atlantic World: African Origins and Diasporic Destinations*, edited by Toyin Falola and Raphael Chijioke Njoku, 82–98. Bloomington: Indiana University Press, 2016.

Moulieras, Auguste. *Une tribu zénète anti-musulmane au Maroc (les Zkara)*. Paris: A.Challamel, 1903.

Mullin, Michael. *Africa in America: Slave Acculturation and Resistance in the American South and British Caribbean, 1736–1831*. Urbana: University of Illinois Press, 1992.

Nadel, Ira. *Modernism's Second Act: A Cultural Narrative*. New York: Palgrave Macmillan, 2013.

Nadel, Siegfried Frederick. "The Kede: A Riverain State in Northern Nigeria." In *African Political Systems*, edited by M. Fortes and E. E. Evans-Pritchard, 164–95. London: Oxford University Press, 1940.

Nash, Joe. "Bamboula to Ballet: The Joe Nash Black Dance Collection." *Dance Research Journal* 15, no. 2 (1983): 50–51.

Ndeffo Fongué, Joseph. "The Market for Works of Art: The Case of African Cultural Goods." *Southern African Journal of Economics* 70, no. 8 (2002): 1320–43.

Nduka, Utonti. *Western Education and Nigerian Cultural Background*. London: Oxford University Press, 1964.

Ndukaihe, Vernantius Emeka. *Achievement as a Value in Igbo/African Identity: The Ethics*. Berlin: Lit Verlag, 2006.

Nesbitt, Nick. "African Music: Ideology and Utopia." *Research in African Literature* 32, no. 2 (2011): 175–86.

Newton, Douglas. *Sculpture: Cefs-d'oeuvre de Musee Barbier-Mueller*. Geneva: Musee Barbier-Mueller, 1995.

Niani, D. T. *Sundiata: An Epic of Old Mali*. London: Longman, 2005.

Nicholls, Robert W. "African Dance: Transition and Continuity." In *African Dance: An Artistic, Historical, and Philosophical Inquiry*, edited by Kariamu Welsh Asante, Trenton, NJ: African World Press, 1998, 63–78.

——. "Igbo Influences on Masquerading and Drum Dances in the Caribbean." In *Igbo in the Atlantic World: African Origins and Diasporic Destinations*, edited by

Toyin Falola and Raphael Chijioke Njoku, 228–52. Bloomington: Indiana University Press, 2016.

———. *Old-Time Masquerading in the Virgin Islands.* St. Thomas: The Virgin Island Humanities Council, 1998.

———. *The Jumbies' Playing Ground: Old World Influences on Afro-Creole Masquerades in the Eastern Caribbean.* Jackson: University Press of Mississippi, 2012.

———. "The Mocko Jumbie of the U.S. Virgin Islands." *African Arts* 32, no. 3 (1999): 48–61, 94–95.

Nicklin, Keith. "Cross River Studies." *African Arts* 18, no. 1 (1984): 24–27

Nicklin, Keith and Jill Salmons. "On Ekkpe, Ekpe, Epo, and Ogbom." *African Arts* 15, no. 4 (1982): 78–79.

The Nigerian Daily Times. "Calabar Improvement League Honour Hon E. E. E. Anwan." Lagos, August 28, 1947.

Nissen, Johan Peter. *Reminiscences of a 46 Years' Residence in the Island of Saint Thomas in the West Indies.* Nazareth, Pennsylvania, 1838.

Njoku, Francis O. C. "The Originality of African Philosophy as a Hermeneutical Problem in Okere." In *African Philosophy and the Herneneutics of Culture: Essays in Honour of Theophilus Okere*, edited by Obi J. Oguejieofor and Godfrey Igwebuike Onah, 93–111. Piscataway, NJ: Transaction Publishers, 2005.

Njoku, Raphael Chijioke. *African Cultural Values: Igbo Political Leadership in Colonial Nigeria.* New York: Routledge, 2016.

———. "Chinua Achebe and the Development of Igbo/African Studies." In *The IgboIntellectual Tradition: Creative Conflict in African and African Diasporic Thought*, edited by Gloria Chuku, 249–66. New York: Palgrave / Macmillan, 2013.

———. "Christian Missions and Social Change in Igboland, Southern Nigeria: Myths, Realities and Continuities." In *Religion, History and Politics in Nigeria: Essays in Honor of Ogbu U. Kalu*, edited by Chima J. Korieh and G. Ugo Nwokeji, 93–116. Washington, DC: University Press of America, 2005.

———. "Igbo Slaves and the Transformation of the Niger Delta." In *The Aftermath of Slavery: Transitions and Transformations in Southeastern Nigeria*, edited by Chima J. Korieh and Femi Kolapo, 70–99. Trenton, NJ: African World Press, 2007.

———. "Neoliberal Globalism in Microcosm: A Study of the Precolonial Igbo of Eastern Nigeria." *Mbari: The International Journal of Igbo Studies* 1, no. 1 (2008): 45–68.

———. "Symbols and Meanings of Igbo Masks and Carnivals of the Black Diaspora." In *Migrations and Creative Expressions in Africa and the African Diaspora*, edited by Toyin Falola, Niyi Afolabi, and Aderonke A. Adesanya, 257–79. Durham, NC: Carolina Academic Press, 2008.

———. *The History of Somalia.* Santa Barbara, CA: Greenwood, 2013.

———. "The Influence of the Family on the Rise of Igbo State Unionism in Urban Colonial Nigeria 1916–1966." In *Urbanization and African Cultures*, edited by Toyin Falola and Steven J. Salm, 385–404. Durham, NC: Carolina Academic Press, 2005.

Njoku, Raphael Chijioke and Yik, King. "Onitsha Market Literature: Narrating Identity and Survival in a Colonial African City." In *Narrative, Identity, and Academic Community in Higher Education*, edited Brian Atterbery, John Gribas, Mark K. McBeth, Paul Sivitz, and Kandi Turley-Ames, 31–46. New York: Routledge, 2016.

Nketia, Kwabena. J. H. *The Music of Africa*. London: Oxford University, 1975.

Nodal, Roberto. "The Social Evolution of the Afro-Cuban Drum." *The Black Perspective in Music* 11, no. 2 (1983): 157–77.

Northrup, David. "Igbo and Myth Igbo: Culture and Ethnicity in the Atlantic World, 1600–1850." *Slavery and Abolition* 21, no. 3 (2000): 1–20.

———. "Precolonial References to the Annang Ibibio." *Ikenga* 2, no. 1 (1973): 1–5.

———. "The Growth Trade among the Igbo before 1800. *Journal of African History* 13 (1972): 217–36.

———. *Trade without Rulers: Pre-Colonial Economic Development in South Eastern Nigeria*. Oxford: Clarendon Press, 1978.

Nunley, John and Judith Bettelheim. *Caribbean Festival Arts: Each and Every Bit of Difference*. Seattle: Saint Louis Art Museum and University of Washington Press, 1988.

Nwabara, S. N. *Iboland: A Century of Contact with Britain 1860–1960*. London: Hodder and Stoughton, 1977.

Nwadike, Chinedu. "Waves of Miracle—Mp3 soundtrack, 2014.

Nwafo, D. C. *Born to Serve: An Autobiography of Dr. Akanu Ibiam*. Yaba, Lagos: Macmillan Publishers, 1988.

Nwafor, Nze Chukwukadibia. *Leopards of the Magical Dawn: Science and the Cosmological Foundations of Igbo Culture*. Morrisville, NC: Lulu Press, 2014.

Nwaka, Geoffrey I. "Secret Societies and Colonial Change: A Nigerian Example." *Cashier d'Etudes africaines* 18, no. 1–2 (1969–1970): 187–209.

Nwala, Uzodinma T. *Igbo Philosophy*. Lagos: Literamed, 1985.

Nwanunobi, Onyeka C. *African Social Institutions*. Nsukka: University of Nigeria Press, 1992.

Nwauwa, Apollos O. "Far Ahead of His Time: James Africanus Horton's Initiatives for a West African University and His Frustrations, 1862–1871." *Cahiers d'Études Africaines* 39, no. 153 (1999): 107–21.

Nwokeji, Ugo G. "The Atlantic Slave Trade and Population Density: A Historical Demography of the Biafran Hinterland." *Canadian Journal of African Studies* 34, no. 3 (2000): 616–55.

———. *The Slave Trade and Culture in the Bight of Biafra: An African Society in the Atlantic World*. Cambridge: Cambridge University Press, 2010.

Nze, C. B. *Aspects of Edeh Philosophy*, vol. 1. Enugu: Madonna University Press, 2011.

Nzekwu, Onuora. "Masquerade." *Nigeria Magazine* 66 (1960): 134–44.

Nzewunwa, Nwanna. *The Niger Delta: Aspects of Its Prehistoric Economy and Culture*. Oxford: Cambridge Monographs in African Archaeology, 1982.

Nzimiro, Ikenna. *Studies in Ibo Political Systems: Chieftaincy and Politics in Four Niger States*. Berkeley: University of California Press, 1972.

Obi, Z. C. Address to the Mammoth Assembly of the Ibo State Union Holding at Enugu. June 6, 1964.

Obiechina, Emmanuel. *Culture, Tradition, and Society in West African Novel.* Cambridge: Cambridge University Press, 1975.

———. "Nchetaka: The Story, Memory, and Continuity of Igbo Culture." *Ahịajọku Lecture 1994*, 17–47. Owerri: Ministry of Information and Social Development/Government Press, 1994.

Offiong, Daniel A. "The Functions of the Ekpo Society of the Ibibio of Nigeria." *African Studies Review* 27, no. 3 (1984): 77–92.

Offonry, Kanu H. "The Strength of Ibo Clan Feelings II." *West Africa,* London, June 2, 1951.

Ogbechie, Sylvester Okwunedu. *Ben Enweonwu: The Making of an African Modernist.* Rochester, NY: University of Rochester Press, 2008.

Ogede, Ode S. *Art, Society and Performance: Igede Praise Poetry.* Gainesville: University of Florida, 1997.

———. "Counters to Male Domination: Images of Pain in Igede Women's Songs." *Research in African Literature* 3 (1994): 105–20.

Ogundeji, Philip. "Ritual as Theatre, Theatre as Ritual: The Nigerian Example." *Ibadan Monograph Series* 2 no.1. Ibadan: Atlantis Books, 2000.

Ojomeyda, Rotimi. "Pandemonium as Muslims, Masquerades Lock Horns in Ikun-Etiti." *Vanguard,* Friday, June 16, 2017.

Okafor, F. U. *Igbo Philosophy of Law.* Enugu: Fourth Dimension, 1991.

Okere, Theophilus. "The Assumption of African Values as Christian Values." *Lucerna* 1 (1978): 6–15.

Olasope, Olakumbi O. "Gender Ambiguity and Iconic Paradox in Ebirra Ekuechi 'Facekuerade Ritualization.'" In *Developments in the Theory and Practice of Contemporary Nigerian Drama and Theatre: A Festschrift in Honour of Dapo Adelugba,* edited by Duro Oni and Sola Adeyemi, 7–26. Rochester, UK: Alpha Crownes Publishers, 2012.

Oldendorp, Christian Georges Andreas. *History of the Missions of the Evangelical Brethren on the Caribbean Islands of St. Thomas, St. Croix, and St. John, ed. by Johann Jakob Bossard. Orig. publication as C.G.A. Olderdorps Geschichte der Mission der evengelisechen Brueder auf den Caraibischen Inseln S. Thomas, S. Croix and S. Jan 2 vols.* Barby: Christian Friedrich Laur. Translated and edited by Highfield, Arnold R. and Bara, Vladimir. Ann Arbor, MI: Karoma Publishers, 1777.

Oliver, Cynthia. "St. Croix Dancing: The Contemporary and Historical Path of Dance on the U.S. Virgin Island of Saint Croix." MA Thesis, Gallatin Division of New York University, 1995.

Oliver, Roland. "Bantu Genesis: An Inquiry into Some Problems of Early Bantu History. *African Affairs* 65 (1966): 245–58.

———. "The Problem of Bantu Expansion." *Journal of African History* 7 (1966): 361–76.

Olusanya, G. O. "The Nationalist Movement in Nigeria." In *Groundwork of Nigerian History,* edited by Obaro Ikime, 545–69. Ibadan, Nigeria: Heinemann, 1980.

Omeje, Kenneth. "*Enyimba Enyi*: The Comeback of Igbo Nationalism in Nigeria." *Review of African Political Economy* 32 (2005): 630–36.

Onsite Real-time. Observation of the Nkwá Love Festivities in Achi Mbieri, December 28, 2008.

Onwu, Emmanuel Elenanya. *Uzo Ndu Na Ezi Okwu: Towards an Understanding of Igbo Traditional Religion, Life and Philosophy 2002 Ahiajoku Lecture*. Owerri, Nigeria: Published by the Ministry of Information and Culture and Printed by Government Press, 2002.

Onwuejeogwu, Angulu M. *An Igbo Civilization: Nri Kingdom and Hegemony*. Benin: Ethiope, 1981.

———. *Evolutionary Trends in the History of the Development of the Igbo Civilization in the Culture Theatre of Igboland in Southern Nigeria (Ahiajoku Lecture)*. Owerri: Culture Division, Ministry of Information, Culture, Youth and Sports, 1987.

Onwumechili, Cyril Agodi. *"Igbo Enwe Eze?" (The Igbo Have No King?), 2000 Ahiajoku Lecture*. Owerri, Nigeria: Published by the Ministry of Information and Culture and Printed by Government Press, 2000.

Onyeji, Christian. "Abigbo Music and Musicians of Mbaise, Igbo: An Introduction." *Ethnomusicology* 48, no. 1 (2004): 52–72.

Onyishi Ngwu Nwa Idoko. Interview with Chinyere Uzor, "Omabe Masquerade Festivals." *Vanguard*, Thursday, May 14, 2015.

Onyishi, Ike E. Prokop, Pavol, Okafor, Chiedozie O. and Pham, Michael N. "Female Genital Cutting Restricts Sociosexuality among the Igbo People of Southeast Nigeria. *Evolutionary Psychology* (2016): 1–7.

Oriji, John Nwachimereze. "Oracular Trade, Okonko Secret Society, and Evolution of Decentralized Authority among the Ngwa-Igbo of South Eastern Nigeria." *Ikenga* 5, no. 1 (1981): 35–52.

———. "The Slave Trade, Warfare, and Aro Expansion in the Igbo Heartland." *Transafrican Journal of History* 16 (1987): 151–66.

Ortiz, Fernandez, Melville J. Herskovits, Núñez Cedeño, Rafael A. "The Abakuá Secret Society in Cuba: Language and Culture." *Hispania* 71, no. 1 (1988): 148–54.

Osaghae, Eghosa E. *Trends in Migrant Political Organizations in Nigeria: The Igbo Union in Kano*. Ibadan: IFRA, 1994.

Osuagwu, Chidi G. *Truth and Chaos: Dynamics of Truth within Igbo Cosmology*. Owerri: African World Communications, 2003.

Ottenberg, Simon. "Humorous Masks and Serious Politics among the Afikpo Ibo." In *African Art & Leadership*, Douglas Fraser and Herbert M. Cole, eds., 99–121 Madison: University of Wisconsin Press, 1972.

———. "Ibo Receptivity to Change." In *Continuity and Change in African Cultures*, edited by William R. Bascom and Melville J. Herskovits, 130–43. Chicago: University of Chicago Press, 1959.

———. "Illusion, Communication, and Psychology in West African Masquerades." *Ethos* 2, no. 2 (1982): 149–85.

————. "Improvement Associations among the Afikpo Ibo." *Africa* 25, no. 1 (1955): 1–28.

Otuka, J. I. J. "Calling on all Ibos: Ibo Day Celebrations 1965." Port Harcourt, November (mimeo), 1965.

Packard, Randall Matthew. *Chiefship and Cosmology: An Historical Study of Competition.* Bloomington: Indiana University Press, 1981.

————. *The Politics of Ritual Control among the Bashu of Eastern Zaire during the 19th Century.* Madison: University of Wisconsin Press, 1978.

Palmer, Bryan D. *Cultures of Darkness: Night Travels in the Histories of Transgression, from Medieval to Modern.* New York: Monthly Review Press, 2000.

Palmer, Colin A. "From Africa to the Americas: Ethnicity in the Early Black Communities of the Americas." *Journal of World History* 6, no.2 (1995): 223–37.

Pearse, Andrew. "Aspects of Change in Caribbean Folk Music." *International Folk Music Journal* 7 (1955): 29–35.

————. "Carnival in Nineteenth Century Trinidad." *Caribbean Quarterly* 3 no. 4 (1956): 175–93.

Peek, Philip M. "Isoko Arts and Their Audiences." *African Arts* 13, no. 3 (1980): 58–60.

Pereira, Duarte Pacheco. "Mr. John Grazilhier's Voyage from Bandy to New Calabar." In Barbot, John [Jean]. "A Description of the Coasts of North and South Guinea." In *A Collection of Voyages and Travels* vol. 5, 380–81 edited by Thomas Astley and John Churchill. London: Awnsham and Churchill, 1732.

————. *Esmeraldo de situ orbis (edicao de Raphael Eduardo de Azevado Basto) [A Description of the World (edition by Raphael Eduardo de Azevado Basto)].* Lisbon: National Press, 1892.

Perry, Warren R. *Landscape Transformations and the Archaeology of Impact: Social Disruption and Formation in Southern Africa.* New York: Kluver, 2002.

Perry, William. *Children of the Sun: A Study in the Early History of Civilizations.* Saint Claire Shores, MI: Scholarly Press, 1923.

Phillips, Ulrich Bonnell. *American Negro Slavery: A Survey of the Supply, Employment, and Control of Negro Slaves.* 1918; reprint New York: D. Appleton and Company, 1966.

Phillipson, D.W. *The Later Prehistory of Eastern and Southern Africa.* London: Heinemann, 1977.

Picket, Elliot. "Animal Horns in African Art. *African Arts* 4, no. 4 (1971): 27–53.

Picton, John. "What Is a Mask?" In *The Performance Arts in Africa—A Reader,* edited by Frances Harding, 49–68. London: Routledge, 2002.

Plato. *The Republic of Plato. Translated With Notes and an Interpretative Essay by Allan Bloom.* New York: Basic Books, 1968.

Popova, Yanna B. *Stories, Meaning, and Experience: Narrativity and Enaction.* New York: Routledge, 2005.

Port of Spain Gazette. Monday, September 12, 1853

Posnansky, Merrick. *Archaeology and Linguistic Reconstruction of African History.* Berkeley: University of California Press, 1982.

Pradel, Lucie. *African Beliefs in the New World: Popular Literary Traditions in the Caribbean*. Trenton, NJ: African World Press, 2000.

Pratten, David. *Man-Leopold Murders: History and Society in Colonial Nigeria*. Edinburgh: Edinburgh University Press, 2007.

Price, Richard and Sally Price. "John Gabriel Stedman's Collections of 18th Century Artifacts from Surinam." *Nieuwe West-Indishe Gids* 53, nos. 3, 4 (1979): 131, 138.

Prichard, Richard Cowles. *Researches into This Physical History of Mankind,* 4th ed., vol 1. London: Houlston and Stoneman, 1851.

Procope, Bruce. "The Dragon Band or Devil Band." *Caribbean Quarterly* 4, nos. 3, 4 (1956): 275–80.

Pulford, Mary H., eds. *Peoples of the Ituri*. Orlando, FL: Harcourt Brace College Publishers, 1993.

Puri, Shalini. "Canonized Hybridities, Resistant Hybridities: Chutney Soca, Carnival, and the Politics of Nationalism." In *Caribbean Romances: The Politics of Regional Representation*. Edited by Belinda Edmondson, 12–38. Charlottesville: University Press of Virginia, 1999.

Raboteau, Albert J. *Slave Religion: The "Invisible Institution" in the Antebellum South*. New York: Oxford University Press, 1978.

Rachewiltz, Boris de. *Introduction to African Art*. Translated by Peter Whigham. New York: The American Library Inc., 1966.

Ravenstein, E. G. Ed. and Translated. *A Journal of the First Voyage of Vasco da Gama, 1497–1499*. London: Hakluyt Society, 1907.

Rea, Will. "Making History: The Modernity of Masquerade in Ikole Ekiti." *African Arts* 41, no. 4 (2008): 10–25.

Reid, Ira De A. "The John Canoe Festival: A New World Africanism." *Phylon* 3, no. 4 (1942): 345–46; 349–70.

Report of the Commission of Inquiry. On the Disturbances in Calabar and Owerri Provinces, December 1929. Lagos: Government Press, 1930, 24–30.

The Republic of Kenya. Kenya National Assembly Official Report Second Parliament Inaugurated 6th February 1970 (Hansard), Second Section, February 23–April 2, 1971. Nairobi: Kenya National Assembly Library, 1971.

Richard D. E. Burton. *Afro Creole: Power, Opposition, and Play in the Caribbean*. Ithaca, NY: Cornell University Press, 1997.

Richards, Sandra L. "Horned Ancestral Masks, Shakespearean Actor Boys, and Scotch-Inspired Set Girls: Social Relations in Nineteenth-Century Jamaican Jonkonnu." In *African Diaspora: African Origins and New World Identities*, edited by Isidore Okpewho, Carole Boyce Davies, and Ali Al'Amin. Mazrui, 254–75. Bloomington: Indiana University Press, 2001.

Rivers, Williams H. R. *History and Ethnology*. New York: Macmillan, 1922.

Robertson, John H. and Rebecca Bradley. "A New Paradigm: The African Early Iron Age without Bantu Migrations." *History in Africa* 27 (2000): 287–323.

Rodriguez, Julius P. *The Historical Encyclopedia of World Slavery Vol. 1 A–K*. Santa Barbara: ABC-CLIO, 1997.

Rotimi, Ola. "Through Whom the Spirits Breathe." In "The Masquerade in Nigeria History and Culture," Proceedings of a Workshop Sponsored by the School of Humanities, University of Port-Harcourt, Nigeria, 1980.

Rouse, Irving. *The Rise and Decline of the People Who Greeted Columbus*. New Haven, CT: Yale University Press, 1996.

Roy, Christopher. *Traduction et adaptation en Français F. Chaffin Art of the Upper Volta Rivers*. [*Tradition and Adaptation in Français F. Chaffin Art of the Upper Volta Rivers*]. Paris: Meudon, 1987.

Rucker, Walter C. *The River Flows On: Black Resistance, Culture and Identity Formation in Early America*. Baton Rouge: Louisiana State University Press, 2007.

Russell, Thembi Fabio Silva, and James Steele. "Modeling the Spread of Farming in the Bantu-Speaking Regions of Africa: An Archaeology-Based Phylogeography." *PLoS ONE* 9 no. 1 (2014): e87854. https://doi.org/10.1371/journal.pone.0087854.

The Saint Crois Avis. "A Watcher Against His Will." Christiansted, Saint Croix [V.I.] (Microfiche), January 3, 1901.

Saint Thomas Tidende. Danish West Indies, December 28, 1872.

Sandoval, Alonso de. *Treaties on Slavery Edited and Translated with an Introduction by Nicole Von Germeten*. Indianapolis: Hackett Publishing Company Inc, 2008.

Sartre, Jean-Paul. *What Is Literature?* Translated from the French by Bernard Frenchman. New York: Philosophical Library, 1949.

Scher, Philip W. "The Devil and the Bed-Wetter: Carnival, Memory, National Culture, and Post-Colonial Consciousness in Trinidad." *Western Folklore* 66, nos. 1, 2 (2007): 107–26.

———. *Carnival and the Formation of a Caribbean Transnation*. Gainesville: University Press of Florida, 2003.

Schiff, Brian. "The Function of Narrative: Towards a Narrative Psychology of Meaning." *Narrative Works* 2, no. 2 (2012): 33–47.

Schmalenbach, Werner, eds. *African Art from the Barbier-Mueller Collection*. Geneva. Munich: Prestel, 1988.

Schmidt, Wilhelm. "Fritz Graebner." *Anthropos* 30, nos. 1, 2 (1935): 203–14.

———. *The Culture Historical Method of Ethnology: The Scientific Approach to the Racial Question*. New York: Fortuyn's, 1939.

Schuler, Monica. "Akán Slave Rebellions in the British Caribbean." *Savacou* 1, no. 1 (1970): 373–86.

Scott, Michael. *Tom Cringle's Log*. Edinburgh: William Blackwood, 1836.

Scott, Michael and Frank Brangwyn. *Tom Cringle's Log by Michael Scott—Volume I*. 1894; reprint London: Gibbings and Co, 1920.

Sékou Touré. *L'Afrique et la revolution [Africa and the Revolution]*. Paris: Présence Africaine, 1967.

Shaw, Thurstan. *Igbo-Ukwu: An Account of Archaeological Discoveries in Eastern Nigeria*, 2 vols. Evanston, IL: Northwestern University Press, 1970.

Sheldon, H. F. "The Bantu Races." *Science Progress in the Twentieth Century* 17, no. 66 (1922): 303.

Sherlock, Philip M. *West Indian Nations: A New History*. Kingston: Jamaica Publishing House, 1973.

Sidky, Hornayun. *Perspectives on Culture: A Critical Introduction to Theory in Anthropology*. New Jersey: Pearson Education, 2004.

Sieber, Roy and Barry Hecht. "Eastern Nigerian Art: From the Toby and Barry Hecht Collection." *African Art* 35, no. 1 (2002): 56–77, 95–96.

Sieber, Roy and Roselyn Adele Walker. *African Art in the Cycle of Life*. Washington, DC: Smithsonian Institution Press, 1987.

Sigler, Allen A. and Shirley Aamidor. "From Positive Reinforcement to Positive Behaviors: An Everyday Guide for the Practitioner." *Early Childhood Education Journal* 32, no. 4 (2005): 249–53.

Sigmund Freud. *The Interpretation of Dreams—New Interdisciplinary Essays*. Edited by Laura Marcus. Manchester: Manchester University Press, 1999.

Simmons, Donald C. "The Depiction of Gangosa on Efik-Ibibio Masks." *Man* 57 (1957): 17–20.

Sims, Patterson. *Anxious Objects: Willie Cole's Favorite Brands*. Montclair, NJ: Montclair Art Museum and Rutgers University Press, 2006.

Sloane, Hans A. *A Voyage to the Islands of Madera, Barbados, Nieves, S. Christopher, and Jamaica Volume 1*. London: Printed by B. M. for the Author, 1707/1725.

Smith, Robert. "The Canoe in West African History." *Journal of African History* 11, no. 4 (1970): 515–33.

Smithsonian National Museum of American History. Onsite Visit, Washington DC, Monday, July 5, 2010.

Smock, Audrey C. *Ibo Politics: The Role of Ethnic Unions in Eastern Nigeria*. Cambridge: Harvard University Press, 1974.

———. "The NCNC and Ethic Unions in Biafra." *Journal of Modern African Studies* 7, no. 1 (1969): 21–34

Soleillet, Paul. *Voyages et Decouvertes de Paul Soleillet Dane Les Sahara et Dane Le Soudan [Voyages and Discoveries of Paul Soleillet in the Sahara and in the Sudan]*. Paris: M. Dreyfour and M. Dalsace, 1881.

Speed, Frank and Peggy Harper. "Gelede—A Yoruba Masquerade." Country/Production, Nigeria/UK, 1970.

Spencer, Flora. *Crop-Over: An Old Barbadian Plantation Festival*. Barbados: Commonwealth Caribbean Center, 1974.

Steiner, Christopher B. *African Art in Transit*. Cambridge: Cambridge University Press, 1994.

Steward, Julian Haynes. *Theory of Culture Change: The Methodology of Multilinear Evolution*. Urbana: University of Illinois Press, 1972.

Stolzoff, Norman C. *Wake the Town and Tell the People: Dancehall Culture in Jamaica.* Durham, NC: Duke University Press, 2000.

Strogatz, Steve H. *Nonlinear Dynamics and Chaos, with Application to Physics, Chemistry, and Engineering.* Boulder, CO: Westview Press, 2015.

Stuckey, Sterling. *Slave Culture: Nationalist Theory and the Foundations of Black America.* Oxford: Oxford University Press, 2013.

———. "Through the Prism of Folklore: The Black Ethos in Slavery." *Massachusetts Review* 9 (1968): 417–37.

Sutton, J. E. G. "The International Factor at Igbo-Ukwu." *The African Archaeological Review* 9 (1991): 145–60.

Tait, Jennifer Woodruff Undated. "Christianity in Early Africa—Ancient Traditions, Profound Impact." *Christian History* 105 undated. https://christianhistoryinstitute.org/magazine/article/early-africa-editors-note.

Talbot, Amaury P. *The Peoples of Southern Nigeria: A Sketch of their History, Ethnology and Languages with an Abstract of the 1921 Census,* 4 vols., 1926; reprint London: Frank Cass, 1969.

Tangri, Roger. *Politics in Sub-Saharan Africa.* London: James Currey and Heinemann, 1985.

Teelucksingh, Jerome. "The 'Invisible Child' in British West Indian Slavery. *Slavery and Abolition* 27, no. 2 (2006): 237–50.

Telegraph Reporters. "What Is Wahhabism: The Reactionary Branch of Islam from Saudi Arabia Said to Be the Main Source of Global Terrorism." *The Telegraph* May 19, 2017.

Thembi Russell, Fabio Silva, and James Steele. "Modelling the Spread of Farming in Bantu-Speaking Regions of Africa: An Archaeological-Based Phytogeography." *PLos* 9, no. 1 (2014): 1–9.

Thompson, Colin J. "Chaos and Strange Attractors: *A Review of Nonlinear Dynamics by Robert H. G. Helleman, Science* 213, no. 4503 (1981): 128.

Thompson, Donald. "Poor Man's Bass Fiddle." *Caribbean Review* 3, no. 1 (1971): 11–12.

Thompson, Robert Farris. *African Art in Motion: Icon and Act.* Berkeley: University of California Press, 1974.

Throsby, David. *Economics and Culture.* Cambridge: Cambridge University Press, 2001.

Time. "Nigeria's Civil War: Hate, Hunger and the Will to Survive." Friday, August 23, 1968.

Tomaselli, Keyan and Handel Kashope Wright. *Africa, Cultural Studies and Differences.* New York: Routledge, 2013.

Trinidad Chronicle, 1883. Cited by Hollis Urban Liverpool, "Origins of Rituals and Customs in the Trinidad Carnival: African or European?" *TDR* 42, no. 3 (1998): 4–37.

The Trinidad Palladium. February 4, 1880.

Trinidad Sentinel. Thursday February 23, 1860.

Trowell, Margaret. *Classical African Sculpture.* London: Faber and Faber, 1964.

Trowell, Margaret and Hans Nevermann. *Africa and Oceanic Art: Texts by Margaret Trowell and Hans Nevermann*. New York: Harry N. Abrams Inc., 1968.

Tuckerman, Joseph. *A Letter Respecting Santa Cruz as a Winter Residence Foe Invalids: Addressed to Dr. John C. Warren of Boston, Mass*. Boston: D. Clapp, 1837.

Turnbull, Colin M. *The Forest People*. New York: Simon and Schuster, 1962.

———. *The Mbuti Pygmies: Change and Adaptation*. New York: Holt, Rinehart and Winston, 1983.

Turton, E. R. "Bantu, Galla, and Somali Migration in the Horn of Africa: A Reassessment of the Juba/Tana Area." *Journal of African History* 16, no. 4 (1975): 519–37.

Uba-Mgbemena, Asonye. "The Role of Ífò in Training the Igbo Child." *Folklore* 96, no. 1 (1985): 57–61.

Uchendu, Victor C. *The Igbo of Southeast Nigeria: The Same Yesterday, Today, and Tomorrow?* New York: Holt, Rinehart and Winston, 1965.

Udal, John Symonds. "Dorsetshire Folklore for Somerset and Dorset." Edited by Rev. G. W. Saunders and Rev. R. G. Bartlet. *Notes and Queries* 17 (1891): 174–81.

Udo, Edet A. *Who Are the Ibibios?* Enugu: Africana-Fep Publishers, 1983.

Udoye, Edwin Anaegboka. *Resolving the Prevailing Conflict between Christianity and African (Igbo) Traditional Religion Through Inculturation*. Zurich: LIT Verlag, 2011.

Ugonna, Nnabuenyi. "Ezeigboezue: An Igbo Masquerade Play." *Nigeria Magazine* 114 (1974): 22–33.

Ukaegbu, Victor Ikechukwu. "The Composite Scene: The Aesthetics of Igbo Mask Theatre." PhD diss., University of Plymouth, Exeter, May 1996.

———. *The Uses of Masks in Igbo Theater in Nigeria: The Aesthetic Flexibility of Performance Traditions*. London: Edwin Mellen, 2008.

UNESCO. "Makishi Masquerade." Tangible Cultural Series, 2005. Inscribed in 2008 (3.com) on the Representative List of the Intangible Cultural Heritage of Humanity, 2008.

———. Slave Trade Project. Voyages: *The Trans-Atlantic Slave Trade Database* (www.slavevoyages.org/).

Ute Röschenthaler. *Purchasing Culture in the Cross River Region of Cameroon and Nigeria*. Trenton, NJ: Africa World Press, 2011.

Uzor, Chinyere. "Omabe Masquerade Festivals: Imufu Community's Cultural Heritage of all Ages." *Vanguard*, Thurs., May 14, 2015.

Vanguard. "Calabar Carnivals Is a Melting-Pot of African Hospitality." Lagos, December 28, 2016.

———. "2016 Calabar Carnival." Lagos, December 28, 2016.

———. "Calabar Carnivals: Residents, Fun Seekers Demand Improvement." Lagos, December 29, 2016.

Vansina, Jan. "Bantu in the Crystal Ball." *History in Africa* 6 (1979): 287–333.

Vasconcellos, Colleen. "And a Child Shall Lead Them?: Slavery, Childhood, and African Cultural Identity in Jamaica, 1750–1838." PhD diss., Florida International University, 2004.

Vershbow, Michael E. "The Sounds of Resistance: The Role of Music in South Africa's Anti-Apartheid Movement." *Inquiries: Social Science, Arts and Humanities* 2, no. 6 (2010): 1–21.

Vinyl, LP of 1960 "Les Ballets Africains De Keita Fodeba Vol. 2." Produced by Disques Vogue—LDM. Track 2—"Soundiata Lounge A L' Emperor Du Manding." 1960.

Visby-Petersen, Thora. *Saint Thomas Tropeminder Fra De Vestindiske Oer.* Translated by Poul Erik Olsen. Aarhus, Copenhagen, 1917.

Vogel, Susan and Mary Jo Arnoldi. "Sòmonò Puppet Masquerades in Kirango, Mali." *African Arts*, 34, no. 1 (2001): 72–77.

Vrije University Brussels (VUB). Consolidated Annotations on African Masks. Accessed October 9, 2017. https://www.vub.ac.be/BIBLIO/nieuwenhuysen/african-art/african-art-collection-masks.htm.

Walker, R. "Open Peer Commentary: Can We Understand the Music of Another Culture." *Psychology of Music* 24 (1996): 103–30.

Wall Malefijt, Annemarie de. *Images of Man: A History of Anthropological Thought.* New York: Alfred Knopf, 1974.

Wallace, A. E. C. "Revitalization Movements." *American Anthropologist* 58 (1956): 264–81.

Wallerstein, Immanuel. *The Modern World System*, 3 vols. Berkeley: California University Press, 2011.

Wang, Yi. "Globalization Enhances Cultural Identity." *Intercultural Communication Studies* 16, no. 1 (2007): 83–86.

Wanyama, Mellitus and Egesah, Omar. "Ethnography and Ethno-Music of Babukusu Traditional Male Circumcision: Messaging, Symbolism and Rationale." *Sociology and Anthropology* 3 (2015): 6–18.

Warner-Lewis, Maureen. *Central Africa in the Caribbean: Transcending Time, Transforming Cultures.* Barbados: University of West Indies, 2003.

———. "Rebels, Tyrants and Saviours: Leadership and Power Relations in Lovelace's Fiction." *Journal of West Indian Literature* 2, no. 1 (1987): 76–89.

Werner, Alice. *Myths and Legends of the Bantu.* 1933, reprint; London: Frank Cass, 1968.

———. "Notes on Clicks in the Bantu Languages." *Journal of the Royal African Society* 2, no. 8 (1903): 416–21.

———. "Some Bantu Language Problems." *Journal of Royal African Anthropology* 28, no. 110 (1929): 155–65.

———. "The Bantu Element in Swahili Folklore." *Folklore* 20, no. 4 (1909): 432–56.

Westermarck, Edvard. *Marriage Ceremonies in Morocco.* London: Macmillan, 1914.

———. *Ritual and Belief in Morocco—Volume II.* 1926 reprint; London: Macmillan, 2014.

Widmer, Ted. "The Invention of a Memory: Congo Square and African Music in Nineteenth-Century New Orleans." *Revue française d'études américaines* 98, no. 2 (2003): 69–78.

Willard, John. "Mokolution: The Evolution of the Moko Jumbie," with post-production editing by WTJX. Virgin Islands: Department of Tourism's Video, 2009.

Willett, Frank. *African Art*. London: Thames and Hudson, 2002.

Williams, Cynric A. *A Tour through the Island of Jamaica, from the Western to the Eastern End, in the Year 1823*. London: Hunt and Clarke, 1826.

Wissler, Clark. *The American Indian: An Introduction to the Anthropology of the New World*. New York: Oxford University Press, 1938.

Wolf, Eric. *Europe and the People without History*. Berkeley: University of California Press, 1982.

Woodward, Richard B. *African Art*. Virginia: Virginia Museum of Fine Arts, 2000.

Wright, Donald. *The World and a Very Small Place in Africa: A History of Globalization in Niume, the Gambia*. New York: Routledge, 2010.

Wrigley, Christopher C. "Speculations on the Economic Prehistory of Africa." *Journal of African History* 1, no. 2 (1960): 189–203.

Young, Jason. "African Religions in the Early South." *The Journal of Southern Religion* 14 (2012): 1–18.

Young, William. *A Tour through the Several Islands of Barbados, St. Vincent, Antiga, Tobago, and Grenada, In the Years 1791–1792*. London, 1801/1823.

Zarate, Christina. *Dia de Los Muertos*. Program of Latino History and Culture, the Smithsonian National Museum of American History: Washington, DC, 2006.

Zwartjes, Otto. *Portuguese Missionary Grammars: Asia, Africa and Brazil 1550–1800*. Amsterdam: Benjamin Publishing Company, 2011.

INDEX

Page numbers in *italics* refer to figures and tables.

Sartre, Jean-Paul, 185–187
sawm, 140
Scott, Michael, 14, 118, 122, 125, 133
Semites, 139
Senegal, 12, 130, 163
Setswana, 75
shahadah, 140–141
Shona, 73–75, 178
Sierra Leone, 13, 15, 90, *92*, 98, *101*, 113,
 129–130, 178, 180–181
Silk Roads, 6
singers, 164, 167, 169, 172, 176, 197
Siwa Oasis, 140
Skull and Bones, 53
Sloane, Hans, 14, 103, 114, 217n15
Smyth, Francis, 107
Smyth, Robert, 107
sociophysics, 30
Sogo Bo, 84, 231n27
Somalia, 81
Sòmonò, 16, 84, 191; elders, 231n27;
 masquerade, 191; parade, 191;
 puppet, 191
Songhai, 146, 217n11
Soninke, 143–144, 147
Sotho, 73, 75
Soussi, 141
Southern Africa, 67, 73, 161
stilt masquerade, 84, 122, 129–132,
 221n91, 222n107
Stolzoff, Norman, 5,
Strogatz, Steven H., 8
Sudan, 39, 81, 83, 85, 123, 136, 217n11;
 western, 141, 143–145
Sundiata Epic, 163
Surinam, 14, 119, 180
Swaziland, 71, 81

Tabula Rasa School, 3, 43, 193
Tallensi, 39, 204n77
Tanker, 167
Tanzania, 64, 71, 73, 81

Temne, 74, 129, 180
Tenda, 90
Thistlewood, Thomas, 176
Thomas (the apostle), 34
Tibetan, 28
Tiv, 95
Tji Wara, 124, 220n68
Tobago, 12, 100–101, 130, 159, 192, 232n32
Tombstone Feast music, 103
Toronto, 138
Touré, Sékou, 163
Toussian masks, 123
Trans-Saharan trade routes, 6, 136,
 141, 143–144
Tres Puntas, 121
Trinidad and Tobago, 12, 130, 159,
 192, 232n32
Trinidadian masquerade carnival, 167,
 192, 220n63, 222n121
Tswana, 75
Tuareg, 139, 141
Tuckerman, Joseph, 14, 119, 149,
Tukulor Empire, 144
Tumbuka, 74
Tunisia, 140
Tutankhamen, 27, 202n27

U.S. Virgin Islands, 109, 112, 121, 130–131,
 232–233n49
Ubangi River, 72
Ubomiri, 16, 84, 129, 167, 196, 221n91
Udi Division, 63, 127
Ùdú, 57, 103, 170
Uganda, 39, 71, 73–74, 79, 81, 83
Úgbè society, 112
Ujda, 142
Ukulunkulu, 81
Ụlágá masquerade, 55, 61, 132–133
umu mmádu, 75
Umuáká, 60
Umuezukwe, 124
Umunnáá Ámáụbụrụ, 196